Eighteenth Century Comedy

Nov

Thurs. 7th 4.15 — 5.45

Fri 15th 12.15 — 1.15

Wed 20th 2 — 4

Thurs 28th 4.15 — 5.45

Dec

Mon 2nd 4.15 — 5.45

Tues 3rd 4.15 — 5.45

Wed 4th 2 — 5

Thurs 5th 4.15 — 5.45

Fri 6th 2pm →

Mon 9th

Eighteenth Century Comedy

SELECTED AND INTRODUCED BY

W. D. TAYLOR

TEXTS NEWLY EDITED
WITH ANNOTATION AND AN INTRODUCTION TO EACH PLAY BY

SIMON TRUSSLER

OXFORD UNIVERSITY PRESS

LONDON   OXFORD   NEW YORK

1969

Oxford University Press

LONDON OXFORD NEW YORK
GLASGOW TORONTO MELBOURNE WELLINGTON
CAPE TOWN SALISBURY IBADAN NAIROBI LUSAKA ADDIS ABABA
BOMBAY CALCUTTA MADRAS KARACHI LAHORE DACCA
KUALA LUMPUR SINGAPORE HONG KONG TOKYO

First published in The World's Classics in 1929, with a
fuller version of the present Introduction by W. D. Taylor

This edition, with new material by Simon Trussler, first
published as an Oxford University Press paperback
by Oxford University Press, London, 1969

PRINTED IN GREAT BRITAIN
BY RICHARD CLAY (THE CHAUCER PRESS) LTD
BUNGAY SUFFOLK

Contents

Introduction

The five plays printed in this volume are all important in the history of eighteenth-century drama. *The Beaux Stratagem* (1707) illustrates a widening of the range of comic interest that took place in the wake of Congreve's *Way of the World* (1700). *The Conscious Lovers* (1722) is an example of the moral and sentimental comedy of the early part of the century, and *She Stoops to Conquer* (1773) a reaction against such comedy when it becomes lachrymose. *The Beggar's Opera* (1728) is the first and best of the ballad-plays, and *The Tragedy of Tragedies; or The Life of Tom Thumb the Great* (1731) a happy effort of the young Fielding in the sublime-ludicrous.

English comedy underwent a marked change at the beginning of the eighteenth century. There were more theatres regularly playing—five in 1730 instead of the two of Restoration times. By the Licensing Act of 1737 their number was again reduced to two, Drury Lane and Covent Garden; but the provisions of the Act could be evaded, as Foote did, for example, by inviting people to take chocolate with him at the Little Theatre in the Haymarket. Actors were becoming persons of greater importance. In King William's reign they could still be treated as if they were vagabonds with less rights than ordinary subjects: Dogget, for whom Congreve wrote Alderman Fondlewife in the *Old Bachelor* and Ben in *Love for Love*, was arrested on one occasion for leaving his company without the Lord Chamberlain's consent: fifty years later Garrick thought himself on a level with Dukes, Earls, and Archbishops. Betterton's salary, exclusive of what he received from benefits (which, however, amounted to a large sum in the last years of his life), was never more than eighty shillings a week; Garrick's first engagement at Drury Lane was at £500 a year; and he made a huge fortune from the theatre.

Then, too, the range of drama was wider. Comedy was no longer always set in London—in Hyde Park or in Westminster Hall or in the New Exchange. Nor was it written any longer solely from the point of view of the rakish gentleman about town; the country wife became more than a deceitful ingenue, and the country squire more than a mark for raillery. Realistic domestic plays ('Tradesmen's Tragedies', as Goldsmith called them), like Lillo's *The London Merchant* (1731) and his revision of *Arden of Feversham* (1759), made a claim for themselves.

Farce, ballad-plays, pantomime, dancers, performing animals of all kinds, also became immensely popular—perhaps because of the new audience, the honest citizens and their wives, who now thronged the theatres. Colley Cibber says of the patentee of Drury Lane in 1707: 'His point was to please the majority, who could more easily comprehend any thing they saw, than the daintiest things that could be said to them.' And Pope writes:

> Loud as the Wolves, on Orcas' stormy steep,
> Howl to the roarings of the Northern deep,
> Such is the shout, the long-applauding note,
> At Quin's high plume, or Oldfield's petticoat,
> Or when from Court a birth-day suit bestow'd
> Sinks the lost Actor in the tawdry load.
> Booth enters—hark! the Universal peal!
> 'But has he spoken?' Not a syllable.
> 'What shook the stage, and made the People stare?'
> Cato's long Wig, flow'rd gown, and lacquer'd chair.
>
> *Epistle to Augustus*, ll. 328–37.

The conception of morals and manners changed in the eighteenth century. In the life Restoration comedy had presented there was no fidelity in marriage, virtue was esteemed a matter of appearance, every citizen was an Alderman Fondlewife and every country girl a Miss Prue. The comedies of the turn of the century, such as Vanbrugh's *Provok'd Wife* (1697) and Farquhar's *Beaux Stratagem*, have similar situations: Constant in the one tempts Lady Brute as in the other Archer tempts the wife of Squire Sullen. But the tone and manner in which the women repulse the temptations are totally different; Lady Brute would be unfaithful without a qualm if time and circumstance suited; Mrs. Sullen flirts with the idea of infidelity, but when Archer appears suddenly in her bed-chamber, she starts back in terror. Sir Harry Wildair in Farquhar's *Constant Couple* (1699) persists through four acts in taking Lady Darling as the keeper of a house of ill fame. Richmore in his *The Twin Rivals* (1702) seduces women and then marries them off to the nincompoops of his acquaintance. Beside the devilry of these fine gentlemen the *Beaux Stratagem* appears an innocent intrigue.

Restoration comedy represents the society of the time as it appeared to its authors, ridiculing its idiosyncrasies and follies. Farquhar by contrast is at his best not in the comic representation of society but in the humorous drawing of low life. Even in his early plays his servants—Dicky in *The Constant Couple* and Teague in *The Twin Rivals*—were far more than the butts of their masters, and drew as much applause. In *The Beaux Stratagem* it is the low characters who are always in the spotlight—Boniface As-the-Saying-Is, Captain Gibbet, Cherry, Gipsey, Scrub, the priest Foigard, Archer in the disguise of a valet.

Steele's method—at least in *The Conscious Lovers*—is to oppose and contrast two or three sets of people. One set are patterns of what fine gentlemen and fine gentlewomen should be. They may have some slight weakness at which one may laugh; but in the main, they are people to be admired or wept over rather than laughed at. Opposed to these is a set of characters with a much lower code of morality who excite our scorn; a conceited rascal, for instance, who plans to marry the heroine because of her fortune; or a widow who, as soon as the old lord she has duped is in his coffin, takes off the mask of fidelity, and launches on an amorous career. Still another set, the servants, provide the pure comic relief.

There are neither fine gentlemen nor servants in *The Beggar's Opera*, which is sometimes said to have sprung from a remark of Swift's, that Gay should write a 'Newgate pastoral, among the whores and thieves there'. Congreve said that the play would 'either take greatly or be damned confoundedly'. It met a success beyond all expectation, ran through the whole season in 1727, and has run ever since.

One reason for its original success was its political satire of Walpole and his Government. But it is a satire, too, on Italian opera, which under Handel's direction was striving to establish itself in England at the expense of native music and native drama. It achieved its effects by setting English sentiments that everyone could understand against foreign high-falutin, and English tunes which everyone could like, against the trills and quavers that delighted Neapolitan audiences.

Yet a third strain of satire is the ironical attack on contemporary manners. There is the suggestion that the manners and opinions of Newgate are better than those of the court and city, or at least as good as they. Macheath's gang merely retrenches the superfluities of mankind out of a hatred of avarice. No courtiers are so faithful to one another as they are. Then, when the characters profess moral opinions contrary to what are usual, which they are always doing, the suggestion is that this morality is not confined to Newgate.

The success of *The Beggar's Opera* is due both to its songs and its dialogue. The ear is pleased with the music and the eye with the picturesque setting and groupings—the prison scene, the dance, the march of the gang, the gallows. One seizes immediately, too, the relations of the principal characters —the genial curmudgeons, Lockit and Peachum, the vixenish Lucy, the matchless Polly, the splendid dare-devilish Macheath. And it repays the close attention the play requires to catch the finenesses of the dialogue, the exquisite cutting of the characters and the neatness of their colouring.

Among the influences that went into the making of Fielding's *Tragedy of Tragedies*, written when he was in his middle twenties, was *The Rehearsal*, which was constantly being revived in the eighteenth century, changed to suit the occasion. *The Tragedy of Tragedies* is, like it, an attack on the bombast and the absurdities of a number of popular tragedies, some of them half a century old but still holding the stage. In the revised version of 1731—the text given here—especially in the annotations to it, it is a satirical hit in the style of the *Dunciad* (published three years before) on pedantic learning or what was thought to be so.

It is not strange that Fielding in his youth should excel in an extravaganza of nonsense and high spirits like *The Tragedy of Tragedies*. One thinks of him first of all as the author of *Tom Jones*, *Joseph Andrews*, and *Amelia*; but even they have burlesque in them—the mock-heroic introduction of certain incidents, the wild hurly-burly of fights with much letting of blood at the nose and loss of hair. It is not the main strand in them, but Fielding never despised it. Speaking of the difference between comedy and the burlesque in the preface to *Joseph Andrews* he says: 'And I apprehend, my Lord Shaftesbury's opinion of mere burlesque agrees with mine, when he asserts, There is no such thing to be found in the writings of the ancients. But, perhaps, I have less abhorrence than he professes for it: and that, not because I have had some little success on the stage this way; but rather as it contributes more to exquisite mirth and laughter than any other; and these are probably more wholesome physic for the mind, and conduce better to purge away spleen, melancholy, and ill affections, than is generally imagined.'

The greatest geniuses of the eighteenth century preferred the novel to plays. The new form gave writers a wider audience, and its untried possibilities and pliability attracted them. It freed them also from the tyrannical requirements of actors and managers. Neither Richardson nor Smollett nor Sterne attempted the dramatic form: Fielding did his utmost in it, but without striking success except in farce. Neither of the authors of the brilliant comedies of the latter part of the century was a dramatist by profession as Dryden, Congreve, and Farquhar had been. Goldsmith and Sheridan only, as it were, strayed into the theatre, and Goldsmith had to face great difficulties before he could have his two plays performed.

What distinguishes *She Stoops to Conquer* from other plays of the period by novelists turned dramatists, is that it was written by Goldsmith, who 'gazed with admiration on happy human faces as some men admire the colours of a tulip or a butterfly'. The elegance and grace of the dialogue are those of *The Citizen of the World* and *The Vicar of Wakefield*. Mrs. Hardcastle who dresses her hair from a fashion print in last year's *Ladies' Memorandum-Book* and Mrs. Primrose with her passion for crimson paduasoy are nearly related; so, too, are Tony Lumpkin, whose knowledge of written-hand does not permit him to taste the cream of the correspondence, and the art connoscento George Primrose met in Paris, whose trump critical remark before every picture was to praise the works of Pietro Perugino. The gay, gentle Goldsmith speaks to us in every line of the play.

Some of the lesser comedies famous in the eighteenth century still make good reading—Hoadly's *Suspicious Husband*, Murphy's *The Way to Keep Him*, *The Clandestine Marriage* of Garrick and Colman. The plots are tightly constructed, the situations ingenious, and in the dialogue one seems to hear the voice of the eighteenth-century middle class and their servants. But they are mere imitations of life; they have not the comic fire which appears in Congreve as brilliant wit and in Farquhar as a blend of wit and humour, and makes their works more intense than life. This kind of elevation or intensity Goldsmith recaptures. In *A Word or Two on the Late Farce, Called High Life Below Stairs* Goldsmith says: 'From a conformity to critic rules, which perhaps on the whole have done more harm than good, our author has sacrificed all the vivacity of the dialogue to Nature; and though he makes his characters talk like servants, they are seldom absurd enough or lively enough, to make us merry. Though he is always natural, he happens seldom to be humorous.' Goldsmith's characters are always absurd enough and lively enough to make us merry. His dialogue does not merely reveal character or carry on the plot; every word of it, open the play where one will, makes us laugh.

1928   W. D. TAYLOR

A Note on This Edition

The texts of the five plays which follow have been newly edited for this edition. I have selected what I consider the most authoritative text of each play published in its author's lifetime, and have reproduced it in as close conformity as possible to this original. Rather than attempt to provide a critically collated text, without space in which to justify chosen readings or note alternatives, I have specified only variants of real substance. Stylistic regularization has been kept to a minimum: catchwords and long *s* have necessarily been abandoned, but capitalization and the use of italics follow the style of the originals, as do abbreviations, forms of character notation, and stage directions. Such features will, hopefully, make the collection useful to scholars without detracting from its interest for the general reader, who will quickly become accustomed to the local colour of eighteenth-century typographical conventions.

More crucial, alike from the scholar's, the student's, and the actor's point of view, is the retention of the original punctuation. The unfortunate modern tendency is to update it—and thus to make grammatical what is essentially theatrical. The interested reader may like to compare regularized versions, where these exist, with the originals here reprinted: I am convinced he will agree that the sensitivity of playwrights and their typesetters to the natural breaks in speech makes not only superfluous but downright unhelpful the painstaking corrections of latter-day editors.

The footnotes, with Fielding's mock-pedantry in *The Tragedy of Tragedies* to serve as an awful warning, attempt to enlighten wherever time has rendered an allusion ambiguous or modified the meaning of a word, but not—except in the rare instances where such information seems essential to the full understanding of a passage—to spot sources of incidents, characters, or ideas. My introductions to the individual texts attempt to set each play within the context of its author's literary career and of contemporary theatrical conditions, rather than to suggest a definitive critical interpretation or to provide a potted plot. Each introduction ends with a brief note on the text reproduced, and on the availability of fuller or complementary commentaries on particular texts, and of reliable collected editions of an author's works. The Selected Bibliography, with which the volume ends, contains suggestions for critical reading.

1969   SIMON TRUSSLER

THE
BEAUX STRATAGEM

George Farquhar

1677–1707

George Farquhar wrote *The Beaux Stratagem* in his thirtieth year, in the fatal throes of tuberculosis. It's a moot point whether the technical mastery of the youthful dramatist or the inextinguishable spirit of the dying man is the more remarkable: and it is tantalizing to surmise that England lost in his premature passing the one playwright who could have guided the regular comedy of his age into paths as pleasing to later audiences as to his own. One thing, at least, is certain: at his death Farquhar alone enjoyed the ability to plot a middle way between the epigrammatic sensuality of the Restoration, and that sentimental moralizing which characterized an increasingly bourgeois comedy in the sober wake of Jeremy Collier's *Short View of the Profaneness and Immorality of the English Stage*.

It is still customary to deal cursorily with Farquhar at the conclusion of a book or a chapter on Restoration comedy—although the dramatist was a mere eight years old when Charles II died, and had scarcely begun his career as a playwright at the turn of the century. His earliest effort, first staged at Drury Lane in December 1698, was admittedly cast in the Restoration mould—its hero adopting the Irish nationality of his emigrant creator, but quickened by a lust that transcends both brogue and birthplace. The play's title, *Love and a Bottle*, is apt enough. But less than a year later, *The Constant Couple* was already asserting the freshness and individuality by which its nominally representative rake, Sir Harry Wildair, is distinguished from his forebears. Sir Harry's debaucheries are rooted in follies of flesh-and-blood rather than in verbal facility. And he has, besides, a more formidable adversary in Lady Lurewell than any female creation of Wycherley or Congreve—coquettes more or less ready to be ravished at the turn of a well-wrought phrase. Emotion that is actual rather than artificial—to adopt Lamb's apologetic use of the word—and an understanding of feminine psychology rather than its mere exploitation, were to contribute to the more organically-conceived comedies of Farquhar's later years.

Like most sequels, *Sir Harry Wildair*—an uncomfortable blend of bawdy and domestic bliss—was a failure. So, commercially, was Farquhar's adaptation of Fletcher's *The Wild Goose Chase*, which he renamed *The Inconstant*, in 1702—and, artistically, his version of Chapelle's *Les Carosses d'Orléans*, which he translated as *The Stage-Coach* in 1703. Between these last two pieces, however, came a fourth original work, *The Twin Rivals*, in which two brothers battle for the heirdom of which the younger has been deprived by half an hour. There is a certain over-intricacy of plotting, to which Farquhar was always prone, and a confusion of authorial point-of-view. The resulting shifts in sympathy may create an interesting ambiguity, but they only hint at the more purposeful complexity of Farquhar's final plays. However, he had first to gain the human experience which contributed to that sense of complexity—by contracting an unwise marriage, and by deserting his dramatic calling to serve as a recruiting officer for the Grenadiers at Litchfield, and subsequently at Shrewsbury. These two towns, in reverse order, were to be Farquhar's settings for *The Recruiting Officer*, first staged at Drury Lane in April 1706, and for *The Beaux Stratagem*, produced at the Haymarket on 8 March 1707, within a few weeks of his death on 29 April. Too much has perhaps been made of his shift from town to country settings: but the broader change in attitude of which this was a symptom did sever Farquhar's remaining links with the artificial manner, and bring him as close in comic sensibility to Shakespeare as any dramatist had come for almost a century.

The social range of *The Recruiting Officer*, which takes in a market township from its taverns to its town hall, and which unashamedly suggests the *shared* sexuality of its love affairs, is complemented rather than developed in *The Beaux Stratagem*. Here, more traditional types—a pair of fortune-hunting rakes—are transplanted into a country inn: and they are taught lessons in personal morality even as Farquhar outraged *public* morality by dramatizing Milton's teachings on divorce-by-consent. No regular comedy rivalled *The Beaux Stratagem* until the masterly throwbacks of Goldsmith and Sheridan: but fortunately modern audiences can be more tolerant than Augustan critics towards the genealogy of those 'illegitimate' kinds of comedy—farces, burlesques, ballad plays—which flourished in between.

The present text of *The Beaux Stratagem* follows that of the first edition of 1707. The fullest modern edition of Farquhar, and critically and textually the most reliable, is *The Complete Works of George Farquhar*, edited in two volumes by Charles Stonehill in 1930, in a limited edition for the Nonesuch Press. More accessible is the Mermaid Edition of the four major plays, edited by William Archer in 1906, and many times reprinted. Its texts are fairly sound, though unnecessarily modernized and tidied up: and Archer's comments now seem over-apologetic in tone.

THE
Beaux Stratagem.

A
COMEDY.

As it is Acted at the

QUEEN's THEATRE

IN THE

HAY-MARKET.

BY

Her MAJESTY's Sworn Comedians.

Written by Mr. Farquhar, *Author of the* Recruiting-Officer.

LONDON:

Printed for BERNARD LINTOTT, at the *Cross-Keys* next
Nando's Coffee-House in *Fleetstreet.*

ADVERTISEMENT.

THE Reader may find some Faults in this Play, which my Illness prevented the amending of, but there is great Amends made in the Representation, which cannot be match'd, no more than the friendly and indefatigable Care of Mr. *Wilks*, to whom I chiefly owe the Success of the Play.

GEORGE FARQUHAR.

Care of Mr. *Wilks*] Robert Wilks, besides excelling in the part of Archer, rendered assistance to Farquhar's widow and two daughters at the dying injunction of his long-standing friend.

PROLOGUE.

Spoken by Mr. WILKS.

*W*HEN *Strife disturbs or Sloth Corrupts an Age,*
    Keen Satyr is the Business of the Stage.
When the Plain-Dealer *writ, he lash'd those Crimes*
Which then infested most—The Modish Times:
But now, when Faction sleeps and Sloth is fled,
And all our Youth in Active Fields are bred;
When thro' GREAT BRITAIN'*s fair extensive Round,*
The Trumps of Fame the Notes of UNION *sound;*
When ANNA'*s Scepter points the Laws their Course,*
And Her Example gives her Precepts Force: 10
There scarce is room for Satyr, all our Lays
Must be, or Songs of Triumph, or of Praise:
But as in Grounds best cultivated, Tares
And Poppies rise among the Golden Ears;
Our Products so, fit for the Field or School,
Must mix with Nature's Favourite Plant—A Fool:
A Weed that has to twenty Summers ran,
Shoots up in Stalk, and Vegetates to Man.
Simpling our Author goes from Field to Field,
And culls such Fools, as may Diversion yield;   20
And, Thanks to Nature, there's no want of those,
For Rain, or Shine, the thriving Coxcomb grows.
Follies, to Night we shew, ne'er lash'd before,
Yet, such as Nature shews you every Hour;
Nor can the Picture's give a Just Offence,
For Fools are made for Jests to Men of Sense.

---

3 *the* Plain-Dealer] William Wycherley, whose play of that name was first performed in 1674.   8 UNION] That is, the Union of the English and Scottish Parliaments, enacted on 6 March 1707, two days before the first performance of *The Beaux Stratagem.* 19 *Simpling*] Gathering—originally, searching for 'simples' or medicinal herbs.

AN
EPILOGUE,

Design'd to be spoke in the Beaux Stratagem.

*I*F *to our Play Your Judgment can't be kind,*
   Let its expiring Author Pity find.
Survey his mournful Case with melting Eyes,
Nor let the Bard be dam'd before he dies.
Forbear you Fair on his last Scene to frown,
But his true Exit with a Plaudit Crown;
Then shall the dying Poet cease to Fear,
The dreadful Knell, while your Applause he hears.
At Leuctra *so, the Conqu'ring* Theban *dy'd,*
Claim'd his Friend's Praises, but their Tears deny'd: 10
Pleas'd in the Pangs of Death he greatly Thought
Conquest with loss of Life but cheaply bought.
The Difference this, the Greek was one wou'd fight
As brave, tho' not so gay as Serjeant Kite;
Ye Sons of Will's *what's that to those who write?*
To Thebes *alone the Grecian ow'd his Bays,* ⎫
You may the Bard above the Hero raise, ⎬
Since yours is greater than Athenian *Praise.* ⎭

---

2 *its expiring Author*] Wilks perpetuated the tradition that Farquhar died on 13 March 1707, the third night of *The Beaux Stratagem*. In fact he was buried—at Wilks's expense — on 3 May.   9 Leuctra] The Thebans defeated the Spartans at Leuctra in 371 B.C. But it was at the battle at Mantinea in 362 B.C. that the Theban leader, Epaminondas, died in the moment of his victory.   14 *Serjeant* Kite] A character in *The Recruiting Officer*.   15 Will's] A coffee house in Bow Street, famous for its literary clientele.   16 *Bays*] The victor's wreath of bay leaves—but also, of course, the laureate's.

Dramatis Personæ.

MEN.

Aimwell, Archer,	Two Gentlemen of broken Fortunes, the first as Master, and the second as Servant.	Mr. *Mills.* Mr. *Wilks.*
Count Bellair,	A French Officer, Prisoner at *Litch-field.*	Mr. *Bowman.*
Sullen,	A Country Blockhead, brutal to his Wife.	Mr. *Verbruggen.*
Freeman,	A Gentleman from *London.*	Mr. *Keen.*
Foigard,	A Priest, Chaplain to the French Officers.	Mr. *Bowen.*
Gibbet,	A High-way-man.	Mr. *Cibber.*
Hounslow, Bagshot,	His Companions.	
Bonniface,	Landlord of the Inn.	Mr. *Bullock.*
Scrub,	Servant to Mr. *Sullen.*	Mr. *Norris.*

WOMEN.

Lady *Bountiful,*	An old civil Country Gentlewoman, that cures all her Neighbours of all Distempers, and foolishly fond of her Son *Sullen.*	Mrs. *Powel.*
Dorinda,	Lady *Bountiful*'s Daughter.	Mrs. *Bradshaw.*
Mrs. *Sullen,*	Her Daughter-in-law.	Mrs. *Oldfield.*
Gipsey,	Maid to the Ladies.	Mrs. *Mills.*
Cherry,	The Landlord's Daughter in the Inn.	Mrs. *Bignal.*

SCENE, *Litchfield.*

THE
Beaux Stratagem.

ACT I. SCENE I.

SCENE, *an Inn.*

Enter Bonniface *running.*

Bon. CHamberlain, Maid, *Cherry*, Daughter *Cherry*, all asleep, all dead?

Enter Cherry *running.*

Cherry. Here, here, Why d'ye baul so, Father? d'ye think we have no Ears?

Bon. You deserve to have none, you young Minx;—The Company of the *Warrington* Coach has stood in the Hall this Hour, and no Body to shew them to their Chambers.

Cher. And let 'em wait farther; there's neither Red-Coat in the Coach, nor Footman behind it.

Bon. But they threaten to go to another Inn to Night.

Cher. That they dare not, for fear the Coachman should overturn them to Morrow——Coming, coming: Here's the *London* Coach arriv'd. 11

Enter several People with Trunks, Band-boxes, and other Luggage, and cross the Stage.

Bon. Welcome, Ladies.

Cher. Very welcome, Gentlemen——Chamberlain, shew the *Lyon* and the *Rose*. [*Exit with the Company.*

Enter Aimwell *in riding Habit*, Archer *as Footman carrying a Portmantle.*

Bon. This way, this way, Gentlemen.

Aim. Set down the things, go to the Stable, and see my Horses well rubb'd.

Arch. I shall, Sir. [*Exit.*

Aim. You're my Landlord, I suppose?

13 the *Lyon* and the *Rose*] Rooms in the inn, at that date known by names.

Bon. Yes, Sir, I'm old *Will. Bonniface*, pretty well known upon this Road, as the saying is.   21

Aim. O Mr. *Bonniface*, your Servant.

Bon. O Sir—What will your Honour please to drink, as the saying is?

Aim. I have heard your Town of *Litchfield* much fam'd for Ale, I think I'll taste that.

Bon. Sir, I have now in my Cellar Ten Tun of the best Ale in *Staffordshire*; 'tis smooth as Oil, sweet as Milk, clear as Amber, and strong as Brandy; and will be just Fourteen Year old the Fifth Day of next *March* old Stile.

Aim. You're very exact, I find, in the Age of your Ale.

Bon. As punctual, Sir, as I am in the Age of my Children: I'll shew you such Ale——Here, Tapster, broach Number 1706. as the saying is;——Sir, you shall taste my *Anno Domini*;—I have liv'd in *Litchfield* Man and Boy above Eight and fifty Years, and I believe have not consum'd Eight and fifty Ounces of Meat.   34

Aim. At a Meal, you mean, if one may guess your Sense by your Bulk.

Bon. Not in my Life, Sir, I have fed purely upon Ale; I have eat my Ale, drank my Ale, and I always sleep upon Ale.

Enter Tapster with a Bottle and Glass.

Now, Sir, you shall see [*filling it out*] your Worship's Health; ha! delicious, delicious,—fancy it *Burgundy*, only fancy it, and 'tis worth Ten Shilling a Quart.   40

Aim. [*Drinks.*] 'Tis confounded strong.

Bon. Strong! It must be so, or how should we be strong that drink it?

Aim. And have you liv'd so long upon this Ale, Landlord?

Bon. Eight and fifty Years upon my Credit, Sir; but it kill'd my Wife, poor Woman, as the saying is.

Aim. How came that to pass?

Bon. I don't know how, Sir; she would not let the Ale take its natural Course, Sir, she was for qualifying it every now and then with a Dram, as the saying is; and an honest Gentleman that came this way from *Ireland*, made her a Present of a dozen Bottles of Usquebaugh—But the poor Woman was never well after: But howe're, I was obliged to the Gentleman, you know.

Aim. Why, was it the Usquebaugh that kill'd her?   52

Bon. My Lady *Bountyful* said so,——She, good Lady, did what could be done, she cured her of Three Tympanies, but the Fourth carry'd her off; but she's happy, and I'm contented, as the saying is.

25 Tun] A cask equivalent to four hogsheads—thus containing about 200 gallons of ale. 28 old Stile] According to the Julian calendar; the Gregorian was not introduced into England until 1752. s.d. *Glass*] That is, glassware—in this case, probably two glasses. 50 Usquebaugh] Whiskey. 54 Tympanies] Swellings.

Aim. Who's that Lady *Bountyful*, you mention'd?

Bon. Ods my Life, Sir, we'll drink her Health. [*Drinks*] My Lady *Bountyful* is one of the best of Women: Her last Husband Sir *Charles Bountyful* left her worth a Thousand Pound a Year; and I believe she lays out one half on't in charitable Uses for the Good of her Neighbours; she cures Rheumatisms, Ruptures, and broken Shins in Men, Green Sickness, Obstructions, and Fits of the Mother in Women;—The Kings-Evil, Chin-Cough, and Chilblains in Children; in short, she has cured more People in and about *Litchfield* within Ten Years than the Doctors have kill'd in Twenty; and that's a bold Word.

Aim. Has the Lady been any other way useful in her Generation?   65

Bon. Yes, Sir, She has a Daughter by Sir *Charles*, the finest Woman in all our Country, and the greatest Fortune. She has a Son too by her first Husband Squire *Sullen*, who marry'd a fine Lady from *London* t'other Day; if you please, Sir, we'll drink his Health?

Aim. What sort of a Man is he?   70

Bon. Why, Sir, the Man's well enough; says little, thinks less, and does—nothing at all, Faith: But he's a Man of a great Estate, and values no Body.

Aim. A Sportsman, I suppose.

Bon. Yes, Sir, he's a Man of Pleasure, he plays at Whisk, and smoaks his Pipe Eight and forty Hours together sometimes.

Aim. And marry'd, you say?

Bon. Ay, and to a curious Woman, Sir,———But he's a——He wants it, here, Sir.   [*Pointing to his Forehead.*

Aim. He has it there, you mean.

Bon. That's none of my Business, he's my Landlord, and so a Man you know, wou'd not,———But—I cod, he's no better than——Sir, my humble Service to you. [*Drinks.*] Tho' I value not a Farthing what he can do to me; I pay him his Rent at Quarter day, I have a good running Trade, I have but one Daughter, and I can give her——But no matter for that.   84

Aim. You're very happy, Mr. *Bonniface*, pray what other Company have you in Town?

Bon. A power of fine Ladies, and then we have the *French* Officers.

Aim. O that's right, you have a good many of those Gentlemen: Pray how do you like their Company?

Bon. So well, as the saying is, that I cou'd wish we had as many more of 'em, they're full of Money, and pay double for every thing they have; they know, Sir, that we pay'd good round Taxes for the taking of 'em, and so they are willing to reimburse us a little; one of 'em lodges in my House.   93

Enter Archer.

61 Green Sickness] A kind of anaemia, most prevalent among young girls during puberty.
61 Fits of the Mother] Hysteria.   62 Kings-Evil] Scrofula.   62 Chin-Cough] Whooping cough.   74 Whisk] Whist.

Arch. Landlord, there are some *French* Gentlemen below that ask for you.

Bon. I'll wait on 'em;——Does your Master stay long in Town, as the saying is?   [*To* Archer.

Arch. I can't tell, as the saying is.

Bon. Come from *London*?

Arch. No.

Bon. Going to *London*, may hap?   100

Arch. No.

Bon. An odd Fellow this. I beg your Worship's Pardon, I'll wait on you in half a Minute.   [*Exit.*

Aim. The Coast's clear, I see,——Now my dear *Archer*, welcome to *Litchfield*.

Arch. I thank thee, my dear Brother in Iniquity.

Aim. Iniquity! prithee leave Canting, you need not change your Stile with your Dress.

Arch. Don't mistake me, *Aimwell*, for 'tis still my Maxim, that there is no Scandal like Rags, nor any Crime so shameful as Poverty.   110

Aim. The World confesses it every Day in its Practice, tho' Men won't own it for their Opinion: Who did that worthy Lord, my Brother, single out of the Side-box to sup with him t'other Night?

Arch. Jack Handycraft, a handsom, well dress'd, mannerly, sharping Rogue, who keeps the best Company in Town.

Aim. Right, and pray who marry'd my Lady *Manslaughter* t'other Day, the great Fortune?

Arch. Why, *Nick Marrabone*, a profess'd Pick-pocket, and a good Bowler; but he makes a handsom Figure, and rides in his Coach, that he formerly used to ride behind.   120

Aim. But did you observe poor *Jack Generous* in the Park last Week?

Arch. Yes, with his Autumnal Perriwig, shading his melancholly Face, his Coat older than any thing but its Fashion, with one Hand idle in his Pocket, and with the other picking his useless Teeth; and tho' the Mall was crowded with Company, yet was poor *Jack* as single and solitary as a Lyon in a Desart.

Aim. And as much avoided, for no Crime upon Earth but the want of Money.

Arch. And that's enough; Men must not be poor, Idleness is the Root of all Evil; the World's wide enough, let 'em bustle; Fortune has taken the weak under her Protection, but Men of Sense are left to their Industry.

Aim. Upon which Topick we proceed, and I think luckily hitherto: Wou'd not any Man swear now that I am a Man of Quality, and you my Servant, when if our intrinsick Value were known——   134

Arch. Come, come, we are the Men of intrinsick Value, who can strike our

Fortunes out of our selves, whose worth is independent of Accidents in Life, or Revolutions in Government; we have Heads to get Money, and Hearts to spend it.

Aim. As to our Hearts, I grant'ye, they are as willing Tits as any within Twenty Degrees; but I can have no great opinion of our Heads from the Service they have done us hitherto, unless it be that they have brought us from *London* hither to *Litchfield*, made me a Lord, and you my Servant.

Arch. That's more than you cou'd expect already. But what Money have we left?   144

Aim. But Two hundred Pound.

Arch. And our Horses, Cloaths, Rings, &c. why we have very good Fortunes now for moderate People; and let me tell you, besides, that this Two hundred Pound, with the experience that we are now Masters of, is a better Estate than the Ten Thousand we have spent.—Our Friends indeed began to suspect that our Pockets were low; but we came off with flying Colours, shew'd no signs of want either in Word or Deed.   151

Aim. Ay, and our going to *Brussels* was a good Pretence enough for our sudden disappearing; and I warrant you, our Friends imagine that we are gone a volunteering.

Arch. Why Faith, if this Prospect fails, it must e'en come to that, I am for venturing one of the Hundreds if you will upon this Knight-Errantry; but in case it should fail, we'll reserve the t'other to carry us to some Counterscarp, where we may die as we liv'd in a Blaze.

Aim. With all my Heart; and we have liv'd justly, *Archer*, we can't say that we have spent our Fortunes, but that we have enjoy'd 'em.   160

Arch. Right, so much Pleasure for so much Money, we have had our Penyworths, and had I Millions, I wou'd go to the same Market again. O *London, London!* well, we have had our share, and let us be thankful; Past Pleasures, for ought I know are best, such as we are sure of, those to come may disappoint us.

Aim. It has often griev'd the Heart of me, to see how some inhumane Wretches murther their kind Fortunes; those that by sacrificing all to one Appetite, shall starve all the rest.—You shall have some that live only in their Palates, and in their sense of tasting shall drown the other Four: Others are only Epicures in Appearances, such who shall starve their Nights to make a Figure a Days, and famish their own to feed the Eyes of others: A contrary Sort confine their Pleasures to the dark, and contract their spacious Acres to the Circuit of a Muff-string.   173

---

139 willing Tits] sound horses.   149 Ten Thousand] The word 'Thousand' is misplaced after 'besides', earlier in the same sentence, in the first edition.   156 one of the Hundreds] That is, 100 of their remaining 200 pounds.   157 Counterscarp] The outer wall of a fortified ditch.

Arch. Right; but they find the *Indies* in that Spot where they consume 'em, and I think your kind Keepers have much the best on't; for they indulge the most Senses by one Expence, there's the Seeing, Hearing, and Feeling amply gratify'd; and some Philosophers will tell you, that from such a Commerce there arises a sixth Sense that gives infinitely more Pleasure than the other five put together.

Aim. And to pass to the other Extremity, of all Keepers, I think those the worst that keep their Money.   181

Arch. Those are the most miserable Wights in being, they destroy the Rights of Nature, and disappoint the Blessings of Providence: Give me a Man that keeps his Five Senses keen and bright as his Sword, that has 'em always drawn out in their just order and strength, with his Reason as Commander at the Head of 'em, that detaches 'em by turns upon whatever Party of Pleasure agreeably offers, and commands 'em to retreat upon the least Appearance of Disadvantage or Danger:—For my part I can stick to my Bottle, while my Wine, my Company, and my Reason holds good; I can be charm'd with *Sappho*'s singing without falling in Love with her Face; I love Hunting, but wou'd not, like *Acteon*, be eaten up by my own Dogs; I love a fine House, but let another keep it; and just so I love a fine Woman.

Aim. In that last particular you have the better of me.   193

Arch. Ay, you're such an amorous Puppy, that I'm afraid you'll spoil our Sport; you can't counterfeit the Passion without feeling it.

Aim. Tho' the whining part be out of doors in Town, 'tis still in force with the Country Ladies;—And let me tell you *Frank*, the Fool in that Passion shall outdoe the Knave at any time.

Arch. Well, I won't dispute it now, you Command for the Day, and so I submit;——At *Nottingham* you know I am to be Master.   200

Aim. And at *Lincoln* I again.

Arch. Then at *Norwich* I mount, which, I think, shall be our last Stage; for if we fail there, we'll imbark for *Holland*, bid adieu to *Venus*, and welcome *Mars*.

Aim. A Match! [*Enter* Bonniface.] Mum.

Bon. What will your Worship please to have for Supper?

Aim. What have you got?

Bon. Sir, we have a delicate piece of Beef in the Pot, and a Pig at the Fire.

Aim. Good Supper-meat, I must confess,——I can't eat Beef, Landlord.

Arch. And I hate Pig.   210

Aim. Hold your prating, Sirrah, do you know who you are?

Bon. Please to bespeak something else, I have every thing in the House.

Aim. Have you any Veal?

Bon. Veal! Sir, we had a delicate Loin of Veal on *Wednesday* last.

Aim. Have you got any Fish or Wildfowl?

Bon. As for Fish, truly Sir, we are an inland Town, and indifferently provided with Fish, that's the Truth ont, and then for Wildfowl,——We have a delicate Couple of Rabbets.

Aim. Get me the Rabbets fricasy'd.

Bon. Fricasy'd! Lard, Sir, they'll eat much better smother'd with Onions.

Arch. Pshaw! damn your Onions.   221

Aim. Again, Sirrah!——Well, Landlord, what you please; but hold, I have a small Charge of Money, and your House is so full of Strangers, that I believe it may be safer in your Custody than mine; for when this Fellow of mine gets drunk, he minds nothing.——Here, Sirrah, reach me the strong Box.

Arch. Yes, Sir,——This will give us a Reputation.   [*Aside.*
                                                      [*Brings the Box.*

Aim. Here, Landlord, the Locks are sealed down both for your Security and mine; it holds somewhat above Two hundred Pound; if you doubt it, I'll count it to you after Supper; but be sure you lay it where I may have it at a Minute's warning; for my Affairs are a little dubious at present, perhaps I may be gone in half an Hour, perhaps I may be your Guest till the best part of that be spent; and pray order your Ostler to keep my Horses always sadled; but one thing above the rest I must beg, that you would let this Fellow have none of your *Anno Domini*, as you call it;——For he's the most insufferable Sot——Here, Sirrah, light me to my Chamber.   236
                                                      [*Exit lighted by* Archer.

Bon. Cherry, Daughter *Cherry!*

Enter Cherry.

Cher. D'ye call, Father?

Bon. Ay, Child, you must lay by this Box for the Gentleman, 'tis full of Money.   240

Cher. Money! all that Money! why, sure Father the Gentleman comes to be chosen Parliament-man. Who is he?

Bon. I don't know what to make of him, he talks of keeping his Horses ready sadled, and of going perhaps at a minute's warning, or of staying perhaps till the best part of this be spent.

Cher. Ay, ten to one, Father, he's a High-way-man.

Bon. A High-way-man! upon my Life, Girl, you have hit it, and this Box is some new purchased Booty.—Now cou'd we find him out, the Money were ours.

Cher. He don't belong to our Gang?   250

Bon. What Horses have they?

242 Parliament-man] Cherry assumes that Aimwell's money is to be expended in purchasing votes.

Cher. The Master rides upon a Black.

Bon. A Black! ten to one the Man upon the black Mare; and since he don't belong to our Fraternity, we may betray him with a safe Conscience; I don't think it lawful to harbour any Rogues but my own.——Look'ye, Child, as the saying is, we must go cunningly to work, Proofs we must have, the Gentleman's Servant loves Drink, I'll ply him that way, and ten to one loves a Wench; you must work him t'other way.

Cher. Father, wou'd you have me give my Secret for his?

Bon. Consider, Child, there's Two hundred Pound to Boot. [*Ringing without.*] Coming, coming.——Child, mind your Business.   261

Cher. What a Rogue is my Father! my Father! I deny it.——My Mother was a good, generous, free-hearted Woman, and I can't tell how far her good Nature might have extended for the good of her Children. This Landlord of mine, for I think I can call him no more, would betray his Guest, and debauch his Daughter into the bargain,——By a Footman too!

Enter Archer.

Arch. What Footman, pray, Mistress, is so happy as to be the subject of your Contemplation?

Cher. Whoever he is, Friend, he'll be but little the better for't.

Arch. I hope so, for I'm sure you did not think of me.   270

Cher. Suppose I had?

Arch. Why then you're but even with me; for the Minute I came in, I was a considering in what manner I should make love to you.

Cher. Love to me, Friend!

Arch. Yes, Child.

Cher. Child! Manners; if you kept a little more distance, Friend, it would become you much better.

Arch. Distance! good night, Sauce-box.   [*Going.*

Cher. A pretty Fellow! I like his Pride,——Sir, pray, Sir, you see, Sir, [*Archer returns.*] I have the Credit to be intrusted with your Master's Fortune here, which sets me a Degree above his Footman; I hope, Sir, you an't affronted.   282

Arch. Let me look you full in the Face, and I'll tell you whether you can affront me or no.——S'death, Child, you have a pair of delicate Eyes, and you don't know what to do with 'em.

Cher. Why, Sir, don't I see every body?

Arch. Ay, but if some Women had 'em, they wou'd kill every body.—— Prithee, instruct me, I wou'd fain make Love to you, but I don't know what to say.

Cher. Why, did you never make Love to any body before?   290

Arch. Never to a Person of your Figure, I can assure you, Madam, my

Addresses have been always confin'd to People within my own Sphere, I never aspir'd so high before.

> But you look so bright,
> And are dress'd so tight,
> That a Man would swear you're Right,
> As arm was e'er laid over.

> Such an Air
> You freely wear
> To ensnare,   300
> As makes each Guest a Lover!

> Since then, my Dear, I'm your Guest,
> Prithee give me of the Best
> Of what is ready Drest:
> Since then, my Dear, &c.   [*A Song.*

Cher. What can I think of this Man? [*Aside.*] Will you give me that Song, Sir?

Arch. Ay, my Dear, take it while 'tis warm. [*Kisses her.*] Death and Fire! her Lips are Honey-combs.

Cher. And I wish there had been Bees too, to have stung you for your Impudence.   311

Arch. There's a swarm of *Cupids*, my little *Venus*, that has done the Business much better.

Cher. This Fellow is misbegotten as well as I. [*Aside.*] What's your Name, Sir?

Arch. Name! I gad, I have forgot it. [*Aside.*] Oh! *Martin.*

Cher. Where were you born?

Arch. In St. *Martin*'s Parish.

Cher. What was your Father?

Arch. St. *Martin*'s Parish.   320

Cher. Then, Friend, good night.

Arch. I hope not.

Cher. You may depend upon't.

Arch. Upon what?

Cher. That you're very impudent.

Arch. That you're very handsome.

Cher. That you're a Footman.

296–305 *That a Man . . . my Dear*] Only the first two lines of the song are given in the first edition.

Arch. That you're an Angel.

Cher. I shall be rude.

Arch. So shall I.   330

Cher. Let go my Hand.

Arch. Give me a Kiss.   [*Kisses her.*
                                          [*Call without,* Cherry, Cherry.

Cher. I'mm——My Father calls; you plaguy Devil, how durst you stop my Breath so?——Offer to follow me one step, if you dare.

Arch. A fair Challenge by this Light; this is a pretty fair opening of an Adventure; but we are Knight-Errants, and so Fortune be our Guide.

[*Exit.*

The End of the First Act.

ACT II.

SCENE, *A Gallery in Lady* Bountyful's *House.*

Mrs. Sullen *and* Dorinda *meeting.*

Dor. MOrrow, my dear Sister; are you for Church this Morning?

Mrs. Sull. Any where to Pray; for Heaven alone can help me: But, I think, *Dorinda*, there's no Form of Prayer in the Liturgy against bad Husbands.

Dor. But there's a Form of Law in *Doctors-Commons;* and I swear, Sister *Sullen*, rather than see you thus continually discontented, I would advise you to apply to that: For besides the part that I bear in your vexatious Broils, as being Sister to the Husband, and Friend to the Wife; your Example gives me such an Impression of Matrimony, that I shall be apt to condemn my Person to a long Vacation all its Life.——But supposing, Madam, that you brought it to a Case of Separation, what can you urge against your Husband? My Brother is, first, the most constant Man alive.

Mrs. Sull. The most constant Husband, I grant'ye.   13

Dor. He never sleeps from you.

Mrs. Sull. No, he always sleeps with me.

Dor. He allows you a Maintenance suitable to your Quality.

Mrs. Sull. A Maintenance! do you take me, Madam, for an hospital Child, that I must sit down, and bless my Benefactors for Meat, Drink and Clothes? As I take it, Madam, I brought your Brother Ten thousand Pounds, out of which, I might expect some pretty things, call'd Pleasures.   20

II. i, 5 *Doctors-Commons*] The College of Civil Law which then dealt in marriage settlements, divorces, and wills.

Dor. You share in all the Pleasures that the Country affords.

Mrs. *Sul.* Country Pleasures! Racks and Torments! dost think, Child, that my Limbs were made for leaping of Ditches, and clambring over Stiles; or that my Parents wisely foreseeing my future Happiness in Country-pleasures, had early instructed me in the rural Accomplishments of drinking fat Ale, playing at Whisk, and smoaking Tobacco with my Husband; or of spreading of Plaisters, brewing of Diet-drinks, and stilling Rosemary-Water with the good old Gentlewoman, my Mother-in-Law.

Dor. I'm sorry, Madam, that it is not more in our power to divert you; I cou'd wish indeed that our Entertainments were a little more polite, or your Taste a little less refin'd: But, pray, Madam, how came the Poets and Philosophers that labour'd so much in hunting after Pleasure, to place it at last in a Country Life?   33

Mrs. *Sull.* Because they wanted Money, Child, to find out the Pleasures of the Town: Did you ever see a Poet or Philosopher worth Ten thousand Pound; if you can shew me such a Man, I'll lay you Fifty Pound you'll find him somewhere within the weekly Bills.——Not that I disapprove rural Pleasures, as the Poets have painted them; in their Landschape every *Phillis* has her *Coridon*, every murmuring Stream, and every flowry Mead gives fresh Alarms to Love.——Besides, you'll find, that their Couples were never marry'd:——But yonder I see my *Coridon*, and a sweet Swain it is, Heaven knows.——Come, *Dorinda*, don't be angry, he's my Husband, and your Brother; and between both is he not a sad Brute?   43

Dor. I have nothing to say to your part of him, you're the best Judge.

Mrs. *Sull.* O Sister, Sister! if ever you marry, beware of a sullen, silent Sot, one that's always musing, but never thinks:——There's some Diversion in a talking Blockhead; and since a Woman must wear Chains, I wou'd have the Pleasure of hearing 'em rattle a little.——Now you shall see, but take this by the way;——He came home this Morning at his usual Hour of Four, waken'd me out of a sweet Dream of something else, by tumbling over the Tea-table, which he broke all to pieces, after his Man and he had rowl'd about the Room like sick Passengers in a Storm, he comes flounce into Bed, dead as a Salmon into a Fishmonger's Basket; his Feet cold as Ice, his Breath hot as a Furnace, and his Hands and his Face as greasy as his Flanel Night-cap.——Oh Matrimony!——He tosses up the Clothes with a barbarous swing over his Shoulders, disorders the whole Oeconomy of my Bed, leaves me half naked, and my whole Night's Comfort is the tuneable Serenade of that wakeful Nightingale, his Nose.——O the Pleasure of counting the

---

26 fat Ale] Full-bodied, strong ale. 37 within the weekly Bills] That is, within the central districts of London for which weekly bills of mortality and of its various causes were issued. 38 every *Phillis* has her *Coridon*] Allusively, every pastoral lover has his or her mate.

melancholly Clock by a snoring Husband!——But now, Sister, you shall see how handsomely, being a well-bred Man, he will beg my Pardon.   60

Enter Sullen.

Sull. My Head akes consumedly.

Mrs. Sull. Will you be pleased, my Dear, to drink Tea with us this Morning? it may do your Head good.

Sull. No.

Dor. Coffee? Brother.

Sull. Pshaw.

Mrs. Sull. Will you please to dress and go to Church with me, the Air may help you.

Sull. Scrub.

Enter Scrub.

Scrub. Sir.   70

Sull. What Day o'th Week is this?

Scrub. Sunday, an't please your Worship.

Sull. Sunday! bring me a Dram, and d'ye hear, set out the Venison-Pasty, and a Tankard of strong Beer upon the Hall-Table, I'll go to breakfast. [*Going.*

Dor. Stay, stay, Brother, you shan't get off so; you were very naughty last Night, and must make your Wife Reparation; come, come, Brother, won't you ask Pardon?

Sull. For what?

Dor. For being drunk last Night.

Sull. I can afford it, can't I?   80

Mrs. Sull. But I can't, Sir.

Sull. Then you may let it alone.

Mrs. Sull. But I must tell you, Sir, that this is not to be born.

Sull. I'm glad on't.

Mrs. Sull. What is the Reason, Sir, that you use me thus inhumanely?

Sull. Scrub?

Scrub. Sir.

Sull. Get things ready to shave my Head.   [*Exit.*

Mrs. Sull. Have a care of coming near his Temples, *Scrub*, for fear you meet something there that may turn the Edge of your Razor.——Inveterate Stupidity! did you ever know so hard, so obstinate a Spleen as his? O Sister, Sister! I shall never ha' Good of the Beast till I get him to Town; *London*, dear *London* is the Place for managing and breaking a Husband.   93

Dor. And has not a Husband the same Opportunities there for humbling a Wife?

Mrs. Sull. No, no, Child, 'tis a standing Maxim in conjugal Discipline, that when a Man wou'd enslave his Wife, he hurries her into the Country;

and when a Lady would be arbitrary with her Husband, she wheedles her
Booby up to Town.——A Man dare not play the Tyrant in *London*, because
there are so many Examples to encourage the Subject to rebel. O *Dorinda*,
Dorinda! a fine Woman may do any thing in *London*: O'my Conscience, she
may raise an Army of Forty thousand Men.   102

Dor. I fancy, Sister, you have a mind to be trying your Power that way here
in *Litchfield*; you have drawn the *French* Count to your Colours already.

Mrs. *Sull.* The *French* are a People that can't live without their Gallantries.

Dor. And some *English* that I know, Sister, are not averse to such Amuse-
ments.

Mrs. *Sull.* Well, Sister, since the Truth must out, it may do as well now as
hereafter; I think one way to rouse my Lethargick sotish Husband, is, to
give him a Rival; Security begets Negligence in all People, and Men must be
alarm'd to make 'em alert in their Duty: Women are like Pictures of no Value
in the Hands of a Fool, till he hears Men of Sense bid high for the Purchase.

Dor. This might do, Sister, if my Brother's Understanding were to be
convinc'd into a Passion for you; but I fancy there's a natural Aversion of his
side; and I fancy, Sister, that you don't come much behind him, if you dealt
fairly.   116

Mrs. *Sull.* I own it, we are united Contradictions, Fire and Water: But
I cou'd be contented, with a great many other Wives, to humour the cen-
sorious Mob, and give the World an Appearance of living well with my
Husband, cou'd I bring him but to dissemble a little Kindness to keep me in
Countenance.   121

Dor. But how do you know, Sister, but that instead of rousing your
Husband by this Artifice to a counterfeit Kindness, he should awake in a real
Fury?

Mrs. *Sull.* Let him:——If I can't entice him to the one, I wou'd provoke
him to the other.

Dor. But how must I behave my self between ye?

Mrs. *Sull.* You must assist me.

Dor. What, against my own Brother!

Mrs. *Sull.* He's but half a Brother, and I'm your entire Friend: If I go a
step beyond the Bounds of Honour, leave me; till then I expect you should go
along with me in every thing, while I trust my Honour in your Hands, you
may trust your Brother's in mine.——The Count is to dine here to Day.

Dor. 'Tis a strange thing, Sister, that I can't like that Man.   134

Mrs. *Sull.* You like nothing, your time is not come; Love and Death have
their Fatalities, and strike home one time or other:——You'll pay for all one
Day, I warrant'ye.——But, come, my Lady's Tea is ready, and 'tis almost
Church-time.   [*Exeunt.*

B

SCENE, *The Inn*.

Enter Aimwell *dress'd, and* Archer.

Aim. And was she the Daughter of the House?

Arch. The Landlord is so blind as to think so; but I dare swear she has better Blood in her Veins.

Aim. Why dost think so?

Arch. Because the Baggage has a pert *Je ne scai quoi*, she reads Plays, keeps a Monkey, and is troubled with Vapours.

Aim. By which Discoveries I guess that you know more of her.

Arch. Not yet, Faith, the Lady gives her self Airs, forsooth, nothing under a Gentleman.

Aim. Let me take her in hand.   10

Arch. Say one Word more o'that, and I'll declare my self, spoil your Sport there, and every where else; look'ye, *Aimwell*, every Man in his own Sphere.

Aim. Right; and therefore you must pimp for your Master.

Arch. In the usual Forms, good Sir, after I have serv'd my self.——But to our Business:——You are so well dress'd, *Tom*, and make so handsome a Figure, that I fancy you may do Execution in a Country Church; the exteriour part strikes first, and you're in the right to make that Impression favourable.

Aim. There's something in that which may turn to Advantage: The Appearance of a Stranger in a Country Church draws as many Gazers as a blazing Star; no sooner he comes into the Cathedral, but a Train of Whispers runs buzzing round the Congregation in a moment;——Who is he? whence comes he? do you know him?——Then I, Sir, tips me the Verger with half a Crown; he pockets the Simony, and Inducts me into the best Pue in the Church, I pull out my Snuff-box, turn my self round, bow to the Bishop, or the Dean, if he be the commanding Officer; single out a Beauty, rivet both my Eyes to hers, set my Nose a bleeding by the Strength of Imagination, and shew the whole Church my concern by my endeavouring to hide it; after the Sermon, the whole Town gives me to her for a Lover, and by perswading the Lady that I am a dying for her, the Tables are turn'd, and she in good earnest falls in Love with me.   32

Arch. There's nothing in this, *Tom*, without a Precedent; but instead of riveting your Eyes to a Beauty, try to fix 'em upon a Fortune, that's our Business at present.

17 do Execution in] Impress your personal distinctions upon.   22 blazing Star] Comet.
25 Simony] A means of purchasing ecclesiastical preferment—hence, here, a bribe to secure a good pew.

Aim. Pshaw, no Woman can be a Beauty without a Fortune.—Let me alone, for I am a Mark'sman.

Arch. Tom.

Aim. Ay.

Arch. When were you at Church before, pray?   40

Aim. Um——I was there at the Coronation.

Arch. And how can you expect a Blessing by going to Church now?

Aim. Blessing! nay, *Frank*, I ask but for a Wife.   [*Exit.*

Arch. Truly the Man is not very unreasonable in his Demands.

[*Exit at the opposite Door.*

Enter Bonniface *and* Cherry.

Bon. Well Daughter, as the saying is, have you brought *Martin* to confess?

Cher. Pray, Father, don't put me upon getting any thing out of a Man; I'm but young you know, Father, and I don't understand Wheedling.

Bon. Young! why you Jade, as the saying is, can any Woman wheedle that is not young? you'r Mother was useless at five and twenty; not wheedle! would you make your Mother a Whore and me a Cuckold, as the saying is? I tell you his Silence confesses it, and his Master spends his Money so freely, and is so much a Gentleman every manner of way that he must be a Highwayman.   53

Enter Gibbet *in a Cloak.*

Gib. Landlord, Landlord, is the Coast clear?

Bon. O, Mr. *Gibbet*, what's the News?

Gib. No matter, ask no Questions, all fair and honourable, here, my dear *Cherry* [*Gives her a Bag.*] Two hundred Sterling Pounds, as good as any that ever hang'd or sav'd a Rogue; lay 'em by with the rest, and here——Three wedding or mourning Rings, 'tis much the same you know——Here, two Silver-hilted Swords; I took those from Fellows that never shew any part of their Swords but the Hilts: Here is a Diamond Necklace which the Lady hid in the privatest place in the Coach, but I found it out: This Gold Watch I took from a Pawn-broker's Wife; it was left in her Hands by a Person of Quality, there's the Arms upon the Case.   64

Cher. But who had you the Money from?

Gib. Ah! poor Woman! I pitied her;——From a poor Lady just elop'd from her Husband, she had made up her Cargo, and was bound for *Ireland*, as hard as she cou'd drive; she told me of her Husband's barbarous Usage, and so I left her half a Crown: But I had almost forgot, my dear *Cherry*, I have a Present for you.   70

Cher. What is't?

41 the Coronation] That is, of Queen Anne—five years before.

Gib. A Pot of Cereuse, my Child, that I took out of a Lady's under Pocket.

Cher. What, Mr. *Gibbet*, do you think that I paint?

Gib. Why, you Jade, your Betters do; I'm sure the Lady that I took it from had a Coronet upon her Handkerchief.——Here, take my Cloak, and go, secure the Premisses.

Cher. I will secure 'em.   [*Exit.*

Bon. But, heark'ye, where's *Hounslow* and *Bagshot*?

Gib. They'll be here to Night.

Bon. D'ye know of any other Gentlemen o'the Pad on this Road?   80

Gib. No.

Bon. I fancy that I have two that lodge in the House just now.

Gib. The Devil! how d'ye smoak 'em?

Bon. Why, the one is gone to Church.

Gib. That's suspitious, I must confess.

Bon. And the other is now in his Master's Chamber; he pretends to be Servant to the other, we'll call him out, and pump him a little.

Gib. With all my Heart.

Bon. Mr. *Martin*, Mr. *Martin*?

Enter Martin *combing a Perrywig, and singing.*

Gib. The Roads are consumed deep; I'm as dirty as old *Brentford* at *Christmas.*——A good pretty Fellow that; who's Servant are you, Friend?

Arch. My Master's.   92

Gib. Really?

Arch. Really.

Gib. That's much.——The Fellow has been at the Bar by his Evasions:——But, pray, Sir, what is your Master's Name?

Arch. Tall, all dall; [*sings and combs the Perrywig.*] This is the most obstinate Curl——

Gib. I ask you his Name?

Arch. Name, Sir,——*Tall, all dal*——I never ask'd him his Name in my Life. *Tall, all dall.*   101

Bon. What think you now?

Gib. Plain, plain, he talks now as if he were before a Judge: But, pray, Friend, which way does your Master travel?

Arch. A Horseback.

Gib. Very well again, an old Offender, right;——But, I mean does he go upwards or downwards?

Arch. Downwards, I fear, Sir: *Tall, all.*

72 Cereuse] A cosmetic for whitening the skin.   76 the Premisses] That is, the articles previously enumerated. A legal phrase, used ironically.   90 old *Brentford*] A 'town of mud', according to Thomson, in his *Castle of Indolence*.

Gib. I'm afraid my Fate will be a contrary way.

Bon. Ha, ha, ha! Mr. *Martin* you're very arch.——This Gentleman is only travelling towards *Chester*, and wou'd be glad of your Company, that's all. ———Come, Captain, you'll stay to Night, I suppose; I'll shew you a Chamber———Come, Captain.   113

Gib. Farewell, Friend———   [*Exit.*

Arch. Captain, your Servant.———Captain! a pretty Fellow; s'death, I wonder that the Officers of the Army don't conspire to beat all Scoundrels in Red, but their own.

Enter Cherry.

Cher. Gone! and *Martin* here! I hope he did not listen; I wou'd have the Merit of the discovery all my own, because I wou'd oblige him to love me. [*Aside.*] Mr. *Martin*, who was that Man with my Father?   120

Arch. Some Recruiting Serjeant, or whip'd out Trooper, I suppose.

Cher. All's safe, I find.   [*Aside.*

Arch. Come, my Dear, have you con'd over the Catechise I taught you last Night?

Cher. Come, question me.

Arch. What is Love?

Cher. Love is I know not what, it comes I know not how, and goes I know not when.

Arch. Very well, an apt Scholar. [*Chucks her under the Chin.*] Where does Love enter?   130

Cher. Into the Eyes.

Arch. And where go out?

Cher. I won't tell'ye.

Arch. What are Objects of that Passion?

Cher. Youth, Beauty, and clean Linen.

Arch. The Reason?

Cher. The two first are fashionable in Nature, and the third at Court.

Arch. That's my Dear: What are the Signs and Tokens of that Passion?

Cher. A stealing Look, a stammering Tongue, Words improbable, Designs impossible, and Actions impracticable.   140

Arch. That's my good Child, kiss me.——What must a Lover do to obtain his Mistress?

Cher. He must adore the Person that disdains him, he must bribe the Chambermaid that betrays him, and court the Footman that laughs at him; ——He must, he must———

Arch. Nay, Child, I must whip you if you don't mind your Lesson; he must treat his———

Cher. O, ay, he must treat his Enemies with Respect, his Friends with

Indifference, and all the World with Contempt; he must suffer much, and fear more; he must desire much, and hope little; in short, he must embrace his Ruine, and throw himself away.   151

Arch. Had ever Man so hopeful a Pupil as mine? come, my Dear, why is Love call'd a Riddle?

Cher. Because being blind, he leads those that see, and tho' a Child, he governs a Man.

Arch. Mighty well.—And why is Love pictur'd blind?

Cher. Because the Painters out of the weakness or privilege of their Art chose to hide those Eyes that they cou'd not draw.

Arch. That's my dear little Scholar, kiss me again.——And why shou'd Love, that's a Child, govern a Man?   16ͼ

Cher. Because that a Child is the end of Love.

Arch. And so ends Love's Catechism.——And now, my Dear, we'll go in, and make my Master's Bed.

Cher. Hold, hold, Mr. *Martin*,——You have taken a great deal of Pains to instruct me, and what d'ye think I have learn't by it?

Arch. What?

Cher. That your Discourse and your Habit are Contradictions, and it wou'd be nonsense in me to believe you a Footman any longer.

Arch. 'Oons, what a Witch it is!

Cher. Depend upon this, Sir, nothing in this Garb shall ever tempt me; for tho' I was born to Servitude, I hate it:——Own your Condition, swear you love me, and then——   172

Arch. And then we shall go make the Bed.

Cher. Yes.

Arch. You must know then, that I am born a Gentleman, my Education was liberal; but I went to *London* a younger Brother, fell into the Hands of Sharpers, who stript me of my Money, my Friends disown'd me, and now my Necessity brings me to what you see.

Cher. Then take my Hand——promise to marry me before you sleep, and I'll make you Master of two thousand Pound.   180

Arch. How!

Cher. Two thousand Pound that I have this Minute in my own Custody; so throw off your Livery this Instant, and I'll go find a Parson.

Arch. What said you? A Parson!

Cher. What! do you scruple?

Arch. Scruple! no, no, but——two thousand Pound you say?

Cher. And better.

Arch. S'death, what shall I do——but heark'e, Child, what need you make me Master of your self and Money, when you may have the same Pleasure out of me, and still keep your Fortune in your Hands.   190

Cher. Then you won't marry me?

Arch. I wou'd marry you, but——

Cher. O sweet, Sir, I'm your humble Servant, you're fairly caught, wou'd you perswade me that any Gentleman who cou'd bear the Scandal of wearing a Livery, wou'd refuse two thousand Pound let the Condition be what it wou'd—no, no, Sir,—but I hope you'll Pardon the Freedom I have taken, since it was only to inform my self of the Respect that I ought to pay you.
                                                                    [*Going.*

Arch. Fairly bit, by *Jupiter*——hold, hold, and have you actually two thousand Pound?

Cher. Sir, I have my Secrets as well as you—when you please to be more open, I shall be more free, and be assur'd that I have Discoveries that will match yours, be what they will—in the mean while be satisfy'd that no Discovery I make shall ever hurt you, but beware of my Father.—   [*Exit.*

Arch. So—we're like to have as many Adventures in our Inn, as *Don Quixote* had in his——let me see,——two thousand Pound! if the Wench wou'd promise to dye when the Money were spent, I gad, one wou'd marry her, but the Fortune may go off in a Year or two, and the Wife may live ——Lord knows how long? then an Inkeeper's Daughter; ay that's the Devil——there my Pride brings me off.   208

> *For whatsoe'er the Sages charge on Pride*
> *The Angels fall, and twenty Faults beside,*
> *On Earth I'm sure, 'mong us of mortal Calling,*
> *Pride saves Man oft, and Woman too from falling.*

                                                                    [*Exit.*

                        End of the Second Act.

ACT III.

SCENE *continues.*

Enter Mrs. Sullen, Dorinda.

Mrs. Sull. Ha, ha, ha, my dear Sister, let me embrace thee, now we are Friends indeed! for I shall have a Secret of yours, as a Pledge for mine——now you'll be good for something, I shall have you conversable in the Subjects of the Sex.

Dor. But do you think that I am so weak as to fall in Love with a Fellow at first sight?

III. SCENE *continues*] In fact, the context demands a scene-change to the Gallery of Lady Bountiful's house.

Mrs. *Sull*. Pshaw! now you spoil all, why shou'd not we be as free in our Friendships as the Men? I warrant you the Gentleman has got to his Confident already, has avow'd his Passion, toasted your Health, call'd you ten thousand Angels, has run over your Lips, Eyes, Neck, Shape, Air and every thing, in a Description that warms their Mirth to a second Enjoyment.   12

Dor. Your Hand, Sister, I an't well.

Mrs. *Sull*. So,—she's breeding already—come Child up with it—hem a little——so——now tell me, don't you like the Gentleman that we saw at Church just now?

Dor. The Man's well enough.

Mrs. *Sull*. Well enough! is he not a Demigod, a *Narcissus*, a Star, the Man i'the Moon?

Dor. O Sister, I'm extreamly ill.   20

Mrs. *Sull*. Shall I send to your Mother, Child, for a little of her Cephalick Plaister to put to the Soals of your Feet, or shall I send to the Gentleman for something for you?——Come, unlace your Steas, unbosome your self—— the Man is perfectly a pretty Fellow, I saw him when he first came into Church.

Dor. I saw him too, Sister, and with an Air that shone, methought like Rays about his Person.

Mrs. *Sull*. Well said, up with it.

Dor. No forward Coquett Behaviour, no Airs to set him off, no study'd Looks nor artful Posture,—but Nature did it all—   30

Mrs. *Sull*. Better and better—one Touch more—come.—

Dor. But then his Looks—did you observe his Eyes?

Mrs. *Sull*. Yes, yes, I did——his Eyes, well, what of his Eyes?

Dor. Sprightly, but not wandring; they seem'd to view, but never gaz'd on any thing but me——and then his Looks so humble were, and yet so noble, that they aim'd to tell me that he cou'd with Pride dye at my Feet, tho' he scorn'd Slavery any where else.

Mrs. *Sull*. The Physick works purely——How d'ye find your self now, my Dear?

Dor. Hem! much better, my Dear——O here comes our Mercury! [*Enter* Scrub.] Well *Scrub*, what News of the Gentleman?   41

Scrub. Madam, I have brought you a Packet of News.

Dor. Open it quickly, come.

Scrub. In the first place I enquir'd who the Gentleman was? they told me he was a Stranger, Secondly, I ask'd what the Gentleman was, they answer'd and said, that they never saw him before. Thirdly, I enquir'd what Country-

9 Confident] Trusted friend, confidant. 21 Cephalick Plaister] A plaster not, of course, for the feet, but for the head.

man he was, they reply'd 'twas more than they knew. Fourthly, I demanded whence he came, their Answer was, they cou'd not tell. And Fifthly, I ask'd whither he went, and they reply'd they knew nothing of the matter,—and this is all I cou'd learn.   50

Mrs. Sull. But what do the People say, can't they guess?

Scrub. Why some think he's a Spy, some guess he's a Mountebank, some say one thing, some another; but for my own part, I believe he's a Jesuit.

Dor. A Jesuit! why a Jesuit?

Scrub. Because he keeps his Horses always ready sadled, and his Footman talks French.

Mrs. Sull. His Footman!

Scrub. Ay, he and the Count's Footman were Gabbering French like two intreaguing Ducks in a Mill-Pond, and I believe they talk'd of me, for they laugh'd consumedly.   60

Dor. What sort of Livery has the Footman?

Scrub. Livery! Lord, Madam, I took him for a Captain, he's so bedizen'd with Lace, and then he has Tops to his Shoes, up to his mid Leg, a silver headed Cane dangling at his Nuckles,—he carries his Hands in his Pockets just so—[*Walks in the French Air*] and has a fine long Perriwig ty'd up in a Bag——Lord, Madam, he's clear another sort of Man than I.

Mrs. Sull. That may easily be——but what shall we do now, Sister?

Dor. I have it—This Fellow has a world of Simplicity, and some Cunning, the first hides the latter by abundance—*Scrub.*

Scrub. Madam.   70

Dor. We have a great mind to know who this Gentleman is, only for our Satisfaction.

Scrub. Yes, Madam, it would be a Satisfaction, no doubt.

Dor. You must go and get acquainted with his Footman, and invite him hither to drink a Bottle of your Ale, because you're Butler to Day.

Scrub. Yes, Madam, I am Butler every Sunday.

Mrs. Sull. O brave, Sister, O my Conscience, you understand the Mathematicks already—'tis the best Plot in the World, your Mother, you know, will be gone to Church, my Spouse will be got to the Ale-house with his Scoundrels, and the House will be our own—so we drop in by Accident and ask the Fellow some Questions our selves. In the Countrey you know any Stranger is Company, and we're glad to take up with the Butler in a Country Dance, and happy if he'll do us the Favour.   83

Scrub. Oh! Madam, you wrong me, I never refus'd your Ladyship the Favour in my Life.

Enter Gipsey.

52 Mountebank] Charlatan, confidence-trickster.

Gip. Ladies, Dinner's upon Table.

Dor. Scrub, We'll excuse your waiting———Go where we order'd you.

Scrub. I shall.   *[Exeunt.*

SCENE *changes to the Inn.*

Enter Aimwell *and* Archer.

Arch. Well, *Tom,* I find you're a Marksman.

Aim. A Marksman! who so blind cou'd be, as not discern a Swan among the Ravens?

Arch. Well, but heark'ee, *Aimwell.*

Aim. Aimwel! call me *Oroondates, Cesario, Amadis,* all that Romance can in a Lover paint, and then I'll answer. O *Archer,* I read her thousands in her Looks, she look'd like *Ceres* in her Harvest, Corn, Wine and Oil, Milk and Honey, Gardens, Groves and Purling Streams play'd on her plenteous Face.

Arch. Her Face! her Pocket, you mean; the Corn, Wine and Oil lies there. In short, she has ten thousand Pound, that's the English on't.   10

Aim. Her Eyes———

Arch. Are Demi-Cannons to be sure, so I won't stand their Battery.

                                                                [Going.

Aim. Pray excuse me, my Passion must have vent.

Arch. Passion! what a plague, d'ee think these Romantick Airs will do our Business? Were my Temper as extravagant as yours, my Adventures have something more Romantick by half.

Aim. Your Adventures!

Arch. Yes, The Nymph that with her twice ten hundred Pounds
        With brazen Engine hot, and Quoif clear starch'd
        Can fire the Guest in warming of the Bed———   20
There's a Touch of Sublime *Milton* for you, and the Subject but an Innkeeper's Daughter; I can play with a Girl as an Angler do's with his Fish; he keeps it at the end of his Line, runs it up the Stream, and down the Stream, till at last, he brings it to hand, tickles the Trout, and so whips it into his Basket.

Enter Bonniface.

Bon. Mr. *Martin,* as the saying is—yonder's an honest Fellow below, my

III. ii, 5 *Oroondates*] A character in La Calprenède's *Cassandra*, first translated in 1652. 5 *Cesario*] In *Twelfth Night.* 5 *Amadis*] The eponymous hero of the *Amadis de Gaul,* a Spanish romance of the fourteenth century.   12 Demi-Cannons] One of the larger kinds of cannon, weighing some 6000 pounds.   19 Quoif] A tightly-fitting white cap.

Lady *Bountiful*'s Butler, who begs the Honour that you wou'd go Home with
him and see his Cellar.

Arch. Do my *Baisemains* to the Gentleman, and tell him I will do my self
the Honour to wait on him immediately.   [*Exit* Bon.

Aim. What do I hear? soft *Orpheus* Play, and fair *Toftida* sing?   31

Arch. Pshaw! damn your Raptures, I tell you here's a Pump going to be
put into the Vessel, and the Ship will get into Harbour, my Life on't. You say
there's another Lady very handsome there.

Aim. Yes, faith.

Arch. I'm in love with her already.

Aim. Can't you give me a Bill upon *Cherry* in the mean time?

Arch. No, no, Friend, all her Corn, Wine and Oil is ingross'd to my
Market.—And once more I warn you to keep your Anchorage clear of mine,
for if you fall foul of me, by this Light you shall go to the Bottom.———
What! make Prize of my little Frigat, while I am upon the Cruise for you.
                                                                [*Exit.*

Enter Bonniface.

Aim. Well, well, I won't——Landlord, have you any tolerable Company
in the House, I don't care for dining alone.   43

Bon. Yes, Sir, there's a Captain below; as the saying is, that arrived about
an Hour ago.

Aim. Gentlemen of his Coat are welcome every where; will you make him
a Complement from me, and tell him I should be glad of his Company.

Bon. Who shall I tell him, Sir, wou'd.——

Aim. Ha! that Stroak was well thrown in———I'm only a Traveller like
himself, and wou'd be glad of his Company, that's all.   50

Bon. I obey your Commands, as the saying is.   [*Exit.*

Enter Archer.

Arch. S'Death! I had forgot, what Title will you give your self?

Aim. My Brother's to be sure, he wou'd never give me any thing else, so
I'll make bold with his Honour this bout——you know the rest of your Cue.
                                                                [*Exit* Bon.

Arch. Ay, ay.

Enter Gibbet.

Gib. Sir, I'm yours.

Aim. 'Tis more than I deserve, Sir, for I don't know you.

Gib. I don't wonder at that, Sir, for you never saw me before, I hope.
                                                                [*Aside.*

---

31 *Toftida*] Katherine Tofts, the native-born prima-donna then at the height of her fame.
She retired from the stage in 1709.

Aim. And pray, Sir, how came I by the Honour of seeing you now?

Gib. Sir, I scorn to intrude upon any Gentleman——but my Landlord——

Aim. O, Sir, I ask your Pardon, you're the Captain he told me of.   61

Gib. At your Service, Sir.

Aim. What Regiment, may I be so bold?

Gib. A marching Regiment, Sir, an old Corps.

Aim. Very old, if your Coat be Regimental, [*Aside.*] You have serv'd abroad, Sir?

Gib. Yes, Sir, in the Plantations, 'twas my Lot to be sent into the worst Service, I wou'd have quitted it indeed, but a Man of Honour, you know ——Besides 'twas for the good of my Country that I shou'd be abroad—— Any thing for the good of one's Country——I'm a *Roman* for that.   70

Aim. One of the first, I'll lay my Life [*Aside.*] You found the *West Indies* very hot, Sir?

Gib. Ay, Sir, too hot for me.

Aim. Pray, Sir, han't I seen your Face at *Will*'s Coffee-house?

Gib. Yes, Sir, and at *White*'s too.

Aim. And where is your Company now, Captain?

Gib. They an't come yet.

Aim. Why, d'ye expect 'em here?

Gib. They'll be here to Night, Sir.

Aim. Which way do they march?   80

Gib. Across the Country——the Devil's in't, if I han't said enough to encourage him to declare—but I'm afraid he's not right, I must tack about.

Aim. Is your Company to quarter in *Litchfield*?

Gib. In this House, Sir.

Aim. What! all?

Gib. My Company's but thin, ha, ha, ha, we are but three, ha, ha, ha.

Aim. You're merry, Sir.

Gib. Ay, Sir, you must excuse me, Sir, I understand the World, especially, the Art of Travelling; I don't care, Sir, for answering Questions directly upon the Road——for I generally ride with a Charge about me.   91

Aim. Three or four, I believe.   [*Aside.*

Gib. I am credibly inform'd that there are Highway-men upon this Quarter, not, Sir, that I cou'd suspect a Gentleman of your Figure—— But truly, Sir, I have got such a way of Evasion upon the Road, that I don't care for speaking Truth to any Man.

---

70 a *Roman*] That is, in military jargon, a foot-soldier ready to fight for his country without payment.   71 One of the first] An ambiguous aside. Strauss plausibly suggests that Gibbet might have been thought by Aimwell to typify the rabble who first took refuge in Rome at the invitation of Romulus its founder

Aim. Your Caution may be necessary——Then I presume you're no Captain?

Gib. Not I, Sir, Captain is a good travelling Name, and so I take it; it stops a great many foolish Inquiries that are generally made about Gentlemen that travel, it gives a Man an Air of something, and makes the Drawers obedient—And thus far I am a Captain, and no farther. 102

Aim. And pray, Sir, what is your true Profession?

Gib. O, Sir, you must excuse me—upon my Word, Sir, I don't think it safe to tell you.

Aim. Ha, ha, ha, upon my word I commend you. [*Enter* Bonniface.] Well, Mr. *Bonniface*, what's the News?

Bon. There's another Gentleman below, as the saying is, that hearing you were but two, wou'd be glad to make the third Man if you wou'd give him leave. 110

Aim. What is he?

Bon. A Clergyman, as the saying is.

Aim. A Clergyman! is he really a Clergyman? or is it only his travelling Name, as my Friend the Captain has it.

Bon. O, Sir, he's a Priest and Chaplain to the French Officers in Town.

Aim. Is he a French-man?

Bon. Yes, Sir, born at *Brussels*.

Gib. A French-man, and a Priest! I won't be seen in his Company, Sir; I have a Value for my Reputation, Sir.

Aim. Nay, but Captain, since we are by our selves——Can he speak English, Landlord? 121

Bon. Very well, Sir, you may know him, as the saying is, to be a Foreigner by his Accent, and that's all.

Aim. Then he has been in *England* before?

Bon. Never, Sir, but he's a Master of Languages, as the saying is, he talks Latin, it do's me good to hear him talk Latin.

Aim. Then you understand Latin, Mr. *Bonniface*?

Bon. Not I, Sir, as the saying is, but he talks it so very fast that I'm sure it must be good.

Aim. Pray desire him to walk up. 130

Bon. Here he is, as the saying is.

Enter Foigard.

Foig. Save you, Gentlemen's, both.

Aim. A French-man! Sir, your most humble Servant.

Foig. Och, dear Joy, I am your most faithful Shervant, and yours alsho.

Gib. Doctor, you talk very good English, but you have a mighty Twang of the Foreigner.

Foig. My English is very vel for the vords, but we Foregners you know cannot bring our Tongues about the Pronunciation so soon.

Aim. A Foreigner! a down-right Teague by this Light. [*Aside.*] Were you born in *France*, Doctor?   140

Foig. I was educated in *France*, but I was borned at *Brussels*, I am a Subject of the King of *Spain*, Joy.

Gib. What King of *Spain*, Sir, speak.

Foig. Upon my Shoul Joy, I cannot tell you as yet.

Aim. Nay, Captain, that was too hard upon the Doctor, he's a Stranger.

Foig. O let him alone, dear Joy, I am of a Nation that is not easily put out of Countenance.

Aim. Come, Gentlemen, I'll end the Dispute.—Here, Landlord, is Dinner ready?

Bon. Upon the Table, as the saying is.

Aim. Gentlemen——pray——that Door——

Foig. No, no fait, the Captain must lead.

Aim. No, Doctor, the Church is our Guide.

Gib. Ay, ay, so it is.——   [*Exit foremost, they follow.*

SCENE, *Changes to a Gallery in Lady* Bountyful'*s House.*

Enter Archer *and* Scrub *singing, and hugging one another,* Scrub *with a Tankard in his Hand,* Gipsey *listning at a distance.*

Scrub. Tall, all dall——Come, my dear Boy——Let's have that Song once more.

Arch. No, no, we shall disturb the Family;——But will you be sure to keep the Secret?

Scrub. Pho! upon my Honour, as I'm a Gentleman.

Arch. 'Tis enough.—You must know then that my Master is the Lord Viscount *Aimwell*; he fought a Duel t'other day in *London*, wounded his Man so dangerously, that he thinks fit to withdraw till he hears whether the Gentleman's Wounds be mortal or not: He never was in this part of *England* before, so he chose to retire to this Place, that's all.   10

Gip. And that's enough for me.   [*Exit.*

Scrub. And where were you when your Master fought?

Arch. We never know of our Masters Quarrels.

Scrub. No! if our Masters in the Country here receive a Challenge, the

---

139 Teague] Then the commonest colloquialism for an Irishman. 143 What King of *Spain*, Sir] Foigard is being asked to declare his allegiance in the War of the Spanish Succession, then being disputed between Philip, grandson of Louis XIV, and the Archduke Charles of Austria.

first thing they do is to tell their Wives; the Wife tells the Servants, the Servants alarm the Tenants, and in half an Hour you shall have the whole County in Arms.

Arch. To hinder two Men from doing what they have no mind for:——— But if you should chance to talk now of my Business?

Scrub. Talk! ay, Sir, had I not learn't the knack of holding my Tongue, I had never liv'd so long in a great Family.   21

Arch. Ay, ay, to be sure there are Secrets in all Families.

Scrub. Secrets, ay;——But I'll say no more.——Come, sit down, we'll make an end of our Tankard: Here———

Arch. With all my Heart; who knows but you and I may come to be better acquainted, eh———Here's your Ladies Healths; you have three, I think, and to be sure there must be Secrets among 'em.

Scrub. Secrets! Ay, Friend; I wish I had a Friend——

Arch. Am not I your Friend? come, you and I will be sworn Brothers.

Scrub. Shall we?   30

Arch. From this Minute.———Give me a kiss——And now Brother *Scrub*———

Scrub. And now, Brother *Martin*, I will tell you a Secret that will make your Hair stand on end:——You must know, that I am consumedly in Love.

Arch. That's a terrible Secret, that's the Truth on't.

Scrub. That Jade, *Gipsey*, that was with us just now in the Cellar, is the arrantest Whore that ever wore a Petticoat; and I'm dying for love of her.

Arch. Ha, ha, ha———Are you in love with her Person, or her Vertue, Brother *Scrub*?

Scrub. I should like Vertue best, because it is more durable than Beauty; for Vertue holds good with some Women long, and many a Day after they have lost it.   42

Arch. In the Country, I grant ye, where no Woman's Vertue is lost, till a Bastard be found.

Scrub. Ay, cou'd I bring her to a Bastard, I shou'd have her all to my self; but I dare not put it upon that Lay, for fear of being sent for a Soldier.——— Pray, Brother, how do you Gentlemen in *London* like that same Pressing Act?

Arch. Very ill, Brother *Scrub*;——'Tis the worst that ever was made for us: Formerly I remember the good Days, when we cou'd dun our Masters for our Wages, and if they refused to pay us, we cou'd have a Warrant to carry 'em before a Justice; but now if we talk of eating, they have a Warrant for us, and carry us before three Justices.   53

46 put it upon that Lay] Take that risk.   47 Pressing Act] The Mutiny and Impress-
ment Acts of 1703–5 enabled magistrates to levy all those 'who have not any lawful calling
or employment . . . to serve as soldiers'.

Scrub. And to be sure we go, if we talk of eating; for the Justices won't give their own Servants a bad Example. Now this is my Misfortune————I dare not speak in the House, while that Jade *Gipsey* dings about like a Fury ———Once I had the better end of the Staff.

Arch. And how comes the Change now?

Scrub. Why, the Mother of all this Mischief is a Priest.

Arch. A Priest!　　　　　　　　　　　　　　　　　　　　　　　60

Scrub. Ay, a damn'd Son of a Whore of *Babylon*, that came over hither to say Grace to the *French* Officers, and eat up our Provisions————There's not a Day goes over his Head without Dinner or Supper in this House.

Arch. How came he so familiar in the Family?

Scrub. Because he speaks *English* as if he had liv'd here all his Life; and tells Lies as if he had been a Traveller from his Cradle.

Arch. And this Priest, I'm afraid has converted the Affections of your *Gipsey.*

Scrub. Converted! ay, and perverted, my dear Friend:—For I'm afraid he has made her a Whore and a Papist.——But this is not all; there's the *French* Count and Mrs. *Sullen*, they're in the Confederacy, and for some private Ends of their own to be sure.　　　　　　　　　　　　　　　72

Arch. A very hopeful Family yours, Brother *Scrub*; I suppose the Maiden Lady has her Lover too.

Scrub. Not that I know;——She's the best on 'em, that's the Truth on't: But they take care to prevent my Curiosity, by giving me so much Business, that I'm a perfect Slave.——What d'ye think is my Place in this Family?

Arch. Butler, I suppose.

Scrub. Ah, Lord help you——I'll tell you————Of a *Monday*, I drive the Coach; of a *Tuesday*, I drive the Plough; on *Wednesday*, I follow the Hounds; a *Thursday*, I dun the Tenants; on *Fryday*, I go to Market; on *Saturday*, I draw Warrants; and a *Sunday*, I draw Beer.　　　　　　　　　　82

Arch. Ha, ha, ha! if variety be a Pleasure in Life, you have enough on't, my dear Brother——But what Ladies are those?

Scrub. Ours, ours; that upon the right Hand is Mrs. *Sullen*, and the other is Mrs. *Dorinda.*————Don't mind 'em, sit still, Man————

Enter Mrs. Sullen, *and* Dorinda.

Mrs. *Sull.* I have heard my Brother talk of my Lord *Aimwell*, but they say that his Brother is the finer Gentleman.

Dor. That's impossible, Sister.

Mrs. *Sull.* He's vastly rich, but very close, they say.　　　　　　90

Dor. No matter for that; if I can creep into his Heart, I'll open his Breast, I

56 dings about] Sets upon those around her.　85 *Scrub*] The first edition impossibly assigns this speech to Archer.

warrant him: I have heard say, that People may be guess'd at by the Behaviour of their Servants; I cou'd wish we might talk to that Fellow.

Mrs. Sull. So do I; for, I think he's a very pretty Fellow: Come this way, I'll throw out a Lure for him presently.

> [*They walk a turn towards the opposite side of the Stage, Mrs. Sullen drops her Glove, Archer runs, takes it up, and gives it to her.*

Arch. Corn, Wine, and Oil, indeed——But, I think, the Wife has the greatest plenty of Flesh and Blood; she should be my Choice———Ah, a, say you so——Madam———Your Ladyship's Glove.

Mrs. Sull. O, Sir, I thank you———what a handsom Bow the Fellow has?   100

Dor. Bow! why I have known several Footmen come down from *London* set up here for Dancing-Masters, and carry off the best Fortunes in the Country.

Arch. [*Aside.*] That Project, for ought I know, had been better than ours. Brother *Scrub*———Why don't you introduce me.

Scrub. Ladies, this is the strange Gentleman's Servant that you see at Church to Day; I understood he came from *London*, and so I invited him to the Cellar, that he might show me the newest Flourish in whetting my Knives.

Dor. And I hope you have made much of him?   110

Arch. O yes, Madam, but the Strength of your Ladyship's Liquor is a little too potent for the Constitution of your humble Servant.

Mrs. Sull. What, then you don't usually drink Ale?

Arch. No, Madam, my constant Drink is Tea, or a little Wine and Water; 'tis prescrib'd me by the Physician for a Remedy against the Spleen.

Scrub. O la, O la!——a Footman have the Spleen.——

Mrs. Sull. I thought that Distemper had been only proper to People of Quality.

Arch. Madam, like all other Fashions it wears out, and so descends to their Servants; tho' in a great many of us, I believe it proceeds from some melancholly Particles in the Blood, occasion'd by the Stagnation of Wages.

Dor. How affectedly the Fellow talks——How long, pray, have you serv'd your present Master?   123

Arch. Not long; my Life has been mostly spent in the Service of the Ladies.

Mrs. Sull. And pray, which Service do you like best?

Arch. Madam, the Ladies pay best; the Honour of serving them is sufficient Wages; there is a Charm in their looks that delivers a Pleasure with their Commands, and gives our Duty the Wings of Inclination.

Mrs. Sull. That Flight was above the pitch of a Livery; and, Sir, wou'd not you be satisfied to serve a Lady again?   131

Arch. As a Groom of the Chamber, Madam, but not as a Footman.

Mrs. *Sull.* I suppose you serv'd as Footman before.

Arch. For that Reason I wou'd not serve in that Post again; for my Memory is too weak for the load of Messages that the Ladies lay upon their Servants in *London*; my Lady *Howd'ye*, the last Mistress I serv'd call'd me up one Morning, and told me, *Martin*, go to my Lady *Allnight* with my humble Service; tell her I was to wait on her Ladyship yesterday, and left word with Mrs. *Rebecca*, that the Preliminaries of the Affair she knows of, are stopt till we know the concurrence of the Person that I know of, for which there are Circumstances wanting which we shall accommodate at the old Place; but that in the mean time there is a Person about her Ladyship, that from several Hints and Surmises, was accessary at a certain time to the disappointments that naturally attend things, that to her knowledge are of more Importance.

Mrs. *Sull.*⎫
          ⎬ Ha, ha, ha! where are you going, Sir?   145
Dor. ⎭

Arch. Why, I han't half done.——The whole Howd'ye was about half an Hour long; so I hapned to misplace two Syllables, and was turn'd off, and render'd incapable——

Dor. The pleasentest Fellow, Sister, I ever saw.——But, Friend, if your Master be marry'd,——I presume you still serve a Lady.   150

Arch. No, Madam, I take care never to come into a marry'd Family; the Commands of the Master and Mistress are always so contrary, that 'tis impossible to please both.

Dor. There's a main point gain'd.—My Lord is not marry'd, I find.

                                                        [*Aside.*

Mrs. *Sull.* But, I wonder, Friend, that in so many good Services, you had not a better Provision made for you.

Arch. I don't know how, Madam.——I had a Lieutenancy offer'd me three or four Times; but that is not Bread, Madam——I live much better as I do.

Scrub. Madam, he sings rarely.——I was thought to do pretty well here in the Country till he came; but alack a day, I'm nothing to my Brother *Martin*.   162

Dor. Does he? Pray, Sir, will you oblige us with a Song?

Arch. Are you for Passion, or Humour?

Scrub. O le! he has the purest Ballad about a Trifle——

Mrs. *Sull.* A Trifle! pray, Sir, let's have it.

Arch. I'm asham'd to offer you a Trifle, Madam: But since you command me——   [*Sings to the Tune of Sir* Simon *the King.*

168 *Sir* Simon *the King*] A popular tune included in Playford's *Musick's Recreation* in 1652, and believed to celebrate the memory of Simon Wardloe, keeper of the Devil Tavern off Fleet Street in the early seventeenth century.

A trifling Song you shall hear,
Begun with a Trifle and ended: 170
All Trifling People draw near,
And I shall be nobly attended.

Were it not for Trifles, a few,
That lately have come into Play;
The Men wou'd want something to do,
And the Women want something to say.

What makes Men trifle in Dressing?
Because the Ladies (they know)
Admire, by often Possessing,
That eminent Trifle a Beau.   180

When the Lover his Moments has trifled,
The Trifle of Trifles to gain:
No sooner the Virgin is Rifled,
But a Trifle shall part 'em again.

What mortal Man wou'd be able
At White's *half an Hour to sit?*
Or who cou'd bear a Tea-Table,
Without talking of Trifles for Wit?

The Court is from Trifles secure,
Gold Keys are no Trifles, we see: 190
White Rods are no Trifles, I'm sure,
Whatever their Bearers may be.

But if you will go to the Place,
Where Trifles abundantly breed,
The Levee will show you his Grace
Makes Promises Trifles indeed.

171–220 *All Trifling People . . . a Trifle to boot*] Only the first two lines of the song are given in the first edition.   190 *Gold Keys*] The insignia of the Lord Chamberlain.   191 *White Rods*] Carried by both the Lord Chamberlain and the Lord High Treasurer as marks of office.   195 *Levee*] Reception for a great man's petitioners and sycophants.   195 *his Grace*] Assumed to be a casual hit at His Grace the Duke of Ormond, who had let Farquhar down after promising to obtain him a commission.

A Coach with six Footmen behind,
I count neither Trifle nor Sin:
But, ye Gods! how oft do we find
A scandalous Trifle within?   200

A flask of Champaign, People think it
A Trifle, or something as bad:
But if you'll contrive how to drink it,
You'll find it no Trifle egad.

A Parson's a Trifle at Sea,
A Widow's a Trifle in Sorrow:
A Peace is a Trifle to-day,
Who knows what may happen to-morrow?

A Black Coat, a Trifle may cloak,
Or to hide it, the Red may endeavour: 210
But if once the Army is broke,
We shall have more Trifles than ever.

The Stage is a Trifle, they say,
The Reason, pray carry along,
Because at ev'ry new Play,
The House they with Trifles so throng.

But with People's Malice to Trifle,
And to set us all on a Foot:
The Author of this is a Trifle,
And his Song is a Trifle to boot.   220

Mrs. *Sull.* Very well, Sir, we're obliged to you.——Something for a pair
of Gloves.   [*Offering him Money.*

Arch. I humbly beg leave to be excused: My Master, Madam, pays me;
nor dare I take Money from any other Hand without injuring his Honour,
and disobeying his Commands.   [*Exit.*

Dor. This is surprising: Did you ever see so pretty a well bred Fellow?

Mrs. *Sull.* The Devil take him for wearing that Livery.

Dor. I fancy, Sister, he may be some Gentleman, a Friend of my Lords,
that his Lordship has pitch'd upon for his Courage, Fidelity, and Discretion
to bear him Company in this Dress, and who, ten to one was his Second
too.   231

Mrs. *Sull.* It is so, it must be so, and it shall be so:——For I like him.

Dor. What! better than the Count?

Mrs. *Sull.* The Count happen'd to be the most agreeable Man upon the Place; and so I chose him to serve me in my Design upon my Husband.——But I shou'd like this Fellow better in a Design upon my self.

Dor. But now, Sister, for an Interview with this Lord, and this Gentleman; how shall we bring that about?

Mrs. *Sull.* Patience! you Country Ladies give no Quarter, if once you be enter'd.——Wou'd you prevent their Desires, and give the Fellows no wishing-time?——Look'ye, *Dorinda*, if my Lord *Aimwell* loves you or deserves you, he'll find a way to see you, and there we must leave it.—My Business comes now upon the Tapis—Have you prepar'd your Brother?

Dor. Yes, yes.   244

Mrs. *Sull.* And how did he relish it?

Dor. He said little, mumbled something to himself, promis'd to be guided by me: But here he comes——

Enter Sullen.

Sull. What singing was that I heard just now?

Mrs. *Sull.* The singing in you're Head, my Dear, you complain'd of it all Day.   250

Sull. You're impertinent.

Mrs. *Sull.* I was ever so, since I became one Flesh with you.

Sull. One Flesh! rather two Carcasses join'd unnaturally together.

Mrs. *Sull.* Or rather a living Soul coupled to a dead Body.

Dor. So, this is fine Encouragement for me.

Sull. Yes, my Wife shews you what you must do.

Mrs. *Sull.* And my Husband shews you what you must suffer.

Sull. S'death, why can't you be silent?

Mrs. *Sull.* S'death, why can't you talk?

Sull. Do you talk to any purpose?   260

Mrs. *Sull.* Do you think to any purpose?

Sull. Sister, heark'ye; [*Whispers.*] I shan't be home till it be late.   [*Exit.*

Mrs. *Sull.* What did he whisper to ye?

Dor. That he wou'd go round the back way, come into the Closet, and listen as I directed him.——But let me beg you once more, dear Sister, to drop this Project; for, as I told you before, instead of awaking him to Kindness, you may provoke him to a Rage; and then who knows how far his Brutality may carry him?

Mrs. *Sull.* I'm provided to receive him, I warrant you: But here comes the Count, vanish.   [*Exit Dorinda.*

243 upon the Tapis] Literally, upon the tapestried council table—thus, under discussion.

Enter Count Bellair.

Don't you wonder, *Monsieur le Count*, that I was not at Church this Afternoon?   272

Count. I more wonder, Madam, that you go dere at all, or how you dare to
lift those Eyes to Heaven that are guilty of so much killing.

Mrs. *Sull*. If Heaven, Sir, has given to my Eyes with the Power of killing,
the Virtue of making a Cure, I hope the one may atone for the other.

Co. O largely, Madam; wou'd your Ladyship be as ready to apply the
Remedy as to give the Wound?—Consider, Madam, I am doubly a Prisoner;
first to the Arms of your General, then to your more conquering Eyes; my
first Chains are easy, there a Ransom may redeem me, but from your Fetters
I never shall get free.   281

Mrs. *Sull*. Alas, Sir, why shou'd you complain to me of your Captivity,
who am in Chains my self? you know, Sir, that I am bound, nay, must be
tied up in that particular that might give you ease: I am like you, a Prisoner
of War——Of War indeed:—I have given my Parole of Honour; wou'd you
break yours to gain your Liberty?

Co. Most certainly I wou'd, were I a Prisoner among the *Turks*; dis is your
Case; you're a Slave, Madam, Slave to the worst of *Turks*, a Husband.

Mrs. *Sull*. There lies my Foible, I confess; no Fortifications, no Courage,
Conduct, nor Vigilancy can pretend to defend a Place, where the Cruelty of
the Governour forces the Garrison to Mutiny.   291

Co. And where de Besieger is resolv'd to die before de Place—Here will I
fix; [*Kneels*.] With Tears, Vows, and Prayers assault your Heart, and never
rise till you surrender; or if I must storm—Love and St. *Michael*—And so I
begin the Attack——

Mrs. *Sull*. Stand off—Sure he hears me not—And I cou'd almost wish he
—did not.——The Fellow makes love very prettily. [*Aside*.] But, Sir, why
shou'd you put such a Value upon my Person, when you see it despis'd by
one that knows it so much better.

Co. He knows it not, tho' he possesses it; if he but knew the Value of the
Jewel he is Master of, he wou'd always wear it next his Heart, and sleep with
it in his Arms.   302

Mrs. *Sull*. But since he throws me unregarded from him.

Count. And one that knows your Value well, comes by, and takes you up, is
it not Justice.   [*Goes to lay hold on her.*

Enter Sullen *with his Sword drawn.*

s.d. *Enter Count* Bellair] A note to the edition of 1736 reads: 'This Scene . . . with the
entire part of the *Count*, was cut out by the Author, after the first Night's Representation;
and where he shou'd enter in the last Scene of the fifth Act, it is added to the Part of
Foigard.'

Sull. Hold, Villain, hold.

Mrs. Sull. [*Presenting a Pistol.*] Do you hold.

Sull. What! Murther your Husband, to defend your Bully.

Mrs. Sull. Bully! for shame, Mr. *Sullen*; Bullies wear long Swords, the
Gentleman has none, he's a Prisoner you know—I was aware of your Out-
rage, and prepar'd this to receive your Violence, and, if Occasion were, to
preserve my self against the Force of this other Gentleman.   312

Count. O Madam, your Eyes be bettre Fire Arms than your Pistol, they
nevre miss.

Sull. What! court my Wife to my Face!

Mrs. Sull. Pray, Mr. *Sullen*, put up, suspend your Fury for a Minute.

Sull. To give you time to invent an Excuse.

Mrs. Sull. I need none.

Sull. No, for I heard every Sillable of your Discourse.

Coun. Ay! and begar, I tink de Dialogue was vera pretty.   320

Mrs. Sull. Then I suppose, Sir, you heard something of your own
Barbarity.

Sull. Barbarity! oons what does the Woman call Barbarity? do I ever
meddle with you?

Mrs. Sull. No.

Sull. As for you, Sir, I shall take another time.

Count. Ah, begar, and so must I.

Sull. Look'e, Madam, don't think that my Anger proceeds from any
Concern I have for your Honour, but for my own, and if you can contrive
any way of being a Whore without making me a Cuckold, do it and welcome.

Mrs. Sull. Sir, I thank you kindly, you wou'd allow me the Sin but rob
me of the Pleasure———No, no, I'm resolv'd never to venture upon the
Crime without the Satisfaction of seeing you punish'd for't.   333

Sull. Then will you grant me this, my Dear? let any Body else do you the
Favour but that French-man, for I mortally hate his whole Generation.

[*Exit.*

Count. Ah, Sir, that he ungrateful, for begar, I love some of your's,
Madam.—   [*Approaching her.*

Mrs. Sull. No, Sir.——

Count. No, Sir,—Garzoon, Madam, I am not your Husband.

Mrs. Sull. 'Tis time to undeceive you, Sir,—I believ'd your Addresses to
me were no more than an Amusement, and I hope you will think the same of
my Complaisance, and to convince you that you ought, you must know, that
I brought you hither only to make you instrumental in setting me right with
my Husband, for he was planted to listen by my Appointment.   344

Count. By your Appointment?

308 Bully] A protector of prostitutes.

Mrs. Sull. Certainly.

Count. And so, Madam, while I was telling twenty Stories to part you from your Husband, begar, I was bringing you together all the while.

Mrs. Sull. I ask your Pardon, Sir, but I hope this will give you a Taste of the Vertue of the English Ladies.   350

Count. Begar, Madam, your Vertue be vera Great, but Garzoon your Honeste de vera little.

Enter Dorinda.

Mrs. Sull. Nay, now you're angry, Sir.

Count. Angry! fair *Dorinda* [*Sings* Dorinda *the Opera Tune, and addresses to* Dorinda,] Madam, when your Ladyship want a Fool, send for me, fair *Dorinda, Revenge, &c.*   [*Exit.*

Mrs. Sull. There goes the true Humour of his Nation, Resentment with good Manners, and the height of Anger in a Song.———Well Sister, you must be Judge, for you have heard the Trial.

Dor. And I bring in my Brother Guilty.   360

Mrs. Sull. But I must bear the Punishment,—'Tis hard Sister.

Dor. I own it—but you must have Patience.

Mrs. Sull. Patience! the Cant of Custom—Providence sends no Evil without a Remedy—shou'd I lie groaning under a Yoke I can shake off, I were accessary to my Ruin, and my Patience were no better than self-Murder.

Dor. But how can you shake off the Yoke?——Your Divisions don't come within the Reach of the Law for a Divorce.

Mrs. Sull. Law! what Law can search into the remote Abyss of Nature, what Evidence can prove the unaccountable Disaffections of Wedlock?—can a Jury sum up the endless Aversions that are rooted in our Souls, or can a Bench give Judgment upon Antipathies?   371

Dor. They never pretended Sister, they never meddle but in case of Uncleanness.

Mrs. Sull. Uncleanness! O Sister, casual Violation is a transient Injury, and may possibly be repair'd, but can radical Hatreds be ever reconcil'd— No, no, Sister, Nature is the first Lawgiver, and when she has set Tempers opposite, not all the golden Links of Wedlock, nor Iron Manacles of Law can keep 'um fast.

> *Wedlock we own ordain'd by Heaven's Decree,*
> *But such as Heaven ordain'd it first to be,*   380
> *Concurring Tempers in the Man and Wife*

354 fair *Dorinda*] Stonehill identifies this as the eleventh song in Owen Swiney's hack opera *Camilla*, translated from the Italian in 1706—although, as he says, 'it does not deal with revenge'.

> *As mutual Helps to draw the Load of Life.*
> *View all the Works of Providence above,*
> *The Stars with Harmony and Concord move;*
> *View all the Works of Providence below,*
> *The Fire, the Water, Earth, and Air, we know*
> *All in one Plant agree to make it grow.*
> *Must Man the chiefest Work of Art Divine,*
> *Be doom'd in endless Discord to repine.*
> *No, we shou'd injure Heaven by that surmise,*   390
> *Omnipotence is just, were Man but wise.*

End of the Third Act.

ACT IV.

SCENE *continues.*

Enter Mrs. Sullen.

Mrs. Sull. WERE I born an humble Turk, where Women have no Soul nor Property there I must sit contented——But in *England*, a Country whose Women are it's Glory, must Women be abus'd, where Women rule, must Women be enslav'd? nay, cheated into Slavery, mock'd by a Promise of comfortable Society into a Wilderness of Solitude ——I dare not keep the Thought about me——O, here comes something to divert me——

Enter a Country Woman.

Wom. I come an't please your Ladyships, you're my Lady *Bountiful* an't ye?

Mrs. Sull. Well, good Woman go on.   10

Wom. I come seventeen long Mail to have a Cure for my Husband's sore Leg.

Mrs. Sull. Your Husband! what Woman, cure your Husband!

Wom. Ay, poor Man, for his Sore Leg won't let him stir from Home.

Mrs. Sull. There, I confess, you have given me a Reason. Well good Woman, I'll tell you what you must do——You must lay your Husbands Leg upon a Table, and with a Choping-knife, you must lay it open as broad as you can, then you must take out the Bone, and beat the Flesh soundly with a rowling-pin, then take Salt, Pepper, Cloves, Mace and Ginger, some sweet

IV. i, 4 where Women rule] Queen Anne was on the throne.

Herbs, and season it very well, then rowl it up like Brawn, and put it into the Oven for two Hours.   21

Wom. Heavens reward your Ladyship—I have two little Babies too that are pitious bad with the Graips, an't please ye.

Mrs. *Sull.* Put a little Pepper and Salt in their Bellies, good Woman. [*Enter Lady* Bountiful.] I beg your Ladyship's Pardon for taking your Business out of your Hands, I have been a tampering here a little with one of your Patients.

L. *Boun.* Come, good Woman, don't mind this mad Creature, I am the Person that you want, I suppose——What wou'd you have, Woman?

Mrs. *Sull.* She wants something for her Husband's sore Leg.   30

L. *Boun.* What's the matter with his Leg, Goody?

Wom. It come first as one might say with a sort of Dizziness in his Foot, then he had a kind of a Laziness in his Joints, and then his Leg broke out, and then it swell'd, and then it clos'd again, and then it broke out again, and then it fester'd, and then it grew better, and then it grew worse again.

Mrs. *Sull.* Ha, ha, ha.

L. *Boun.* How can you be merry with the Misfortunes of other People?

Mrs. *Sull.* Because my own make me sad, Madam.

L. *Boun.* The worst Reason in the World, Daughter, your own Misfortunes shou'd teach you to pitty others.   40

Mrs. *Sull.* But the Woman's Misfortunes and mine are nothing alike, her Husband is sick, and mine, alas, is in Health.

L. *Boun.* What! wou'd you wish your Husband sick?

Mrs. *Sull.* Not of a sore Leg, of all things.

L. *Boun.* Well, good Woman, go to the Pantrey, get your Belly-full of Victuals, then I'll give you a Receipt of Diet-drink for your Husband—— But d'ye hear Goody, you must not let your Husband move too much.

Wom. No, no, Madam, the poor Man's inclinable enough to lye still.

[*Exit.*

L. *Boun.* Well, Daughter *Sullen*, tho' you laugh, I have done Miracles about the Country here with my Receipts.   50

Mrs. *Sull.* Miracles, indeed, if they have cur'd any Body, but, I believe, Madam, the Patient's Faith goes farther toward the Miracle than your Prescription.

L. *Boun.* Fancy helps in some Cases, but there's your Husband who has as little Fancy as any Body, I brought him from Death's-door.

Mrs. *Sull.* I suppose, Madam, you made him drink plentifully of Asse's Milk.

Enter Dor. *runs to Mrs.* Sull.

Dor. News, dear Sister, news, news.

Enter Archer *running.*

Arch. Where, where is my Lady *Bountiful*———Pray which is the old
Lady of you three?   60

L. Boun. I am.

Arch. O, Madam, the Fame of your Ladyship's Charity, Goodness,
Benevolence, Skill and Ability have drawn me hither to implore your Ladyship's Help in behalf of my unfortunate Master, who is this Moment breath-
ing his last.

L. Boun. Your Master! where is he?

Arch. At your Gate, Madam, drawn by the Appearance of your handsome
House to view it nearer, and walking up the Avenue within five Paces of the
Court-Yard, he was taken ill of a sudden with a sort of I know not what, but
down he fell, and there he lies.   70

L. Boun. Here, *Scrub, Gipsey*, all run, get my easie Chair down Stairs, put
the Gentleman in it, and bring him in quickly, quickly.

Arch. Heaven will reward your Ladyship for this charitable Act.

L. Boun. Is your Master us'd to these Fits?

Arch. O yes, Madam, frequently———I have known him have five or six
of a Night.

L. Boun. What's his Name?

Arch. Lord, Madam, he's a dying, a Minute's Care or Neglect may save
or destroy his Life.

L. Boun. Ah, poor Gentleman! come Friend, show me the way, I'll see him
brought in my self.   [*Exit with* Archer.

Dor. O Sister my Heart flutters about strangely, I can hardly forbear
running to his Assistance.   83

Mrs. Sull. And I'll lay my Life, he deserves your Assistance more than he
wants it; did not I tell you that my Lord wou'd find a way to come at you.
Love's his Distemper, and you must be the Physitian; put on all your
Charms, summon all your Fire into your Eyes, plant the whole Artillery of
your Looks against his Breast, and down with him.

Dor. O Sister, I'm but a young Gunner, I shall be afraid to shoot, for fear
the Piece shou'd recoil and hurt my self.   90

Mrs. Sull. Never fear, you shall see me shoot before you, if you will.

Dor. No, no, dear Sister, you have miss'd your Mark so unfortunately,
that I shan't care for being instructed by you.

Enter Aimwell *in a Chair, carry'd by* Archer *and* Scrub, *L.* Bountiful,
Gipsey. Aimwell *counterfeiting a Swoon.*

L. Boun. Here, here, let's see the Hartshorn-drops—*Gipsey* a Glass of fair
Water, his Fit's very strong—Bless me, how his Hands are clinch'd.

94 fair Water] Pure, untainted water.

Arch. For shame, Ladies, what d'ye do? why don't you help us—Pray,
Madam, [*To Dorinda.*] Take his Hand and open it if you can, whilst I hold
his Head.   [*Dorinda takes his Hand.*

Dor. Poor Gentleman,—Oh—he has got my Hand within his, and squeezes
it unmercifully——   100

L. *Boun.* 'Tis the Violence of his Convulsion, Child.

Arch. O, Madam, he's perfectly possess'd in these Cases——he'll bite if
you don't have a care.

Dor. Oh, my Hand, my Hand.

L. *Boun.* What's the matter with the foolish Girl? I have got this Hand
open, you see, with a great deal of Ease.

Arch. Ay, but, Madam, your Daughter's Hand is somewhat warmer than
your Ladyship's, and the Heat of it draws the Force of the Spirits that way.

Mrs. *Sull.* I find, Friend, you're very learned in these sorts of Fits.

Arch. 'Tis no wonder, Madam, for I'm often troubled with them my self, I
find my self extreamly ill at this Minute.   [*Looking hard at Mrs.* Sull.

Mrs. *Sull.* [*Aside.*] I fancy I cou'd find a way to cure you.   112

L. *Boun.* His Fit holds him very long.

Arch. Longer than usual, Madam,——Pray, young Lady, open his
Breast, and give him Air.

L. *Boun.* Where did his Illness take him first, pray?

Arch. To Day at Church, Madam.

L. *Boun.* In what manner was he taken?

Arch. Very strangely, my Lady. He was of a sudden touch'd with something in his Eyes, which at the first he only felt, but cou'd not tell whether
'twas Pain or Pleasure.   121

L. *Boun.* Wind, nothing but Wind.

Arch. By soft Degrees it grew and mounted to his Brain, there his Fancy
caught it; there form'd it so beautiful, and dress'd it up in such gay pleasing
Colours, that his transported Appetite seiz'd the fair Idea, and straight
convey'd it to his Heart. That hospitable Seat of Life sent all its sanguine
Spirits forth to meet, and open'd all its sluicy Gates to take the Stranger in.

L. *Boun.* Your Master shou'd never go without a Bottle to smell to—Oh!—
He recovers—The Lavender Water—Some Feathers to burn under his
Nose——Hungary-water to rub his Temples—O, he comes to himself. Hem
a little, Sir, hem—*Gipsey*, bring the Cordial-water.   131

[*Aimwell seems to awake in amaze.*

Dor. How d'ye, Sir?

Aim. Where am I?   [*Rising.*

     Sure I have pass'd the Gulph of silent Death,

     And now I land on the *Elisian* Shore——

---

130 Hungary-water] A perfume compounded of rosemary flowers and spirit.

Behold the Goddess of those happy Plains,
Fair *Proserpine*—Let me adore thy bright Divinity.

> [*Kneels to* Dorinda *and kisses her Hand.*

Mrs. *Sull.* So, so, so, I knew where the Fit wou'd end.
Aim. Euridice perhaps—

How cou'd thy *Orpheus* keep his word, 140
And not look back upon thee;
No Treasure but thy self cou'd sure have brib'd him
To look one Minute off thee.

L. *Boun.* Delirious, poor Gentleman.
Arch. Very Delirious, Madam, very Delirious.
Aim. Martin's Voice, I think.
Arch. Yes, my Lord—How do's your Lordship?
L. *Boun.* Lord! did you mind that, Girls.
Aim. Where am I?
Arch. In very good Hands, Sir,—You were taken just now with one of your old Fits under the Trees just by this good Lady's House, her Ladyship had you taken in, and has miraculously brought you to your self, as you see——
Aim. I am so confounded with Shame, Madam, that I can now only beg Pardon——And refer my Acknowledgements for your Ladyship's Care, till an Opportunity offers of making some Amends——I dare be no longer troublesome——*Martin*, give two Guineas to the Servants. [*Going.*
Dor. Sir, you may catch cold by going so soon into the Air, you don't look, Sir, as if you were perfectly recover'd.

> [*Here* Archer *talks to L.* Bountiful *in dumb shew.*

Aim. That I shall never be, Madam, my present Illness is so rooted, that I must expect to carry it to my Grave. 160
Mrs. *Sull.* Don't despair, Sir, I have known several in your Distemper shake it off, with a Fortnight's Physick.
L. *Boun.* Come, Sir, your Servant has been telling me that you're apt to relapse if you go into the Air——Your good Manners shan't get the better of ours——You shall sit down again, Sir,——Come, Sir, we don't mind Ceremonies in the Country——Here, Sir, my Service t'ye——You shall taste my Water; 'tis a Cordial I can assure you, and of my own making—— drink it off, Sir, [Aimwell *drinks.*] And how d'ye find your self now, Sir?
Aim. Somewhat better——Tho' very faint still.
L. *Boun.* Ay, ay, People are always faint after these Fits——Come Girls, you shall show the Gentleman the House, 'tis but an old Family Building, Sir, but you had better walk about and cool by Degrees than venture immediately into the Air——You'll find some tolerable Pictures—*Dorinda*, show the Gentleman the way. I must go to the poor Woman below. [*Exit.*
Dor. This way, Sir. 175

Aim. Ladies shall I beg leave for my Servant to wait on you, for he understands Pictures very well.

Mrs. *Sull.* Sir, we understand Originals, as well as he do's Pictures, so he may come along.   [*Ex.* Dor. *Mrs.* Sull. Aim. Arch. Aim. *leads* Dor.

Enter Foigard *and* Scrub, *meeting.*

Foig. Save you, Master *Scrub*.   180

Scrub. Sir, I won't be sav'd your way—I hate a Priest, I abhor the French, and I defie the Devil———Sir, I'm a bold *Briton*, and will spill the last drop of my Blood to keep out Popery and Slavery.

Foig. Master *Scrub*, you wou'd put me down in Politicks, and so I wou'd be speaking with Mrs. *Shipsey*.

Scrub. Good Mr. Priest, you can't speak with her, she's sick, Sir, she's gone abroad, Sir, she's—dead two Months ago, Sir.

Enter Gipsey.

Gip. How now, Impudence; how dare you talk so saucily to the Doctor? Pray, Sir, don't take it ill; for the Common-people of *England* are not so civil to Strangers, as———   190

Scrub. You lie, you lie—'Tis the Common People that are civilest to Strangers.

Gip. Sirrah, I have a good mind to——Get you out, I say.

Scrub. I won't.

Gip. You won't, Sauce-box——Pray, Doctor, what is the Captain's Name that came to your Inn last Night?

Scrub. The Captain! Ah, the Devil, there she hampers me again;——The Captain has me on one side, and the Priest on t'other:——So between the Gown and the Sword, I have a fine time on't.——But, *Cedunt Arma togæ.*
                                                          [*Going.*

Gip. What, Sirrah, won't you march?   200

Scrub. No, my Dear, I won't march——But I'll walk——And I'll make bold to listen a little too.   [*Goes behind the side-Scene, and listens.*

Gip. Indeed, Doctor, the Count has been barbarously treated, that's the Truth on't.

Foig. Ah, Mrs. *Gipsey*, upon my Shoul, now, *Gra*, his Complainings wou'd mollifie the Marrow in your Bones, and move the Bowels of your Commiseration; he veeps, and he dances, and he fistles, and he swears, and he laughs, and he stamps, and he sings: In Conclusion, Joy, he's afflicted, *a la Francois*, and a Stranger wou'd not know whider to cry, or to laugh with him.

Gip. What wou'd you have me do, Doctor?   210

178 Originals] That is, in the additional sense of eccentric or unique characters.
199 *Cedunt Arma togæ*] That is, 'the sword gives way to the gown'.

Foig. Noting, Joy, but only hide the Count in Mrs. *Sullen*'s Closet when it is dark.

Gip. Nothing! Is that nothing? it wou'd be both a Sin and a shame, Doctor.

Foig. Here is twenty *Lewidores*, Joy, for your shame; and I will give you an Absolution for the Shin.

Gip. But won't that Money look like a Bribe?

Foig. Dat is according as you shall tauk it.——If you receive the Money beforehand, 'twill be *Logicè* a Bribe; but if you stay till afterwards, 'twill be only a Gratification. 220

Gip. Well, Doctor, I'll take it *Logicè*.——But what must I do with my Conscience, Sir?

Foig. Leave dat wid me, Joy; I am your Priest, *Gra*; and your Conscience is under my Hands.

Gip. But shou'd I put the Count into the Closet——

Foig. Vel, is dere any Shin for a Man's being in a Closhet; one may go to Prayers in a Closhet.

Gip. But if the Lady shou'd come into her Chamber, and go to Bed?

Foig. Vel, and is dere any Shin in going to Bed, Joy?

Gip. Ay, but if the Parties shou'd meet, Doctor? 230

Foig. Vel den——The Parties must be responsible.——Do you be after putting the Count in the Closet; and leave the Shins wid themselves.——I will come with the Count to instruct you in your Chamber.

Gip. Well, Doctor, your Religion is so pure——Methinks I'm so easie after an Absolution, and can sin afresh with so much security, that I'm resolv'd to die a Martyr to't.——Here's the Key of the Garden-door, come in the back way when 'tis late,—I'll be ready to receive you; but don't so much as whisper, only take hold of my Hand, I'll lead you, and do you lead the Count, and follow me. [*Exeunt.*

Enter Scrub.

Scrub. What Witchcraft now have these two Imps of the Devil been a hatching here?——There's twenty *Lewidores*, I heard that, and saw the Purse: But I must give room to my Betters. 242

Enter Aimwell *leading* Dorinda, *and making Love in dumb Show*——Mrs. Sull. *and* Archer.

Mrs. *Sull.* Pray, Sir, [*To* Archer.] how d'ye like that Piece?

Arch. O, 'tis *Leda*.——You find, Madam, how *Jupiter* comes disguis'd to make Love——

Mrs. *Sull.* But what think you there of *Alexander*'s Battles?

Arch. We want only a *Le Brun*, Madam, to draw greater Battles, and a greater General of our own.————The *Danube*, Madam, wou'd make a greater Figure in a Picture than the *Granicus*; and we have our *Ramelies* to match their *Arbela*.   250

Mrs. *Sull*. Pray, Sir, what Head is that in the Corner there?

Arch. O, Madam, 'tis poor *Ovid* in his Exile.

Mrs. *Sull*. What was he banish'd for?

Arch. His ambitious Love, Madam. [*Bowing*.] His Misfortune touches me.

Mrs. *Sull*. Was he successful in his Amours?

Arch. There he has left us in the dark.————He was too much a Gentleman to tell.

Mrs. *Sull*. If he were secret, I pity him.

Arch. And if he were successful, I envy him.   260

Mrs. *Sull*. How d'ye like that *Venus* over the Chimney?

Arch. *Venus!* I protest, Madam, I took it for your Picture; but now I look again, 'tis not handsome enough.

Mrs. *Sull*. Oh, what a Charm is Flattery! if you wou'd see my Picture, there it is, over that Cabinet;——How d'ye like it?

Arch. I must admire any thing, Madam, that has the least Resemblance of you——But, methinks, Madam——[*He looks at the Picture and Mrs. Sullen three or four times, by turns*.] Pray, Madam, who drew it?

Mrs. *Sull*. A famous Hand, Sir.   [*Here* Aimwell *and* Dorinda *go off*.

Arch. A famous Hand, Madam————Your Eyes, indeed, are featur'd there; but where's the sparkling Moisture shining fluid, in which they swim. The Picture indeed has your Dimples; but where's the Swarm of killing *Cupids* that shou'd ambush there? the Lips too are figur'd out; but where's the Carnation Dew, the pouting Ripeness that tempts the Taste in the Original?   275

Mrs. *Sull*. Had it been my Lot to have match'd with such a Man!

Arch. Your Breasts too, presumptuous Man! what! paint Heaven! *Apropo*, Madam, in the very next Picture is *Salmoneus*, that was struck dead with Lightning, for offering to imitate *Jove*'s Thunder; I hope you serv'd the Painter so, Madam?   280

Mrs. *Sull*. Had my Eyes the power of Thunder, they shou'd employ their Lightning better.

Arch. There's the finest Bed in that Room, Madam, I suppose 'tis your Ladyship's Bed-Chamber.

Mrs. *Sull*. And what then, Sir?

Arch. I think the Quilt is the richest that ever I saw:——I can't at this

---

247-50 *Le Brun . . . Arbela*] The French artist Le Brun was commissioned by Louis XIV to depict the battles of Alexander the Great. Archer contrasts battles fought under the Duke of Marlborough with those of Alexander.

Distance, Madam, distinguish the Figures of the Embroidery; will you give
me leave, Madam———

Mrs. Sull. The Devil take his Impudence.——Sure if I gave him an
opportunity, he durst not offer it.——I have a great mind to try.——
[*Going.*] [*Returns.*] S'death, what am I doing?—And alone too!———Sister,
Sister?   [*Runs out.*

Arch. I'll follow her close———   293
      For where a French-*man durst attempt to storm,*
      A Briton *sure may well the Work perform.*   [*Going.*

Enter Scrub.

Scrub. Martin, Brother *Martin.*

Arch. O, Brother *Scrub,* I beg your Pardon, I was not a going; here's a
Guinea, my Master order'd you.

Scrub. A Guinea, hi, hi, hi, a Guinea! eh—by this Light it is a Guinea; but
I suppose you expect One and twenty Shillings in change.   300

Arch. Not at all; I have another for *Gipsey.*

Scrub. A Guinea for her! Faggot and Fire for the Witch.—Sir, give me
that Guinea, and I'll discover a Plot.

Arch. A Plot!

Scrub. Ay, Sir, a Plot, and a horrid Plot.—First, it must be a Plot because
there's a Woman in't; secondly, it must be a Plot because there's a Priest
in't; thirdly, it must be a Plot because there's *French* Gold in't; and fourthly,
it must be a Plot, because I don't know what to make on't.

Arch. Nor any body else, I'm afraid, Brother *Scrub.*

Scrub. Truly I'm afraid so too; for where there's a Priest and a Woman,
there's always a Mystery and a Riddle.——This I know, that here has been
the Doctor with a Temptation in one Hand, and an Absolution in the other;
and *Gipsey* has sold her self to the Devil; I saw the Price paid down, my Eyes
shall take their Oath on't.   314

Arch. And is all this bustle about *Gipsey.*

Scrub. That's not all; I cou'd hear but a Word here and there; but
I remember they mention'd a Count, a Closet, a back Door, and a
Key.

Arch. The Count! did you hear nothing of Mrs. *Sullen?*

Scrub. I did hear some word that sounded that way; but whether it was
Sullen or *Dorinda,* I cou'd not distinguish.   321

Arch. You have told this matter to no Body, Brother?

Scrub. Told! No, Sir, I thank you for that; I'm resolv'd never to speak one
word *pro* nor *con,* till we have a Peace.

Arch. You're i'th right, Brother *Scrub;* here's a Treaty a foot between the
Count and the Lady.——The Priest and the Chamber-maid are the Pleni-

C

potentiaries.——It shall go hard but I find a way to be included in the Treaty.——Where's the Doctor now?

Scrub. He and *Gipsey* are this moment devouring my Lady's Marmalade in the Closet.   330

Aim. [*From without.*] *Martin, Martin.*

Arch. I come, Sir, I come.

Scrub. But you forget the other Guinea, Brother *Martin.*

Arch. Here, I give it with all my Heart.

Scrub. And I take it with all my Soul.   [*Exeunt severally.*

I'cod, I'll spoil your Plotting, Mrs. *Gipsey;* and if you shou'd set the Captain upon me, these two Guineas will buy me off.   [*Exit.*

Enter Mrs. Sullen *and* Dorinda *meeting.*

Mrs. Sull. Well, Sister.

Dor. And well, Sister.

Mrs. Sull. What's become of my Lord?   340

Dor. What's become of his Servant?

Mrs. Sull. Servant! he's a prettier Fellow, and a finer Gentleman by fifty Degrees than his Master.

Dor. O'my Conscience, I fancy you cou'd beg that Fellow at the Gallows-foot.

Mrs. Sull. O'my Conscience, I cou'd, provided I cou'd put a Friend of yours in his Room.

Dor. You desir'd me, Sister to leave you, when you transgress'd the Bounds of Honour.

Mrs. Sull. Thou dear censorious Country-Girl—What dost mean? you can't think of the Man without the Bedfellow, I find.   351

Dor. I don't find any thing unnatural in that thought, while the Mind is conversant with Flesh and Blood, it must conform to the Humours of the Company.

Mrs. Sull. How a little Love and good Company improves a Woman; why, Child, you begin to live—you never spoke before.

Dor. Because I was never spoke to.——My Lord has told me that I have more Wit and Beauty than any of my Sex; and truly I begin to think the Man is sincere.

Mrs. Sull. You're in the right, *Dorinda,* Pride is the Life of a Woman, and Flattery is our daily Bread; and she's a Fool that won't believe a Man there, as much as she that believes him in any thing else——But I'll lay you a Guinea, that I had finer things said to me than you had.   363

Dor. Done——What did your Fellow say to'ye?

344 beg that Fellow at the Gallows-foot] That is, save him from hanging by an offer of marriage at the scaffold.

Mrs. *Sull*. My Fellow took the Picture of *Venus* for mine.

Dor. But my Lover took me for *Venus* her self.

Mrs. *Sull*. Common Cant! had my Spark call'd me a *Venus* directly, I shou'd have believ'd him a Footman in good earnest.

Dor. But my Lover was upon his Knees to me.

Mrs. *Sullen*. And mine was upon his Tiptoes to me. 370

Dor. Mine vow'd to die for me.

Mrs. *Sull*. Mine swore to die with me.

Dor. Mine spoke the softest moving things.

Mrs. *Sull*. Mine had his moving things too.

Dor. Mine kiss'd my Hand Ten thousand times.

Mrs. *Sull*. Mine has all that Pleasure to come.

Dor. Mine offer'd Marriage.

Mrs. *Sull*. O lard! D'ye call that a moving thing?

Dor. The sharpest Arrow in his Quiver, my dear Sister,——Why, my Ten thousand Pounds may lie brooding here this seven Years, and hatch nothing at last but some ill natur'd Clown like yours:——Whereas, If I marry my Lord *Aimwell*, there will be Title, Place and Precedence, the Park, the Play, and the drawing-Room, Splendor, Equipage, Noise and Flambeaux—— Hey, my Lady *Aimwell*'s Servants there——Lights, Lights to the Stairs—— My Lady *Aimwell*'s Coach put forward———Stand by, make room for her Ladyship——Are not these things moving?——What! melancholly of a sudden? 387

Mrs. *Sull*. Happy, happy Sister! your Angel has been watchful for your Happiness, whilst mine has slept regardless of his Charge.———Long smiling Years of circling Joys for you, but not one Hour for me! [*Weeps*.

Dor. Come, my Dear, we'll talk of something else. 391

Mrs. *Sull*. O *Dorinda*, I own my self a Woman, full of my Sex, a gentle, generous Soul,——easie and yielding to soft Desires; a spacious Heart, where Love and all his Train might lodge. And must the fair Apartment of my Breast be made a Stable for a Brute to lie in?

Dor. Meaning your Husband, I suppose.

Mrs. *Sull*. Husband! no,—Even Husband is too soft a Name for him. ——But, come, I expect my Brother here to Night or to Morrow; he was abroad when my Father marry'd me; perhaps he'll find a way to make me easy. 400

Dor. Will you promise not to make your self easy in the mean time with my Lord's Friend?

Mrs. *Sull*. You mistake me, Sister—It happens with us, as among the Men, the greatest Talkers are the greatest Cowards; and there's a Reason for it; those Spirits evaporate in prattle, which might do more Mischief if

370 upon his Tiptoes] In eager anticipation—by implication, of sexual favours.

they took another Course;——Tho' to confess the Truth, I do love that Fellow;——And if I met him drest as he shou'd be, and I undrest as I shou'd be—Look'ye, Sister, I have no supernatural Gifts;—I can't swear I cou'd resist the Temptation,—tho' I can safely promise to avoid it; and that's as much as the best of us can do.   [*Ex.* Mrs. *Sull.* and *Dor.*

Enter Aimwell *and* Archer *laughing.*

Arch. And the awkward Kindness of the good motherly old Gentle-woman——   412

Aim. And the coming Easiness of the young one——S'death, 'tis pity to deceive her.

Arch. Nay, if you adhere to those Principles, stop where you are.

Aim. I can't stop; for I love her to distraction.

Arch. S'death, if you love her a hair's breadth beyond discretion, you must go no farther.

Aim. Well, well, any thing to deliver us from sauntering away our idle Evenings at *White*'s, *Tom*'s, or *Will*'s, and be stinted to bear looking at our old Acquaintance, the Cards; because our impotent Pockets can't afford us a Guinea for the mercenary Drabs.   422

Arch. Or be oblig'd to some Purse-proud Coxcomb for a scandalous Bottle, where we must not pretend to our share of the Discourse, because we can't pay our Club o'th Reckoning;—dam it, I had rather spunge upon *Morris*, and sup upon a Dish of *Bohee* scor'd behind the Door.

Aim. And there expose our want of Sense by talking Criticisms, as we shou'd our want of Money by railing at the Government.

Arch. Or be oblig'd to sneak into the side-Box, and between both Houses steal two Acts of a Play, and because we han't Money to see the other three, we come away discontented, and damn the whole five.   431

Aim. And Ten thousand such rascally Tricks,—had we outliv'd our Fortunes among our Acquaintance.—But now——

Arch. Ay, now is the time to prevent all this.——Strike while the Iron is hot.—This Priest is the luckiest part of our Adventure;——He shall marry you, and pimp for me.

Aim. But I shou'd not like a Woman that can be so fond of a *Frenchman.*

Arch. Alas, Sir, Necessity has no Law; the Lady may be in Distress; per-haps she has a confounded Husband, and her Revenge may carry her farther

425 pay our Club o'th Reckoning] Contribute to the pool of money for settling the account.   426 *Morris*] A coffee-house keeper.   426 *Bohee*] A kind of black tea.   430 steal two Acts of a Play] That is, avoid payment for a side box, since this was not demanded till the end of the second act. The context also seems to suggest that successive acts of the same play have been seen on a single day's outing, one at each of the licensed theatres. For this the opportunity would have been most infrequent.

than her Love.———I gad, I have so good an Opinion of her, and of my self, that I begin to fancy strange things; and we must say this for the Honour of our Women, and indeed of our selves, that they do stick to their Men, as they do to their *Magna Charta.*—If the Plot lies as I suspect,—I must put on the Gentleman.———But here comes the Doctor.———I shall be ready.

[*Exit.*

Enter Foigard.

Foig. Sauve you, noble Friend.   445
Aim. O Sir, your Servant; pray Doctor, may I crave your Name?
Foig. Fat Naam is upon me? my Naam is *Foigard,* Joy.
Aim. Foigard, a very good Name for a Clergyman: Pray, Doctor *Foigard,* were you ever in *Ireland?*
Foig. Ireland! No Joy.——Fat sort of Plaace is dat saam *Ireland?* dey say de People are catcht dere when dey are young.   451
Aim. And some of 'em when they're old;—as for Example.

[*Takes* Foigard *by the Shoulder.*

Sir, I arrest you as a Traytor against the Government; you're a Subject of *England,* and this Morning shew'd me a Commission, by which you serv'd as Chaplain in the *French* Army: This is Death by our Law, and your Reverence must hang for't.

Foig. Upon my Shoul, Noble Friend, dis is strange News you tell me, Fader *Foigard* a Subject of *England,* de Son of a *Burgomaster* of *Brussels,* a Subject of *England!* Ubooboo———
Aim. The Son of a Bogtrotter in *Ireland;* Sir, your Tongue will condemn you before any Bench in the Kingdom.   461
Foig. And is my Tongue all your Evidensh, Joy?
Aim. That's enough.
Foig. No, no, Joy, for I vill never spake *English* no more.
Aim. Sir, I have other Evidence———Here, *Martin,* you know this Fellow.   [*Enter* Archer.
Arch. [*In a Brogue.*] Saave you, my dear Cussen, how do's your Health?
Foig. Ah! upon my Shoul dere is my Countryman, and his Brogue will hang mine. [*Aside.*] *Mynheer, Ick wet neat watt hey zacht, Ick universton ewe neat, sacramant.*   470
Aim. Altering your Language won't do, Sir, this Fellow knows your Person, and will swear to your Face.
Foig. Faace! fey, is dear a Brogue upon my Faash, too?
Arch. Upon my Soulvation dere ish Joy——But Cussen *Mack-shane* vil you not put a remembrance upon me?
Foig. Mack-shane! by St. *Paatrick,* dat is Naame, shure enough. [*Aside.*
Aim. I fancy *Archer,* you have it.

Foig. The Devil hang you, Joy——By fat Acquaintance are you my Cussen.

Arch. O, de Devil hang your shelf, Joy, you know we were little Boys togeder upon de School, and your foster Moder's Son was marry'd upon my Nurse's Chister, Joy, and so we are Irish Cussens.   482

Foig. De Devil taak the Relation! vel, Joy, and fat School was it?

Arch. I tinks it vas——Aay——'Twas *Tipperary*.

Foig. No, no, Joy, it vas *Kilkenny*.

Aim. That's enough for us—Self-Confession—Come, Sir, we must deliver you into the Hands of the next Magistrate.

Arch. He sends you to Gaol, you're try'd next Assizes, and away you go swing into Purgatory.

Foig. And is it so wid you, Cussen?   490

Arch. It vil be sho wid you, Cussen, if you don't immediately confess the Secret between you and Mrs. *Gipsey*—Look'e, Sir, the Gallows or the Secret, take your Choice.

Foig. The Gallows! upon my Shoul I hate that saam Gallow, for it is a Diseash dat is fatal to our Family——Vel den, dere is nothing, Shentlemens, but Mrs. *Shullen* wou'd spaak wid the Count in her Chamber at Midnight, and dere is no Haarm, Joy, for I am to conduct the Count to the Plash, my shelf.

Arch. As I guess'd——Have you communicated the matter to the Count?

Foig. I have not sheen him since.   500

Arch. Right agen; why then, Doctor—you shall conduct me to the Lady instead of the Count.

Foig. Fat my Cussen to the Lady! upon my Shoul, gra, dat is too much upon the Brogue.

Arch. Come, come, Doctor, consider we have got a Rope about your Neck, and if you offer to squeek, we'll stop your Wind-pipe, most certainly, we shall have another Job for you in a Day or two, I hope.

Aim. Here's Company coming this way, let's into my Chamber, and there concert our Affair farther.

Arch. Come, my dear Cussen, come along.   [*Exeunt.*

Enter Bonniface, Hounslow *and* Bagshot *at one Door*,
Gibbet *at the opposite*.

Gib. Well, Gentlemen, 'tis a fine Night for our Enterprise.   511

Houns. Dark as Hell.

Bag. And blows like the Devil; our Landlord here has show'd us the Window where we must break in, and tells us the Plate stands in the Wainscoat Cupboard in the Parlour.

Bon. Ay, ay, Mr. *Bagshot*, as the saying is, Knives and Forks, and Cups,

and Canns, and Tumblers, and Tankards——There's one Tankard, as the
saying is, that's near upon as big as me, it was a Present to the Squire from
his Godmother, and smells of Nutmeg and Toast like an *East India* Ship.

Houns. Then you say we must divide at the Stair-head?   520

Bon. Yes, Mr. *Hounslow*, as the saying is—At one end of that Gallery lies
my Lady *Bountifull* and her Daughter, and at the other Mrs. *Sullen*——As
for the Squire——

Gib. He's safe enough, I have fairly enter'd him, and he's more than half
seas over already—But such a Parcel of Scoundrels are got about him now,
that I gad I was asham'd to be seen in their Company.

Bon. 'Tis now Twelve, as the saying is——Gentlemen, you must set out at
One.

Gib. Hounslow, do you and *Bagshot* see our Arms fix'd, and I'll come to you
presently.   530

Houns. }
Bag.   } We will.   [*Exeunt.*

Gib. Well, my dear *Bonny*, you assure me that *Scrub* is a Coward.

Bon. A Chicken, as the saying is——You'll have no Creature to deal
with but the Ladies.

Gib. And I can assure you, Friend, there's a great deal of Address and good
Manners in robbing a Lady, I am the most a Gentleman that way that ever
travell'd the Road—But, my dear *Bonny*, this Prize will be a Galleon, a *Vigo*
Business—I warrant you we shall bring off three or four thousand Pound.

Bon. In Plate, Jewels and Money, as the saying is, you may.

Gib. Why then, *Tyburn*, I defie thee, I'll get up to Town, sell off my
Horse and Arms, buy my self some pretty Employment in the Houshold, and
be as snug, and as honest as any Courtier of 'um all.   542

Bon. And what think you then of my Daughter *Cherry* for a Wife?

Gib. Look'ee, my dear *Bonny*—Cherry *is the Goddess I adore*, as the Song
goes; but it is a Maxim that Man and Wife shou'd never have it in their
Power to hang one another, for if they should, the Lord have Mercy on 'um
both.   [*Exeunt.*

End of the Fourth Act.

---

524 half seas over] Drunk.   537 a *Vigo* Business] An affair as profitable as Sir George
Rook's action off Vigo in October 1702.

ACT V.

SCENE *continues*　*Knocking without.*

Enter Bonniface.

Bon. COming, coming—A Coach and six foaming Horses at this time
o'Night! Some great Man, as the saying is, for he scorns to travel
with other People.

Enter Sir Charles Freeman.

Sir Ch. What, Fellow! a Publick-house, and a Bed when other People
Sleep.

Bon. Sir, I an't a Bed, as the saying is.

Sir Ch. Is Mr. *Sullen*'s Family, a Bed, think'e?

Bon. All but the Squire himself, Sir, as the saying is, he's in the House.

Sir Ch. What Company has he?

Bon. Why, Sir, there's the Constable, Mr. *Gage* the Exciseman, the
Hunchback'd-Barber, and two or three other Gentlemen.　　　　　11

Sir Ch. I find my Sister's Letters gave me the true Picture of her Spouse.

Enter Sullen *Drunk.*

Bon. Sir, here's the Squire.

Sull. The Puppies left me asleep——Sir.

Sir Ch. Well, Sir.

Sull. Sir, I'm an unfortunate Man—I have three thousand Pound a Year,
and I can't get a Man to drink a Cup of Ale with me.

Sir Ch. That's very hard.

Sull. Ay, Sir—And unless you have pitty upon me, and smoke one Pipe
with me, I must e'en go home to my Wife, and I had rather go the Devil by
half.　　　　　21

Sir Ch. But, I presume, Sir, you won't see your Wife to Night, she'll be
gone to Bed—you don't use to lye with your Wife in that Pickle?

Sull. What! not lye with my Wife! why, Sir, do you take me for an Atheist
or a Rake?

Sir Ch. If you hate her, Sir, I think you had better lye from her.

Sull. I think so too, Friend——But I'm a Justice of Peace, and must do
nothing against the Law.

Sir Ch. Law! as I take it, Mr. Justice, no Body observes Law for Law's
Sake, only for the good of those for whom it was made.　　　　　30

Sull. But if the Law orders me to send you to Goal, you must ly there, my Friend.

Sir *Ch.* Not unless I commit a Crime to deserve it.

Sull. A Crime! Oons an't I marry'd?

Sir *Ch.* Nay, Sir, if you call Marriage a Crime, you must disown it for a Law.

Sull. Eh!—I must be acquainted with you, Sir—But, Sir, I shou'd be very glad to know the Truth of this Matter.

Sir *Ch.* Truth, Sir, is a profound Sea, and few there be that dare wade deep enough to find out the bottom on't. Besides, Sir, I'm afraid the Line of your Understanding mayn't be long enough.   41

Sull. Look'e, Sir, I have nothing to say to your Sea of Truth, but if a good Parcel of Land can intitle a Man to a little Truth, I have as much as any He in the Country.

Bon. I never heard your Worship, as the saying is, talk so much before.

Sull. Because I never met with a Man that I lik'd before—

Bon. Pray, Sir, as the saying is, let me ask you one Question, are not Man and Wife one Flesh?

Sir *Ch.* You and your Wife, Mr. Guts, may be one Flesh, because ye are nothing else——but rational Creatures have minds that must be united.

Sull. Minds.   51

Sir *Ch.* Ay, Minds, Sir, don't you think that the Mind takes place of the Body?

Sull. In some People.

Sir *Ch.* Then the Interest of the Master must be consulted before that of his Servant.

Sull. Sir, you shall dine with me to Morrow.———Oons I always thought that we were naturally one.

Sir *Ch.* Sir, I know that my two Hands are naturally one, because they love one another, kiss one another, help one another in all the Actions of Life, but I cou'd not say so much, if they were always at Cuffs.   61

Sull. Then 'tis plain that we are two.

Sir *Ch.* Why don't you part with her, Sir?

Sull. Will you take her, Sir?

Sir *Ch.* With all my Heart.

Sull. You shall have her to Morrow Morning, and a Venison-pasty into the Bargain.

Sir *Ch.* You'll let me have her Fortune too?

Sull. Fortune! why, Sir, I have no Quarrel at her Fortune—I only hate the Woman, Sir, and none but the Woman shall go.   70

Sir *Ch.* But her Fortune, Sir——

31 Goal] Old spelling of 'gaol'.

Sull. Can you play at Whisk, Sir?

Sir *Ch.* No, truly, Sir.

Sull. Nor at All-fours?

Sir *Ch.* Neither!

Sull. Oons! where was this Man bred. [*Aside.*] Burn me, Sir, I can't go home, 'tis but two a Clock.

Sir *Ch.* For half an Hour, Sir, if you please—But you must consider 'tis late.

Sull. Late! that's the Reason I can't go to Bed——Come, Sir.——

[*Exeunt.*

Enter Cherry, *runs across the Stage and knocks at* Aimwell's *Chamberdoor.*
Enter Aimwell *in his Night-cap and Gown.*

Aim. What's the matter, you tremble, Child, you're frighted.   81

Cher. No wonder, Sir——But in short, Sir, this very Minute a Gang of Rogues are gone to rob my Lady *Bountiful*'s House.

Aim. How!

Cher. I dogg'd 'em to the very Door, and left 'em breaking in.

Aim. Have you alarm'd any Body else with the News?

Cher. No, no, Sir, I wanted to have discover'd the whole Plot, and twenty other things to your Man *Martin*; but I have search'd the whole House and can't find him; where is he?

Aim. No matter, Child, will you guide me immediately to the House?

Cher. With all my Heart, Sir, my Lady *Bountiful* is my Godmother; and I love Mrs. *Dorinda* so well——   92

Aim. Dorinda! The Name inspires me, the Glory and the Danger shall be all my own——Come, my Life, let me but get my Sword.   [*Exeunt.*

SCENE, *Changes to a Bed-chamber in Lady* Bountiful's *House.*

Enter Mrs. Sull. Dor. *undress'd, a Table and Lights.*

Dor. 'Tis very late, Sister, no News of your Spouse yet?

Mrs. *Sull.* No, I'm condemn'd to be alone till towards four, and then perhaps I may be executed with his Company.

Dor. Well, my Dear, I'll leave you to your rest; you'll go directly to Bed, I suppose.

Mrs. *Sull.* I don't know what to do? hey-hoe.

Dor. That's a desiring Sigh, Sister.

Mrs. *Sull.* This is a languishing Hour, Sister.

74 All-fours] A card game for two.

Dor. And might prove a Critical Minute, if the pretty Fellow were here.

Mrs. Sull. Here! what, in my Bed-chamber, at two a Clock o'th' Morning, I undress'd, the Family asleep, my hated Husband abroad, and my lovely Fellow at my Feet—O gad, Sister! 12

Dor. Thoughts are free, Sister, and them I allow you—So, my Dear, good Night.

Mrs. Sull. A good Rest to my dear *Dorinda*——Thoughts free! are they so? why then suppose him here, dress'd like a youthful, gay and burning Bridegroom, [*Here* Archer *steals out of the Closet.*] with Tongue enchanting, Eyes bewitching, Knees imploring. [*Turns a little o' one side, and sees* Archer *in the Posture she describes.*] Ah! [*Shreeks, and runs to the other Side of the Stage.*] Have my Thoughts rais'd a Spirit?——What are you, Sir, a Man or a Devil? 21

Arch. A Man, a Man, Madam. [*Rising.*

Mrs. Sull. How shall I be sure of it?

Arch. Madam, I'll give you Demonstration this Minute.

[*Takes her Hand.*

Mrs. Sull. What, Sir! do you intend to be rude?

Arch. Yes, Madam, if you please.

Mrs. Sull. In the Name of Wonder, Whence came ye?

Arch. From the Skies, Madam———I'm a *Jupiter* in Love, and you shall be my *Alcmena*.

Mrs. Sull. How came you in? 30

Arch. I flew in at the Window, Madam, your Cozen *Cupid* lent me his Wings, and your Sister *Venus* open'd the Casement.

Mrs. Sull. I'm struck dumb with Admiration.

Arch. And I with wonder. [*Looks passionately at her.*

Mrs. Sull. What will become of me?

Arch. How beautiful she looks——The teeming Jolly Spring Smiles in her blooming Face, and when she was conceiv'd, her Mother smelt to Roses, look'd on Lillies—

> *Lillies unfold their white, their fragrant Charms,*
> *When the warm Sun thus Darts into their Arms.* 40

[*Runs to her.*

Mrs. Sull. Ah! [*Shreeks.*]

Arch. Oons, Madam, what d'ye mean? you'll raise the House.

Mrs. Sull. Sir, I'll wake the Dead before I bear this———What! approach me with the Freedoms of a Keeper; I'm glad on't, your Impudence has cur'd me.

---

29 *Alcmena*] Mother of Hercules. The night of his conception was said to have been extended to three times its proper length at the command of Zeus, for his mistress's better pleasure. The name was misprinted *Alimena* in the first edition.

Arch. If this be Impudence [*Kneels*] I leave to your partial self; no panting Pilgrim after a tedious, painful Voyage, e'er bow'd before his Saint with more Devotion.

Mrs. *Sull.* Now, now, I'm ruin'd, if he kneels! [*Aside*] rise thou prostrate Ingineer, not all thy undermining Skill shall reach my Heart———Rise, and know, I am a Woman without my Sex, I can love to all the Tenderness of Wishes, Sighs and Tears———But go no farther———Still to convince you that I'm more than Woman, I can speak my Frailty, confess my Weakness even for you—But——— 54

Arch. For me!   [*Going to lay hold on her.*

Mrs. *Sull.* Hold, Sir, build not upon that—For my most mortal hatred follows if you disobey what I command you now—leave me this Minute—— If he denies, I'm lost.   [*Aside.*

Arch. Then you'll promise———

Mrs. *Sull.* Any thing another time.   60

Arch. When shall I come?

Mrs. *Sull.* To Morrow when you will.

Arch. Your Lips must seal the Promise.

Mrs. *Sull.* Pshaw!

Arch. They must, they must [*Kisses her*] Raptures and Paradice! and why not now, my Angel? the Time, the Place, Silence and Secresy, all conspire ———And the now conscious Stars have preordain'd this Moment for my Happiness.   [*Takes her in his Arms.*

Mrs. *Sull.* You will not, cannot sure.

Arch. If the Sun rides fast, and disappoints not Mortals of to Morrow's Dawn, this Night shall crown my Joys.   71

Mrs. *Sull.* My Sex's Pride assist me.

Arch. My Sex's Strength help me.

Mrs. *Sull.* You shall kill me first.

Arch. I'll dye with you.   [*Carrying her off.*

Mrs. *Sull.* Thieves, Thieves, Murther———

Enter Scrub *in his Breeches, and one Shoe.*

Scrub. Thieves, Thieves, Murther, Popery.

Arch. Ha! the very timorous Stag will kill in rutting time.

                         [*Draws and offers to Stab* Scrub.

Scrub. [*Kneeling.*] O, Pray, Sir, spare all I have and take my Life.

Mrs. *Sull.* [*Holding* Archer's *Hand.*] What do's the Fellow mean?   80

Scrub. O, Madam, down upon your Knees, your Marrow-bones——He's one of 'um.

Arch. Of whom?

50 Ingineer] Plotter.

Scrub. One of the Rogues—I beg your Pardon, Sir, one of the honest Gentlemen that just now are broke into the House.

Arch. How!

Mrs. Sull. I hope, you did not come to rob me?

Arch. Indeed I did, Madam, but I wou'd have taken nothing but what you might ha' spar'd, but your crying Thieves has wak'd this dreaming Fool, and so he takes 'em for granted.   90

Scrub. Granted! 'tis granted, Sir, take all we have.

Mrs. Sull. The Fellow looks as if he were broke out of *Bedlam*.

Scrub. Oons, Madam, they're broke in to the House with Fire and Sword, I saw them, heard them, they'll be here this Minute.

Arch. What, Thieves!

Scrub. Under Favour, Sir, I think so.

Mrs. Sull. What shall we do, Sir?

Arch. Madam, I wish your Ladyship a good Night.

Mrs. Sull. Will you leave me?

Arch. Leave you! Lord, Madam, did not you command me to be gone just now upon pain of your immortal Hatred.   101

Mrs. Sull. Nay, but pray, Sir——   [*Takes hold of him.*

Arch. Ha, ha, ha, now comes my turn to be ravish'd.—You see now, Madam, you must use Men one way or other; but take this by the way, good Madam, that none but a Fool will give you the benefit of his Courage, unless you'll take his Love along with it.——How are they arm'd, Friend?

Scrub. With Sword and Pistol, Sir.

Arch. Hush——I see a dark Lanthorn coming thro' the Gallery.—— Madam, be assur'd I will protect you, or lose my Life.

Mrs. Sull. Your Life! no, Sir, they can rob me of nothing that I value half so much; therefore, now, Sir, let me intreat you to be gone.   111

Arch. No, Madam, I'll consult my own Safety for the sake of yours, I'll work by Stratagem: Have you Courage enough to stand the appearance of 'em?

Mrs. Sull. Yes, yes, since I have scap'd your Hands, I can face any thing.

Arch. Come hither, Brother *Scrub*, don't you know me?

Scrub. Eh! my dear Brother, let me kiss thee.   [*Kisses* Archer.

Arch. This way—Here—   [Archer *and* Scrub *hide behind the Bed.*

Enter Gibbet *with a dark Lanthorn in one Hand*
and a Pistol in t'other.

Gib. Ay, ay, this is the Chamber, and the Lady alone.

Mrs. Sull. Who are you, Sir? what wou'd you have? d'ye come to rob me?   121

Gib. Rob you! alack a day, Madam, I'm only a younger Brother, Madam;

and so, Madam, if you make a Noise, I'll shoot you thro' the Head; but don't be afraid, Madam.   [*Laying his Lanthorn and Pistol upon the Table.*
These Rings, Madam, don't be concern'd, Madam, I have a profound Respect for you, Madam; your Keys, Madam, don't be frighted, Madam, I'm the most of a Gentleman.   [*Searching her Pockets.*
This Necklace, Madam, I never was rude to a Lady;—I have a Veneration— for this Necklace———

> [*Here* Archer *having come round and seiz'd the Pistols, takes* Gibbet *by the Collar, trips up his Heels, and claps the Pistol to his Breast.*

Arch. Hold, profane Villain, and take the Reward of thy Sacrilege.   130
Gib. Oh! Pray, Sir, don't kill me; I an't prepar'd.
Arch. How many is there of 'em, *Scrub*?
Scrub. Five and Forty, Sir.
Arch. Then I must kill the Villain to have him out of the way.
Gib. Hold, hold, Sir, we are but three upon my Honour.
Arch. Scrub, will you undertake to secure him?
Scrub. Not I, Sir; kill him, kill him.
Arch. Run to *Gipsey*'s Chamber, there you'll find the Doctor; bring him hither presently.   [*Exit* Scrub *running.*
Come, Rogue, if you have a short Prayer, say it.   140
Gib. Sir, I have no Prayer at all; the Government has provided a Chaplain to say Prayers for us on these Occasions.
Mrs. *Sull.* Pray, Sir, don't kill him;—You fright me as much as him.
Arch. The Dog shall die, Madam, for being the Occasion of my disappointment.———Sirrah, this Moment is your last.
Gib. Sir, I'll give you Two hundred Pound to spare my Life.
Arch. Have you no more, Rascal?
Gib. Yes, Sir, I can command Four hundred; but I must reserve Two of 'em to save my Life at the Sessions.

Enter Scrub *and* Foigard.

Arch. Here, Doctor, I suppose *Scrub* and you between you may manage him.——Lay hold of him, Doctor.   151
> [Foig. *lays hold of* Gibbet.

Gib. What! turn'd over to the Priest already.———Look'ye, Doctor, you come before your time; I an't condemn'd yet, I thank'ye.
Foig. Come, my dear Joy, I vill secure your Body and your Shoul too; I vill make you a good Catholick, and give you an Absolution.
Gib. Absolution! can you procure me a Pardon, Doctor?
Foig. No, Joy.———
Gib. Then you and your Absolution may go to the Devil.
Arch. Convey him into the Cellar, there bind him:—Take the Pistol, and

if he offers to resist, shoot him thro' the Head,—and come back to us with all
the speed you can.   161

Scrub. Ay, ay, come, Doctor, do you hold him fast, and I'll guard him.

Mrs. Sull. But how came the Doctor?

Arch. In short, Madam—[*Shreeking without.*] S'death! the Rogues are at
work with the other Ladies.———I'm vex'd I parted with the Pistol; but I
must fly to their Assistance.——Will you stay here, Madam, or venture your
self with me.

Mrs. Sull. O, with you, dear Sir, with you.

                                    [*Takes him by the Arm and Exeunt.*

SCENE, *Changes to another Apartment in the same House.*

Enter Hounslow *dragging in Lady* Bountyfull, *and* Bagshot *halling in*
            Dorinda; *the Rogues with Swords drawn.*

Houn. Come, come, your Jewels, Mistriss.

Bag. Your Keys, your Keys, old Gentlewoman.

Enter Aimwell *and* Cherry.

Aim. Turn this way, Villains; I durst engage an Army in such a Cause.
                                            [*He engages 'em both.*

Dor. O, Madam, had I but a Sword to help the brave Man?

L. Boun. There's three or four hanging up in the Hall; but they won't
draw. I'll go fetch one however.   [*Exit.*

Enter Archer *and Mrs.* Sullen.

Arch. Hold, hold, my Lord, every Man his Bird, pray.
            [*They engage Man to Man, the Rogues are thrown and disarm'd.*

Cher. What! the Rogues taken! then they'll impeach my Father; I must
give him timely Notice.   [*Runs out.*

Arch. Shall we kill the Rogues?   10

Aim. No, no, we'll bind them.

Arch. Ay, ay; here, Madam, lend me your Garter?
                                    [*To Mrs.* Sullen *who stands by him.*

Mrs. Sull. The Devil's in this Fellow; he fights, loves, and banters, all in a
Breath.———Here's a Cord that the Rogues brought with 'em, I suppose.

Arch. Right, right, the Rogue's Destiny, a Rope to hang himself.——
Come, my Lord,——This is but a scandalous sort of an Office, [*Binding
the Rogues together.*] if our Adventures shou'd end in this sort of Hangman-
work; but I hope there is something in prospect that———[*Enter* Scrub.]
Well, *Scrub,* have you secur'd your *Tartar?*

Scrub. Yes, Sir, I left the Priest and him disputing about Religion.   20

Aim. And pray carry these Gentlemen to reap the Benefit of the Controversy.   [*Delivers the Prisoners to* Scrub, *who leads 'em out.*

Mrs. *Sull.* Pray, Sister, how came my Lord here?

Dor. And pray, how came the Gentleman here?

Mrs. *Sull.* I'll tell you the greatest piece of Villainy——

[*They talk in dumb show.*

Aim. I fancy, *Archer*, you have been more successful in your Adventures than the House-breakers.

Arch. No matter for my Adventure, yours is the principal.—Press her this Minute to marry you,——now while she's hurry'd between the Palpitation of her Fear, and the Joy of her Deliverance, now while the Tide of her Spirits are at High-flood——Throw your self at her Feet; speak some *Romantick* Nonsense or other;——Address her like *Alexander* in the height of his Victory, confound her Senses, bear down her Reason, and away with her——The Priest is now in the Cellar, and dare not refuse to do the work.   35

Enter Lady Bountifull.

Aim. But how shall I get off without being observ'd?

Arch. You a Lover! and not find a way to get off—Let me see.

Aim. You bleed, *Archer*.

Arch. S'death, I'm glad on't; this Wound will do the Business——I'll amuse the old Lady and Mrs. *Sullen* about dressing my Wound, while you carry off *Dorinda*.   41

L. *Boun.* Gentlemen, cou'd we understand how you wou'd be gratified for the Services——

Arch. Come, come, my Lady, this is no time for Complements, I'm wounded, Madam.

L. *Boun.* } How! wounded!
Mrs. *Sull.*

Dor. I hope, Sir, you have receiv'd no Hurt?

Aim. None but what you may cure.   [*Makes Love in dumb show.*

L. *Boun.* Let me see your Arm, Sir.——I must have some Powder-sugar to stop the Blood——O me! an ugly Gash upon my Word, Sir, you must go into Bed.   51

Arch. Ay, my Lady a Bed wou'd do very well.——Madam, [*To Mrs.* Sull.] Will you do me the Favour to conduct me to a Chamber?

L. *Boun.* Do, do, Daughter——while I get the Lint and the Probe and the Plaister ready.

[*Runs out one way,* Aimwell *carries off* Dorinda *another.*

49 Powder-sugar] Crushed sugar.

Arch. Come, Madam, why don't you obey your Mother's Commands?

Mrs. Sull. How can you, after what is past, have the Confidence to ask me?

Arch. And if you go to that, how can you after what is past, have the Confidence to deny me?——Was not this Blood shed in your Defence, and my Life expos'd for your Protection.——Look'ye, Madam, I'm none of your *Romantick* Fools, that fight Gyants and Monsters for nothing; my Valour is downright *Swiss*; I'm a Soldier of Fortune and must be paid.

Mrs. Sull. 'Tis ungenerous in you, Sir, to upbraid me with your Services.

Arch. 'Tis ungenerous in you, Madam, not to reward 'em.   65

Mrs. Sull. How! at the Expence of my Honour.

Arch. Honour! can Honour consist with Ingratitude? if you wou'd deal like a Woman of Honour, do like a Man of Honour, d'ye think I wou'd deny you in such a Case?   [*Enter a Servant.*

Ser. Madam, my Lady order'd me to tell you that your Brother is below at the Gate?   71

Mrs. Sull. My Brother? Heavens be prais'd.——Sir, he shall thank you for your Services, he has it in his Power.

Arch. Who is your Brother, Madam?

Mrs. Sull. Sir *Charles Freeman.*——You'll excuse me, Sir; I must go and receive him.

Arch. Sir *Charles Freeman!* S'death and Hell!——My old Acquaintance. Now unless *Aimwell* has made good use of his time, all our fair Machine goes souse into the Sea like the *Edistone*.   [*Exit.*

SCENE, *Changes to the Gallery in the same House.*

Enter Aimwell *and* Dorinda.

Dor. Well, well, my Lord, you have conquer'd; your late generous Action will I hope, plead for my easie yielding, tho' I must own your Lordship had a Friend in the Fort before.

Aim. The Sweets of *Hybla* dwell upon her Tongue.——Here, Doctor——   [*Enter* Foigard *with a Book.*

Foig. Are you prepar'd boat?

Dor. I'm ready: But, first, my Lord one Word;——I have a frightful Example of a hasty Marriage in my own Family; when I reflect upon't, it shocks me. Pray, my Lord, consider a little——

Aim. Consider! Do you doubt my Honour or my Love?   10

---

63 *Swiss*] Mercenary.   79 the *Edistone*] The first, wooden Eddystone Lighthouse was completed in 1699, but destroyed in a storm on 27 November 1703. Winstanley, its builder, was among those who lost their lives.

Dor. Neither: I do believe you equally Just as Brave.——And were your whole Sex drawn out for me to chuse, I shou'd not cast a look upon the Multitude if you were absent.——But my Lord, I'm a Woman; Colours, Concealments may hide a thousand Faults in me;——Therefore know me better first; I hardly dare affirm I know my self in any thing except my Love.

Aim. Such Goodness who cou'd injure; I find my self unequal to the Task of Villain; she has gain'd my Soul, and made it honest like her own;——I cannot, cannot hurt her.   [*Aside*.

Doctor, retire.   [*Exit* Foigard.

Madam, behold your Lover and your Proselite, and judge of my Passion by my Conversion.—I'm all a Lie, nor dare I give a Fiction to your Arms; I'm all Counterfeit except my Passion.   23

Dor. Forbid it Heaven! a Counterfeit!

Aim. I am no Lord, but a poor needy Man, come with a mean, a scandalous Design to prey upon your Fortune:—But the Beauties of your Mind and Person have so won me from my self, that like a trusty Servant, I prefer the Interest of my Mistress to my own.

Dor. Sure I have had the Dream of some poor Mariner, a sleepy image of a welcome Port, and wake involv'd in Storms.——Pray, Sir, who are you?

Aim. Brother to the Man whose Title I usurp'd, but Stranger to his Honour or his Fortune.   32

Dor. Matchless Honesty——Once I was proud, Sir, of your Wealth and Title, but now am prouder that you want it: Now I can shew my Love was justly levell'd, and had no Aim but Love. Doctor, come in.

Enter Foigard *at one Door*, Gipsey *at another, who whispers* Dorinda.

Your Pardon, Sir, we shannot; won't you now, Sir? you must excuse me,— I'll wait on you presently.   [*Exit with* Gipsey.

Foig. Upon my Shoul, now, dis is foolish.   [*Exit*.

Aim. Gone! and bid the Priest depart.——It has an ominous Look.

Enter Archer.

Arch. Courage, *Tom*——Shall I wish you Joy?   40

Aim. No.

Arch. Oons, Man, what ha' you been doing?

Aim. O, *Archer*, my Honesty, I fear has ruin'd me.

Arch. How!

Aim. I have discover'd my self.

Arch. Discover'd! and without my Consent? what! have I embark'd my

21 Proselite] A convert—one now won over to a cause.

small Remains in the same bottom with yours, and you dispose of all without my Partnership?

Aim. O, *Archer*, I own my Fault.

Arch. After Conviction—'Tis then too late for Pardon.—You may remember, Mr. *Aimwell*, that you propos'd this Folly—As you begun, so end it.—Henceforth I'll hunt my Fortune single.—So farewel.   52

Aim. Stay, my dear *Archer*, but a Minute.

Arch. Stay! what to be despis'd, expos'd and laugh'd at—No, I wou'd sooner change Conditions with the worst of the Rogues we just now bound, than bear one scornful Smile from the proud Knight that once I treated as my equal.

Aim. What Knight?

Arch. Sir *Charles Freeman*, Brother to the Lady that I had almost——But no matter for that, 'tis a cursed Night's Work, and so I leave you to make your best on't.   [*Going.*

Aim. Freeman!——One Word, *Archer.* Still I have Hopes; methought she receiv'd my Confession with Pleasure.   63

Arch. S'death! who doubts it?

Aim. She consented after to the Match; and still I dare believe she will be just.

Arch. To her self, I warrant her, as you shou'd have been.

Aim. By all my Hopes, she comes, and smiling comes.

Enter Dorinda *mighty gay.*

Dor. Come, my dear Lord,——I fly with Impatience to your Arms.—The Minutes of my Absence was a tedious Year. Where's this tedious Priest?

Enter Foigard.

Arch. Oons! a brave Girl.   71

Dor. I suppose, my Lord, this Gentleman is privy to our Affairs?

Arch. Yes, yes, Madam, I'm to be your Father.

Dor. Come, Priest, do your Office.

Arch. Make hast, make hast, couple 'em any way. [*Takes* Aimwell's *Hand.*] Come, Madam, I'm to give you——

Dor. My Mind's alter'd, I won't.

Arch. Eh——

Aim. I'm confounded.

Foig. Upon my Shoul, and sho is my shelf.   80

Arch. What's the matter now, Madam?

Dor. Look'ye, Sir, one generous Action deserves another—This Gentleman's Honour oblig'd him to hide nothing from me; my Justice engages me to conceal nothing from him: In short, Sir, you are the Person that you

thought you counterfeited; you are the true Lord Viscount *Aimwell*; and I
wish your Lordship Joy. Now, Priest, you may be gone; if my Lord is
pleas'd now with the Match, let his Lordship marry me in the face of the
World.

Aim. Arch. What do's she mean?

Dor. Here's a Witness for my Truth. [*Enter Sir* Ch. *and Mrs.* Sul.

Sir Ch. My dear Lord *Aimwell*, I wish you Joy.   91

Aim. Of what?

Sir Ch. Of your Honour and Estate: Your Brother died the Day before I
left *London*; and all your Friends have writ after you to *Brussels*; among the
rest I did my self the Honour.

Arch. Hark'ye, Sir Knight, don't you banter now?

Sir Ch. 'Tis Truth upon my Honour.

Aim. Thanks to the pregnant Stars that form'd this Accident.

Arch. Thanks to the Womb of Time that brought it forth; away with it.

Aim. Thanks to my Guardian Angel that led me to the Prize——   100
[*Taking* Dorinda's *Hand.*

Arch. And double Thanks to the noble Sir *Charles Freeman*. My Lord,
I wish you Joy. My Lady I wish you Joy.—I Gad, Sir *Freeman*, you're the
honestest Fellow living.——S'death, I'm grown strange airy upon this
matter—My Lord, how d'ye?—a word, my Lord; don't you remember
something of a previous Agreement, that entitles me to the Moyety of this
Lady's Fortune, which, I think will amount to Five thousand Pound.

Aim. Not a Penny, *Archer*; You wou'd ha' cut my Throat just now, because
I wou'd not deceive this Lady.

Arch. Ay, and I'll cut your Throat again, if you shou'd deceive her now.

Aim. That's what I expected; and to end the Dispute, the Lady's Fortune
is Ten thousand Pound; we'll divide Stakes; take the Ten thousand Pound,
or the Lady.   112

Dor. How! is your Lordship so indifferent?

Arch. No, no, no, Madam, his Lordship knows very well, that I'll take the
Money; I leave you to his Lordship, and so we're both provided for.
[*Enter Count* Bellair.

Co. Mesdames, & Massieurs, I am your Servant trice humble: I hear you be
rob, here.

Aim. The Ladies have been in some danger, Sir.

Co. And Begar, our Inn be rob too.

Aim. Our Inn! by whom?   120

Count. By the Landlord, begar—Garzoon he has rob himself and run
away.

Arch. Rob'd himself!

103 airy] Gay, flippant.   s.d. *Enter Count* Bellair.] Cf. note on Act III, Scene iii, p. 42.

Count. Ay, begar, and me too of a hundre Pound.

Arch. A hundred Pound.

Count. Yes, that I ow'd him.

Aim. Our Money's gone, *Frank*.

Arch. Rot the Money, my Wench is gone——*Scavez vous quelque chose de Madamoiselle* Cherry?

Enter a Fellow with a strong Box and a Letter.

Fell. Is there one *Martin* here? 130

Arch. Ay, ay,——who wants him?

Fell. I have a Box here and Letter for him.

Arch. [*Taking the Box.*] Ha, ha, ha, what's here? *Legerdemain!* by this Light, my Lord, our Money again; but this unfolds the Riddle. [*Opening the Letter, reads.*] Hum, hum, hum——O, 'tis for the Publick good, and must be communicated to the Company.

Mr. MARTIN,

MY *Father being afraid of an Impeachment by the Rogues that are taken to Night is gone off, but if you can procure him a Pardon he will maake great Discoveries that may be useful to the Country; cou'd I have met you instead of your Master to Night, I wou'd have deliver'd my self into your Hands with a Sum that much exceeds that in your strong Box, which I have sent you, with an Assurance to my dear* Martin, *that I shall ever be his most faithful Friend till Death.* 144

CHERRY BONNIFACE.

there's a Billet-doux for you——As for the Father I think he ought to be encouraged, and for the Daughter,——Pray, my Lord, persuade your Bride to take her into her Service instead of *Gipsey*.

Aim. I can assure you, Madam, your Deliverance was owing to her Discovery. 150

Dor. Your Command, my Lord, will do without the Obligation. I'll take care of her.

Sir Ch. This good Company meets oportunely in favour of a Design I have in behalf of my unfortunate Sister, I intend to part her from her Husband ——Gentlemen will you assist me?

Arch. Assist you! S'Death, who wou'd not.

Count. Assist! Garzoon, we all assest.

Enter Sullen.

Sull. What's all this?——They tell me Spouse that you had like to have been rob'd.

Mrs. *Sull*. Truly, Spouse, I was pretty near it——Had not these two
Gentlemen interpos'd.   161

Sull. How came these Gentlemen here?

Mrs. *Sull*. That's his way of returning Thanks you must know.

Count. Garzoon, the Question be a propo for all dat.

Sir *Ch*. You promis'd last Night, Sir, that you wou'd deliver your Lady to
me this Morning.

Sull. Humph.

Arch. Humph. What do you mean by humph—Sir, you shall deliver her—
In short, Sir, we have sav'd you and your Family, and if you are not civil
we'll unbind the Rogues, join with 'um and set fire to your House—What
do's the Man mean? not part with his Wife!   171

Count. Ay, Garzoon de Man no understan Common Justice.

Mrs. *Sull*. Hold, Gentlemen, all things here must move by consent,
Compulsion wou'd Spoil us, let my Dear and I talk the matter over, and you
shall judge it between us.

Sull. Let me know first who are to be our Judges——Pray, Sir, who are
you?

Sir *Ch*. I am Sir *Charles Freeman*, come to take away your Wife.

Sull. And you, good Sir?

Aim. Charles Viscount Aimwell, come to take away your Sister.   180

Sull. And you pray, Sir?

Arch. Francis Archer, Esq; come———

Sull. To take away my Mother, I hope—Gentlemen, you're heartily
welcome, I never met with three more obliging People since I was born——
And now, my Dear, if you please, you shall have the first word.

Arch. And the last for five Pound.

Mrs. *Sull*. Spouse.

Sull. Ribb.

Mrs. *Sull*. How long have we been marry'd?

Sull. By the Almanak fourteen Months——But by my Account fourteen
Years.   191

Mrs. *Sull*. 'Tis thereabout by my reckoning.

Count. Garzoon, their Account will agree.

Mrs. *Sull*. Pray, Spouse, what did you marry for?

Sull. To get an Heir to my Estate.

Sir *Ch*. And have you succeeded?

Sull. No.

Arch. The Condition fails of his side———Pray, Madam, what did you
marry for?

Mrs. *Sull*. To support the Weakness of my Sex by the Strength of his, and
to enjoy the Pleasures of an agreeable Society.   201

Sir *Ch.* Are your Expectations answer'd?

Mrs. *Sull.* No.

Count. A clear Case, a clear Case.

Sir *Ch.* What are the Bars to your mutual Contentment.

Mrs. *Sull.* In the first Place I can't drink Ale with him.

Sull. Nor can I drink Tea with her.

Mrs. *Sull.* I can't hunt with you.

Sull. Nor can I dance with you.

Mrs. *Sull.* I hate Cocking and Racing.   210

Sull. And I abhor Ombre and Piquet.

Mrs. *Sull.* Your Silence is intollerable.

Sull. Your Prating is worse.

Mrs. *Sull.* Have we not been a perpetual Offence to each other——A gnawing Vulture at the Heart.

Sull. A frightful Goblin to the Sight.

Mrs. *Sull.* A Porcupine to the Feeling.

Sull. Perpetual Wormwood to the Taste.

Mrs. *Sull.* Is there on Earth a thing we cou'd agree in?

Sull. Yes——To part.   220

Mrs. *Sull.* With all my Heart.

Sull. Your Hand.

Mrs. *Sull.* Here.

Sull. These Hands join'd us, these shall part us——away——

Mrs. *Sull.* North.

Sul. South.

Mrs. *Sull.* East.

Sull. West——far as the Poles asunder.

Count. Begar the Ceremony be vera pretty.

Sir *Ch.* Now, Mr. *Sullen*, there wants only my Sister's Fortune to make us easie.   231

Sull. Sir *Charles*, you love your Sister, and I love her Fortune; every one to his Fancy.

Arch. Then you won't refund?

Sull. Not a Stiver.

Arch. Then I find, Madam, you must e'en go to your Prison again.

Count. What is the Portion.

Sir *Ch.* Ten thousand Pound, Sir.

Count. Garzoon, I'll pay it, and she shall go home wid me.

Arch. Ha, ha, ha, French all over—Do you know, Sir, what ten thousand Pound English is?   241

Count. No, begar, not justement.

235 Stiver] A Dutch coin, roughly equivalent to a penny.

Arch. Why, Sir, 'tis a hundred thousand Livres.

Count. A hundre tousand Livres——A Garzoon, me canno' do't, your Beauties and their Fortunes are both too much for me.

Arch. Then I will——This Nights Adventure has prov'd strangely lucky to us all——For Captain *Gibbet* in his Walk had made bold, Mr. *Sullen*, with your Study and Escritore, and had taken out all the Writings of your Estate, all the Articles of Marriage with his Lady, Bills, Bonds, Leases, Receipts to an infinite Value, I took 'em from him, and I deliver them to Sir *Charles*.

[Gives him a Parcel of Papers and Parchments.

Sull. How, my Writings! my Head akes consumedly——Well, Gentlemen, you shall have her Fortune, but I can't talk. If you have a mind, Sir *Charles*, to be merry, and celebrate my Sister's Wedding, and my Divorce, you may command my House—but my Head akes consumedly——*Scrub*, bring me a Dram.   255

Arch. Madam, [*To Mrs.* Sull.] there's a Country Dance to the Trifle that I sung to Day; your Hand, and we'll lead it up.   [*Here a Dance.*

Arch. 'Twou'd be hard to guess which of these Parties is the better pleas'd, the Couple Join'd, or the Couple Parted? the one rejoycing in hopes of an untasted Happiness, and the other in their Deliverance from an experienc'd Misery.   261

> *Both happy in their several States we find,*
> *Those parted by consent, and those conjoin'd.*
> *Consent, if mutual, saves the Lawyer's Fee,*
> *Consent is Law enough to set you free.*

FINIS.

---

248 with your Study and Escritore] In your private room and writing-desk.   256 to the Trifle] That is, as an accompaniment to the song assigned to Archer in the third act.

THE
CONSCIOUS LOVERS

Sir Richard Steele

1672–1729

The Conscious Lovers qualifies for a collection of *Eighteenth Century Comedy* by the standards of Steele's age rather than those of our own. With the exception of its scenes below-stairs—their purpose all too evidently to sugar a didactic pill—it is, in fact, a distinctly unfunny play. The clue to its claim to comic stature has therefore to be sought in its author's preface, where it is claimed that 'any thing that has its Foundation in Happiness and Success must be allow'd to be the Object of Comedy'. According to Steele, an audience's pleasure might be 'too exquisite for Laughter', and thus better expressed in the tears evoked by his play's appeal to sentiment—the word then denoting fine feelings movingly realized, and not the disproportion between emotion and object it now unflatteringly describes. An imbalance of this kind *did* flaw *The Conscious Lovers*—as it did the sentimental school Steele's play has alone survived, in the study if not on the stage. And the imbalance was recognized by the play's more perceptive critics: but not by the mass of its audiences, nor, to do him justice, by Steele himself.

The dividing line between sentimental comedy and a tragedy tempered by the demands of 'strict poetical justice' was becoming increasingly hard to draw, and those who made the attempt usually got tied up in neoclassical knots over rules and regularity. Meanwhile, the theatre managers got on with the job of catering for the new taste in tears. Indeed, the first sentimental comedy in the language was by one of their number—the pragmatic Colley Cibber, whose *Love's Last Shift* was first performed as early as 1696. This was four years before Congreve's *Way of the World*, and it stimulated Vanbrugh's very first play, *The Relapse*—his purpose of vitiating Cibber's moral climax apparent in his choice of title. But Cibber was no leader of fashion: he merely had a good nose for it, and continued to prosper as playwright, actor, and manager long after Congreve and Vanbrugh had quitted an increasingly unsympathetic stage.

Richard Steele was born in 1672—one year after Cibber, two after Congreve. But the drama was for him a means neither to subsistence nor to

reputation. Rather, it was one of several genres he tailored to the requirements of his own reformist gospel—incidentally establishing, in mid-career,
the periodical essay as a literary form in its own right. But in the *Tatler* and
the *Spectator*, Steele could fashion a style appropriate to his subject, and was
unconstricted by theatrical conventions which subordinated 'telling' to
'showing'. Unlike, for example, Gay and Fielding, he was unable to practice
while he preached: and the mercantile morality of *The Conscious Lovers* is
thus at once over-explicit and interruptive. Its characters are neither humorous nor mannered, but *ethical* absolutes. No wonder that Parson Adams, in
Fielding's *Joseph Andrews*—written, it's worth noting, in reaction to that
most sentimental of novels, Richardson's *Pamela*—considered it the first play
fit for a Christian to read since the pagan tragedies. But then Parson Adams, as
Fielding intended, lacked both irony and a sense of incongruity. And *The
Conscious Lovers*, as Steele could scarcely have sensed, suffered from very
similar defects.

A more assured theatrical craftsman and a less self-conscious moralist had
been at work in two of Steele's earlier plays—*The Funeral* and *The Tender
Husband*, written and staged between 1701 and 1705. But *The Lying Lover*,
written between these two, was ahead of its time, and therefore 'damn'd
for its Piety', whilst its companion pieces were hangovers from an earlier
tradition—and their morals taken no more seriously than those of any
morning-after. *The Conscious Lovers*, undoubtedly long in gestation, was not
performed until 7 November 1722: and by this time it both met and represented its public's taste. It duly represents its author and its kind in the
present collection. It is at least a salutary reminder that comedy in the
eighteenth century was, in what long remained its most fashionable form,
no laughing matter.

The present text of *The Conscious Lovers* follows that of the first edition—dated
1723, but in fact published late in 1722. A collected edition of Steele's plays appeared in the Mermaid Series, under the editorship of G. A. Aitken, in 1903, but
has long been out of print. A collated, critical edition of *The Conscious Lovers* is
available in the Regents Restoration Drama Series. Edited in 1968 by Shirley
Strum Kenny, it is flawed only by the updated, over-grammatical punctuation
common to its imprint—under which *The Tender Husband* also appeared, in 1967.

THE
Conscious Lovers.

A
COMEDY.

As it is Acted at the

Theatre Royal in *Drury-Lane*,

By His MAJESTY's Servants.

Written by
Sir *RICHARD STEELE.*

Illud Genus Narrationis, quod in Personis positum est, debet habere Sermonis Festivitatem, Animorum Dissimilitudinem, Gravitatem, Lenitatem, Spem, Metum, Suspicionem, Desiderium, Dissimulationem, Misericordiam, Rerum Varietates, Fortunæ Commutationem, Insperatum Incommodum, Subitam Letitiam, Jucundum Exitum Rerum. Cic. Rhetor. ad Herenn. Lib. 1.

LONDON:

Printed for J. TONSON at *Shakespear's Head* over-against *Katharine-Street* in the *Strand.* 1723.

TO THE
KING.

AFter having aspir'd to the Highest and most Laudable Ambition, that of following the Cause of Liberty, I should not have humbly petition'd Your Majesty for a Direction of the Theatre, had I not believ'd Success in that Province an Happiness much to be wish'd by an Honest Man, and highly conducing to the Prosperity of the Common-wealth. It is in this View I lay before Your Majesty a Comedy, which the Audience, in Justice to themselves, has supported and encouraged, and is the Prelude of what, by Your Majesty's Influence and Favour, may be attempted in future Representations.   9

The Imperial Mantle, the Royal Vestment, and the shining Diadem, are what strike ordinary Minds; But Your Majesty's Native Goodness, Your Passion for Justice, and Her constant Assessor Mercy, is what continually surrounds you, in the View of intelligent Spirits, and gives Hope to the Suppliant, who sees he has more than succeeded in giving Your Majesty an Opportunity of doing Good. Our King is above the Greatness of Royalty, and every Act of His Will which makes another Man happy, has ten times more Charms in it, than one that makes Himself appear rais'd above the Condition of others; but even this carries Unhappiness with it; for, Calm Dominion, Equal Grandeur and Familiar Greatness do not easily affect the Imagination of the Vulgar, who cannot see Power but in Terror; and as Fear moves mean Spirits, and Love prompts Great ones to obey, the Insinuations of Malecontents are directed accordingly; and the unhappy People are insnar'd, from Want of Reflection, into Disrespectful Ideas of their Gracious and Amiable Sovereign; and then only begin to apprehend the Greatness of their Master, when they have incurr'd his Displeasure.   25

As Your Majesty was invited to the Throne of a Willing People, for their own sakes, and has ever enjoy'd it with Contempt of the Ostentation of it, we beseech You to Protect us who revere Your Title as we love Your Person. 'Tis to be a Savage to be a Rebel, and they who have fall'n from You have not so much forfeited their Allegiance, as lost their Humanity. And therefore, if it were only to preserve my self from the Imputation of being amongst the

---

4 a Direction of the Theatre] George I had made Steele a Governor of Drury Lane Theatre in 1714.   19 Equal] Equable.

Insensible and Abandon'd, I would beg Permission in the most publick manner possible, to profess my self, with the utmost Sincerity and Zeal,

SIRE,

Your MAJESTY's
Most Devoted Subject
and Servant,

RICHARD STEELE.

THE
PREFACE.

THIS Comedy has been receiv'd with universal Acceptance, for it was in
every Part excellently perform'd; and there needs no other Applause of
the Actors, but that they excell'd according to the Dignity and Difficulty of
the Character they represented. But this great Favour done to the Work in
Acting, renders the Expectation still the greater from the Author, to keep up
the Spirit in the Representation of the Closet, or any other Circumstance of
the Reader, whether alone or in Company: To which I can only say, that it
must be remember'd a Play is to be Seen, and is made to be Represented with
the Advantage of Action, nor can appear but with half the Spirit, without it;
for the greatest Effect of a Play in reading is to excite the Reader to go see it;
and when he does so, it is then a Play has the Effect of Example and Precept.

The chief Design of this was to be an innocent Performance, and the
Audience have abundantly show'd how ready they are to support what is
visibly intended that way; nor do I make any Difficulty to acknowledge, that
the whole was writ for the sake of the Scene of the Fourth Act, wherein Mr.
Bevill evades the Quarrel with his Friend, and hope it may have some Effect
upon the *Goths* and *Vandals* that frequent the Theatres, or a more polite
Audience may supply their Absence.   18

But this Incident, and the Case of the Father and Daughter, are esteem'd
by some People no Subjects of Comedy; but I cannot be of their Mind: for
any thing that has its Foundation in Happiness and Success, must be allow'd
to be the Object of Comedy, and sure it must be an Improvement of it, to
introduce a Joy too exquisite for Laughter, that can have no Spring but in
Delight, which is the Case of this young Lady. I must therefore contend, that
the Tears which were shed on that Occasion flow'd from Reason and Good
Sense, and that Men ought not to be laugh'd at for weeping, till we are come
to a more clear Notion of what is to be imputed to the Hardness of the Head,
and the Softness of the Heart; and I think it was very politely said of Mr.
Wilks to one who told him there was a *General* weeping for *Indiana*, I'll
warrant he'll fight ne'er the worse for that. To be apt to give way to the
Impressions of Humanity is the Excellence of a right Disposition, and the
natural Working of a well-turn'd Spirit. But as I have suffer'd by Criticks
who are got no farther than to enquire whether they ought to be pleas'd or
not, I would willingly find them properer Matter for their Employment, and
revive here a Song which was omitted for want of a Performer, and design'd

29 a *General* weeping] Said by Egerton to have been Brigadier-General Charles Churchill,
whose mistress, Anne Oldfield, took the part of Indiana.

for the Entertainment of *Indiana*; Sig. *Carbonelli* instead of it play'd on the Fiddle, and it is for want of a Singer that such advantageous things are said of an Instrument which were design'd for a Voice. The Song is the Distress of a Love-sick Maid, and may be a fit Entertainment for some small Criticks to examine whether the Passion is just, or the Distress Male or Female.

I.

From Place to Place forlorn I go,   41
  With downcast Eyes a silent Shade;
Forbidden to declare my Woe;
  To speak, till spoken to, afraid.

II.

My inward Pangs, my secret Grief,
  My soft consenting Looks betray:
He Loves, but gives me no Relief:
  Why speaks not he who may?

It remains to say a Word concerning *Terence*, and I am extremely surpris'd to find what Mr. *Cibber* told me, prove a Truth, That what I valued my self so much upon, the Translation of him, should be imputed to me as a Reproach. Mr. *Cibber*'s Zeal for the Work, his Care and Application in instructing the Actors, and altering the Disposition of the Scenes, when I was, through Sickness, unable to cultivate such Things my self, has been a very obliging Favour and Friendship to me. For this Reason, I was very hardly persuaded to throw away *Terence*'s celebrated Funeral, and take only the bare Authority of the young Man's Character, and how I have work'd it into an *Englishman*, and made Use of the same Circumstances of discovering a Daughter, when we least hop'd for one, is humbly submitted to the Learned Reader.   60

---

36 Sig. *Carbonelli*] An Italian violinist of recent immigration.   49 *Terence*] The basic situation of *The Conscious Lovers* is adapted from his *Andria*.   52 a Reproach] Dennis and others had criticized Steele's adaptation of Terence, and his misuse of the comic genre. 56 *Terence*'s celebrated Funeral] The funeral of Chrysis in the *Andria*, which fulfilled a similar function to Steele's masquerade.   57 the young Man's Character] That is, the character of Pamphilus in the *Andria*.

PROLOGUE,

By Mr. *WELSTED*.

Spoken by Mr. *WILKS*.

TO *win your Hearts, and to secure your Praise,*
  The Comic-Writers strive by various Ways:
By subtil Stratagems they act their Game,
And leave untry'd no Avenue to Fame.
One writes the Spouse a beating from his Wife;
And says, Each stroke was Copy'd from the Life.
Some fix all Wit and Humour in Grimace,
And make a Livelyhood of Pinkey's *Face:*
Here, One gay Shew and costly Habits tries,
Confiding to the Judgment of your Eyes: 10
Another smuts his Scene (a cunning Shaver)
Sure of the Rakes and of the Wenches Favour.
Oft have these Arts prevail'd; and one may guess,
If practis'd o'er again, would find Success.
But the bold Sage, the Poet of To-night,
By new and desp'rate Rules resolv'd to Write;
Fain would he give more just Applauses Rise,
And please by Wit that scorns the Aids of Vice;
The Praise he seeks, from worthier Motives springs,
Such Praise, as Praise to those that give, it brings.   20
    Your Aid, most humbly sought, then Britons *lend,*
And Lib'ral Mirth, like Lib'ral Men, defend:
No more let Ribaldry, with Licence writ,
Usurp the Name of Eloquence or Wit;
No more let lawless Farce uncensur'd go,
The lewd dull Gleanings of a Smithfield *Show.*

Mr. *WELSTED*] A minor poet encouraged by Steele. He was attacked by Pope in the *Dunciad*.   8 Pinkey] William Pinkethman, the comic actor.   25 *lawless Farce*] That is, irregular drama, which ignored both moral and aesthetic 'rules', and which was often staged at the unlicensed playhouses.   26 Smithfield *Show*] An entertainment at Bartholomew Fair, which took place at Smithfield.

D

'Tis yours, with Breeding to refine the Age,
To Chasten Wit, and Moralize the Stage.
  Ye Modest, Wise and Good, ye Fair, ye Brave,
To-night the Champion of your Virtues save,   30
Redeem from long Contempt the Comic Name,
And judge Politely for your Countrey's Fame.

Dramatis Personæ.

MEN.

Sir John Bevil.	*Mr.* Mills.
Mr. Sealand.	*Mr.* Williams.
Bevil *jun. in Love with* Indiana.	*Mr.* Booth.
Myrtle, *in Love with* Lucinda.	*Mr.* Wilks.
Cimberton, *a Coxcomb.*	*Mr.* Griffin.
Humphry, *an old Servant to Sir* John.	*Mr.* Shepard.
Tom, *Servant to* Bevil *jun.*	*Mr.* Cibber.
Daniel, *a Country Boy, Servant to* Indiana.	*Mr.* Theo. Cibber.

WOMEN.

Mrs. Sealand, *second Wife to* Sealand.	*Mrs.* Moore.
Isabella, *Sister to* Sealand.	*Mrs.* Thurmond.
Indiana, Sealand'*s Daughter by his first Wife.*	*Mrs.* Oldfield.
Lucinda, Sealand'*s Daughter by his second Wife.*	*Mrs.* Booth.
Phillis, *Maid to* Lucinda.	*Mrs.* Younger.

SCENE *LONDON.*

THE
Conscious Lovers.

***

ACT I. SCENE I.

SCENE, *Sir* John Bevil's *House.*

Enter Sir John Bevil, *and* Humphrey.

Sir JOHN BEVIL.

HAVE you order'd that I should not be interrupted while I am dressing?

Humph. Yes, Sir: I believ'd you had something of Moment to say to me.

Sir. J. Bev. Let me see, *Humphrey;* I think it is now full forty Years since I first took thee, to be about my Self.

Humph. I thank you, Sir, it has been an easy forty Years; and I have pass'd 'em without much Sickness, Care, or Labour.

Sir J. Bev. Thou hast a brave Constitution; you are a Year or two older than I am, Sirrah.

Humph. You have ever been of that mind, Sir.   10

Sir J. Bev. You Knave, you know it; I took thee for thy Gravity and Sobriety, in my wild Years.

Humph. Ah Sir! our Manners were form'd from our different Fortunes, not our different Age. Wealth gave a Loose to your Youth, and Poverty put a Restraint upon mine.

Sir J. Bev. Well, *Humphrey,* you know I have been a kind Master to you; I have us'd you, for the ingenuous Nature I observ'd in you from the beginning, more like an humble Friend than a Servant.

Humph. I humbly beg you'll be so tender of me, as to explain your Commands, Sir, without any farther Preparation.   20

Sir J. Bev. I'll tell thee then. In the first Place, this Wedding of my Son's, in all Probability, (shut the Door) will never be at all.

Humph. How, Sir! not be at all? for what reason is it carry'd on in Appearance?

Sir J. Bev. Honest *Humphrey,* have patience; and I'll tell thee all in Order. I have my self, in some part of my Life, liv'd (indeed) with Freedom, but, I hope, without Reproach: Now, I thought Liberty wou'd be as little injurious to my Son; therefore, as soon as he grew towards Man, I indulg'd him in living after his own manner: I knew not how, otherwise, to judge of his Inclination; for what can be concluded from a Behaviour under Restraint and Fear? But what charms me above all Expression is, that my Son has never in the least Action, the most distant Hint or Word, valued himself upon that great Estate of his Mother's, which, according to our Marriage Settlement, he has had ever since he came to Age.   34

Humph. No, Sir; on the contrary, he seems afraid of appearing to enjoy it, before you or any belonging to you——He is as dependant and resign'd to your Will, as if he had not a Farthing but what must come from your immediate Bounty——You have ever acted like a good and generous Father, and he like an obedient and grateful Son.

Sir J. Bev. Nay, his Carriage is so easy to all with whom he converses, that he is never assuming, never prefers himself to others, nor ever is guilty of that rough Sincerity which a Man is not call'd to, and certainly disobliges most of his Acquaintance; to be short, *Humphrey*, his Reputation was so fair in the World, that Old *Sealand*, the great *India* Merchant, has offer'd his only Daughter, and sole Heiress to that vast Estate of his, as a Wife for him; you may be sure I made no Difficulties, the Match was agreed on, and this very Day named for the Wedding.   47

Humph. What hinders the Proceeding?

Sir J. Bev. Don't interrupt me. You know, I was last *Thursday* at the Masquerade; my Son, you may remember, soon found us out——He knew his Grandfather's Habit, which I then wore; and tho' it was the Mode, in the last Age, yet the Maskers, you know, follow'd us as if we had been the most monstrous Figures in that whole Assembly.   53

Humph. I remember indeed a young Man of Quality in the Habit of a Clown, that was particularly troublesome.

Sir J. Bev. Right—He was too much what he seem'd to be. You remember how impertinently he follow'd, and teiz'd us, and wou'd know who we were.

Humph. I know he has a mind to come into that Particular.   [*Aside.*

Sir J. Bev. Ay, he follow'd us, till the Gentleman who led the Lady in the *Indian* Mantle presented that gay Creature to the Rustick, and bid him (like *Cymon* in the Fable) grow Polite, by falling in Love, and let that worthy old Gentleman alone, meaning me: The Clown was not reform'd, but rudely persisted, and offer'd to force off my Mask; with that the Gentleman throwing off his own, appear'd to be my Son, and in his Concern for me, tore

50 Masquerade] A fashionable assembly, at which it was customary to adopt some form of disguise.   55 a Clown] A rustic, a yokel.   61 *Cymon* in the Fable] The story of a dullard who falls in love with the sleeping Iphigenia is in the *Decameron*, but was also used by Dryden in his *Fables*.

off that of the Nobleman; at this they seiz'd each other; the Company call'd the Guards: and in the Surprize, the Lady swoon'd away: Upon which my Son quitted his Adversary, and had now no Care but of the Lady,——when raising her in his Arms, Art thou gone, cry'd he, for ever——forbid it Heav'n!—She revives at his known Voice,——and with the most familiar tho' modest Gesture hangs in Safety over his Shoulder weeping, but wept as in the Arms of one before whom she could give her self a Loose, were she not under Observation: while she hides her Face in his Neck, he carefully conveys her from the Company.   73

Humph. I have observ'd this Accident has dwelt upon you very strongly.

Sir J. Bev. Her uncommon Air, her noble Modesty, the Dignity of her Person, and the Occasion it self, drew the whole Assembly together; and I soon heard it buzz'd about, she was the adopted Daughter of a famous Sea-Officer, who had serv'd in *France.* Now this unexpected and publick Discovery of my Son's so deep Concern for her——

Humph. Was what I suppose alarm'd Mr. *Sealand,* in behalf of his Daughter, to break off the Match.   81

Sir J. Bev. You are right———He came to me yesterday, and said, he thought himself disengag'd from the Bargain; being credibly informed my Son was already marry'd, or worse, to the Lady at the Masquerade. I palliated matters, and insisted on our Agreement; but we parted with little less than a direct Breach between us.

Humph. Well, Sir: and what Notice have you taken of all this to my young Master?

Sir J. Bev. That's what I wanted to debate with you——I have said nothing to him yet——But look you, *Humphrey*———if there is so much in this Amour of his, that he denies upon my Summons to marry, I have Cause enough to be offended; and then by my insisting upon his marrying to-day, I shall know how far he is engag'd to this Lady in Masquerade, and from thence only shall be able to take my Measures: in the mean time I would have you find out how far that Rogue his Man is let into his Secret—— He, I know, will play Tricks as much to cross me, as to serve his Master.

Humph. Why do you think so of him, Sir? I believe he is no worse than I was for you, at your Son's Age.   98

Sir J. Bev. I see it in the Rascal's Looks. But I have dwelt on these things too long; I'll go to my Son immediately, and while I'm gone, your Part is to convince his Rogue *Tom* that I am in Earnest. I'll leave him to you.

[*Exit Sir* John Bevil.

Humph. Well, tho' this Father and Son live as well together as possible, yet their fear of giving each other Pain, is attended with constant mutual Un-easiness. I'm sure I have enough to do to be honest, and yet keep well with

71 give her self a Loose] Feel free to give vent to her emotions.

them both: But they know I love 'em, and that makes the Task less painful however——Oh, here's the Prince of poor Coxcombs, the Representative of All the better fed than taught.—Ho! ho! *Tom*, whither so gay and so airy this Morning?   108

Enter Tom, *Singing.*

Tom. Sir, we Servants of Single Gentlemen are another kind of People than you domestick ordinary Drudges that do Business: We are rais'd above you: The Pleasures of Board-Wages, Tavern-Dinners, and many a clear Gain; Vails, alas! you never heard or dreamt of.   112

Humph. Thou hast Follies and Vices enough for a Man of Ten thousand a Year, tho' 'tis but as t'other Day that I sent for you to Town, to put you into Mr. *Sealand*'s Family, that you might learn a little before I put you to my young Master, who is too gentle for training such a rude Thing as you were into proper Obedience——You then pull'd off your Hat to every one you met in the Street, like a bashful great aukward Cub as you were. But your great Oaken Cudgel when you were a Booby, became you much better than that dangling Stick at your Button now you are a Fop. That's fit for nothing, except it hangs there to be ready for your Master's Hand when you are impertinent.   122

Tom. Uncle *Humphrey*, you know my Master scorns to strike his Servants. You talk as if the World was now, just as it was when my old Master and you were in your Youth—when you went to dinner because it was so much a Clock, when the great Blow was given in the Hall at the Pantrey-door, and all the Family came out of their Holes in such strange Dresses and formal Faces as you see in the Pictures in our long Gallery in the Country.

Humph. Why, you wild Rogue!

Tom. You could not fall to your Dinner till a formal Fellow in a black Gown said something over the Meat, as if the Cook had not made it ready enough.   132

Humph. Sirrah, who do you prate after?—Despising Men of Sacred Characters! I hope you never heard my good young Master talk so like a Profligate.

Tom. Sir, I say you put upon me, when I first came to Town, about being Orderly, and the Doctrine of wearing Shams to make Linnen last clean a Fortnight, keeping my Cloths fresh, and wearing a Frock within Doors.

Humph. Sirrah, I gave you those Lessons, because I suppos'd at that time your Master and you might have din'd at home every Day, and cost you nothing; then you might have made a good Family Servant. But the Gang

112 Vails] Tips.   120 that dangling Stick at your Button] A kind of walking-stick attachable to a manservant's coat.   137 Shams] False shirt-fronts.   138 a Frock] A kind of loose-fitting overall.

you have frequented since at Chocolate Houses and Taverns, in a continual round of Noise and Extravagance——————   143

Tom. I don't know what you heavy Inmates call Noise and Extravagance; but we Gentlemen, who are well fed, and cut a Figure, Sir, think it a fine Life, and that we must be very pretty Fellows who are kept only to be looked at.

Humph. Very well, Sir,—I hope the Fashion of being lewd and extravagant, despising of Decency and Order, is almost at an End, since it is arrived at Persons of your Quality.

Tom. Master *Humphrey*, Ha! Ha! you were an unhappy Lad to be sent up to Town in such Queer Days as you were: Why now, Sir, the Lacquies are the Men of Pleasure of the Age; the Top-Gamesters; and many a lac'd Coat about Town have had their Education in our Party-colour'd Regiment,—We are false Lovers; have a Taste of Musick, Poetry, Billet-doux, Dress, Politicks; ruin Damsels; and when we are weary of this lewd Town, and have a mind to take up, whip into our Masters Whigs and Linnen, and marry Fortunes.   157

Humph. Hey-day!

Tom. Nay, Sir, our Order is carry'd up to the highest Dignities and Distinctions; step but into the *Painted Chamber*——and by our Titles you'd take us all for Men of Quality——————then again come down to the *Court of Requests*, and you see us all laying our broken Heads together for the Good of the Nation: and tho' we never carry a Question *Nemine Contradicente*, yet this I can say with a safe Conscience, (and I wish every Gentleman of our Cloth could lay his Hand upon his Heart and say the same) that I never took so much as a single Mug of Beer for my Vote in all my Life.   166

Humph. Sirrah, there is no enduring your Extravagance; I'll hear you prate no longer. I wanted to see you, to enquire how things go with your Master, as far as you understand them; I suppose he knows he is to be married to-day.   170

Tom. Ay, Sir, he knows it, and is dress'd as gay as the Sun; but, between you and I, my Dear, he has a very heavy Heart under all that Gayety. As soon as he was dress'd I retir'd, but overheard him sigh in the most heavy manner. He walk'd thoughtfully to and fro in the Room, then went into his Closet; when he came out, he gave me this for his Mistress, whose Maid you know——————

Humph. Is passionately fond of your fine Person.

153 our Party-colour'd Regiment] That is, the regiment of menservants.   156 to take up] To slacken the pace: to settle down and enjoy one's estate.   160 the *Painted Chamber*] A decorated room in which servants of members of Parliament waited—and meanwhile adopted their masters' names.   161 the *Court of Requests*] A room in the old Palace of Westminster, in which the House of Lords then met.   162 our broken Heads] That is, heads broken when political disputants came to more than verbal blows.

Tom. The poor Fool is so tender, and loves to hear me talk of the World, and the Plays, Opera's, and *Ridotto's*, for the Winter; the Parks and *Bellsize*, for our Summer Diversions; and Lard! says she, you are so wild——but you have a world of Humour——   181

Humph. Coxcomb! Well, but why don't you run with your Master's Letter to Mrs. *Lucinda*, as he order'd you?

Tom. Because Mrs. *Lucinda* is not so easily come at as you think for.

Humph. Not easily come at? Why Sirrah, are not her Father and my old Master agreed, that she and Mr. *Bevil* are to be One Flesh before to-morrow Morning?

Tom. It's no Matter for that; her Mother, it seems, Mrs. *Sealand*, has not agreed to it: and you must know, Mr. *Humphrey*, that in that Family the Grey Mare is the better Horse.   191

Humph. What do'st thou mean?

Tom. In one Word, Mrs. *Sealand* pretends to have a Will of her own, and has provided a Relation of hers, a stiff, starch'd Philosopher, and a wise Fool for her Daughter; for which Reason, for these ten Days past, she has suffer'd no Message nor Letter from my Master to come near her.

Humph. And where had you this Intelligence?

Tom. From a foolish fond Soul, that can keep nothing from me——One that will deliver this Letter too, if she is rightly manag'd.

Humph. What! Her pretty Hand-maid, Mrs. *Phillis*?   200

Tom. Even she, Sir; this is the very Hour, you know, she usually comes hither, under a Pretence of a Visit to your Housekeeper forsooth, but in reality to have a Glance at——

Humph. Your sweet Face, I warrant you.

Tom. Nothing else in Nature; you must know, I love to fret, and play with the little Wanton.——

Humph. Play with the little Wanton! What will this World come to!

Tom. I met her, this Morning, in a new Manteau and Petticoat, not a bit the worse for her Lady's wearing: and she has always new Thoughts and new Airs with new Cloaths——then she never fails to steal some Glance or Gesture from every Visitant at their House; and is indeed the whole Town of Coquets at second hand. But here she comes; in one Motion she speaks and describes herself better than all the Words in the World can.   213

Humph. Then I hope, dear Sir, when your own Affair is over, you will be so good as to mind your Master's with her.

179 *Ridotto's*] Entertainments of music and dancing, the first of which had been held at the Haymarket Theatre in 1722.   179 *Bellsize*] Gardens of public amusement similar to those later opened at Vauxhall and Ranelagh, but much smaller.   208 Manteau and Petticoat] An open-fronted gown, and the decorous undergarment it partially revealed to public view.

Tom. Dear *Humphrey*, you know my Master is my Friend, and those are People I never forget.——

Humph. Sawciness itself! but I'll leave you to do your best for him.

[*Exit.*

Enter Phillis.

Phil. Oh, Mr. *Thomas*, is Mrs. *Sugar-key* at home?—Lard, one is almost asham'd to pass along the Streets. The Town is quite empty, and no Body of Fashion left in it; and the ordinary People do so stare to see any thing (dress'd like a Woman of Condition) as it were on the same Floor with them pass by. Alas! Alas! it is a sad thing to walk. Oh Fortune! Fortune! 223

Tom. What! a sad thing to walk? Why, Madam *Phillis*, do you wish your self lame?

Phil. No, Mr. *Tom*, but I wish I were generally carry'd in a Coach or Chair, and of a Fortune neither to stand nor go, but to totter, or slide, to be short-sighted, or stare, to fleer in the Face, to look distant, to observe, to overlook, yet all become me; and, if I was rich, I cou'd twire and loll as well as the best of them. Oh *Tom! Tom!* is it not a pity, that you shou'd be so great a Coxcomb, and I so great a Coquet, and yet be such poor Devils as we are? 232

Tom. Mrs. *Phillis*, I am your humble Servant for that——

Phil. Yes, Mr. *Thomas*, I know how much you are my humble Servant, and know what you said to Mrs. *Judy*, upon seeing her in one of her Lady's Cast Manteaus; That any one wou'd have thought her the Lady, and that she had ordered the other to wear it till it sat easy—for now only it was becoming:—To my Lady it was only a Covering, to Mrs. *Judy* it was a Habit. This you said, after some Body or other. Oh, *Tom! Tom!* thou art as false and as base, as the best Gentleman of them all: but, you Wretch, talk to me no more on the old odious Subject. Don't, I say. 241

Tom. I know not how to resist your Commands, Madam.

[*In a submissive Tone, retiring.*

Phil. Commands about Parting are grown mighty easy to you of late.

Tom. Oh, I have her; I have nettled and put her into the right Temper to be wrought upon, and set a prating. [*Aside.*]——Why truly, to be plain with you, Mrs. *Phillis*, I can take little Comfort of late in frequenting your House.

Phil. Pray, Mr. *Thomas*, what is it all of a sudden offends your Nicety at our House?

Tom. I don't care to speak Particulars, but I dislike the Whole.

Phil. I thank you, Sir, I am a Part of that Whole. 250

Tom. Mistake me not, good *Phillis*.

228 to fleer] To look scornfully, to sneer.   229 twire] Throw covert, flirtatious glances.
236 Cast] Cast-off, discarded.

Phil. Good *Phillis*! Saucy enough. But however————

Tom. I say, it is that thou art a Part, which gives me Pain for the Disposition of the Whole. You must know, Madam, to be serious, I am a Man, at the Bottom, of prodigious nice Honour. You are too much expos'd to Company at your House: To be plain, I don't like so many, that wou'd be your Mistress's Lovers, whispering to you.

Phil. Don't think to put that upon me. You say this, because I wrung you to the Heart, when I touch'd your guilty Conscience about *Judy.*

Tom. Ah *Phillis! Phillis!* if you but knew my Heart!   260

Phil. I know too much on't.

Tom. Nay then, poor *Crispo*'s Fate and mine are one————Therefore give me Leave to say, or sing at least, as he does upon the same Occasion————

Se vedette, &c. [*sings.*]

Phil. What, do you think I'm to be fob'd off with a Song? I don't question but you have sung the same to Mrs. *Judy* too.

Tom. Don't disparage your Charms, good *Phillis*, with Jealousy of so worthless an Object; besides, she is a poor Hussey, and if you doubt the Sincerity of my Love, you will allow me true to my Interest. You are a Fortune, *Phillis*————   270

Phil. What wou'd the Fop be at now? In good time indeed, you shall be setting up for a Fortune!

Tom. Dear Mrs. *Phillis*, you have such a Spirit that we shall never be dull in Marriage, when we come together. But I tell you, you are a Fortune, and you have an Estate in my Hands.   [*He pulls out a Purse, she eyes it.*

Phil. What Pretence have I to what is in your Hands, Mr. *Tom*?

Tom. As thus: there are Hours, you know, when a Lady is neither pleas'd or displeas'd, neither sick or well, when she lolls or loiters, when she's without Desires, from having more of every thing than she knows what to do with.   280

Phil. Well, what then?

Tom. When she has not Life enough to keep her bright Eyes quite open, to look at her own dear Image in the Glass.

Phil. Explain thy self, and don't be so fond of thy own prating.

Tom. There are also prosperous and good-natur'd Moments, as when a Knot or a Patch is happily fix'd; when the Complexion particularly flourishes.

Phil. Well, what then? I have not Patience!

---

262 poor *Crispo*] Hero of an opera by G. B. Bononcini, composed in 1721. Crispo's fate was to be unjustly accused of deceit.   264 *Se vedette*, &c.] A song in which Crispo defends his innocence. It begins, in Thomas Wood's contemporary English translation of Rolli's libretto, 'If you see my Thoughts ye just Gods, defend the Innocence of my Heart.' 286 Knot] Ribbon tied in a bow.   286 Patch] Beauty spot.

Tom. Why then————or on the like Occasions—we Servants who have Skill to know how to time Business, see when such a pretty folded thing as this [*shews a Letter*] may be presented, laid, or dropp'd, as best suits the present Humour. And, Madam, because it is a long wearisome Journey to run through all the several Stages of a Lady's Temper, my Master, who is the most reasonable Man in the World, presents you this to bear your Charges on the Road.   [*Gives her the Purse.*

Phil. Now you think me a corrupt Hussey.   295

Tom. Oh fie, I only think you'll take the Letter.

Phil. Nay, I know you do, but I know my own Innocence; I take it for my Mistress's Sake.

Tom. I know it, my Pretty One, I know it.

Phil. Yes, I say I do it, because I wou'd not have my Mistress deluded by one who gives no Proof of his Passion; but I'll talk more of this, as you see me on my Way home————No, *Tom*, I assure thee, I take this Trash of thy Master's, not for the Value of the thing, but as it convinces me he has a true Respect for my Mistress. I remember a Verse to the Purpose.   304

>   They may be false who Languish and Complain,
>   But they who part with Money never feign.   [*Exeunt.*

SCENE II.

Bevil *Junior's Lodgings.*

Bevil *junior, Reading.*

Bev. jun. These Moral Writers practise Virtue after Death: This charming Vision of *Mirza*! Such an Author consulted in a Morning, sets the Spirit for the Vicissitudes of the Day, better than the Glass does a Man's Person: But what a Day have I to go thro'! to put on an Easy Look with an Aking Heart. ————If this Lady my Father urges me to marry should not refuse me, my Dilemma is insupportable. But why should I fear it? is not she in equal Distress with me? has not the Letter, I have sent her this Morning, confest my Inclination to another? Nay, have I not moral Assurances of her Engagements too, to my Friend *Myrtle*? It's impossible but she must give in to it: For, sure to be deny'd is a Favour any Man may pretend to. It must be so ————Well then, with the Assurance of being rejected, I think I may confidently say to my Father, I am ready to marry her————Then let me resolve upon (what I am not very good at, tho' it is) an honest Dissimulation.

Enter Tom.

I. ii, 2 Vision of *Mirza*] A visionary story by Addison, which appeared in the *Spectator*. Addison had died in 1719.   3 Glass] That is, looking-glass.

Tom. Sir *John Bevil*, Sir, is in the next Room.   14

Bev. jun. Dunce! Why did not you bring him in?

Tom. I told him, Sir, you were in your Closet.

Bev. jun. I thought you had known, Sir, it was my Duty to see my Father
any where.   [*Going himself to the Door.*

Tom. The Devil's in my Master! he has always more Wit than I have.
                                                              [*Aside.*

Bevil *Jun. introducing* Sir John.

Bev. jun. Sir, you are the most Gallant, the most Complaisant of all
Parents———Sure 'tis not a Compliment to say these Lodgings are yours
———Why wou'd you not walk in, Sir?   22

Sir J. Bev. I was loth to interrupt you unseasonably on your Wedding-
day.

Bev. jun. One to whom I am beholden for my Birth-day, might have used
less Ceremony.

Sir J. Bev. Well, Son, I have Intelligence you have writ to your Mistress
this Morning: It would please my Curiosity to know the Contents of a
Wedding-day Letter; for Courtship must then be over.

Bev. jun. I assure you, Sir, there was no Insolence in it, upon the Prospect
of such a vast Fortune's being added to our Family; but much Acknowledg-
ment of the Lady's greater Desert.   32

Sir J. Bev. But, dear *Jack*, are you in earnest in all this? And will you really
marry her?

Bev. jun. Did I ever disobey any Command of yours, Sir? nay, any
Inclination that I saw you bent upon?

Sir J. Bev. Why, I can't say you have, Son; but methinks in this whole
Business, you have not been so warm as I could have wish'd you: You have
visited her, it's true, but you have not been particular. Every one knows you
can say and do as handsome Things as any Man; but you have done nothing,
but liv'd in the General; been Complaisant only.   41

Bev. jun. As I am ever prepar'd to marry if you bid me, so I am ready to let
it alone if you will have me.   [Humphrey *enters unobserv'd.*

Sir J. Bev. Look you there now! why what am I to think of this so absolute
and so indifferent a Resignation?

Bev. jun. Think? that I am still your Son, Sir,——Sir———you have
been married, and I have not. And you have, Sir, found the Inconvenience
there is, when a Man weds with too much Love in his Head. I have been told,
Sir, that at the Time you married, you made a mighty Bustle on the Occasion.
There was challenging and fighting, scaling Walls———locking up the Lady
———and the Gallant under an Arrest for fear of killing all his Rivals———

---

41 in the General] With no particular object of affection, but in equal amity   with all.

Now, Sir, I suppose you having found the ill Consequences of these strong
Passions and Prejudices, in preference of one Woman to another, in Case of a
Man's becoming a Widower——   54

Sir J. Bev. How is this!

Bev. jun. I say Sir, Experience has made you wiser in your Care of me
——for, Sir, since you lost my dear Mother, your time has been so heavy,
so lonely, and so tasteless, that you are so good as to guard me against the like
Unhappiness, by marrying me prudentially by way of Bargain and Sale. For,
as you well judge, a Woman that is espous'd for a Fortune, is yet a better
Bargain, if she dies; for then a Man still enjoys what he did marry, the
Money; and is disencumber'd of what he did not marry, the Woman.

Sir J. Bev. But pray, Sir, do you think *Lucinda* then a Woman of such little
Merit?   64

Bev. jun. Pardon me, Sir, I don't carry it so far neither; I am rather afraid
I shall like her too well; she has, for one of her Fortune, a great many needless
and superfluous good Qualities.

Sir J. Bev. I am afraid, Son, there's something I don't see yet, something
that's smother'd under all this Raillery.

Bev. jun. Not in the least, Sir: If the Lady is dress'd and ready, you see I
am. I suppose the Lawyers are ready too.   71

Hum. This may grow warm, if I don't interpose.   [*Aside.*
Sir, Mr. *Sealand* is at the Coffee-house, and has sent to speak with you.

Sir J. Bev. Oh! that's well! Then I warrant the Lawyers are ready. Son,
you'll be in the Way, you say——

Bev. jun. If you please, Sir, I'll take a Chair, and go to Mr. *Sealand*'s,
where the young Lady and I will wait your Leisure.

Sir J. Bev. By no means——The old Fellow will be so vain, if he
sees——

Bev. jun. Ay——But the young Lady, Sir, will think me so indifferent——   81

Humph. Ay——there you are right——press your Readiness to go to
the Bride——he won't let you.   [*Aside to* Bev. jun.

Bev. jun. Are you sure of that?   [*Aside to* Humph.

Humph. How he likes being prevented.   [*Aside.*

Sir J. Bev. No, no: You are an Hour or two too early.
                                                   [*Looking on his Watch.*

Bev. jun. You'll allow me, Sir, to think it too late to visit a beautiful,
virtuous young Woman, in the Pride and Bloom of Life, ready to give her
self to my Arms: and to place her Happiness or Misery, for the future, in
being agreeable or displeasing to me, is a——Call a Chair.   90

Sir J. Bev. No, no, no, dear *Jack*; this *Sealand* is a moody old Fellow:

58 tasteless] Insipid.   76 a Chair] That is, a sedan chair.

There's no dealing with some People, but by managing with Indifference. We must leave to him the Conduct of this Day. It is the last of his commanding his Daughter.

Bev. jun. Sir, he can't take it ill, that I am impatient to be hers.

Sir J. Bev. Pray let me govern in this Matter: you can't tell how humoursome old Fellows are:———There's no offering Reason to some of 'em, especially when they are Rich——If my Son should see him, before I've brought old *Sealand* into better Temper, the Match would be impracticable.

                                                      [*Aside.*

Humph. Pray, Sir, let me beg you, to let Mr. *Bevil* go.—See, whether he will or not. [*aside to Sir* John]——[*Then to* Bev.] Pray, Sir, command your self; since you see my Master is positive, it is better you should not go.

Bev. jun. My Father commands me, as to the Object of my Affections; but I hope he will not, as to the Warmth and Height of them.   104

Sir J. Bev. So! I must even leave things as I found them: And in the mean time, at least, keep Old *Sealand* out of his sight.——Well, Son, I'll go myself and take orders in your Affair——You'll be in the way, I suppose, if I send to you—I'll leave your Old Friend with you.———*Humphrey*—don't let him stir, d'ye hear: Your Servant, your Servant.   [*Ex. Sir* John.

Humph. I have a sad time on't, Sir, between you and my Master———I see you are unwilling, and I know his violent Inclinations for the Match———I must betray neither, and yet deceive you both, for your common Good——Heav'n grant a good End of this matter: But there is a Lady, Sir, that gives your Father much Trouble and Sorrow———You'll pardon me.

Bev. jun. Humphrey, I know thou art a Friend to both; and in that Confidence, I dare tell thee———That Lady——is a Woman of Honour and Virtue. You may assure your self, I never will Marry without my Father's Consent: But give me leave to say too, this Declaration does not come up to a Promise, that I will take whomsoever he pleases.   119

Humph. Come Sir, I wholly understand you: You would engage my Services to free you from this Woman, whom my Master intends you, to make way, in time, for the Woman you have really a mind to.

Bev. jun. Honest *Humphrey*, you have always been an useful Friend to my Father, and my self; I beg you continue your good Offices, and don't let us come to the Necessity of a Dispute; for, if we should dispute, I must either part with more than Life, or lose the best of Fathers.   126

Humph. My dear Master, were I but worthy to know this Secret, that so near concerns you, my Life, my All should be engag'd to serve you. This, Sir, I dare promise, that I am sure I will and can be secret: your Trust, at worst, but leaves you where you were; and if I cannot serve you, I will at once be plain, and tell you so.   131

---

107 take orders] Make suitable arrangements.

Bev. jun. That's all I ask: Thou hast made it now my Interest to trust thee
————Be patient then, and hear the Story of my Heart.

Humph. I am all Attention, Sir.

Bev. jun. You may remember, *Humphrey*, that in my last Travels, my Father grew uneasy at my making so long a Stay at *Toulon*.

Humph. I remember it; he was apprehensive some Woman had laid hold of you.

Bev. jun. His Fears were just; for there I first saw this Lady: She is of *English* Birth: Her Father's Name was *Danvers*, a Younger Brother of an Ancient Family, and originally an Eminent Merchant of *Bristol*; who, upon repeated Misfortunes, was reduced to go privately to the *Indies*. In this Retreat Providence again grew favourable to his Industry, and, in six Years time, restored him to his former Fortunes: On this he sent Directions over, that his Wife and little Family should follow him to the *Indies*. His Wife, impatient to obey such welcome Orders, would not wait the leisure of a Convoy, but took the first occasion of a single Ship, and with her Husband's Sister only, and this Daughter, then scarce seven Years old, undertook the fatal Voyage: For here, poor Creature, she lost her Liberty, and Life; she, and her Family, with all they had, were unfortunately taken by a Privateer from *Toulon*. Being thus made a Prisoner, though, as such, not ill treated, yet the Fright, the Shock, and cruel Disappointment, seiz'd with such Violence upon her unhealthy Frame, she sicken'd, pined and died at Sea. 154

Humph. Poor Soul! O the helpless Infant!

Bev. Her Sister yet surviv'd, and had the Care of her: The Captain too proved to have Humanity, and became a Father to her; for having himself married an *English* Woman, and being Childless, he brought home into *Toulon* this her little Country-woman; presenting her, with all her dead Mother's Moveables of Value, to his Wife, to be educated as his own adopted Daughter. 161

Humph. Fortune here seem'd, again, to smile on her.

Bev. Only to make her Frowns more terrible: For, in his Height of Fortune, this Captain too, her Benefactor, unfortunately was kill'd at Sea, and dying intestate, his Estate fell wholly to an Advocate his Brother, who coming soon to take Possession, there found (among his other Riches) this blooming Virgin, at his Mercy.

Humph. He durst not, sure, abuse his Power!

Bev. No wonder if his pamper'd Blood was fired at the Sight of her————in short, he lov'd: but, when all Arts and gentle Means had fail'd to move, he offer'd too his Menaces in vain, denouncing Vengeance on her Cruelty; demanding her to account for all her Maintenance, from her Childhood; seiz'd on her little Fortune, as his own Inheritance, and was dragging her by

Violence to Prison; when Providence at the Instant interpos'd, and sent me, by Miracle, to relieve her.   175

Humph. 'Twas Providence indeed; But pray, Sir, after all this Trouble, how came this Lady at last to *England*?

Bev. The disappointed Advocate, finding she had so unexpected a Support, on cooler Thoughts, descended to a Composition; which I, without her Knowledge, secretly discharg'd.   180

Humph. That generous Concealment made the Obligation double.

Bev. Having thus obtain'd her Liberty, I prevail'd, not without some Difficulty, to see her safe to *England*; where no sooner arrived, but my Father, jealous of my being imprudently engaged, immediately proposed this other fatal Match that hangs upon my Quiet.

Humph. I find, Sir, you are irrecoverably fix'd upon this Lady.

Bev. As my vital Life dwells in my Heart———and yet you see———what I do to please my Father: Walk in this Pageantry of dress, this splendid Covering of Sorrow———But, *Humphrey* you have your Lesson.

Humph. Now, Sir, I have but one material Question———   190

Bev. Ask it freely.

Humph. Is it, then, your own Passion for this secret Lady, or hers for you, that gives you this Aversion to the Match your Father has proposed you?

Bev. I shall appear, *Humphrey*, more Romantick in my Answer, than in all the rest of my Story: For tho' I doat on her to death, and have no little Reason to believe she has the same Thoughts for me; yet in all my Acquaintance, and utmost Privacies with her, I never once directly told her, that I loved.

Humph. How was it possible to avoid it?

Bev. My tender Obligations to my Father have laid so inviolable a Restraint upon my Conduct, that 'till I have his Consent to speak, I am determin'd, on that Subject, to be dumb for ever———   202

Humph. Well Sir, to your Praise be it spoken, you are certainly the most unfashionable Lover in *Great-Britain*.

Enter Tom.

Tom. Sir, Mr. *Myrtle*'s at the next door, and, if you are at Leisure, will be glad to wait on you.

Bev. Whenever he pleases——hold, *Tom!* did you receive no Answer to my Letter?

Tom. Sir, I was desir'd to call again; for I was told, her Mother would not let her be out of her Sight; but about an Hour hence, Mrs. *Lettice* said, I should certainly have one.   211

179 descended to a Composition] Agreed to a compromise.   210 *Lettice*] Thus all the early editions: but Steele surely intended *Phillis*.

Bev. Very well.

Humph. Sir, I will take another Opportunity: in the mean time, I only think it proper to tell you, that from a Secret I know, you may appear to your Father as forward as you please, to marry *Lucinda*, without the least Hazard of its coming to a Conclusion——Sir, your most obedient Servant.

Bev. Honest *Humphrey*, continue but my Friend, in this Exigence, and you shall always find me yours.   [*Exit* Humph.

I long to hear how my Letter has succeeded with *Lucinda*——but I think, it cannot fail: for, at worst, were it possible she could take it ill, her Resentment of my Indifference may as probably occasion a Delay, as her taking it right. ——Poor *Myrtle*, what Terrors must he be in all this while?——Since he knows she is offer'd to me, and refused to him, there is no conversing, or taking any measures, with him, for his own Service——But I ought to bear with my Friend, and use him as one in Adversity;   225

> All his Disquiets by my own I prove,
> The greatest Grief's Perplexity in Love.   [*Exeunt.*

End of the First ACT.

The Conscious Lovers.

ACT II. SCENE I.

SCENE *Continues.*

Enter Bevil *jun. and* Tom.

Tom. SIR, Mr. *Myrtle.*
    Bev. jun. Very well,——do you step again, and wait for an Answer to my Letter.

Enter Myrtle.

Bev. jun. Well *Charles*, why so much Care in thy Countenance? Is there any thing in this World deserves it? You, who used to be so Gay, so Open, so Vacant!

Myrt. I think we have of late chang'd Complexions. You, who us'd to be much the graver Man, are now all Air in your Behaviour——But the Cause of my Concern, may, for ought I know, be the same Object that gives you all

II. i, 6 Vacant] Free from anxiety.

this Satisfaction. In a word, I am told that you are this very Day (and your
Dress confirms me in it) to be married to *Lucinda*.   11

Bev. jun. You are not misinform'd.—Nay, put not on the Terrors of a
Rival, till you hear me out. I shall disoblige the best of Fathers, if I don't
seem ready to marry *Lucinda*: And you know I have ever told you, you
might make use of my secret Resolution never to marry her, for your own
service, as you please. But I am now driven to the extremity of immediately
refusing, or complying, unless you help me to escape the Match.

Myrt. Escape? Sir, neither her Merit or her Fortune are below your
Acceptance.—Escaping, do you call it!

Bev. jun. Dear Sir, do you wish I should desire the Match?   20

Myrt. No—but such is my humorous and sickly state of Mind, since it has
been able to relish nothing but *Lucinda*, that tho' I must owe my Happiness
to your Aversion to this Marriage, I can't bear to hear her spoken of with
Levity or Unconcern.

Bev. jun. Pardon me, Sir; I shall transgress that way no more. She has
Understanding, Beauty, Shape, Complexion, Wit——

Myrt. Nay, dear *Bevil*, don't speak of her as if you lov'd her, neither.

Bev. jun. Why then, to give you Ease at once, tho' I allow *Lucinda* to have
good Sense, Wit, Beauty and Virtue; I know another, in whom these
Qualities appear to me more amiable than in her.   30

Myrt. There you spoke like a reasonable and good-natur'd Friend. When
you acknowledge her Merit, and own your Prepossession for another, at
once, you gratify my Fondness, and cure my Jealousie.

Bev. jun. But all this while you take no notice, you have no Apprehension of
another Man, that has twice the Fortune of either of us.

Myrt. Cimberton! Hang him, a Formal, Philosophical, Pedantick Cox-
comb—For the Sot, with all these crude notions of divers things, under the
direction of great Vanity, and very little Judgment, shews his strongest
Biass is Avarice; which is so predominant in him, that he will examine the
Limbs of his Mistress with the Caution of a Jockey, and pays no more
Compliment to her personal Charms, than if she were a meer breeding
Animal.   42

Bev. jun. Are you sure that is not affected? I have known some Women
sooner set on fire by that sort of Negligence, than by——

Myrt. No, no; hang him, the Rogue has no Art, it is pure simple Insolence
and Stupidity.

Bev. jun. Yet, with all this, I don't take him for a Fool.

Myrt. I own the Man is not a Natural; he has a very quick Sense, tho' very
slow Understanding.——He says indeed many things, that want only the
circumstances of Time and Place to be very just and agreeable.   50

48 a Natural] A simpleton, a half-wit.

Bev. jun. Well, you may be sure of me, if you can disappoint him; but my
Intelligence says, the Mother has actually sent for the Conveyancer, to draw
Articles for his Marriage with *Lucinda*; tho' those for mine with her, are, by
her Father's Order, ready for signing: but it seems she has not thought fit to
consult either him or his Daughter in the matter.

Myrt. Pshaw! A poor troublesome Woman——Neither *Lucinda* nor her
Father will ever be brought to comply with it,—besides, I am sure *Cimberton*
can make no Settlement upon her, without the Concurrence of his great
Uncle Sir *Geoffry* in the West.

Bev. jun. Well Sir, and I can tell you, that's the very Point that is now laid
before her Council; to know whether a firm Settlement can be made, without
this Uncle's actual joyning in it.——Now pray consider, Sir, when my
affair with *Lucinda* comes, as it soon must, to an open Rupture, how are you
sure that *Cimberton*'s Fortune may not then tempt her Father too, to hear his
Proposals?   65

Myrt. There you are right indeed, that must be provided against.——Do
you know who are her Council?

Bev. jun. Yes, for your Service I have found out that too, they are Serjeant
Bramble and Old *Target*—by the way, they are neither of 'em known in the
Family; now I was thinking why you might not put a couple of false Council
upon her, to delay and comfound matters a little—besides, it may probably
let you into the bottom of her whole Design against you.   72

Myrt. As how pray?

Bev. jun. Why can't you slip on a Black Whig and a Gown, and be Old
Bramble your self?

Myrt. Ha! I don't dislike it——but what shall I do for a Brother in the
Case?

Bev. jun. What think you of my Fellow, *Tom*? the Rogue's intelligent, and
is a good Mimick; all his part will be but to stutter heartily, for that's Old
Target's Case——Nay, it would be an immoral thing to mock him, were it
not that his Impertinence is the occasion of its breaking out to that degree
——the Conduct of the Scene will chiefly lye upon you.   82

Myrt. I like it of all things; if you'll send *Tom* to my Chambers, I will give
him full Instructions: This will certainly give me occasion to raise Difficulties, to puzzle, or confound her Project for a while, at least.

Bev. jun. I'll warrant you Success: so far we are right then: And now,
Charles, your apprehension of my marrying her, is all you have to get over.

Myrt. Dear *Bevil*! tho' I know you are my Friend, yet when I abstract my
self from my own interest in the thing, I know no Objection she can make to
you, or you to her, and therefore hope——   90

Bev. jun. Dear *Myrtle*, I am as much obliged to you for the Cause of your
Suspicion, as I am offended at the Effect: but be assured, I am taking mea-

sures for your certain Security, and that all things with regard to me will end in your entire Satisfaction.

Myrt. Well, I'll promise you to be as easy and as confident as I can; tho' I cannot but remember that I have more than Life at stake on your Fidelity.   [*Going.*

Bev. jun. Then depend upon it, you have no Chance against you.

Myrt. Nay, no Ceremony, you know I must be going.   [*Exit* Myrt.

Bev. Well! this is another Instance of the Perplexities which arise too, in faithful Friendship: We must often, in this Life, go on in our good Offices, even under the Displeasure of those to whom we do them, in Compassion to their Weaknesses and Mistakes——But all this while poor *Indiana* is tortured with the Doubt of me! she has no Support or Comfort, but in my Fidelity, yet sees me daily press'd to Marriage with another! How painful, in such a Crisis, must be every Hour she thinks on me? I'll let her see, at least, my Conduct to her is not chang'd: I'll take this Opportunity to visit her; for tho' the Religious Vow, I have made to my Father, restrains me from ever marrying, without his Approbation, yet that confines me not from seeing a virtuous Woman, that is the pure Delight of my Eyes, and the guiltless Joy of my Heart: But the best Condition of Human Life is but a gentler Misery.

> To hope for perfect Happiness is vain,   III
> And Love has ever its Allays of Pain.   [*Exit.*

Enter Isabella, *and* Indiana *in her own Lodgings.*

Isab. Yes—I say 'tis Artifice, dear Child; I say to thee again and again, 'tis all Skill and Management.

Ind. Will you persuade me there can be an ill Design, in supporting me in the Condition of a Woman of Quality? attended, dress'd, and lodg'd like one; in my Appearance abroad, and my Furniture at home, every way in the most sumptuous manner, and he that does it has an Artifice, a Design in it?

Isab. Yes, yes.

Ind. And all this without so much as explaining to me, that all about me comes from him!

Isab. Ay, ay,—the more for that——that keeps the Title to all you have, the more in Him.   II

Ind. The more in Him!——He scorns the Thought——

Isab. Then He—He—He—

Ind. Well, be not so eager.—If he is an ill Man, let us look into his Stratagems. Here is another of them. [*Shewing a Letter.*] Here's two hundred and fifty Pound in Bank Notes, with these Words, 'To pay for the Set of Dressing-plate, which will be brought home To-morrow.' Why dear Aunt,

II. ii 16 Set of Dressing-plate] Toilet set in silver plate.

now here's another Piece of Skill for you, which I own I cannot comprehend
—and it is with a bleeding Heart I hear you say any thing to the Disadvantage
of Mr. *Bevil*. When he is present, I look upon him as one to whom I owe my
Life, and the Support of it; Then again, as the Man who loves me with
Sincerity and Honour. When his Eyes are cast another way, and I dare survey
him, my Heart is painfully divided between Shame and Love——Oh! cou'd
I tell you:——— 24

Isab. Ah! You need not: I imagine all this for you.

Ind. This is my State of Mind in his Presence; and when he is absent, you
are ever dinning my Ears with Notions of the Arts of Men; that his hidden
Bounty, his respectful Conduct, his careful Provision for me, after his pre-
serving me from utmost Misery, are certain Signs he means nothing, but to
make I know not what of me? 30

Isab. Oh! You have a sweet Opinion of him, truly.

Ind. I have, when I am with him, ten thousand Things, besides my Sex's
natural Decency and Shame, to suppress my Heart, that yearns to thank, to
praise, to say it loves him: I say, thus it is with me while I see him; and in his
Absence I am entertain'd with nothing but your Endeavours to tear this
amiable Image from my Heart; and, in its stead, to place a base Dissembler,
an artful Invader of my Happiness, my Innocence, my Honour.

Isab. Ah poor Soul! has not his Plot taken? don't you die for him? has
not the way he has taken, been the most proper with you? Oh! ho! He has
Sense, and has judg'd the thing right. 40

Ind. Go on then, since nothing can answer you: say what you will of him.
Heigh! ho!

Isab. Heigh! ho! indeed. It is better to say so, as you are now, than as many
others are. There are, among the Destroyers of Women, the Gentle, the
Generous, the Mild, the Affable, the Humble, who all, soon after their
Success in their Designs, turn to the contrary of those Characters. I will own
to you, Mr. *Bevil* carries his Hypocrisie the best of any Man living, but still
he is a Man, and therefore a Hypocrite. They have usurp'd an Exemption
from Shame, for any Baseness, any Cruelty towards us. They embrace without Love; they make Vows, without Conscience of Obligation; they are
Partners, nay, Seducers to the Crime, wherein they pretend to be less
guilty. 52

Ind. That's truly observ'd. [*Aside.*
But what's all this to *Bevil*?

Isab. This it is to *Bevil*, and all Mankind. Trust not those, who will think
the worse of you for your Confidence in them. Serpents, who lie in wait for
Doves. Won't you be on your Guard against those who would betray you?
Won't you doubt those who would contemn you for believing 'em? Take it
from me: Fair and natural Dealing is to invite Injuries, 'tis bleating to escape

Wolves who would devour you! Such is the World,—and such (since the Behaviour of one Man to my self) have I believ'd all the rest of the Sex.

                                                            [*Aside.*

Ind. I will not doubt the Truth of *Bevil*, I will not doubt it; He has not spoke it by an Organ that is given to lying: His Eyes are all that have ever told me that he was mine: I know his Virtue, I know his filial Piety, and ought to trust his Management with a Father, to whom he has uncommon Obligations. What have I to be concern'd for? my Lesson is very short. If he takes me for ever, my purpose of Life is only to please him. If he leaves me (which Heaven avert) I know he'll do it nobly; and I shall have nothing to do but to learn to die, after worse than Death has happen'd to me.   69

Isab. Ay do, persist in your Credulity! flatter your self that a Man of his Figure and Fortune will make himself the Jest of the Town, and marry a handsome Beggar for Love.

Ind. The Town! I must tell you, Madam, the Fools that laugh at Mr. *Bevil*, will but make themselves more ridiculous; his Actions are the Result of Thinking, and he has Sense enough to make even Virtue fashionable.

Isab. O' my Conscience he has turn'd her Head—Come, come; if he were the honest Fool you take him for, why has he kept you here these three Weeks, without sending you to *Bristol*, in search of your Father, your Family, and your Relations?

Ind. I am convinc'd he still designs it; and that nothing keeps him here, but the Necessity of not coming to a Breach with his Father, in regard to the Match he has propos'd him: Beside, has he not writ to *Bristol*? and has not he Advice that my Father has not been heard of there, almost these twenty Years?   84

Isab. All Sham, meer Evasion; he is afraid, if he should carry you thither, your honest Relations may take you out of his hands, and so blow up all his wicked Hopes at once.

Ind. Wicked Hopes! did I ever give him any such?

Isab. Has he ever given you any honest ones? can you say, in your Conscience, he has ever once offer'd to marry you?   90

Ind. No! but by his Behaviour I am convinc'd he will offer it, the Moment 'tis in his Power, or consistent with his Honour, to make such a Promise good to me.

Isab. His Honour!

Ind. I will rely upon it; therefore desire you will not make my Life uneasie, by these ungrateful Jealousies of one, to whom I am, and wish to be oblig'd: For from his Integrity alone, I have resolv'd to hope for Happiness.

Isab. Nay, I have done my Duty; if you won't see, at your Peril be it——

Ind. Let it be——This is his hour of visiting me.

Isab. Oh! to be sure, keep up your Form; don't see him in a Bed-chamber:

This is pure Prudence, when she is liable, where-ever he meets her, to be convey'd where-e'er he pleases. [*Apart.*

Ind. All the rest of my Life is but waiting till he comes: I live only when I'm with him. [*Exit.*

Isab. Well, go thy ways, thou willful Innocent! I once had almost as much Love for a Man, who poorly left me, to marry an Estate——And I am now, against my Will, what they call an Old Maid——but I will not let the Peevishness of that Condition grow upon me——only keep up the Suspicion of it, to prevent this Creature's being any other than a Virgin, except upon proper Terms. [*Exit.*

Re-enter Indiana *speaking to a Servant.*

Ind. Desire Mr. *Bevil* to walk in——Design! impossible! A base designing Mind could never think of what he hourly puts in practice——And yet, since the late Rumour of his Marriage, he seems more reserv'd than formerly ——he sends in too, before he sees me, to know if I am at leisure——such new Respect may cover Coldness in the Heart——it certainly makes me thoughtful——I'll know the worst, at once; I'll lay such fair Occasions in his way, that it shall be impossible to avoid an Explanation——for these Doubts are insupportable!——But see! he comes, and clears them all. 118

Enter Bevil.

Bev. Madam, your most Obedient——I am afraid I broke in upon your Rest last Night——'twas very late before we parted; but 'twas your own Fault: I never saw you in such agreeable Humour. 121

Ind. I am extremely glad we were both pleas'd; so I thought I never saw you better Company.

Bev. Me, Madam! you rally; I said very little.

Ind. But, I am afraid, you heard me say a great deal; and when a Woman is in the talking Vein, the most agreeable thing a Man can do, you know, is to have Patience, to hear her.

Bev. Then it's pity, Madam, you should ever be silent, that we might be always agreeable to one another.

Ind. If I had your Talent, or Power, to make my Actions speak for me, I might indeed be silent, and yet pretend to something more than the Agreeable. 132

Bev. If I might be vain of any thing, in my Power, Madam, 'tis that my Understanding, from all your Sex, has mark'd you out, as the most deserving Object of my Esteem.

Ind. Should I think I deserve this, 'twere enough to make my Vanity forfeit the very Esteem you offer me.

Bev. How so, Madam?

Ind. Because Esteem is the Result of Reason, and to deserve it from good Sense, the Height of Human Glory: Nay, I had rather a Man of Honour should pay me that, than all the Homage of a sincere and humble Love.

Bev. jun. You certainly distinguish right, Madam; Love often kindles from external Merit only——   143

Ind. But Esteem arises from a higher Source, the Merit of the Soul——

Bev. jun. True——And great Souls only can deserve it.

                                                                              [*Bowing respectfully*.

Ind. Now, I think, they are greater still, that can so charitably part with it.

Bev. jun. Now, Madam, you make me vain, since the utmost Pride, and Pleasure of my Life is, that I esteem you——as I ought.

Ind. [*Aside*.] As he ought! still more perplexing! he neither saves, nor kills my Hope.   150

Bev. jun. But Madam, we grow grave methinks—Let's find some other Subject——Pray how did you like the Opera last Night?

Ind. First give me leave to thank you, for my Tickets.

Bev. jun. O! your Servant, Madam——But pray tell me, you now, who are never partial to the Fashion, I fancy, must be the properest Judge of a mighty Dispute among the Ladies, that is, whether *Crispo* or *Griselda* is the more agreeable Entertainment.

Ind. With submission now, I cannot be a proper Judge of this Question.

Bev. jun. How so, Madam?

Ind. Because I find I have a Partiality for one of them.   160

Bev. jun. Pray which is that?

Ind. I do not know——there's something in that Rural Cottage of *Griselda*, her forlorn Condition, her Poverty, her Solitude, her Resignation, her Innocent Slumbers, and that lulling *Dolce Sogno* that's sung over her; it had an Effect upon me, that—in short I never was so well deceiv'd, at any of them.

Bev. jun. Oh! Now then, I can account for the Dispute: *Griselda*, it seems, is the Distress of an injur'd Innocent Woman: *Crispo*, that only of a Man in the same Condition; therefore the Men are mostly concern'd for *Crispo*, and, by a Natural Indulgence, both Sexes for *Griselda*.   170

Ind. So that Judgment, you think, ought to be for one, tho' Fancy and Complaisance have got ground for the other. Well! I believe you will never give me leave to dispute with you on any Subject; for I own, *Crispo* has its Charms for me too: Though in the main, all the Pleasure the best Opera

---

156 *Griselda*] Like *Crispo*, an opera by G. B. Bononcini, with libretto by Rolli, staged at the King's Theatre shortly before the first performance of *The Conscious Lovers* in 1722. 162 that Rural Cottage] The retreat of the persecuted Griselda in Bononcini's opera. 164 that lulling *Dolce Sogno*] The lullaby sung over the sleeping Griselda by her husband, upon her discovery in hiding.

gives us, is but meer Sensation.——Methinks it's Pity the Mind can't have a
little more Share in the Entertainment.——The Musick's certainly fine; but,
in my Thoughts, there's none of your Composers come up to Old *Shakespear*
and *Otway*.

Bev. How, Madam! why if a Woman of your Sense were to say this in the
Drawing-Room—   180

Enter a Servant.

Serv. Sir, here's Signior *Carbonelli* says he waits your Commands, in the
next Room.

Bev. A propos! You were saying Yesterday, Madam, you had a mind to
hear him——will you give him leave to entertain you now?

Ind. By all means: desire the Gentleman to walk in.   [*Ex. Servant.*

Bev. I fancy you will find something in this Hand, that is uncommon.

Ind. You are always finding ways, Mr. *Bevil*, to make Life seem less tedious
to me.——

Enter Musick Master.

When the Gentleman pleases.

After a Sonata is play'd, Bevil *waits on the
Master to the Door*, &c.

Bev. You smile, Madam, to see me so Complaisant to one, whom I pay
for his Visit: Now, I own, I think it is not enough barely to pay those, whose
Talents are superior to our own (I mean such Talents, as would become our
Condition, if we had them.) Methinks we ought to do something more, than
barely gratify them, for what they do at our Command, only because their
Fortune is below us.   195

Ind. You say I smile: I assure you it was a Smile of Approbation; for indeed, I cannot but think it the distinguishing part of a Gentleman, to make
his Superiority of Fortune as easy to his Inferiors, as he can.——Now once
more to try him. [*Aside*.]——I was saying just now, I believed you would
never let me dispute with you, and I dare say, it will always be so: However I
must have your Opinion upon a Subject, which created a Debate between my
Aunt and me, just before you came hither; she would needs have it, that no
Man ever does any extraordinary Kindness or Service for a Woman, but for
his own sake.

Bev. Well Madam! Indeed I can't but be of her Mind.   205

Ind. What, tho' he should maintain, and support her, without demanding
any thing of her, on her part?

Bev. Why, Madam, is making an Expence, in the Service of a Valuable

s.d. *a Sonata*] Steele gives the words to which this music was originally meant as an
accompaniment in his Preface.   194 gratify] Reward with money.

Woman (for such I must suppose her) though she should never do him any Favour, nay, though she should never know who did her such Service, such a mighty Heroick Business?   211

Ind. Certainly! I should think he must be a Man of an uncommon Mold.

Bev. Dear Madam, why so? 'tis but, at best, a better Taste in Expence: To bestow upon one, whom he may think one of the Ornaments of the whole Creation, to be conscious, that from his Superfluity, an Innocent, a Virtuous Spirit is supported above the Temptations and Sorrows of Life! That he sees Satisfaction, Health and Gladness in her Countenance, while he enjoys the Happiness of seeing her (as that I will suppose too, or he must be too abstracted, too insensible) I say, if he is allowed to delight in that Prospect; alas! what mighty matter is there, in all this?   220

Ind. No mighty matter, in so disinterested a Friendship!

Bev. Disinterested! I can't think him so; your Hero, Madam, is no more, than what every Gentleman ought to be, and I believe very many are——He is only one, who takes more delight in Reflections, than in Sensations: He is more pleased with Thinking, than Eating; that's the utmost you can say of him——Why, Madam, a greater Expence, than all this, Men lay out upon an unnecessary Stable of Horses.

Ind. Can you be sincere, in what you say?

Bev. You may depend upon it, if you know any such Man, he does not love Dogs inordinately.   230

Ind. No, that he does not.

Bev. Nor Cards, nor Dice.

Ind. No.

Bev. Nor Bottle Companions.

Ind. No.

Bev. Nor loose Women.

Ind. No, I'm sure he does not.

Bev. Take my Word then, if your admired Hero is not liable to any of these kind of Demands, there's no such Preheminence in this, as you imagine: Nay this way of Expence you speak of, is what exalts and raises him, that has a Taste for it: And, at the same time, his Delight is incapable of Satiety, Disgust, or Penitence.   242

Ind. But still I insist his having no private Interest in the Action, makes it Prodigious, almost Incredible.

Bev. Dear Madam, I never knew you more mistaken: Why, who can be more an Usurer, than he, who lays out his Money in such Valuable Purchases? If Pleasure be worth purchasing, how great a Pleasure is it to him, who has a true Taste of Life, to ease an Aking Heart, to see the humane Countenance lighted up, into Smiles of Joy, on the Receipt of a Bit of Oar,

215 Superfluity] That is, excess of wealth.   249 Oar] That is, ore, gold.

which is superfluous, and otherwise useless in a Man's own Pocket? What
could a Man do better with his Cash? This is the Effect of an humane
Disposition, where there is only a general Tye of Nature, and common
Necessity. What then must it be, when we serve an Object of Merit, of
Admiration!   254

Ind. Well! the more you argue against it, the more I shall admire the
Generosity.

Bev. Nay, nay——Then, Madam, 'tis time to fly, after a Declaration, that
my Opinion strengthens my Adversary's Argument——I had best hasten to
my Appointment with Mr. *Myrtle*, and begone, while we are Friends, and—
before things are brought to an Extremity——   [*Exit carelessly.*

Enter Isabella.

Isab. Well, Madam, what think you of him now pray?   261

Ind. I protest, I begin to fear he is wholly disinterested, in what he does for
me. On my Heart, he has no other View, but the meer Pleasure of doing it,
and has neither Good or Bad Designs upon me.

Isab. Ah! dear Neice! don't be in fear of both! I'll warrant you, you will
know time enough, that he is not indifferent.

Ind. You please me, when you tell me so: For, if he has any Wishes towards
me, I know he will not pursue them, but with Honour.

Isab. I wish, I were as confident of one, as t'other—I saw the respectful
Downcast of his Eye, when you catcht him gazing at you during the Musick:
He, I warrant, was surpriz'd, as if he had been taken stealing your Watch. O!
the undissembled Guilty Look!   272

Ind. But did you observe any such thing, Really? I thought he look'd most
Charmingly Graceful! How engaging is Modesty, in a Man, when one knows
there is a great Mind within——So tender a Confusion! and yet, in other
Respects, so much himself, so collected, so dauntless, so determin'd!

Isab. Ah! Neice! there is a sort of Bashfulness, which is the best Engine to
carry on a shameless Purpose: some Men's Modesty serves their Wickedness,
as Hypocrisy gains the Respect due to Piety: But I will own to you, there is
one hopeful Symptom, if there could be such a thing, as a disinterested
Lover; But it's all a Perplexity, till—till——till——   281

Ind. Till what?

Isab. Till I know whether Mr. *Myrtle* and Mr. *Bevil* are really Friends, or
Foes——And that I will be convinced of, before I sleep: For you shall not be
deceiv'd.

Ind. I'm sure, I never shall, if your Fears can guard me: In the mean time,
I'll wrap my self up, in the Integrity of my own Heart, nor dare to doubt of
his.

277 Engine] Means of ensnarement, wily device.

As Conscious Honour all his Actions steers;   289
So Conscious Innocence dispels my Fears.   [*Ex.*

End of the Second ACT.

The Conscious Lovers.

ACT III. SCENE I.

SCENE, *Sealand's* House.

Enter Tom *meeting* Phillis.

Tom. WELL, *Phillis!*—what, with a Face, as if you had never seen me
before———What a Work have I to do now? She has seen some
new Visitant, at their House, whose Airs she has catch'd, and is resolv'd to
practice them upon me. Numberless are the Changes she'll dance thro',
before she'll answer this plain Question; *videlicet*, Have you deliver'd my
Master's Letter to your Lady? Nay, I know her too well, to ask an Account of
it, in an ordinary Way; I'll be in my Airs as well as she.   [*Aside.*
———Well, Madam, as unhappy as you are, at present pleased to make me, I
would not, in the general, be any other than what I am; I would not be a bit
wiser, a bit richer, a bit taller, a bit shorter, than I am at this Instant.   10
                                              [*Looking stedfastly at her.*

Phil. Did ever any body doubt, Master *Thomas*, but that you were extremely satisfied with your sweet self?

Tom. I am indeed——The Thing I have least reason to be satisfied with, is
my Fortune, and I am glad of my Poverty; Perhaps, if I were rich, I should
overlook the finest Woman in the World, that wants nothing but Riches, to be
thought so.

Phil. How prettily was that said? But, I'll have a great deal more, before
I'll say one Word.   [*Aside.*

Tom. I should, perhaps, have been stupidly above her, had I not been her
Equal; and by not being her Equal, never had Opportunity of being her
Slave. I am my Master's Servant, for Hire; I am my Mistress's, from Choice;
wou'd she but approve my Passion.   22

Phil. I think, it's the first Time I ever heard you speak of it, with any
Sense of the Anguish, if you really do suffer any.

Tom. Ah! *Phillis*, can you doubt, after what you have seen?

Phil. I know not what I have seen, nor what I have heard; but since I'm at
Leisure, you may tell me, When you fell in Love with me; How you fell in
Love with me; and what you have suffer'd, or are ready to suffer for me.

Tom. Oh! the unmerciful Jade! when I'm in haste about my Master's Letter———But, I must go thro' it. [*Aside.*]———Ah! too well I remember when, and how, and on what Occasion I was first surpriz'd. It was on the first of *April*, one thousand seven hundred and fifteen, I came into Mr. *Sealand's* Service; I was then a Hobble-de-Hoy, and you a pretty little tight Girl, a favourite Handmaid of the Housekeeper.——At that Time, we neither of us knew what was in us: I remember, I was order'd to get out of the Window, one pair of Stairs, to rub the Sashes clean,—the Person employ'd, on the innerside, was your Charming self, whom I had never seen before.   37

Phil. I think, I remember the silly Accident: What made ye, you Oaf, ready to fall down into the Street?

Tom. You know not, I warrant you—You could not guess what surpriz'd me. You took no Delight, when you immediately grew wanton, in your Conquest, and put your Lips close, and breath'd upon the Glass, and when my Lips approach'd, a dirty Cloth you rubb'd against my Face, and hid your beauteous Form; when I again drew near, you spit, and rubb'd, and smil'd at my Undoing.   45

Phil. What silly Thoughts you Men have!

Tom. We were *Pyramus* and *Thisbe*——but ten times harder was my Fate; *Pyramus* could peep only through a Wall, I saw her, saw my *Thisbe* in all her Beauty, but as much kept from her as if a hundred Walls between, for there was more, there was her Will against me—Would she but yet relent!——Oh, *Phillis! Phillis!* shorten my Torment, and declare you pity me.

Phil. I believe, it's very sufferable; the Pain is not so exquisite, but that you may bear it, a little longer.

Tom. Oh! my charming *Phillis*, if all depended on my Fair One's Will, I could with Glory suffer—But, dearest Creature, consider our miserable State.

Phil. How! Miserable!   56

Tom. We are miserable to be in Love, and under the Command of others than those we love—with that generous Passion in the Heart, to be sent to and fro on Errands, call'd, check'd and rated for the meanest Trifles. Oh, *Phillis!* you don't know how many *China* Cups, and Glasses, my Passion for you has made me break: You have broke my Fortune, as well as my Heart.

Phil. Well, Mr. *Thomas*, I cannot but own to you, that I believe, your Master writes and you speak the best of any Men in the World. Never was Woman so well pleas'd with a Letter, as my young Lady was with his, and this is an Answer to it.   [*Gives him a Letter.*

Tom. This was well done, my Dearest; consider, we must strike out some pretty Livelihood for our selves, by closing their Affairs: It will be nothing for them to give us a little Being of our own, some small Tenement, out of

---

33 tight] Neat and shapely.   36 one pair of Stairs] On the second floor.   68 give us a little Being] Allow us a subsistence.

their large Possessions: whatever they give us, 'twill be more than what they keep for themselves: one Acre, with *Phillis*, wou'd be worth a whole County without her.   71

Phil. O, could I but believe you!

Tom. If not the Utterance, believe the Touch of my Lips.   [*Kisses her.*

Phil. There's no contradicting you; how closely you argue, *Tom*!

Tom. And will closer, in due time. But I must hasten with this Letter, to hasten towards the Possession of you.——Then, *Phillis*, consider, how I must be reveng'd, look to it, of all your Skittishness, shy Looks, and at best but coy Compliances.

Phil. Oh! *Tom*, you grow wanton, and sensual, as my Lady calls it, I must not endure it; Oh! Foh! you are a Man, an odious filthy Male Creature; you should behave, if you had a right Sense, or were a Man of Sense, like Mr. *Cimberton*, with Distance, and Indifference; or let me see some other becoming hard Word, with seeming in-in-inadvertency, and not rush on one as if you were seizing a Prey. But Hush——the Ladies are coming——God *Tom*, don't kiss me above once, and be gone——Lard, we have been Fooling and Toying, and not consider'd the main Business of our Masters and Mistresses.   87

Tom. Why, their Business is to be Fooling and Toying, as soon as the Parchments are ready.

Phil. Well remember'd——Parchments—— my Lady, to my Knowledge, is preparing Writings between her Coxcomb Cousin *Cimberton*, and my Mistress; though my Master has an Eye to the Parchments already prepar'd between your Master Mr. *Bevil*, and my Mistress; and I believe, my Mistress herself has sign'd, and seal'd, in her Heart, to Mr. *Myrtle*.——Did I not bid you kiss me but once, and be gone? but I know you won't be satisfy'd.

Tom. No, you smooth Creature, how should I!   [*Kissing her Hand.*

Phil. Well, since you are so humble, or so cool, as to ravish my Hand only, I'll take my Leave of you like a great Lady, and you a Man of Quality.

                                         [*They Salute formally.*

Tom. Pox of all this State.   [*Offers to kiss her more closely.*

Phil. No, pr'ythee, *Tom*, mind your Business. We must follow that Interest which will take; but endeavour at that which will be most for us, and we like most——O here's my young Mistress! [*Tom* taps her Neck behind, and kisses her Fingers.] Go, ye liquorish Fool.   [*Exit* Tom.

Enter Lucinda.

Luc. Who was that you was hurrying away?   104

Phil. One that I had no mind to part with.

89 Parchments] Marriage contracts.   100 that Interest which will take] Whichever side will come off best.

Luc. Why did you turn him away then?

Phil. For your Ladyship's Service, to carry your Ladyship's Letter to his Master: I could hardly get the Rogue away.

Luc. Why, has he so little Love for his Master?

Phil. No; but he has so much Love for his Mistress.   110

Luc. But, I thought, I heard him kiss you. Why do you suffer that?

Phil. Why, Madam, we Vulgar take it to be a Sign of Love; we Servants, we poor People, that have nothing but our Persons to bestow, or treat for, are forc'd to deal, and bargain by way of Sample; and therefore, as we have no Parchments, or Wax necessary in our Agreements, we squeeze with our Hands, and seal with our Lips, to ratifie Vows and Promises.

Luc. But can't you trust one another, without such Earnest down?

Phil. We don't think it safe, any more than you Gentry, to come together without Deeds executed.

Luc. Thou art a pert merry Hussy.   120

Phil. I wish, Madam, your Lover and you were as happy, as *Tom* and your Servant are.

Luc. You grow impertinent.

Phil. I have done, Madam; and I won't ask you, what you intend to do with Mr. *Myrtle*, what your Father will do with Mr. *Bevil*, nor what you all, especially my Lady, mean by admitting Mr. *Cimberton* as particularly here, as if he were married to you already; nay, you are married actually as far as People of Quality are.

Luc. How's that?

Phil. You have different Beds in the same House.   130

Luc. Pshaw! I have a very great Value for Mr. *Bevil*, but have absolutely put an End to his Pretensions, in the Letter I gave you for him: But, my Father, in his Heart, still has a mind to him, were it not for this Woman they talk of; and, I am apt to imagine he is married to her, or never designs to marry at all.

Phil. Then Mr. *Myrtle*———

Luc. He had my Parents Leave to apply to me, and by that he has won me, and my Affections: who is to have this Body of mine, without 'em, it seems, is nothing to me; my Mother says, it's indecent for me to let my Thoughts stray about the Person of my Husband: nay, she says, a Maid, rigidly Virtuous, tho' she may have been where her Lover was a thousand times, should not have made Observations enough, to know him from another Man, when she sees him in a third Place.   143

Phil. That is more than the Severity of a Nun, for not to see, when one may, is hardly possible; not to see when one can't, is very easy: at this rate, Madam, there are a great many whom you have not seen who———

Luc. Mamma says, the first time you see your Husband should be at that

E

Instant he is made so; when your Father, with the help of the Minister, gives you to him; then you are to see him, then you are to Observe and take Notice of him, because then you are to Obey him.   150

Phil. But does not my Lady remember, you are to Love, as well as Obey?

Luc. To Love is a Passion, 'tis a Desire, and we must have no Desires. Oh! I cannot endure the Reflection! With what Insensibility on my Part, with what more than Patience, have I been expos'd, and offer'd to some aukward Booby or other, in every County of *Great Britain?*

Phil. Indeed, Madam, I wonder, I never heard you speak of it before, with this Indignation.

Luc. Every Corner of the Land has presented me with a wealthy Coxcomb. As fast as one Treaty has gone off, another has come on, till my Name and Person have been the Tittle Tattle of the whole Town: What is this World come to! No Shame left! To be barter'd for, like the Beasts of the Fields, and that, in such an Instance, as coming together, to an intire Familiarity, and Union of Soul and Body; Oh! and this, without being so much as Well-wishers to each other, but for encrease of Fortune.   164

Phil. But, Madam, all these Vexations will end, very soon, in one for all: Mr. *Cimberton* is your Mother's Kinsman, and three hundred Years an older Gentleman than any Lover you ever had; for which Reason, with that of his prodigious large Estate, she is resolved on him, and has sent to consult the Lawyers accordingly. Nay, has (whether you know it or no) been in Treaty with Sir *Geoffry*, who, to join in the Settlement, has accepted of a Sum to do it, and is every Moment expected in Town for that Purpose.   171

Luc. How do you get all this Intelligence?

Phil. By an Art I have, I thank my Stars, beyond all the Waiting-maids in *Great-Britain*; the Art of List'ning, Madam, for your Ladyship's Service.

Luc. I shall soon know as much as you do; leave me, leave me, *Phillis*, be gone: Here, here, I'll turn you out. My Mother says I must not converse with my Servants; tho' I must converse with no one else. [*Exit* Phillis.] How un-happy are we, who are born to great Fortunes! No one looks at us, with Indifference, or acts towards us on the Foot of Plain Dealing; yet, by all I have been heretofore offer'd to, or treated for, I have been us'd with the most agreeable of all Abuses, Flattery; but now, by this Flegmatick Fool, I am us'd as nothing, or a meer Thing; He, forsooth! is too wise, too learned to have any regard to Desires, and, I know not what the learned Oaf calls Sentiments of Love and Passion——Here he comes with my Mother——It's much if he looks at me; or if he does, takes no more Notice of me, than of any other Moveable in the Room.   186

Enter Mrs. Sealand, *and Mr.* Cimberton.

181 Flegmatick] Cold-blooded, dull.

Mrs. Seal. How do I admire this noble, this learned Taste of yours, and the worthy Regard you have to our own ancient and honourable House, in consulting a Means, to keep the Blood as pure, and as regularly descended as may be.   190

Cim. Why, really Madam, the young Women of this Age are treated with Discourses of such a Tendency, and their Imaginations so bewilder'd in Flesh and Blood, that a Man of Reason can't talk to be understood: They have no Ideas of Happiness, but what are more gross than the Gratification of Hunger and Thirst.

Luc. With how much Reflection he is a Coxcomb?   [*Aside.*

Cim. And in Truth, Madam, I have consider'd it, as a most brutal Custom, that Persons, of the first Character in the World, should go as ordinarily, and with as little Shame, to Bed, as to Dinner with one another. They proceed to the Propagation of the Species, as openly, as to the Preservation of the Individual.   201

Luc. She that willingly goes to Bed to thee, must have no Shame, I'm sure.
                                                                            [*Aside.*

Mrs. Seal. Oh Cousin *Cimberton*! Cousin *Cimberton*! how abstracted, how refin'd, is your Sense of Things! But, indeed, it is too true, there is nothing so ordinary as to say, in the best govern'd Families, my Master and Lady are gone to Bed; one does not know but it might have been said of one's self.
                                                  [*Hiding her Face with her Fan.*

Cim. Lycurgus, Madam, instituted otherwise; among the *Lacedæmonians*, the whole Female World was pregnant, but none, but the Mothers themselves, knew by whom; their Meetings were secret, and the Amorous Congress always by Stealth; and no such professed Doings between the Sexes, as are tolerated among us, under the audacious Word, Marriage.

Mrs. Seal. Oh! had I liv'd, in those Days, and been a Matron of *Sparta*, one might, with less Indecency, have had ten Children, according to that modest Institution, than one, under the Confusion of our modern, barefac'd manner.   215

Luc. And yet, poor Woman, she has gone thro' the whole Ceremony, and here I stand a melancholy Proof of it.   [*Aside.*

Mrs. Seal. We will talk then of Business. That Girl walking about the Room there is to be your Wife. She has, I confess, no Ideas, no Sentiments, that speak her born of a thinking Mother.   220

Cimb. I have observ'd her; her lively Look, free Air, and disengag'd Countenance speak her very——

Luc. Very, What?

Cimb. If you please, Madam—to set her a little that way.

Mrs. Seal. Lucinda, say nothing to him, you are not a Match for him; when

207 *Lycurgus*] Legendary lawgiver to the Spartans.

you are married, you may speak to such a Husband, when you're spoken to. But, I am disposing of you, above your self, every way.

Cimb. Madam, you cannot but observe the Inconveniences I expose my self to, in hopes that your Ladyship will be the Consort of my better Part: As for the young Woman, she is rather an Impediment, than a Help, to a Man of Letters and Speculation. Madam, there is no Reflection, no Philosophy, can, at all times, subdue the Sensitive Life, but the Animal shall sometimes carry away the Man: Ha! ay, the Vermilion of her Lips.   233

Luc. Pray, don't talk of me thus.

Cimb. The pretty enough—Pant of her Bosom.

Luc. Sir; Madam, don't you hear him?

Cimb. Her forward Chest.

Luc. Intollerable!

Cimb. High Health.

Luc. The grave, easy Impudence of him!   240

Cimb. Proud Heart.

Luc. Stupid Coxcomb!

Cimb. I say, Madam, her Impatience, while we are looking at her, throws out all Attractions—her Arms—her Neck—what a Spring in her Step!

Luc. Don't you run me over thus, you strange Unaccountable!

Cimb. What an Elasticity in her Veins and Arteries!

Luc. I have no Veins, no Arteries.

Mrs. Seal. Oh, Child, hear him, he talks finely, he's a Scholar, he knows what you have.

Cimb. The speaking Invitation of her Shape, the Gathering of her self up, and the Indignation you see in the pretty little thing——now, I am considering her, on this Occasion, but as one that is to be pregnant.   252

Luc. The familiar, learned, unseasonable Puppy!   [*Aside.*

Cimb. And pregnant undoubtedly she will be yearly. I fear, I shan't, for many Years, have Discretion enough to give her one fallow Season.

Luc. Monster! there's no bearing it. The hideous Sot!——there's no enduring it, to be thus survey'd like a Steed at Sale.

Cimb. At Sale! she's very illiterate——But she's very well limb'd too; turn her in; I see what she is.   [*Exit* Lucinda *in a Rage.*

Mrs. Seal. Go, you Creature, I am asham'd of you.   260

Cimb. No harm done——you know, Madam, the better sort of People, as I observ'd to you, treat by their Lawyers of Weddings [*adjusting himself at the Glass*] and the Woman in the Bargain, like the Mansion-House in the Sale of the Estate, is thrown in, and what that is, whether good or bad, is not at all consider'd.

229 my better Part] That is, the mind rather than the body.   232 Sensitive] Sensual.
258 turn her in] Take her away. Cimberton sustains the horsebreeding imagery.

Mrs. Seal. I grant it, and therefore make no Demand for her Youth, and Beauty, and every other Accomplishment, as the common World think 'em, because she is not Polite.

Cimb. Madam, I know, your exalted Understanding, abstracted, as it is, from vulgar Prejudices, will not be offended, when I declare to you, I Marry to have an Heir to my Estate, and not to beget a Colony, or a Plantation: This young Woman's Beauty, and Constitution, will demand Provision for a tenth Child at least.   273

Mrs. Seal. With all that Wit, and Learning, how considerate! What an Oeconomist! [*aside.*]—Sir, I cannot make her any other than she is; or say she is much better than the other young Women of this Age, or fit for much, besides being a Mother; but I have given Directions for the Marriage Settlements, and Sir *Geoffrey Cimberton*'s Council is to meet ours here, at this Hour, concerning his joyning in the Deed, which when executed, makes you capable of settling what is due to *Lucinda*'s Fortune: Her self, as I told you, I say nothing of.   281

Cimb. No, no, no, indeed, Madam, it is not usual, and I must depend upon my own Reflection, and Philosophy, not to overstock my Family.

Mrs. Seal. I cannot help her, Cousin *Cimberton*; but she is, for ought I see, as well as the Daughter of any body else.

Cimb. That is very true, Madam.

Enter a Servant, who whispers Mrs. Sealand.

Mrs. Seal. The Lawyers are come, and now we are to hear what they have resolv'd as to the point whether it's necessary that Sir *Geoffry* should join in the Settlement, as being what they call in the Remainder. But, good Cousin, you must have Patience with 'em. These Lawyers, I am told, are of a different kind, one is what they call a Chamber-Council, the other a Pleader: The Conveyancer is slow, from an Imperfection in his Speech, and therefore shun'd the Bar, but extremely Passionate, and impatient of Contradiction: The other is as warm as he; but has a Tongue so voluble, and a Head so conceited, he will suffer no body to speak but himself.   295

Cimb. You mean old Serjeant *Target*, and Counsellor *Bramble?* I have heard of 'em.

Mrs. Seal. The same: shew in the Gentlemen.   [*Exit Servant.*

Re-enter Servant, introducing Myrtle *and* Tom,
disguis'd as Bramble *and* Target.

Mrs. Seal. Gentlemen, this is the Party concern'd, Mr. *Cimberton*; and I hope you have consider'd of the matter.   300

275 Oeconomist] Manager of domestic affairs.   289 in the Remainder] That is, among those holding a residual interest in an estate.   291 Chamber-Council] That is, a private adviser rather than an advocate in open court.   291 Pleader] A lawyer who puts his case in court.

Tar. Yes, Madam, we have agreed that it must be by Indent——dent——dent——dent——

Bram. Yes, Madam, Mr. Serjeant and my self have agreed, as he is pleas'd to inform you, that it must be an Indenture Tripartite, and Tripartite let it be, for Sir *Geoffry* must needs be a Party; old *Cimberton*, in the Year 1619, says, in that ancient Roll, in Mr. Serjeant's Hands, as recourse thereto being had, will more at large appear——

Tar. Yes, and by the Deeds in your Hands, it appears, that——

Bram. Mr. Serjeant, I beg of you to make no Inferences upon what is in our Custody; but speak to the Titles in your own Deeds——I shall not show that Deed till my Client is in Town.   311

Cimb. You know best your own Methods.

Mrs. Seal. The single Question is, whether the Intail is such, that my Cousin Sir *Geoffry* is necessary in this Affair?

Bram. Yes, as to the Lordship of *Tretriplet*, but not as to the Messuage of *Grimgribber*.

Tar. I say that *Gr—gr*—that *Gr—gr—Grimgribber, Grimgribber* is in us. That is to say the remainder thereof, as well as that of *Tr——tr—Triplet.*

Bram. You go upon the Deed of Sir *Ralph*, made in the middle of the last Century, precedent to that in which old *Cimberton* made over the Remainder, and made it pass to the Heirs general, by which your Client comes in; and I question whether the Remainder even of *Tretriplet* is in him——But we are willing to wave that, and give him a valuable Consideration. But we shall not purchase what is in us for ever, as *Grimgribber* is, at the rate as we guard against the Contingent of Mr. *Cimberton* having no Son——Then we know Sir *Geoffry* is the first of the Collateral Male Line in this Family——Yet——   327

Tar. Sir, *Gr—gr—ber* is——

Bram. I apprehend you very well, and your Argument might be of Force, and we would be inclin'd to hear that in all its Parts——But, Sir, I see very plainly what you are going into——I tell you, it is as probable a Contingent that Sir *Geoffry* may die before Mr. *Cimberton*, as that he may outlive him.

Tar. Sir, we are not ripe for that yet, but I must say——

Bram. Sir, I allow you the whole extent of that Argument; but that will go no farther than as to the Claimants under old *Cimberton*,——I am of Opinion, that according to the Instruction of Sir *Ralph*, he could not dock the Entail, and then create a new Estate for the Heirs General.   338

Tar. Sir, I have not patience to be told that, when *Gr—gr—ber*——

315 Lordship] That is, overlordship, rightful jurisdiction over.   315 the Messuage] The dwelling-house, together with its outbuildings and adjacent lands.   337 dock the Entail] Amend the line of succession to an estate.

Bram. I will allow it you, Mr. Serjeant; but there must be the word Heirs for ever, to make such an Estate as you pretend. 341

Cimb. I must be impartial, tho' you are Council for my side of the Question —Were it not that you are so good as to allow him what he has not said, I should think it very hard you should answer him without hearing him—But Gentlemen, I believe you have both consider'd this matter, and are firm in your different Opinions: 'Twere better therefore you proceeded according to the particular Sense of each of you, and gave your Thoughts distinctly in Writing—And do you see, Sirs, pray let me have a Copy of what you say, in *English*.

Bram. Why, what is all we have been saying?—In *English*! Oh! but I forgot my self, you're a Wit—But however, to please you, Sir, you shall have it, in as plain terms, as the Law will admit of. 352

Cimb. But I would have it, Sir, without delay.

Bram. That, Sir, the Law will not admit of: the Courts are sitting at *Westminster*, and I am this moment oblig'd to be at every one of them, and 'twould be wrong if I should not be in the Hall to attend one of 'em at least, the rest would take it ill else———Therefore, I must leave what I have said to Mr. Serjeant's Consideration, and I will digest his Arguments on my part, and you shall hear from me again, Sir.   [*Exit* Bramble.

Tar. Agreed, agreed. 360

Cimb. Mr. *Bramble* is very quick—He parted a little abruptly.

Tar. He could not bear my Argument, I pincht him to the quick about that *Gr—gr—ber*.

Mrs. Seal. I saw that, for he durst not so much as hear you——I shall send to you, Mr. Serjeant, as soon as Sir *Geoffry* comes to Town, and then I hope all may be adjusted.

Tar. I shall be at my Chambers, at my usual Hours.   [*Exit.*

Cimb. Madam, if you please, I'll now attend you to the Tea-Table, where I shall hear from your Ladyship, Reason, and good Sense, after all this Law and Gibberish. 370

Mrs. Seal. 'Tis a wonderful thing, Sir, that Men of Professions do not study to talk the Substance of what they have to say, in the Language of the rest of the World: Sure, they'd find their Account in it.

Cimb. They might, perhaps, Madam, with People of your good Sense; but, with the generality 'twould never do: The Vulgar would have no respect for Truth and Knowledge, if they were exposed to naked View.

> Truth is too simple, of all Art bereav'd:
> Since the World will—why let it be deceiv'd.   [*Exeunt.*

End of the Third ACT.

373 their Account] Their due reward.

The Conscious Lovers.

ACT IV. SCENE I.

SCENE, Bevil *Junior's Lodgings.*

Bevil jun. with a Letter in his Hand, follow'd by Tom.

Tom. UPON my Life, Sir, I know nothing of the matter: I never open'd my Lips to Mr. *Myrtle*, about any thing of your Honour's Letter to Madam *Lucinda.*

Bev. What's the Fool in such a fright for? I don't suppose you did: What I would know is, whether Mr. *Myrtle* shew'd any Suspicion, or ask'd you any Questions, to lead you to say casually, that you had carry'd any such Letter, for me, this Morning.

Tom. Why, Sir, if he did ask me any Questions, how could I help it?

Bev. I don't say you could, Oaf! I am not questioning you, but him: What did he say to you?   10

Tom. Why, Sir, when I came to his Chambers, to be dress'd for the Lawyer's Part, your Honour was pleas'd to put me upon, he ask'd me, if I had been at Mr. *Sealand's* this Morning?—So I told him, Sir, I often went thither—because, Sir, if I had not said that, he might have thought, there was something more, in my going now, than at another time.

Bev. Very well!——This Fellow's Caution, I find, has given him this Jealousy. [*aside.*] Did he ask you no other Questions?

Tom. Yes, Sir——now I remember, as we came away in the Hackney Coach, from Mr. *Sealand's, Tom,* says he, as I came in to your Master, this Morning, he bad you go for an Answer to a Letter he had sent. Pray did you bring him any? says he—Ah! says I, Sir, your Honour is pleas'd to joke with me, you have a mind to know whether I can keep a Secret, or no?   22

Bev. And so, by shewing him you could, you told him you had one?

Tom. Sir——   [*confus'd.*

Bev. What means Actions does Jealousy make a Man stoop to? How poorly has he us'd Art, with a Servant, to make him betray his Master? Well! and when did he give you this Letter for me?

Tom. Sir, he writ it, before he pull'd off his Lawyer's Gown, at his own Chambers.

Bev. Very well; and what did he say, when you brought him my Answer to it?   31

Tom. He look'd a little out of Humour, Sir, and said, It was very well.

Bev. I knew he would be grave upon't,——wait without.

Tom. Humh! 'gad, I don't like this; I am afraid we are all in the wrong Box here.— [*Exit* Tom.

Bev. I put on a Serenity, while my Fellow was present: But I have never been more thoroughly disturb'd; This hot Man! to write me a Challenge, on supposed artificial Dealing, when I profess'd my self his Friend! I can live contented without Glory; but I cannot suffer Shame. What's to be done? But first, let me consider *Lucinda*'s Letter again. [*Reads.*

SIR, 41

I Hope it is consistent with the Laws a Woman ought to impose upon her self, to acknowledge, that your manner of declining a Treaty of Marriage, in our Family, and desiring the Refusal may come from hence, has something more engaging in it, than the Courtship of him, who, I fear, will fall to my Lot; except your Friend exerts himself, for our common Safety, and Happiness: I have Reasons for desiring Mr. Myrtle *may not know of this Letter, till hereafter, and am your most oblig'd humble Servant,* Lucinda Sealand.

Well, but the Postscript. [*Reads.*

I won't, upon second Thoughts, hide any thing from you. But, my Reason for concealing this is, that Mr. Myrtle *has a Jealousy in his Temper, which gives me some Terrors; but my Esteem for him inclines me to hope that only an ill Effect, which sometimes accompanies a Tender Love; and what may be cur'd, by a careful and unblameable Conduct.* 54

Thus has this Lady made me her Friend and Confident, and put her self, in a kind, under my Protection: I cannot tell him immediately the Purport of her Letter, except I could cure him of the violent and untractable Passion of Jealousy, and so serve him, and her, by disobeying her, in the Article of Secrecy, more than I should by complying with her Directions——But then this Duelling, which Custom has impos'd upon every Man, who would live with Reputation and Honour in the World:——How must I preserve my self from Imputations there? He'll, forsooth, call it, or think it Fear, if I explain without Fighting——But his Letter—I'll read it again.——

SIR, 64

Y OU have us'd me basely, in corresponding, and carrying on a Treaty, where you told me you were indifferent: I have chang'd my Sword, since I saw you; which Advertisement I thought proper to send you against the next Meeting, between you, and the injur'd

Charles Myrtle.

Enter Tom.

Tom. Mr. *Myrtle*, Sir: would your Honour please to see him? 70

Bev. Why you stupid Creature! Let Mr. *Myrtle* wait at my Lodgings!

34 in the wrong Box] In error, in an untenable position.   38 artificial] Deceitful, cunning.

Shew him up. [*Exit* Tom.] Well! I am resolv'd upon my Carriage to him——
He is in Love, and in every circumstance of Life a little distrustful, which I
must allow for—but here he is.

Enter Tom introducing Myrtle.

Sir, I am extremely oblig'd to you for this Honour,——But, Sir, You, with
your very discerning Face, leave the Room. [*Exit* Tom.] Well, Mr. *Myrtle*,
your Commands with me?

Myrt. The Time, the Place, our long Acquaintance, and many other
Circumstances, which affect me on this Occasion, oblige me, without farther
Ceremony, or Conference, to desire you would not only, as you already have,
acknowledge the Receipt of my Letter, but also comply with the Request in
it. I must have farther Notice taken of my Message than these half Lines,
——I have yours,——I shall be at home.——   83

Bev. Sir, I own, I have received a Letter from you, in a very unusual
Style; But as I design every thing, in this Matter, shall be your own Action,
your own Seeking, I shall understand nothing, but what you are pleas'd to
confirm, Face to Face, and I have already forgot the Contents of your
Epistle.

Myrt. This cool Manner is very agreeable to the Abuse you have already
made of my Simplicity and Frankness; and I see your Moderation tends to
your own Advantage, and not mine; to your own Safety, not Consideration
of your Friend.   92

Bev. My own Safety, Mr. *Myrtle*!

Myrt. Your own Safety, Mr. *Bevil*.

Bev. Look you, Mr. *Myrtle*, there's no disguising that I understand what
you would be at—But, Sir, you know, I have often dared to disapprove of the
Decisions a Tyrant Custom has introduc'd, to the Breach of all Laws, both
Divine and Human.

Myrt. Mr. *Bevil*, Mr. *Bevil*, it would be a good first Principle, in those who
have so tender a Conscience that way, to have as much Abhorrence of doing
Injuries, as—   101

Bevil. As what?

Myrt. As Fear of answering for 'em.

Bev. As Fear of answering for 'em! But that Apprehension is Just or
Blameable, according to the Object of that Fear.——I have often told you in
Confidence of Heart, I abhorr'd the Daring to offend the Author of Life, and
rushing into his Presence.—I say, by the very same Act, to commit the
Crime against him, and immediately to urge on to his Tribunal.

Myrt. Mr. *Bevil*, I must tell you, this Coolness, this Gravity, this Shew of
Conscience, shall never cheat me of my Mistress. You have, indeed, the best
Excuse for Life, the Hopes of possessing *Lucinda*: But consider, Sir, I have

as much Reason to be weary of it, if I am to lose her; and my first Attempt to recover her, shall be to let her see the Dauntless Man, who is to be her Guardian and Protector. 114

Bev. Sir, shew me but the least Glimpse of Argument, that I am authoriz'd, by my own Hand, to vindicate any lawless Insult of this nature, and I will shew thee—to chastize thee—hardly deserves the Name of Courage—— slight, inconsiderate Man!—There is, Mr. *Myrtle*, no such Terror in quick Anger; and you shall, you know not why, be cool, as you have, you know not why, been warm. 120

Myrt. Is the Woman one loves, so little an Occasion of Anger? You perhaps, who know not what it is to love, who have your Ready, your Commodious, your Foreign Trinket, for your loose Hours; and from your Fortune, your specious outward Carriage, and other lucky Circumstances, as easie a Way to the Possession of a Woman of Honour; you know nothing of what it is to be alarm'd, to be distracted, with Anxiety and Terror of losing more than Life: Your Marriage, happy Man! goes on like common Business, and in the interim, you have your Rambling Captive, your *Indian* Princess, for your soft Moments of Dalliance, your Convenient, your Ready *Indiana*.

Bev. You have touch'd me beyond the Patience of a Man; and I'm excusable, in the Guard of Innocence (or from the Infirmity of Human Nature, which can bear no more) to accept your Invitation, and observe your Letter———Sir, I'll attend you. 133

Enter Tom.

Tom. Did you call, Sir? I thought you did: I heard you speak aloud.

Bev. Yes, go call a Coach.

Tom. Sir,——Master——Mr. *Myrtle*,——Friends——Gentlemen—— what d'ye mean? I am but a Servant, or——

Bev. Call a Coach. [*Exit* Tom.

[*A long Pause, walking sullenly by each other.*

[*Aside*] Shall I (though provok'd to the Uttermost) recover my self at the Entrance of a third Person, and that my Servant too, and not have Respect enough to all I have ever been receiving from Infancy, the Obligation to the best of Fathers, to an unhappy Virgin too, whose Life depends on mine.

[*Shutting the Door.*

[*To* Myrtle.] I have, thank Heaven, had time to recollect my self, and shall not, for fear of what such a rash Man as you think of me, keep longer unexplain'd the false Appearances, under which your Infirmity of Temper makes you suffer; when, perhaps, too much Regard to a false Point of Honour, makes me prolong that Suffering. 147

Myrt. I am sure, Mr. *Bevil* cannot doubt, but I had rather have Satisfaction from his Innocence, than his Sword.

Bev. Why then would you ask it first that Way?   150

Myrt. Consider, you kept your Temper your self no longer than till I spoke to the Disadvantage of her you lov'd.

Bev. True. But let me tell you, I have sav'd you from the most exquisite Distress, even tho' you had succeeded in the Dispute: I know you so well, that I am sure, to have found this Letter about a Man you had kill'd, would have been worse than Death to your self—Read it——. When he is thoroughly mortify'd, and Shame has got the better of Jealousie, when he has seen himself throughly, he will deserve to be assisted towards obtaining *Lucinda.*

Myrt. With what a Superiority has he turn'd the Injury on me, as the Aggressor? I begin to fear, I have been too far transported—*A Treaty in our Family!* is not that saying too much? I shall relapse—But, I find (on the Postscript) *something like Jealousie*—with what Face can I see my Benefactor? my Advocate? whom I have treated like a Betrayer.——Oh! *Bevil,* with what Words shall I——   165

Bev. There needs none; to convince, is much more than to conquer.

Myrt. But can you——

Bev. You have o'erpaid the Inquietude you gave me, in the Change I see in you towards me: Alas! what Machines are we! thy Face is alter'd to that of another Man; to that of my Companion, my Friend.   170

Myrt. That I could be such a precipitant Wretch!

Bev. Pray no more.

Myrt. Let me reflect how many Friends have died, by the Hands of Friends, for want of Temper; and you must give me Leave to say again, and again, how much I am beholden to that Superior Spirit you have subdu'd me with——what had become of one of us, or perhaps both, had you been as weak as I was, and as incapable of Reason?

Bev. I congratulate to us both the Escape from our selves, and hope the Memory of it will make us Dearer Friends than ever.

Myrt. Dear *Bevil,* your Friendly Conduct has convinc'd me that there is nothing manly, but what is conducted by Reason, and agreeable to the Practice of Virtue and Justice. And yet, how many have been sacrific'd to that Idol, the Unreasonable Opinion of Men! Nay, they are so ridiculous in it, that they often use their Swords against each other, with Dissembled Anger, and Real Fear.   185

> Betray'd by Honour, and compell'd by Shame,
> They hazard Being, to preserve a Name:
> Nor dare enquire into the dread Mistake,
> 'Till plung'd in sad Eternity they Wake.   [*Exeunt.*

168 o'erpaid the Inquietude] More than made recompense for the discomfiture.
169 Machines] That is, human machines, acting without intelligence.

SCENE *St.* James's *Park.*

Enter Sir John Bevil, *and Mr.* Sealand.

Sir J. Bev. Give me leave, however, Mr. *Sealand*, as we are upon a Treaty
for Uniting our Families, to mention only the Business of an ancient House
————Genealogy and Descent are to be of some Consideration, in an Affair
of this sort————

Mr. Seal. Genealogy, and Descent!——Sir, there has been in our
Family a very large one. There was *Galfrid* the Father of *Edward*, the Father
of *Ptolomey*, the Father of *Crassus*, the Father of Earl *Richard*, the Father of
Henry the Marquis, the Father of Duke *John*————

Sir J. Bev. What, do you rave, Mr. *Sealand*? all these great Names in your
Family?   10

Mr. Seal. These? yes, Sir——I have heard my Father name 'em all, and
more.

Sir J. Bev. Ay, Sir?——and did he say they were all in your Family?

Mr. Seal. Yes, Sir, he kept 'em all——he was the greatest Cocker in
England—he said, Duke *John* won him many Battles, and never lost
one.

Sir J. Bev. Oh Sir, your Servant, you are laughing at my laying any Stress
upon Descent——but I must tell you Sir, I never knew any one, but he that
wanted that Advantage, turn it into Ridicule.

Mr. Seal. And I never knew any one, who had many better Advantages,
put that into his Account————But, Sir *John*, value your self as you please
upon your ancient House, I am to talk freely of every thing, you are pleas'd to
put into your Bill of Rates, on this Occasion——yet, Sir, I have made no
Objections to your Son's Family——'Tis his Morals, that I doubt.   24

Sir J. Bev. Sir, I can't help saying, that what might injure a Citizen's
Credit, may be no Stain to a Gentleman's Honour.

Mr. Seal. Sir *John*, the Honour of a Gentleman is liable to be tainted, by as
small a matter as the Credit of a Trader; we are talking of a Marriage, and in
such a Case, the Father of a young Woman will not think it an Addition, to
the Honour, or Credit of her Lover—that he is a Keeper——   30

Sir J. Bev. Mr. *Sealand*, don't take upon you, to spoil my Son's Marriage,
with any Woman else.

Mr. Seal. Sir *John*, let him apply to any Woman else, and have as many
Mistresses as he pleases——

Sir J. Bev. My Son, Sir, is a discreet and sober Gentleman——

Mr. Seal. Sir, I never saw a Man that wench'd soberly and discreetly, that
ever left it off——the Decency observ'd in the Practice, hides, even from the

14 Cocker] Patron of cock-fighting.

Sinner, the Iniquity of it. They pursue it, not that their Appetites hurry 'em away; but, I warrant you, because, 'tis their Opinion, they may do it.

Sir J. Bev. Were what you suspect a Truth——do you design to keep your Daughter a Virgin, 'till you find a Man unblemish'd that way?   41

Mr. Seal. Sir, as much a Cit as you take me for—I know the Town, and the World—and give me leave to say, that we Merchants are a Species of Gentry, that have grown into the World this last Century, and are as honourable, and almost as useful, as you landed Folks, that have always thought your selves so much above us; For your trading, forsooth! is extended no farther, than a Load of Hay, or a fat Ox——You are pleasant People, indeed; because you are generally bred up to be lazy, therefore, I warrant you, Industry is dishonourable.

Sir J. Bev. Be not offended, Sir; let us go back to our Point.   50

Mr. Seal. Oh! not at all offended—but I don't love to leave any part of the Account unclos'd—look you, Sir *John*, Comparisons are odious, and more particularly so, on Occasions of this Kind, when we are projecting Races, that are to be made out of both Sides of the Comparisons.

Sir J. Bev. But, my Son, Sir, is, in the Eye of the World, a Gentleman of Merit.

Mr. Seal. I own to you, I think him so.——But, Sir *John*, I am a Man exercis'd, and experienc'd in Chances, and Disasters; I lost, in my earlier Years, a very fine Wife, and with her a poor little Infant; this makes me, perhaps, over cautious, to preserve the second Bounty of Providence to me, and be as careful, as I can, of this Child——you'll pardon me, my poor Girl, Sir, is as valuable to me, as your boasted Son, to you.   62

Sir J. Bev. Why, that's one very good Reason, Mr. *Sealand*, why I wish my Son had her.

Mr. Seal. There is nothing, but this strange Lady here, this *Incognita*, that can be objected to him——here and there a Man falls in Love with an artful Creature, and gives up all the Motives of Life, to that one Passion.

Sir. J. Bev. A Man of my Son's Understanding, cannot be suppos'd to be one of them.

Mr. Seal. Very wise Men have been so enslav'd; and, when a Man marries with one of them upon his Hands, whether mov'd from the Demand of the World, or slighter Reasons; such a Husband soils with his Wife for a Month perhaps——then Good B'w'y' Madam——the Show's over——ah! *John Dryden* points out such a Husband to a Hair, where he says,   74

> And while abroad so prodigal the Dolt is,
> Poor Spouse at home as ragged as a Colt is.

---

42 Cit] Contemptuous term for a bourgeois man of trade.   72 soils] Has sexual dealings.
74 *John Dryden* points out] In his Epilogue to Vanbrugh's *The Pilgrim*, 1700.

Now in plain Terms, Sir, I shall not care to have my poor Girl turn'd a grazing, and that must be the Case, when——

Sir J. Bev. But pray consider, Sir, my Son—

Mr. Seal. Look you Sir, I'll make the Matter short. This unknown Lady, as I told you, is all the Objection I have to him: But, one way or other, he is, or has been, certainly engag'd to her—I am therefore resolv'd, this very Afternoon, to visit her: Now from her Behaviour, or Appearance, I shall soon be let into, what I may fear, or hope for.   84

Sir J. Bev. Sir, I am very confident, there can be Nothing enquir'd into, relating to my Son, that will not, upon being understood, turn to his Advantage.

Mr. Seal. I hope that, as sincerely, as you believe it——Sir *John Bevil*, when I am satisfied, in this great Point, if your Son's Conduct answers the Character you give him, I shall wish your Alliance more than that of any Gentleman in *Great Britain*, and so your Servant.   [*Exit.*

Sir J. Bev. He is gone, in a Way but barely Civil; but his great Wealth, and the Merit of his only Child, the Heiress of it, are not to be lost for a little Peevishness——
                                                                                94

Enter Humphrey.

Oh! *Humphrey*, you are come in a seasonable Minute; I want to talk to thee, and to tell thee, that my Head and Heart are on the Rack, about my Son.

Humph. Sir, you may trust his Discretion, I am sure you may.

Sir J. Bev. Why, I do believe I may, and yet I'm in a thousand Fears, when I lay this vast Wealth before me: When I consider his Prepossessions, either generous, to a Folly, in an honourable Love; or abandon'd, past Redemption, in a vicious One; and, from one or the other, his Insensibility to the fairest Prospect, towards doubling our Estate: a Father, who knows how useful Wealth is, and how necessary, even to those who despise it, I say a Father, *Humphrey*, a Father cannot bear it.   105

Humph. Be not transported, Sir; you will grow incapable of taking any Resolution, in your perplexity.

Sir J. Bev. Yet, as angry as I am with him, I would not have him surpriz'd in any thing———This Mercantile rough Man may go grosly into the Examination of this matter, and talk to the Gentlewoman so as to———

Humph. No, I hope, not in an abrupt manner.

Sir J. Bev. No, I hope not! Why, dost thou know any thing of her, or of him, or of any thing of it, or all of it?   113

Humph. My dear Master, I know so much; that I told him this very Day, you had Reason to be secretly out of Humour about her.

Sir J. Bev. Did you go so far? Well, what said he to that?

Humph. His Words were, looking upon me stedfastly: *Humphrey*, says he,
That Woman is a Woman of Honour.   120

Sir J. Bev. How! Do you think he is married to her, or designs to marry
her?

Humph. I can say nothing to the latter———But he says, he can marry no
one without your Consent, while you are living.

Sir J. Bev. If he said so much, I know he scorns to break his Word with me.

Humph. I am sure of that.

Sir J. Bev. You are sure of that———Well! that's some Comfort———Then
I have nothing to do but to see the bottom of this matter, during this present
Ruffle———Oh, *Humphrey*———

Humph. You are not ill, I hope, Sir.

Sir J. Bev. Yes, a Man is very ill, that's in a very ill Humour: To be a
Father, is to be in Care for one, whom you oftner disoblige, than please, by
that very Care———Oh! that Sons could know the Duty to a Father, before
they themselves are Fathers———But, perhaps, you'll say now, that I am
one of the happiest Fathers in the World; but, I assure you, that of the very
happiest is not a Condition to be envied.   134

Humph. Sir, your Pain arises, not from the Thing it self, but your particular Sense of it———You are over-fond, nay, give me leave to say, you are
unjustly apprehensive from your Fondness: My Master *Bevil* never dis-
oblig'd you, and he will, I know he will, do every thing you ought to expect.

Sir J. Bev. He won't take all this Money with this Girl———For ought I
know, he will, forsooth, have so much Moderation, as to think he ought not
to force his Liking for any Consideration.   141

Humph. He is to marry her, not you; he is to live with her, not you, Sir.

Sir J. Bev. I know not what to think: But, I know, nothing can be more
miserable than to be in this Doubt.—Follow me; I must come to some
Resolution.   [*Exeunt.*

SCENE, Bevil *junior's Lodgings.*

Enter Tom *and* Phillis.

Tom. Well, Madam, if you must speak with Mr. *Myrtle*, you shall; he is
now with my Master in the Library.

Phil. But you must leave me alone with him, for he can't make me a Present, nor I so handsomly take any thing from him, before you; it would not be
decent.

Tom. It will be very decent, indeed, for me to retire, and leave my Mistress
with another Man.   7

127 Ruffle] Upheaval, commotion.

Phil. He is a Gentleman, and will treat one properly——

Tom. I believe so—but, however, I won't be far off, and therefore will venture to trust you: I'll call him to you.   [*Exit* Tom.

Phil. What a deal of Pother, and Sputter here is, between my Mistress, and Mr. *Myrtle*, from meer Punctilio? I could any hour of the Day get her to her Lover, and would do it———But she, forsooth, will allow no Plot to get him; but, if he can come to her, I know she would be glad of it: I must therefore do her an acceptable Violence, and surprize her into his Arms. I am sure I go by the best Rule imaginable: If she were my Maid, I should think her the best Servant in the World for doing so by me.   17

Enter Myrtle *and* Tom.

Oh Sir! You and Mr. *Bevil* are fine Gentlemen, to let a Lady remain under such Difficulties as my poor Mistress, and no Attempt to set her at Liberty, or release her from the Danger of being instantly married to *Cimberton*.

Myrt. Tom has been telling———But what is to be done?   21

Phil. What is to be done———when a Man can't come at his Mistress! ———Why, can't you fire our House, or the next House to us, to make us run out and you take us?

Myrt. How, Mrs. *Phillis*———

Phil. Ay——let me see that Rogue deny to fire a House, make a Riot, or any other little thing, when there were no other Way to come at me.

Tom. I am oblig'd to you, Madam.

Phil. Why, don't we hear every day of People's hanging themselves for Love, and won't they venture the Hazard of being hang'd for Love?—Oh! were I a Man——   31

Myrt. What manly thing would you have me undertake? according to your Ladyship's Notion of a Man.

Phil. Only be at once, what, one Time or other, you may be, and wish to be, or must be.

Myrt. Dear Girl, talk plainly to me, and consider, I, in my Condition, can't be in very good Humour—you say, to be at once what I must be.

Phil. Ay, ay,——I mean no more than to be an old Man; I saw you do it very well at the Masquerade: In a Word, old Sir *Geoffry Cimberton* is every Hour expected in Town, to join in the Deeds and Settlements for marrying Mr. *Cimberton*——He is half blind, half lame, half deaf, half dumb; tho', as to his Passions and Desires, he is as warm and ridiculous as when in the Heat of Youth.———   43

Tom. Come to the Business, and don't keep the Gentleman in Suspense for the Pleasure of being courted, as you serve me.

11 Pother, and Sputter] Fuss and clamour. 12 meer Punctilio] Over-nicety, over-scrupulousness. 26 that Rogue] That is, indicating Tom.

Phil. I saw you at the Masquerade act such a one to Perfection; Go, and put on that very Habit, and come to our House as Sir *Geoffry*. There is not one there, but my self, knows his Person; I was born in the Parish where he is Lord of the Manor. I have seen him often and often at Church in the Country. Do not hesitate; but come thither; they will think you bring a certain Security against Mr. *Myrtle*, and you bring Mr. *Myrtle*; leave the rest to me, I leave this with you, and expect—They don't, I told you, know you; they think you out of Town, which you had as good be for ever, if you lose this Opportunity.——I must be gone; I know I am wanted at home.

Myrt. My dear *Phillis*! [*Catches and kisses her, and gives her Money.*

Phil. O Fie! my Kisses are not my own; you have committed Violence; but I'll carry 'em to the right Owner. [*Tom kisses her*] Come, see me down Stairs, [*to* Tom] and leave the Lover to think of his last Game for the Prize.
          [*Exeunt* Tom *and* Phillis.

Myrt. I think I will instantly attempt this wild Expedient——The Extravagance of it will make me less suspected, and it will give me Opportunity to assert my own Right to *Lucinda*, without whom I cannot live: But I am so mortify'd at this Conduct of mine, towards poor *Bevil*; He must think meanly of me——I know not how to reassume my self, and be in Spirit enough, for such an Adventure as this——Yet I must attempt it, if it be only to be near *Lucinda*, under Her present Perplexities; and sure——

   The next Delight to Transport, with the Fair,   66
   Is to relieve her, in her hours of Care.   [*Exit.*

      End of the Fourth ACT.

The Conscious Lovers.

ACT V. SCENE I.

SCENE, *Sealand*'s House.

Enter Phillis, *with Lights, before* Myrtle, *disguis'd like old Sir* Geoffry; *supported by Mrs.* Sealand, Lucinda, *and* Cimberton.

Mrs. Seal. NOW I have seen you thus far, Sir *Geoffry*, will you excuse me a Moment, while I give my necessary Orders for your Accommodation?   [*Ex. Mrs.* Seal.

Myrt. I have not seen you, Cousin *Cimberton*, since you were ten Years

58 his last Game for the Prize] The final intrigue to achieve his purpose.

old; and as it is incumbent on you, to keep up our Name and Family, I shall, upon very reasonable Terms, join with you, in a Settlement to that purpose. Tho' I must tell you, Cousin this is the first Merchant that has married into our House.

Luc. Deuce on 'em! am I a Merchant, because my Father is?   [*Aside.*

Myrt. But is he directly a Trader, at this time?   10

Cimb. There's no hiding the Disgrace, Sir; he trades to all parts of the World.

Myrt. We never had one of our Family before, who descended from Persons that did any thing.

Cimb. Sir, since it is a Girl that they have, I am, for the Honour of my Family, willing to take it in again; and to sink her into our Name, and no harm done.

Myrt. 'Tis prudently, and generously resolv'd—Is this the young thing?

Cimb. Yes, Sir.

Phil. Good Madam, don't be out of Humour, but let them run to the utmost of their Extravagance—Hear them out.   21

Myrt. Can't I see her nearer? My Eyes are but weak.

Phil. Beside, I am sure the Unkle has something worth your Notice. I'll take care to get off the young one, and leave you to observe what may be wrought out of the old one, for your good.   [*Exit.*

Cimb. Madam, this old Gentleman, your Great Unkle, desires to be introduced to you, and to see you nearer!——Approach, Sir.

Myrt. By your leave, young Lady——[*Puts on Spectacles.*]—Cousin *Cimberton*! She has exactly that sort of Neck, and Bosom, for which my Sister *Gertrude* was so much admired, in the Year sixty one, before the *French* Dresses first discovered any thing in Women, below the Chin.

Luc. [*Aside.*] What a very odd Situation am I in? Tho' I cannot but be diverted, at the extravagance of their Humours, equally unsuitable to their Age—Chin, quotha——I don't believe my passionate Lover there knows whether I have one or not. Ha! ha!   35

Myrt. Madam, I would not willingly offend, but I have a better Glass——   [*Pulls out a large one.*

Enter Phillis *to* Cimberton.

Phil. Sir, my Lady desires to shew the Apartment to you, that she intends for Sir *Geoffry*.

Cimb. Well Sir! by that time you have sufficiently gazed, and sunned your self in the Beauties of my Spouse there, I will wait on you again.   41

[*Ex.* Cimb. *and* Phil.

Myrt. Were it not, Madam, that I might be troublesome, there is something

37 Glass] Magnifying glass.

of Importance, tho' we are alone, which I would say more safe from being heard.

Luc. There is something, in this old Fellow methinks, that raises my Curiosity.

Myrt. To be free, Madam, I as heartily contemn this Kinsman of mine, as you do, and am sorry to see so much Beauty and Merit devoted, by your Parents, to so insensible a Possessor.

Luc. Surprizing!—I hope then, Sir, you will not contribute to the Wrong you are so generous as to pity, whatever may be the Interest of your Family.

Myrt. This Hand of mine shall never be employ'd, to sign any thing, against your Good and Happiness.   35

Luc. I am sorry, Sir, it is not in my Power to make you proper Acknowledgments; but there is a Gentleman in the World, whose Gratitude will, I am sure, be worthy of the Favour.

Myr. All the Thanks I desire, Madam, are in your Power to give.

Luc. Name them, and Command them.

Myr. Only, Madam, that the first time you are alone with your Lover, you will, with open Arms, receive him.   60

Luc. As willingly as his Heart could wish it.

Myr. Thus then he claims your Promise! O *Lucinda*!

Luc. O! a Cheat! a Cheat! a Cheat!

Myr. Hush! 'tis I, 'tis I, your Lover, *Myrtle* himself, Madam.

Luc. O bless me! what a Rashness, and Folly to surprize me so——But hush——my Mother——

Enter Mrs. Sealand, Cimberton, *and* Phillis.

Mrs. Seal. How now! what's the matter?

Luc. O Madam! as soon as you left the Room, my Uncle fell into a sudden Fit, and—and—so I cry'd out for help, to support him, and conduct him to his Chamber.   70

Mrs. Seal. That was kindly done! Alas! Sir, how do you find your self?

Myr. Never was taken, in so odd a way in my Life——pray lead me! Oh! I was talking here——(*pray carry me*) to my Cousin *Cimberton's* young Lady——

Mrs. Seal. [*Aside.*] My Cousin *Cimberton's* young Lady! How zealous he is, even in his Extremity, for the Match! a right *Cimberton*.

[Cimberton *and* Lucinda *lead him, as one in Pain*, &c.

Cimb. Pox! Uncle, you will pull my Ear off.

Luc. Pray Uncle! you will squeeze me to Death.

Mrs. Seal. No matter, no matter——he knows not what he does. Come, Sir, shall I help you out?   81

Myr. By no means; I'll trouble no body, but my young Cousins here.

[They lead him off.

Phil. But pray, Madam, does your Ladyship intend that Mr. *Cimberton* shall really marry my young Mistress at last? I don't think he likes her.

Mrs. Seal. That's not material! Men of his Speculation are above Desires ——but be it as it may; now I have given old Sir *Geoffry* the Trouble of coming up to Sign and Seal, with what Countenance can I be off?

Phil. As well as with twenty others, Madam; It is the Glory and Honour of a Great Fortune, to live in continual Treaties, and still to break off: it looks Great, Madam.   90

Mrs. Seal. True, *Phillis*——yet to return our Blood again into the *Cimberton*'s, is an Honour not to be rejected——but were not you saying, that Sir *John Bevil*'s Creature *Humphrey* has been with Mr. *Sealand*?

Phil. Yes, Madam; I overheard them agree, that Mr. *Sealand* should go himself, and visit this unknown Lady that Mr. *Bevil* is so great with; and if he found nothing there to fright him, that Mr. *Bevil* should still marry my young Mistress.

Mrs. Seal. How! nay then he shall find she is my Daughter, as well as his: I'll follow him this Instant, and take the whole Family along with me: The disputed Power of Disposing of my own Daughter shall be at an end this very Night——I'll live no longer in Anxiety for a little Hussey, that hurts my Appearance, wherever I carry her: and, for whose sake, I seem to be at all regarded, and that in the best of my Days.   103

Phil. Indeed, Madam, if she were married, your Ladyship might very well be taken for Mr. *Sealand*'s Daughter.

Mrs. Seal. Nay, when the Chit has not been with me, I have heard the Men say as much——I'll no longer cut off the greatest Pleasure of a Woman's Life, (the shining in Assemblies) by her Forward Anticipation of the Respect, that's due to her Superior——she shall down to *Cimberton-Hall*——she shall——she shall.   110

Phil. I hope, Madam, I shall stay with your Ladyship.

Mrs. Seal. Thou shalt, *Phillis*, and I'll place thee then more about me.—— But order Chairs immediately——I'll be gone this Minute.   [*Exeunt.*

SCENE, *Charing-Cross.*

Enter Mr. Sealand, *and* Humphrey.

Mr. Seal. I am very glad, Mr. *Humphrey*, that you agree with me, that it is for our Common Good, I should look thoroughly into this Matter.

Humph. I am, indeed, of that Opinion; for there is no Artifice, nothing

85 Speculation] Vision, understanding.

concealed, in our Family, which ought in Justice to be known; I need not desire you, Sir, to treat the Lady with Care and Respect.

Mr. Seal. Master *Humphrey*—I shall not be rude, tho' I design to be a little abrupt, and come into the Matter at once, to see how she will bear, upon a Surprize.

Humph. That's the Door, Sir I wish you Success—[*While* Humphrey *speaks*, Sealand *consults his Table-Book*] I am less concern'd what happens there, because I hear Mr. *Myrtle* is well-lodg'd, as old Sir *Geoffry*, so I am willing to let this Gentleman employ himself here, to give them time at home: for I am sure, 'tis necessary for the Quiet of our Family, *Lucinda* were disposed of, out of it, since Mr. *Bevil's* Inclination is so much otherwise engaged.   [*Exit.*

Mr. Seal. I think this is the Door——[*Knocks*] I'll carry this Matter with an Air of Authority, to enquire, tho' I make an Errand, to begin Discourse. [*Knocks again, and Enter a Foot-Boy.*] So young Man! is your Lady within?

Boy. Alack, Sir! I am but a Country Boy——I dant know, whether she is, or noa: but an you'll stay a bit, I'll goa, and ask the Gentlewoman that's with her.   21

Mr. Seal. Why, Sirrah, tho' you are a Country Boy, you can see, can't you? you know whether she is at home, when you see her, don't you?

Boy. Nay, nay, I'm not such a Country Lad neither, Master, to think she's at home, because I see her: I have been in Town but a Month, and I lost one Place already, for believing my own Eyes.

Mr. Seal. Why, Sirrah! have you learnt to lie already?

Boy. Ah! Master! things that are Lies in the Country, are not Lies at *London*——I begin to know my Business a little better than so——but an you please to walk in, I'll call a Gentlewoman to you, that can tell you for certain——she can make bold to ask my Lady her self.   31

Mr. Seal. O! then, she is within, I find, tho' you dare not say so.

Boy. Nay, nay! that's neither here, nor there: what's matter, whether she is within or no, if she has not a mind to see any Body?

Mr. Seal. I can't tell, Sirrah, whether you are Arch, or Simple, but however get me a direct Answer, and here's a Shilling for you.

Boy. Will you please to walk in, I'll see what I can do for you.

Mr. Seal. I see you will be fit for your Business, in time, Child. But I expect to meet with nothing but Extraordinaries, in such a House.

Boy. Such a House! Sir, you han't seen it yet: Pray walk in.   40

Mr. Seal. Sir, I'll wait upon you.   [*Exeunt.*

---

s.d. *Table-Book*] Pocket-book for memoranda.   17 make] Make up, counterfeit.
35 Arch] Cunning.

SCENE, Indiana's *House.*

Enter Isabella.

Isab. What Anxiety do I feel for this poor Creature! What will be the End of her? Such a languishing unreserv'd Passion, for a Man, that at last must certainly leave, or ruin her! and perhaps both! then the Aggravation of the Distress is, that she does not believe he will————not but, I must own, if they are both what they would seem, they are made for one another, as much as *Adam* and *Eve* were, for there is no other, of their Kind, but themselves.

Enter Boy.

So *Daniel*! what News with you?

Boy. Madam, there's a Gentleman below would speak with my Lady.

Isab. Sirrah! don't you know Mr. *Bevil* yet?   10

Boy. Madam, 'tis not the Gentleman who comes every Day, and asks for you, and won't go in till he knows whether you are with her or no.

Isab. Ha! that's a Particular I did not know before: Well! be it who it will, let him come up to me.   [*Ex.* Boy; *and re-enters with Mr.* Sealand.

Isabella *looks amaz'd!*

Mr. Seal. Madam, I can't blame your being a little surpriz'd, to see a perfect Stranger make a Visit, and————

Isab. I am indeed surpriz'd!————I see he does not know me.

Mr. Seal. You are very prettily lodg'd here, Madam; in troth you seem to have every thing in Plenty————a Thousand a Year, I warrant you, upon this pretty Nest of Rooms, and the dainty One within them.   20

[*Aside, and looking about.*

Isab. [*Apart.*] Twenty Years, it seems, have less Effect in the Alteration of a Man of Thirty, than of a Girl of Fourteen—he's almost still the same; but alas! I find, by other Men, as well as himself, I am not what I was————As soon as he spoke, I was convinc'd 'twas He—How shall I contain my Surprize and Satisfaction! he must not know me yet.

Mr. Seal. Madam, I hope I don't give you any Disturbance; But there is a young Lady here, with whom I have a particular Business to discourse, and I hope she will admit me to that Favour.

Isab. Why, Sir, have you had any Notice concerning her? I wonder who could give it you.   30

Mr. Seal. That, Madam, is fit only to be communicated to herself.

Isab. Well, Sir! you shall see her:————I find he knows nothing yet, nor shall from me: I am resolv'd, I will observe this Interlude, this Sport of

Nature, and of Fortune.——You shall see her presently, Sir; For now I am as a Mother, and will trust her with you.   [*Exit.*

Mr. Seal. As a Mother! right; that's the old Phrase, for one of those Commode Ladies, who lend out Beauty, for Hire, to young Gentlemen that have pressing Occasions. But here comes the precious Lady her self. In troth a very sightly Woman——

Enter Indiana.

Ind. I am told, Sir, you have some Affair that requires your speaking with me.   41

Mr. Seal. Yes, Madam: There came to my Hands a Bill drawn by Mr. *Bevil*, which is payable tomorrow; and he, in the Intercourse of Business, sent it to me, who have Cash of his, and desired me to send a Servant with it; but I have made bold to bring you the Money my self.

Ind. Sir! was that necessary?

Mr. Seal. No, Madam; but, to be free with you, the Fame of your Beauty, and the Regard, which Mr. *Bevil* is a little too well known to have for you, excited my Curiosity.

Ind. Too well known to have for me! Your sober Appearance, Sir, which my Friend describ'd, made me expect no Rudeness, or Absurdity, at least ——Who's there? Sir, if you pay the Money to a Servant, 'twill be as well.

Mr. Seal. Pray, Madam, be not offended; I came hither on an Innocent, nay a Virtuous Design; and, if you will have Patience to hear me, it may be as useful to you, as you are in a Friendship with Mr. *Bevil*, as to my only Daughter, whom I was this Day disposing of.   56

Ind. You make me hope, Sir, I have mistaken you; I am composed again; be free, say on—what I am afraid to hear——   [*Aside.*

Mr. Seal. I fear'd, indeed, an unwarranted Passion here, but I did not think it was in Abuse of so worthy an Object, so accomplish'd a Lady, as your Sense and Mien bespeak——but the Youth of our Age care not what Merit and Virtue they bring to Shame, so they gratify——   62

Ind. Sir—you are going into very great Errors—but, as you are pleas'd to say you see something in me that has chang'd, at least, the Colour of your Suspicions; so has your Appearance alter'd mine, and made me earnestly attentive to what has any way concern'd you, to enquire into my Affairs, and Character.

Mr. Seal. How sensibly! with what an Air she Talks!

Ind. Good Sir, be seated——and tell me tenderly——keep all your Suspicions concerning me alive, that you may in a proper and prepared way ——acquaint me why the Care of your Daughter obliges a Person of your seeming Worth and Fortune, to be thus inquisitive about a wretched, help-

37 Commode Ladies] Accommodating ladies—that is, bawds.

less, friendless———[*weeping*.] But I beg your Pardon—tho' I am an
Orphan, your Child is not; and your Concern for her, it seems, has brought
you hither——I'll be composed—pray go on, Sir. 75

Mr. Seal. How could Mr. *Bevil* be such a Monster, to injure such a
Woman?

Ind. No, Sir—you wrong him—he has not injur'd me—my Support is
from his Bounty.

Mr. Seal. Bounty! when Gluttons give high Prices for Delicates, they are
prodigious Bountiful. 81

Ind. Still, still you will persist in that Error——But my own Fears tell me
all—You are the Gentleman, I suppose, for whose happy Daughter he is
design'd a Husband, by his good Father; and he has, perhaps, consented to
the Overture: He was here this Morning, dress'd beyond his usual Plainness,
nay most sumptuously—and he is to be, perhaps, this Night a Bridegroom.

Mr. Seal. I own he was intended such: But, Madam, on your Account, I
have determin'd to defer my Daughter's Marriage, till I am satisfied from
your own Mouth, of what Nature are the Obligations you are under to
him. 90

Ind. His Actions, Sir, his Eyes have only made me think, he design'd to
make me the Partner of his Heart. The Goodness and Gentleness of his
Demeanour made me misinterpret all———'Twas my own Hope, my own
Passion, that deluded me———he never made one Amorous Advance to
me———His large Heart, and bestowing Hand, have only helpt the Miserable: Nor know I why, but from his mere Delight in Virtue, that I have been
his Care, the Object on which to indulge and please himself, with pouring
Favours.

Mr. Seal. Madam, I know not why it is, but I, as well as you, am methinks
afraid of entring into the Matter I came about; but 'tis the same thing, as if
we had talk'd never so distinctly——he ne'er shall have a Daughter of
mine. 102

Ind. If you say this from what you think of me, you wrong your self and
him——Let not me, miserable tho' I may be, do Injury to my Benefactor
——No, Sir, my Treatment ought rather to reconcile you to his Virtues——
If to bestow, without a Prospect of Return; if to delight in supporting, what
might, perhaps, be thought an Object of Desire, with no other View than to
be her Guard against those who would not be so disinterested; if these
Actions, Sir, can in a careful Parent's Eye commend him to a Daughter, give
yours, Sir, give her to my honest, generous *Bevil*——What have I to do,
but sigh, and weep, to rave, run wild, a Lunatick in Chains, or hid in Dark-
ness, mutter in distracted Starts, and broken Accents, my strange, strange
Story! 113

Mr. Seal. Take Comfort, Madam.

Ind. All my Comfort must be to expostulate in Madness, to relieve with Frenzy my Despair, and shrieking to demand of Fate, why—why was I born to such Variety of Sorrows?

Mr. Seal. If I have been the least Occasion———

Ind. No———'twas Heaven's high Will, I should be such—to be plunder'd in my Cradle! Toss'd on the Seas! and even there, an Infant Captive! to lose my Mother, hear but of my Father—To be adopted! lose my Adopter! then plung'd again in worse Calamities!   122

Mr. Seal. An Infant Captive!

Ind. Yet then! to find the most Charming of Mankind, once more to set me free, (from what I thought the last Distress) to load me with his Services, his Bounties, and his Favours; to support my very Life, in a way, that stole, at the same time, my very Soul it self from me.

Mr. Seal. And has young *Bevil* been this worthy Man?

Ind. Yet then again, this very Man to take another! without leaving me the Right, the Pretence of easing my fond Heart with Tears! For oh! I can't reproach him, though the same Hand that rais'd me to this Height, now throws me down the Precipice.   132

Mr. Seal. Dear Lady! O yet one Moment's Patience: my Heart grows full with your Affliction: But yet, there's something in your Story that———

Ind. My Portion here is Bitterness, and Sorrow.

Mr. Seal. Do not think so: Pray answer me: Does *Bevil* know your Name, and Family?

Ind. Alas! too well! O, could I be any other Thing, than what I am———I'll tear away all Traces of my former Self, my little Ornaments, the Remains of my first State, the Hints of what I ought to have been———   140

[*In her Disorder she throws away a Bracelet, which*
Sealand *takes up, and looks earnestly on it.*

Mr. Seal. Ha! what's this? my Eyes are not deceiv'd? It is, it is the same! the very Bracelet which I bequeath'd my Wife, at our last mournful Parting.

Ind. What said you, Sir! Your Wife! Whither does my Fancy carry me? What means this unfelt Motion at my Heart? And yet again my Fortune but deludes me; for if I err not, Sir, your Name is *Sealand*: But my lost Father's Name was———

Mr. Seal. Danvers! was it not?

Ind. What new Amazement! That is indeed my Family.

Mr. Seal. Know then, when my Misfortunes drove me to the *Indies*, for Reasons too tedious now to mention, I chang'd my Name of *Danvers* into *Sealand*.   151

Enter Isabella.

Isab. If yet there wants an Explanation of your Wonder, examine well this

Face, (yours, Sir, I well remember) gaze on, and read, in me, your Sister *Isabella*!

Mr. Seal. My Sister!

Isab. But here's a Claim more tender yet———your *Indiana*, Sir, your long lost Daughter.

Mr. Seal. O my Child! my Child!

Ind. All-Gracious Heaven! is it possible! do I embrace my Father!

Seal. And I do hold thee———These Passions are too strong for Utterance ———Rise, rise, my Child, and give my Tears their Way———O my Sister!

[Embracing her.

Isab. Now, dearest Neice, my groundless Fears, my painful Cares no more shall vex thee. If I have wrong'd thy noble Lover with too hard Suspicions; my just Concern for thee, I hope, will plead my Pardon.   164

Mr. Seal. O! make him then the full Amends, and be your self the Messenger of Joy: Fly this Instant! tell him all these wondrous Turns of Providence in his Favour! Tell him I have now a Daughter to bestow, which he no longer will decline: that this Day he still shall be a Bridegroom: nor shall a Fortune, the Merit which his Father seeks, be wanting: tell him the Reward of all his Virtues waits on his Acceptance.   *[Exit.* Isab

My dearest *Indiana*!   *[Turns, and embraces her.*

Ind. Have I then at last a Father's Sanction on my Love! His bounteous Hand to give, and make my Heart a Present worthy of *Bevil*'s Generosity?

Mr. Seal. O my Child! how are our Sorrows past o'erpaid by such a Meeting! Though I have lost so many Years of soft paternal Dalliance with thee, Yet, in one Day, to find thee thus, and thus bestow thee, in such perfect Happiness! is ample! ample Reparation! And yet again the Merit of thy Lover.

Ind. O! had I Spirits left to tell you of his Actions! how strongly Filial Duty has suppressed his Love; and how Concealment still has doubled all his Obligations; the Pride, the Joy of his Alliance, Sir, would warm your Heart, as he has conquer'd mine.   182

Mr. Seal. How laudable is Love, when born of Virtue!
I burn to embrace him———

Ind. See, Sir, my Aunt already has succeeded, and brought him to your Wishes.

Enter Isabella, *with Sir* John Bevil, Bevil *jun.* Mrs. Sealand,
Cimberton, Myrtle, *and* Lucinda.

Sir J. Bev. [*Entring*] Where! where's this Scene of Wonder!———Mr. *Sealand*, I congratulate, on this Occasion, our mutual Happiness———Your good Sister, Sir, has, with the Story of your Daughter's Fortune, fill'd us with Surprize and Joy! Now all Exceptions are remov'd; my Son has now avow'd

his Love, and turn'd all former Jealousies and Doubts to Approbation, and, I
am told, your Goodness has consented to reward him.   192

Mr. Seal. If, Sir, a Fortune equal to his Father's Hopes, can make this
Object worthy his Acceptance.

Bev. jun. I hear your Mention, Sir, of Fortune, with Pleasure only, as it
may prove the Means to reconcile the best of Fathers to my Love————Let
him be Provident, but let me be Happy————My ever-destin'd, my
acknowledg'd Wife!   [*Embracing* Indiana.

Ind. Wife!————O! my ever loved! my Lord! my Master!

Sir J. Bev. I congratulate my self, as well as you, that I had a Son, who
could, under such Disadvantages, discover your great Merit.   201

Mr. Seal. O! Sir *John*! how vain, how weak is Humane Prudence? What
Care, what Foresight, what Imagination could contrive such blest Events, to
make our Children happy, as Providence in one short Hour has laid before
us?

Cimb. [*To Mrs.* Sealand] I am afraid, Madam, Mr. *Sealand* is a little too
busy for our Affair, if you please we'll take another Opportunity.

Mrs. Seal. Let us have patience, Sir.

Cimb. But we make Sir *Geoffry* wait, Madam.

Myrt. O Sir! I am not in haste.

> *During this*, Bev. *jun. presents* Lucinda *to* Indiana.
> 210

Mr. Seal. But here! here's our general Benefactor! Excellent young Man,
that could be, at once, a Lover to her Beauty, and a Parent to her Virtue.

Bev. jun. If you think That an Obligation, Sir, give me leave to overpay
my self, in the only Instance, that can now add to my Felicity, by begging you
to bestow this Lady on Mr. *Myrtle.*

Mr. Seal. She is his without reserve, (I beg he may be sent for)————Mr.
Cimberton, notwithstanding you never had my Consent, yet there is, since I
last saw you, another Objection to your Marriage with my Daughter.

Cimb. I hope, Sir, your Lady has conceal'd nothing from me?

Mr. Seal. Troth, Sir! nothing but what was conceal'd from my self;
another Daughter, who has an undoubted Title to half my Estate.   221

Cimb. How! Mr. *Sealand*! why then if half Mrs. *Lucinda*'s Fortune is gone,
you can't say, that any of my Estate is settled upon her: I was in Treaty for
the whole; but if that is not to be come at, to be sure, there can be no Bargain,
————Sir,————I have nothing to do but to take my leave of your good
Lady, my Cousin, and beg Pardon for the Trouble I have given this Old
Gentleman.

Myrt. That you have, Mr. *Cimberton*, with all my Heart.

[*Discovers himself.*

Omn. Mr. *Myrtle*!

Myrt. And I beg Pardon of the whole Company, that I assumed the Person
of Sir *Geoffry*, only to be present at the Danger of this Lady's being disposed

of, and in her utmost Exigence to assert my Right to her: Which if her
Parents will ratifie, as they once favour'd my Pretensions, no Abatement of
Fortune shall lessen her Value to me.   234

Luc. Generous Man!

Mr. Seal. If, Sir, you can overlook the Injury of being in Treaty with one,
who as meanly left her, as you have generously asserted your Right in her, she
is Yours.

Luc. Mr. *Myrtle,* tho' you have ever had my Heart, yet now I find I love
you more, because I bring you less.   240

Myrt. We have much more than we want, and I am glad any Event has
contributed to the Discovery of our real Inclinations to each other.

Mrs. Seal. Well! however I'm glad the Girl's disposed of any way.

　　　　　　　　　　　　　　　　　　　　　　　　　　　　[Aside.

Bev. Myrtle! no longer Rivals now, but Brothers.

Myrt. Dear *Bevil!* you are born to triumph over me! but now our Competi-
tion ceases: I rejoyce in the Preheminence of your Virtue, and your Alliance
adds Charms to *Lucinda.*

Sir J. Bev. Now, Ladies and Gentlemen, you have set the World a fair
Example: Your Happiness is owing to your Constancy and Merit: And the
several Difficulties you have struggled with, evidently shew   250

> Whate'er the generous Mind it self denies,
> The secret Care of Providence supplies.   *[Exeunt.*

EPILOGUE,

By Mr. *WELSTED*.

Intended to be Spoken by *Indiana*.

O<small>UR</small> *Author, whom Intreaties cannot move,*
 Spight of the Dear Coquetry that you love,
Swears he'll not frustrate (so he plainly means)
By a loose Epilogue, his decent Scenes.
Is it not, Sirs, hard Fate I meet To-day,
To keep me Rigid Still beyond the Play?
And yet I'm sav'd a World of Pains that way.
I now can look, I now can move at Ease,
Nor need I torture these poor Limbs, to please;
Nor with the Hand or Foot attempt Surprize,   10
Nor wrest my Features, nor fatigue my Eyes:
Bless me! What freakish Gambols have I play'd!
What Motions try'd, and wanton Looks betray'd!
Out of pure Kindness all! to Over-rule
The threaten'd Hiss, and screen some scribling Fool.
With more Respect I'm entertain'd To-night:
Our Author thinks, I can with Ease delight.
My Artless Looks while modest Graces arm,
He says, I need but to appear; and charm.
A Wife so form'd, by these Examples bred,   20
Pours Joy and Gladness 'round the Marriage Bed;
Soft Source of Comfort, kind Relief from Care,
And 'tis her least Perfection to be Fair.
The Nymph with Indiana's *Worth who vies,*
A Nation will behold with Bevil's *Eyes.*

FINIS.

Intended to be Spoken by *Indiana*] The Epilogue actually spoken by Mrs. Oldfield was
written by Benjamin Victor, and first published in his *Epistle to Sir Richard Steele*, 1722.

THE
BEGGAR'S OPERA

John Gay

1685–1732

It was scarcely Gay's fault that his *Beggar's Opera*, first performed at Lincoln's Inn Fields on 29 January 1728, should have spawned a host of third-rate imitations—still less that his ballad-play is now more often set in prettified prisons than in a truly vicious criminal underworld made ironically more real by its touches of mock-pastoral. But it remains to his credit that he freed comedy almost overnight from its sentimental straitjacket. True, most aspiring dramatists continued to wear that comfortable corset from choice. But it was the unprecedented success of Gay's irregular entertainment— which he could only get staged at a theatre usually given over to pantomime— that enabled such writers as Fielding, Henry Carey, and Robert Dodsley to follow in his experimental footsteps, and to prove that comedy need not be exclusively concerned with love-chases in five acts, but might exploit the possibilities of the social and political situation, and seek freer, less stereo-typed forms for the purpose.

Of course, *The Conscious Lovers* had resonated with social significance, in its assurance of the superiority of middle class to aristocratic values. But Steele's play had simply *defined* a changed social order—and satisfied a new theatrical audience, with its demonstration that comedy could as well be bourgeois as genteel. *The Beggar's Opera*, on the other hand, totally inverted social and moral norms, throwing political and polite society into a new and harsh perspective in the process. That the most successful translator of politics into performance in our own century, Bertolt Brecht, should have adapted Gay's work into his *Threepenny Opera* was thus triply appropriate. It confirmed the strength of the tradition which Gay established of musical drama as a form quite distinct from opera. It suggested the social purpose underlying *The Beggar's Opera* itself, which was revolutionary in implication if not in intention. And it utilized just such techniques of modifying and merging existing methods and materials as Gay had himself adopted.

Thus, no simple label can sum up *The Beggar's Opera*. Its intention of ridiculing Italian opera has perhaps been overstated, but almost every other aim ever attributed to the piece can be justified from its text. It attacked Walpole, cunningly because ambiguously—never absolutely identifying him with any single villain. It parodied poetic justice, by exaggerating its arbitrariness and, of course, by inverting it. It gave a healthy jolt to lazy minds by presenting the lowest of low life as a microcosm of society. And, more positively, it put well-known ballad tunes to its own uses, ignoring the categories by which dramatists had increasingly tended to let their work be confined. It is comedy, farce, satire, ballad-play, and burlesque all at once: it is *The Beggar's Opera*.

The time-honoured anecdote that Swift suggested the idea of a 'Newgate pastoral' to Gay may well make more critical than chronological sense. But as early as 1716, his *Trivia* had shown Gay capable of evoking the everyday life of the London streets in verse, and such plays of about the same period as *The What D'ye Call It* and *Three Hours After Marriage*—the latter too often condemned unread—had proved him a technically capable and refreshingly unorthodox dramatist. He may or may not have been as indolent as tradition holds: in any case, the collected canon of his plays and poems would be a not discreditable life's work for any man. *The Shepherd's Week*, a gloriously forthright mock-pastoral which appeared in 1714, his two series of *Fables*, and his sequel to *The Beggar's Opera*—named after its heroine *Polly*, in which Macheath and several of the *Opera*'s characters are transported to the West Indies—are perhaps most noteworthy among his other pieces. The close friend of Pope, Swift, and Arbuthnot, Gay was in some ways more farsighted, because more detached, than his Scriblerian colleagues. That he was not their inferior in wit, when circumstances combined in his favour, the following pages should amply demonstrate.

The present text of *The Beggar's Opera* follows that of the third edition of 1729. An excellent collected edition of Gay's works, under G. C. Faber's editorship, was added to the Oxford Standard Authors series in 1926, and an undated two-volume edition of his plays has appeared in The Abbey Classics. Both these editions are unfortunately out of print, and neither contains *The Wife of Bath* or *Three Hours After Marriage*. This latter work, together with *The What D'ye Call It*, is included in my own edition of *Burlesque Plays of the Eighteenth Century*, (Oxford Paperbacks, 1969.)

THE
BEGGAR's
OPERA.

As it is Acted at the

THEATRE-ROYAL

IN

LINCOLNS-INN FIELDS.

Written by Mr. *G A Y.*

———— *Nos hæc noviſſimus eſſe nihil.*　　Mart.

The THIRD EDITION:
With the OUVERTURE in SCORE,
The SONGS, *and the* BASSES,
The OUVERTURE and BASSES Compos'd by Dr. *PEPUSCH)*
Curiouſly Engrav'd on COPPER PLATES.

L O N D O N:
Printed for JOHN WATTS, at the Printing-Office in *Wild.*
Court, near *Lincoln's-Inn Fields.*
MDCCXXIX.

F

A

TABLE of the SONGS.

ACT I.

ACT II.

AIR 33. *If you at an office solicit your due.*
     34. *Thus when the Swallow, seeking prey.*
     35. *How happy could I be with either.*
     36. *I'm bubbled.*
     37. *Cease your funning.*
     38. *Why how now, Madam* Flirt.
     39. *No power on earth can e'er divide.*
     40. *I like the Fox shall grieve.*

ACT III.

AIR 41. *When young at the bar you first taught me to score.*
     42. *My love is all madness and folly.*
     43. *Thus gamesters united in friendship,* &c.
     44. *The modes of the court so common are grown.*
     45. *What gudgeons are we men!*
     46. *In the days of my youth I could bill like a Dove,* fa, la, la, &c.
     47. *I'm like a skiff on the ocean tost.*
     48. *When a wife's in her pout.*
     49. *A curse attends that woman's love.*
     50. *Among the men, Coquets we find.*
     51. *Come, sweet lass.*
     52. *Hither, dear husband, turn your eyes.*
     53. *Which way shall I turn me?—*
     54. *When my Hero in court appears.*
     55. *When he holds up his hand, arraign'd for his life.*
     56. *Our selves, like the Great, to secure a retreat.*
     57. *The charge is prepar'd; the Lawyers are met.*
     58. *O cruel, cruel, cruel case.*
     59. *Of all the friends in time of grief.*
     60. *Since I must swing,—I scorn, I scorn to wince or whine.*
     61. *But now again my spirits sink.*
     62. *But valour the stronger grows.*
     63. *If thus—A Man can die.*
     64. *So I drink off this Bumper.—And now I can stand the test.*
     65. *But can I leave my pretty hussies.*
     66. *Their eyes, their lips, their busses.*
     67. *Since laws were made for ev'ry degree.*
     68. *Would I might be hang'd!*
     69. *Thus I stand like the* Turk, *with his doxies around.*

Dramatis Personæ

M E N.

Peachum.		Mr. *Hippesley.*
Lockit.		Mr. *Hall.*
Macheath.		Mr. *Walker.*
Filch.		Mr. *Clark.*
Jemmy Twitcher.		Mr. *H. Bullock.*
Crook-finger'd Jack.		Mr. *Houghton.*
Wat Dreary.		Mr. *Smith.*
Robin *of* Bagshot.	} *Macheath*'s Gang. {	Mr. *Lacy.*
Nimming Ned.		Mr. *Pit.*
Harry Padington.		Mr. *Eaton.*
Mat *of the* Mint.		Mr. *Spiller.*
Ben Budge.		Mr. *Morgan.*
Beggar.		Mr. *Chapman.*
Player.		Mr. *Milward.*

Constables, Drawer, Turnkey, &c.

W O M E N.

Mrs. Peachum.		Mrs. *Martin.*
Polly Peachum.		Miss *Fenton.*
Lucy Lockit.		Mrs. *Egleton.*
Diana Trapes.		Mrs. *Martin.*
Mrs. Coaxer.		Mrs. *Holiday.*
Dolly Trull.		Mrs. *Lacy.*
Mrs. Vixen.		Mrs. *Rice.*
Betty Doxy.	} *Women of the Town.* {	Mrs. *Rogers.*
Jenny Diver.		Mrs. *Clarke.*
Mrs. Slammekin.		Mrs. *Morgan.*
Suky Tawdry.		Mrs. *Palin.*
Molly Brazen.		Mrs. *Sallee.*

INTRODUCTION.

BEGGAR. PLAYER.

BEGGAR.

IF Poverty be a title to Poetry, I am sure no-body can dispute mine. I own myself of the company of Beggars; and I make one at their weekly festivals at St. *Giles*'s. I have a small yearly Salary for my Catches, and am welcome to a dinner there whenever I please, which is more than most Poets can say.

Player. As we live by the Muses, it is but gratitude in us to encourage poetical merit where-ever we find it. The Muses, contrary to all other ladies, pay no distinction to dress, and never partially mistake the pertness of embroidery for wit, nor the modesty of want for dulness. Be the author who he will, we push his Play as far as it will go. So (though you are in want) I wish you success heartily.   10

Beggar. This piece I own was originally writ for the celebrating the marriage of *James Chanter* and *Moll Lay*, two most excellent ballad-singers. I have introduc'd the Similes that are in all your celebrated *Operas*: The *Swallow*, the *Moth*, the *Bee*, the *Ship*, the *Flower*, &c. Besides, I have a prison Scene, which the ladies always reckon charmingly pathetick. As to the parts, I have observ'd such a nice impartiality to our two ladies, that it is impossible for either of them to take offence. I hope I may be forgiven, that I have not made my Opera throughout unnatural, like those in vogue; for I have no Recitative: excepting this, as I have consented to have neither Prologue nor Epilogue, it must be allow'd an Opera in all its forms. The piece indeed hath been heretofore frequently represented by ourselves in our great room at St. *Giles*'s, so that I cannot too often acknowledge your charity in bringing it now on the Stage.   23

Player. But I see 'tis time for us to withdraw; the Actors are preparing to begin. Play away the Ouverture.   [*Exeunt*.

---

2 weekly festivals at St. *Giles*'s] The Parish of St. Giles was among the first to build its own workhouses: but it also contained many cheap lodging-houses frequented by criminals, prostitutes, and receivers of stolen goods. The reference to its 'weekly festivals' is ambiguous. The processions from Newgate to Tyburn were a weekly occurrence—and it was at the Angel tavern, beside St. Giles's Churchyard, that common criminals received their last bowl of ale before proceeding to the gibbet. But festivals of ballad-singing at St. Giles's were customarily an *annual* occasion.   3 Catches] That is, songs in the form of 'rounds'.
12 *James Chanter* and *Moll Lay*] Archetypal names for street ballad-singers.

THE
BEGGAR's OPERA.

ACT I. SCENE I.

SCENE Peachum's *House*.

Peachum *sitting at a Table with a large Book of Accounts before him.*

AIR I. An old woman cloathed in gray.

THROUGH *all the employments of life*
Each neighbour abuses his brother;
Whore and Rogue they call Husband and Wife:
All professions be-rogue one another.
The Priest calls the Lawyer a cheat,
The Lawyer be-knaves the Divine;
And the Statesman, because he's so great,
Thinks his trade as honest as mine.

A Lawyer is an honest employment, so is mine. Like me too he acts in a double capacity, both against Rogues and for 'em; for 'tis but fitting that we should protect and encourage Cheats, since we live by 'em.   11

SCENE II.

PEACHUM, FILCH.

Filch. Sir, black *Moll* hath sent word her tryal comes on in the afternoon, and she hopes you will order matters so as to bring her off.

Peach. Why, she may plead her belly at worst; to my knowledge she hath taken care of that security. But as the wench is very active and industrious, you may satisfy her that I'll soften the evidence.

Filch. Tom Gagg, Sir, is found guilty.   6

Peach. A lazy dog! When I took him the time before, I told him what he

I. ii, 3 she may plead her belly] It was not the custom to hang a pregnant woman: and after the birth of a child, death sentences were frequently commuted to transportation.

would come to if he did not mend his hand. This is death with
I may venture to book him. [*Writes.*] For *Tom Gag*, forty poun
Sly know that I'll save her from Transportation, for I can get
staying in *England.*

Filch. *Betty* hath brought more goods into our Lock to-year than any five
of the gang; and in truth, 'tis a pity to lose so good a customer.   11

Peach. If none of the gang take her off, she may, in the common course of
business, live a twelve-month longer. I love to let women scape. A good
sportsman always lets the Hen-Partridges fly, because the breed of the game
depends upon them. Besides, here the Law allows us no reward; there is
nothing to be got by the death of women——except our wives.

Filch. Without dispute, she is a fine woman! 'Twas to her I was oblig'd
for my education, and (to say a bold word) she hath train'd up more young
fellows to the business than the Gaming-table.   21

Peach. Truly, *Filch*, thy observation is right. We and the Surgeons are
more beholden to women than all the professions besides.

AIR II.   The bonny gray-ey'd morn, &c.

Filch.   *'Tis woman that seduces all mankind,*
        By her we first were taught the wheedling arts:
        Her very eyes can cheat; when most she's kind,
          She tricks us of our money with our hearts.
        For her, like Wolves by night we roam for prey,
          And practise ev'ry fraud to bribe her charms;
        For suits of love, like law, are won by pay,   30
          And Beauty must be fee'd into our arms.

Peach. But make haste to *Newgate*, boy, and let my friends know what I
intend; for I love to make them easy one way or other.

Filch. When a gentleman is long kept in suspence, penitence may break
his spirit ever after. Besides, certainty gives a man a good air upon his tryal,
and makes him risque another without fear or scruple. But I'll away, for 'tis a
pleasure to be the messenger of comfort to friends in affliction.

SCENE III.

PEACHUM.

But 'tis now high time to look about me for a decent Execution against next
Sessions. I hate a lazy rogue, by whom one can get nothing 'till he is hang'd.

12 Lock] A repository for stolen goods.   12 to-year] This year.

A Register of the Gang. [*Reading.*] Crook-finger'd *Jack*. A year and a half in
the service: Let me see how much the stock owes to his industry; one, two,
three, four, five gold Watches, and seven silver ones. A mighty clean-handed
fellow! sixteen Snuff-boxes, five of them of true gold. Six dozen of Handkerchiefs, four silver-hilted Swords, half a dozen of Shirts, three Tye-
perriwigs, and a piece of Broad Cloth. Considering these are only the fruits of
his leisure hours, I don't know a prettier fellow, for no man alive hath a more
engaging presence of mind upon the road. *Wat Dreary*, alias *Brown Will*, an
irregular dog, who hath an underhand way of disposing of his goods. I'll try
him only for a Sessions or two longer upon his good behaviour. *Harry
Padington*, a poor petty-larceny rascal, without the least genius; that fellow,
though he were to live these six months, will never come to the gallows with
any credit. Slippery *Sam*; he goes off the next Sessions, for the villain hath
the impudence to have views of following his trade as a Taylor, which he calls
an honest employment. *Mat* of the *Mint*; listed not above a month ago, a
promising sturdy fellow, and diligent in his way; somewhat too bold and
hasty, and may raise good contributions on the publick, if he does not cut
himself short by murder. *Tom Tipple*, a guzzling soaking sot, who is always
too drunk to stand himself, or to make others stand. A cart is absolutely
necessary for him. *Robin* of *Bagshot*, alias *Gorgon*, alias *Bluff Bob*, alias
Carbuncle, alias *Bob Booty*.   23

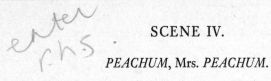

SCENE IV.

PEACHUM, Mrs. *PEACHUM*.

Mrs. *Peach.* What of *Bob Booty*, husband? I hope nothing bad hath be-
tided him. You know, my dear, he's a favourite customer of mine. 'Twas he
made me a present of this ring.

Peach. I have set his name down in the black-list, that's all, my dear; he
spends his life among women, and as soon as his money is gone, one or other
of the ladies will hang him for the reward, and there's forty pound lost to us
for-ever.   7

Mrs. *Peach.* You know, my dear, I never meddle in matters of Death;
I always leave those affairs to you. Women indeed are bitter bad judges in

---

7 Tye-perriwigs] Wigs with the lower part tied; smaller than the full-dress wigs of the
time.   13 a poor petty-larceny rascal] That is, a person convicted of stealing goods less
than a shilling in value, for which the punishment was corporal rather than capital.
22–3 *Robin* of *Bagshot* ... *Bob Booty*] A string of aliases for Sir Robert Walpole. I. iv,
9 bitter bad judges] Prejudiced judges.

these cases, for they are so partial to the brave that they think every man handsome who is going to the Camp or the Gallows.   11

AIR III.   Cold and raw, &c.

If any wench Venus's *girdle wear,*
   Though she be never so ugly,
Lillies and roses will quickly appear,
   And her face look wond'rous smuggly.
Beneath the left ear so fit but a cord,
   (A rope so charming a Zone is!)
The youth in his cart hath the air of a lord,
   And we cry, There dies an Adonis!

But really, husband, you should not be too hard-hearted, for you never had a finer, braver set of men than at present. We have not had a murder among them all, these seven months. And truly, my dear, that is a great blessing.

Peach. What a dickens is the woman always a whimpring about murder for? No gentleman is ever look'd upon the worse for killing a man in his own defence; and if business cannot be carried on without it, what would you have a gentleman do?   26

Mrs. *Peach.* If I am in the wrong, my dear, you must excuse me, for nobody can help the frailty of an over-scrupulous Conscience.

Peach. Murder is as fashionable a crime as a man can be guilty of. How many fine gentlemen have we in *Newgate* every year, purely upon that article? If they have wherewithal to perswade the jury to bring it in manslaughter, what are they the worse for it? So, my dear, have done upon this subject. Was captain *Macheath* here this morning, for the bank-notes he left with you last week?   34

Mrs. *Peach.* Yes, my dear; and though the Bank hath stopt payment, he was so cheerful and so agreeable! Sure there is not a finer gentleman upon the road than the Captain! If he comes from *Bagshot* at any reasonable hour he hath promis'd to make one this evening with *Polly*, and me, and *Bob Booty*, at a party of Quadrille. Pray, my dear, is the Captain rich?

Peach. The Captain keeps too good company ever to grow rich. *Marybone* and the Chocolate-houses are his undoing. The man that proposes to get money by play should have the education of a fine gentleman, and be train'd up to it from his youth.   43

Mrs. *Peach.* Really, I am sorry upon *Polly*'s account the Captain hath not

---

11 the Camp] That is, transportation.   17 *a Zone*] A girdle, an enclosing band.
23 What a dickens] What the devil.   40 *Marybone*] Then a country pleasure garden, in which gaming was one of the main attractions.

more discretion. What business hath he to keep company with lords and gentlemen? he should leave them to prey upon one another.

Peach. Upon *Polly*'s account! What, a plague, does the woman mean?— Upon *Polly*'s account!

Mrs. *Peach.* Captain *Macheath* is very fond of the girl.

Peach. And what then?   50

Mrs. *Peach.* If I have any skill in the ways of women, I am sure *Polly* thinks him a very pretty man.

Peach. And what then? you would not be so mad to have the wench marry him! Gamesters and highwaymen are generally very good to their whores, but they are very devils to their wives.

Mrs. *Peach.* But if *Polly* should be in love, how should we help her, or how can she help herself? Poor girl, I am in the utmost concern about her.

AIR IV.   Why is your faithful slave disdain'd?

If love the virgin's heart invade,
How, like a Moth, the simple maid
Still plays about the flame!   60
If soon she be not made a wife,
Her honour's sing'd, and then for life,
She's—what I dare not name.

Peach. Look ye, wife. A handsome wench in our way of business is as profitable as at the bar of a *Temple* coffee-house, who looks upon it as her livelihood to grant every liberty but one. You see I would indulge the girl as far as prudently we can. In any thing, but marriage! after that, my dear, how shall we be safe? are we not then in her husband's power? for a husband hath the absolute power over all a wife's secrets but her own. If the girl had the discretion of a court lady, who can have a dozen young fellows at her ear without complying with one, I should not matter it; but *Polly* is tinder, and a spark will at once set her on a flame. Married! If the wench does not know her own profit, sure she knows her own pleasure better than to make herself a property! My daughter to me should be, like a court lady to a minister of state, a key to the whole gang. Married! If the affair is not already done, I'll terrify her from it, by the example of our neighbours.   76

Mrs. *Peach.* May-hap, my dear, you may injure the girl. She loves to imitate the fine ladies, and she may only allow the Captain liberties in the view of interest.

Peach. But 'tis your duty, my dear, to warn the girl against her ruin, and

<hr>

64 wench . . . at the bar of a *Temple* coffee-house] Attractive women decorated the bars of coffee-houses long before they took such employment in taverns. They poured coffee for the waiters to serve, effected introductions—and expected to be ogled.

to instruct her how to make the most of her beauty. I'll go to her this moment, and sift her. In the mean time, wife, rip out the coronets and marks of these dozen of cambric handkerchiefs, for I can dispose of them this afternoon to a chap in the city.   84

SCENE V.

Mrs. *PEACHUM*.

Never was a man more out of the way in an argument than my husband! Why must our *Polly*, forsooth, differ from her sex, and love only her husband? And why must our *Polly*'s marriage, contrary to all observation, make her the less followed by other men? All men are thieves in love, and like a woman the better for being another's property.

AIR V.   Of all the simple things we do, *&c.*

A Maid is like the golden oar,
Which hath guineas intrinsical in't,
  Whose worth is never known, before
It is try'd and imprest in the mint.
  A Wife's like a guinea in gold,   10
Stampt with the name of her spouse;
  Now here, now there; is bought, or is sold;
And is current in every house.

SCENE VI.

Mrs. *PEACHUM, FILCH*.

Mrs. Peach. Come hither, *Filch.* I am as fond of this child, as though my mind misgave me he were my own. He hath as fine a hand at picking a pocket as a woman, and is as nimble-finger'd as a juggler. If an unlucky session does not cut the rope of thy life, I pronounce, boy, thou wilt be a great man in history. Where was your post last night, my boy?
Filch. I ply'd at the Opera, madam; and considering 'twas neither dark nor rainy, so that there was no great hurry in getting chairs and coaches, made a tolerable hand on't. These seven handkerchiefs, madam.   8

82 sift her] Question her closely.

Mrs. *Peach.* Colour'd ones, I see. They are of sure sale from our warehouse at *Redriff* among the sea-men.   10

Filch. And this snuff-box.

Mrs. *Peach.* Set in gold! A pretty encouragement this to a young beginner.

Filch. I had a fair tug at a charming gold watch. Pox take the Taylors for making the fobs so deep and narrow! It stuck by the way, and I was forc'd to make my escape under a coach. Really, madam, I fear I shall be cut off in the flower of my youth, so that every now and then (since I was pumpt) I have thoughts of taking up and going to Sea.

Mrs. *Peach.* You should go to *Hockley in the hole*, and to *Marybone*, child, to learn valour. These are the schools that have bred so many brave men. I thought, boy, by this time, thou hadst lost fear as well as shame. Poor lad! how little does he know as yet of the *Old-Baily!* For the first fact I'll ensure thee from being hang'd; and going to Sea, *Filch*, will come time enough upon a sentence of transportation. But now, since you have nothing better to do, ev'n go to your book, and learn your catechism; for really a man makes but an ill figure in the Ordinary's paper, who cannot give a satisfactory answer to his questions. But, hark you, my lad. Don't tell me a lye; for you know I hate a lyar. Do you know of any thing that hath past between captain *Macheath* and our *Polly*?

Filch. I beg you, Madam, don't ask me; for I must either tell a lye to you or to Miss *Polly*; for I promis'd her I would not tell.   30

Mrs. *Peach.* But when the honour of our family is concern'd—

Filch. I shall lead a sad life with Miss *Polly*, if ever she come to know that I told you. Besides, I would not willingly forfeit my own honour by betraying any body.

Mrs. *Peach.* Yonder comes my husband and *Polly*. Come *Filch*, you shall go with me into my own room, and tell me the whole story. I'll give thee a glass of a most delicious cordial that I keep for my own drinking.

SCENE VII.

PEACHUM, POLLY.

Polly. I know as well as any of the fine ladies how to make the most of my self and of my man too. A woman knows how to be mercenary, though she

10 *Redriff*] A riverside district south of the Thames, opposite Wapping.   16 pumpt] Interrogated—or, possibly, exhausted by his new profession of child-getter to condemned women. Cf. Act III, Scene iii.   17 taking up] Reforming and settling down.   18 *Hockley in the hole*] Public garden near Clerkenwell, notorious for bear-baiting, cock-fighting, and other 'sports' involving animals.   25 the Ordinary] The prison chaplain at Newgate.

hath never been in a court or at an assembly. We have it in our natures, papa. If I allow captain *Macheath* some trifling liberties, I have this watch and other visible marks of his favour to show for it. A girl who cannot grant some things, and refuse what is most material, will make but a poor hand of her beauty, and soon be thrown upon the common.

AIR VI.   What shall I do to show how much I love her?

> *Virgins are like the fair flower in its lustre,*
>   *Which in the garden enamels the ground;*
> *Near it the Bees in play flutter and cluster,*   10
>   *And gaudy Butterflies frolick around.*
> *But, when once pluck'd, 'tis no longer alluring,*
>   *To* Covent-garden *'tis sent, (as yet sweet,)*
> *There fades, and shrinks, and grows past all enduring,*
>   *Rots, stinks, and dies, and is trod under feet.*

Peach. You know, *Polly*, I am not against your toying and trifling with a customer in the way of business, or to get out a secret, or so. But if I find out that you have play'd the fool and are married, you jade you, I'll cut your throat, hussy. Now you know my mind.

SCENE VIII.

PEACHUM, POLLY, Mrs. PEACHUM.

AIR VII.   Oh *London* is a fine Town.

> *Mrs.* Peachum, [*in a very great passion.*]
> *Our* Polly *is a sad slut! nor heeds what we have taught her.*
> *I wonder any man alive will ever rear a daughter!*
> *For she must have both hoods and gowns, and hoops to swell her pride,*
> *With scarfs and stays, and gloves and lace; and she will have men beside;*
> *And when she's drest with care and cost, all-tempting, fine and gay,*
> *As men should serve a Cowcumber, she flings herself away.*

You baggage! you hussy! you inconsiderate jade! had you been hang'd, it would not have vex'd me, for that might have been your misfortune; but to do such a mad thing by choice! The wench is married, husband.   9

Peach. Married? the Captain is a bold man, and will risque any thing for

13 Covent-garden] The piazzas there were regularly thronged with prostitutes. The vegetable market provides the imagery for Polly's song. I. viii, 6 *should serve a Cowcumber*] Should deal with their tailors.

money; to be sure he believes her a fortune. Do you think your mother and
I should have liv'd comfortably so long together, if ever we had been married?
Baggage!   13

Mrs. *Peach.* I knew she was always a proud slut; and now the wench hath
play'd the fool and married, because forsooth she would do like the Gentry.
Can you support the expence of a husband, hussy, in gaming, drinking and
whoring? have you money enough to carry on the daily quarrels of man and
wife about who shall squander most? There are not many husbands and
wives, who can bear the charges of plaguing one another in a handsome way.
If you must be married, could you introduce no-body into our family but a
highwayman? Why, thou foolish jade, thou wilt be as ill us'd, and as much
neglected, as if thou hadst married a Lord!   22

Peach. Let not your anger, my dear, break through the rules of decency,
for the Captain looks upon himself in the military capacity, as a gentleman by
his profession. Besides what he hath already, I know he is in a fair way of
getting, or of dying; and both these ways, let me tell you, are most excellent
chances for a wife. Tell me hussy, are you ruin'd or no?

Mrs. *Peach.* With *Polly*'s fortune, she might very well have gone off to a
person of distinction. Yes, that you might, you pouting slut!

Peach. What, is the wench dumb? Speak, or I'll make you plead by
squeezing out an answer from you. Are you really bound wife to him, or are
you only upon liking?   [*Pinches her.*
Polly. Oh!   [*Screaming.*

Mrs. *Peach.* How the mother is to be pitied who hath handsome daughters!
Locks, bolts, bars, and lectures of morality are nothing to them: they break
through them all. They have as much pleasure in cheating a father and
mother, as in cheating at cards.   37

Peach. Why, *Polly*, I shall soon know if you are married, by *Macheath*'s
keeping from our house.

AIR VIII.   Grim King of the Ghosts, &c.

Polly.   *Can Love be controul'd by advice?*   40
   Will Cupid *our mothers obey?*
 Though my heart were as frozen as Ice,
  At his flame 'twould have melted away.
 When he kist me so closely he prest,
  'Twas so sweet that I must have comply'd:
 So I thought it both safest and best
  To marry, for fear you should chide.

Mrs. *Peach.* Then all the hopes of our family are gone for ever and ever!

32 upon liking] On approval, on trial.

Peach. And *Macheath* may hang his father and mother-in-law, in hope to get into their daughter's fortune.   50

Polly. I did not marry him (as 'tis the fashion) cooly and deliberately for honour or money. But, I love him.

Mrs. *Peach.* Love him! worse and worse! I thought the girl had been better bred. Oh husband, husband! her folly makes me mad! my head swims! I'm distracted! I can't support myself—Oh!   [*Faints.*

Peach. See, wench, to what a condition you have reduced your poor mother! a glass of cordial, this instant. How the poor woman takes it to heart!   [Polly *goes out, and returns with it.*
Ah, hussy, now this is the only comfort your mother has left!

Polly. Give her another glass, Sir; my Mamma drinks double the quantity whenever she is out of order. This, you see, fetches her.   61

Mrs. *Peach.* The girl shows such a readiness, and so much concern, that I could almost find in my heart to forgive her.

> AIR IX.   O *Jenny*, O *Jenny*, where hast thou been.
>
> | | O Polly, *you might have toy'd and kist.* |
> | -------- | -- |
> | | *By keeping men off, you keep them on.* |
> | Polly. | *But he so teaz'd me,* |
> | | *And he so pleas'd me,* |
> | | *What I did, you must have done.* |

Mrs. *Peach.* Not with a highway-man.——You sorry slut!

Peach. A word with you, wife. 'Tis no new thing for a wench to take man without consent of Parents. You know 'tis the frailty of woman, my dear.

Mrs. *Peach.* Yes, indeed, the sex is frail. But the first time a woman is frail, she should be somewhat nice methinks, for then or never is the time to make her fortune. After that, she hath nothing to do but to guard herself from being found out, and she may do what she pleases.   75

Peach. Make your self a little easy; I have a thought shall soon set all matters again to rights. Why so melancholy, *Polly*? since what is done cannot be undone, we must all endeavour to make the best of it.

Mrs. *Peach.* Well, *Polly*; as far as one woman can forgive another, I forgive thee.—Your father is too fond of you, hussy.   80

Polly. Then all my sorrows are at an end.

Mrs. *Peach.* A mighty likely speech in troth, for a wench who is just married!

> AIR X.   *Thomas*, I cannot, &c.
>
> | Polly. | I, *like a ship in storms, was tost;* |
> | -------- | ------------------------------------- |
> | | *Yet afraid to put in to Land;* |
> | | *For seiz'd in the port the vessel's lost,* |

> *Whose treasure is contreband.*
> *The waves are laid,*
> *My duty's paid.*
> *O joy beyond expression!*   90
> *Thus, safe a-shore,*
> *I ask no more,*
> *My all is in my possession.*

Peach. I hear customers in t'other room; go, talk with 'em, *Polly*; but come to us again, as soon as they are gone.—But, heark ye, child, if 'tis the gentleman who was here yesterday about the repeating watch; say, you believe we can't get intelligence of it, till to-morrow. For I lent it to *Suky Straddle*, to make a figure with it to-night at a tavern in *Drury-Lane*. If t'other gentleman calls for the silver-hilted sword; you know beetle-brow'd *Jemmy* hath it on, and he doth not come from *Tunbridge* till *Tuesday* night; so that it cannot be had till then.   101

SCENE IX.

PEACHUM, Mrs. *PEACHUM*.

Peach. Dear wife, be a little pacified. Don't let your passion run away with your senses. *Polly*, I grant you, hath done a rash thing.

Mrs. Peach. If she had had only an intrigue with the fellow, why the very best families have excus'd and huddled up a frailty of that sort. 'Tis marriage, husband, that makes it a blemish.

Peach. But money, wife, is the true fuller's earth for reputations, there is not a spot or a stain but what it can take out. A rich rogue now-a-days is fit company for any gentleman; and the world, my dear, hath not such a contempt for roguery as you imagine. I tell you, wife, I can make this match turn to our advantage.   10

Mrs. Peach. I am very sensible, husband, that captain *Macheath* is worth money, but I am in doubt whether he hath not two or three wives already, and then if he should dye in a Session or two, *Polly*'s dower would come into dispute.

Peach. That, indeed, is a point which ought to be consider'd.

AIR XI.   A Soldier and a Sailor.

> *A Fox may steal your hens, sir,*
> *A whore your health and pence, sir,*

I. ix, 6 the true fuller's earth] A certain cleanser.

> *Your daughter rob your chest, sir,*
> *Your wife may steal your rest, sir,*
>   *A thief your goods and plate.*   20
> *But this is all but picking,*
> *With rest, pence, chest and chicken;*
> *It ever was decreed, sir,*
> *If Lawyer's hand is fee'd, sir,*
>   *He steals your whole estate.*

The Lawyers are bitter enemies to those in our way. They don't care that any body should get a clandestine livelihood but themselves.

<hr>

SCENE X.

Mrs. *PEACHUM, PEACHUM, POLLY.*

Polly. 'Twas only Nimming *Ned.* He brought in a damask window-curtain, a hoop-petticoat, a pair of silver candlesticks, a perriwig, and one silk stocking, from the fire that happen'd last night.

Peach. There is not a fellow that is cleverer in his way, and saves more goods out of the fire than *Ned.* But now, *Polly,* to your affair; for matters must not be left as they are. You are married then, it seems?

Polly. Yes, Sir.

Peach. And how do you propose to live, child?

Polly. Like other women, Sir, upon the industry of my husband.

Mrs. *Peach.* What, is the wench turn'd fool? A highway-man's wife, like a soldier's, hath as little of his pay, as of his company.   11

Peach. And had not you the common views of a gentlewoman in your marriage, *Polly?*

Polly. I don't know what you mean, Sir.

Peach. Of a jointure, and of being a widow.

Polly. But I love him, Sir: how then could I have thoughts of parting with him?

Peach. Parting with him! Why, that is the whole scheme and intention of all Marriage-articles. The comfortable estate of widowhood, is the only hope that keeps up a wife's spirits. Where is the woman who would scruple to be a wife, if she had it in her power to be a widow whenever she pleas'd? If you have any views of this sort, *Polly,* I shall think the match not so very un-reasonable.   23

15 a jointure] That part of a man's estate secured to his wife or widow.

Polly. How I dread to hear your advice! Yet I must beg you to explain yourself.

Peach. Secure what he hath got, have him peach'd the next Sessions, and then at once you are made a rich widow.

Polly. What, murder the man I love! The blood runs cold at my heart with the very thought of it.

Peach. Fye, *Polly!* what hath murder to do in the affair? Since the thing sooner or later must happen, I dare say, the Captain himself would like that we should get the reward for his death sooner than a stranger. Why, *Polly,* the Captain knows, that as 'tis his employment to rob, so 'tis ours to take Robbers; every man in his business. So that there is no malice in the case.

Mrs. *Peach.* Ay, husband, now you have nick'd the matter. To have him peach'd is the only thing could ever make me forgive her.   36

AIR XII.   Now ponder well, ye parents dear.

Polly.   *Oh, ponder well! be not severe;*
                 So save a wretched wife!
              For on the rope that hangs my dear
                 Depends poor Polly's *life.*   40

Mrs. *Peach.* But your duty to your parents, hussy, obliges you to hang him. What would many a wife give for such an opportunity!

Polly. What is a jointure, what is widow-hood to me? I know my heart. I cannot survive him.

AIR XIII.   Le printemps rappelle aux armes.

            The Turtle thus with plaintive crying,
                 Her lover dying,
            The turtle thus with plaintive crying
                 Laments her Dove.
            Down she drops quite spent with sighing
            Pair'd in death, as pair'd in love.   50

Thus, Sir, it will happen to your poor *Polly.*

Mrs. *Peach.* What, is the fool in love in earnest then? I hate thee for being particular: Why, wench, thou art a shame to thy very Sex.

Polly. But hear me, mother.—If you ever lov'd—

Mrs. *Peach.* Those cursed Play-books she reads have been her ruin. One word more, hussy, and I shall knock your brains out, if you have any.

Peach. Keep out of the way, *Polly,* for fear of mischief, and consider of what is propos'd to you.

Mrs. *Peach.* Away, hussy. Hang your husband, and be dutiful.

***

26 peach'd] Impeached, informed against.   35 nick'd the matter] Hit the mark, come to the point.

SCENE XI.

Mrs. *PEACHUM, PEACHUM.*

[Polly *listning.*

Mrs. *Peach.* The thing, husband, must and shall be done. For the sake of intelligence we must take other measures, and have him peach'd the next Session without her consent. If she will not know her duty, we know ours.

Peach. But really, my dear, it grieves one's heart to take off a great man. When I consider his personal bravery, his fine stratagem, how much we have already got by him, and how much more we may get, methinks I can't find in my heart to have a hand in his death. I wish you could have made *Polly* undertake it.

Mrs. *Peach.* But in a case of necessity—our own lives are in danger.

Peach. Then, indeed, we must comply with the customs of the world, and make gratitude give way to interest.—He shall be taken off.   12

Mrs. *Peach.* I'll undertake to manage *Polly.*

Peach. And I'll prepare matters for the *Old-Baily.*

SCENE XII.

POLLY.

Now I'm a wretch, indeed.—Methinks I see him already in the cart, sweeter and more lovely than the nosegay in his hand!—I hear the crowd extolling his resolution and intrepidity!—What vollies of sighs are sent from the windows of *Holborn*, that so comely a youth should be brought to disgrace!—I see him at the tree! the whole Circle are in tears!—even Butchers weep!——*Jack Ketch* himself hesitates to perform his duty, and would be glad to lose his fee, by a reprieve. What then will become of *Polly*!—As yet I may inform him of their design, and aid him in his escape.—It shall be so.—But then he flies, absents himself, and I bar my self from his dear dear conversation! that too will distract me.—If he keeps out of the way, my Papa and Mama may in time relent, and we may be happy.—If he stays, he is

I. xii, 4 the windows of *Holborn*] A condemned man's cart passed along Holborn on its way from Newgate to the gallows at Tyburn.   6 *Jack Ketch*] That is, the public executioner. Generally so-called, after the notorious hangman of that name who plied his trade late in the seventeenth century.

hang'd, and then he is lost for ever!—He intended to lye conceal'd in my room, 'till the dusk of the evening: If they are abroad I'll this instant let him out, lest some accident should prevent him.   [*Exit, and returns.*

SCENE XIII.

POLLY, MACHEATH.

AIR XIV.   Pretty Parrot, say, *&c.*

Mach.   *Pretty* Polly, *say,*
                        When I was away,
                        Did your fancy never stray
                        To some newer lover?

Polly.   *Without disguise,*
                            Heaving sighs,
                            Doating eyes,
                        My constant heart discover.
                        Fondly let me loll!

Mach.   *O pretty, pretty* Poll.   10

Polly. And are *you* as fond as ever, my dear?

Mach. Suspect my honour, my courage, suspect any thing but my love.—May my pistols miss fire, and my mare slip her shoulder while I am pursu'd, if I ever forsake thee!

Polly. Nay, my dear, I have no reason to doubt you, for I find in the Romance you lent me, none of the great Heroes were ever false in love.

AIR XV.   Pray, fair one, be kind.

Mach.   *My heart was so free,*
                        It rov'd like the Bee,
                        'Till Polly *my passion requited;*
                        I sipt each flower,   20
                        I chang'd ev'ry hour,
                        But here ev'ry flower is united.

Polly. Were you sentenc'd to Transportation, sure, my dear, you could not leave me behind you——could you?

Mach. Is there any power, any force that could tear me from thee? You might sooner tear a pension out of the hands of a Courtier, a fee from a Lawyer, a pretty woman from a looking-glass, or any woman from *Quadrille.* --But to tear me from thee is impossible!

AIR XVI.   Over the hills and far away.

Were I laid on Greenland's *coast,*
   And in my arms embrac'd my lass;   30
Warm amidst eternal frost,
   Too soon the half year's night would pass.

Polly.   *Were I sold on* Indian *soil.*
   Soon as the burning day was clos'd,
I could mock the sultry toil,
   When on my charmer's breast repos'd.

Mach.   *And I would love you all the day,*
Polly.   *Every night would kiss and play,*
Mach.   *If with me you'd fondly stray*
Polly.   *Over the hills and far away.*   40

Polly. Yes, I would go with thee. But oh!——how shall I speak it? I must be torn from thee. We must part.

Mach. How! Part!

Polly. We must, we must.—My Papa and Mama are set against thy life. They now, even now are in search after thee. They are preparing evidence against thee. Thy life depends upon a moment.

AIR XVII.   Gin thou wert mine awn thing.

O what pain it is to part!
   Can I leave thee, can I leave thee?
O what pain it is to part!
   Can thy Polly *ever leave thee?*   50
But lest death my love should thwart,
And bring thee to the fatal cart,
Thus I tear thee from my bleeding heart!
   Fly hence, and let me leave thee.

One kiss and then—one kiss—begone—farewell.

Mach. My hand, my heart, my dear, is so riveted to thine, that I cannot unloose my hold.

Polly. But my Papa may intercept thee, and then I should lose the very glimmering of hope. A few weeks, perhaps, may reconcile us all. Shall thy *Polly* hear from thee?   60

Mach. Must I then go?

Polly. And will not absence change your love?

Mach. If you doubt it, let me stay——and be hang'd.

Polly. O how I fear! how I tremble!—Go—but when safety will give you leave, you will be sure to see me again; for 'till then *Polly* is wretched.

AIR XVIII.   O the broom, &c.

Mach.	*The Miser thus a shilling sees,*	[Parting and looking
	Which he's oblig'd to pay,	back at each other with
	With sighs resigns it by degrees,	fondness; he at one door,
	And fears 'tis gone for aye.	she at the other.
Polly.	*The Boy thus, when his Sparrow's flown,*	
	The bird in silence eyes;	
	But soon as out of sight 'tis gone,	
	Whines, whimpers, sobs and cries.	

ACT II.   SCENE I.

A Tavern near Newgate.

Jemmy Twitcher, *Crook-finger'd* Jack, Wat Dreary, Robin *of* Bagshot, Nimming Ned, Henry Padington, Matt *of the* Mint, Ben Budge, *and the rest of the Gang, at the Table, with Wine, Brandy and Tobacco.*

BEN.

BUT pr'ythee, *Matt*, what is become of thy brother *Tom?* I have not seen him since my return from transportation.

Matt. Poor brother *Tom* had an accident this time twelvemonth, and so clever a made fellow he was, that I could not save him from those fleaing rascals the Surgeons; and now, poor man, he is among the Otamys at *Surgeon's-Hall.*

Ben. So it seems, his time was come.

Jem. But the present time is ours, and no body alive hath more. Why are the laws levell'd at us? are we more dishonest than the rest of mankind? what we win, gentlemen, is our own by the law of arms, and the right of conquest.   11

Crook. Where shall we find such another set of practical philosophers, who to a man are above the fear of Death?

Wat. Sound men, and true!

Robin. Of try'd courage, and indefatigable industry!

Ned. Who is there here that would not dye for his friend?

Harry. Who is there here that would betray him for his interest?

II. i, 4 fleaing] Mean, miserly—and possibly also intended in its literal sense, to describe the process of anatomizing: peeling away the corpse's skin. 5 Otamys] Anatomies: corpses to be anatomized after execution.

Matt. Show me a gang of Courtiers that can say as much.

Ben. We are for a just partition of the world, for every man hath a right to enjoy life. 20

Matt. We retrench the superfluities of mankind. The world is avaritious, and I hate avarice. A covetous fellow, like a Jack-daw, steals what he was never made to enjoy, for the sake of hiding it. These are the robbers of mankind, for money was made for the free-hearted and generous, and where is the injury of taking from another, what he hath not the heart to make use of?

Jem. Our several stations for the day are fixt. Good luck attend us all. Fill the glasses.

AIR XIX.   Fill ev'ry glass, &c.

Matt.
> *Fill ev'ry glass, for wine inspires us,*
> > *And fires us*
>
> *With courage, love and joy.*   30
> *Women and wine should life employ.*
> *Is there ought else on earth desirous?*

Chorus.   *Fill ev'ry glass,* &c.

SCENE II.

To them enter MACHEATH.

Mach. Gentlemen, well met. My heart hath been with you this hour; but an unexpected affair hath detain'd me. No ceremony, I beg you.

Matt. We were just breaking up to go upon duty. Am I to have the honour of taking the air with you, Sir, this evening upon the Heath? I drink a dram now and then with the Stage-coachmen in the way of friendship and intelligence; and I know that about this time there will be passengers upon the western road, who are worth speaking with.

Mach. I was to have been of that party—but——

Matt. But what, Sir?

Mach. Is there any man who suspects my courage? 10

Matt. We have all been witnesses of it.

Mach. My honour and truth to the gang?

Matt. I'll be answerable for it.

Mach. In the division of our booty, have I ever shown the least marks of avarice or injustice!

Matt. By these questions something seems to have ruffled you. Are any of us suspected?

Mach. I have a fixt confidence, gentlemen, in you all, as men of honour, and as such I value and respect you. *Peachum* is a man that is useful to us.

Matt. Is he about to play us any foul play? I'll shoot him through the head.   21

Mach. I beg you, gentlemen, act with conduct and discretion. A pistol is your last resort.

Matt. He knows nothing of this meeting.

Mach. Business cannot go on without him. He is a man who knows the world, and is a necessary agent to us. We have had a slight difference, and till it is accommodated I shall be oblig'd to keep out of his way. Any private dispute of mine shall be of no ill consequence to my friends. You must continue to act under his direction, for the moment we break loose from him, our gang is ruin'd.   30

Matt. As a bawd to a whore, I grant you, he is to us of great convenience.

Mach. Make him believe I have quitted the gang, which I can never do but with life. At our private quarters I will continue to meet you. A week or so will probably reconcile us.

Matt. Your instructions shall be observ'd. 'Tis now high time for us to repair to our several duties; so till the evening at our quarters in *Moor-fields* we bid you farewell.

Mach. I shall wish my self with you. Success attend you.

                                                [*Sits down melancholy at the Table.*

         AIR XX.   March in *Rinaldo*, with Drums and Trumpets.

Matt.   *Let us take the road.*
                            Hark! I hear the sound of coaches!   40
                            The hour of attack approaches,
                     To your arms, brave boys, and load.
                            See the ball I hold!
                     Let the Chymists toil like asses,
                     Our fire their fire surpasses,
                            And turns all our lead to gold.

[*The Gang, rang'd in the front of the Stage, load their pistols, and stick them under their girdles; then go off singing the first part in Chorus.*

Air: *Rinaldo*] Handel's opera, first performed in 1710. 44 *Chymists*] Alchemists. 45–6 *Our fire . . . to gold*] That is, a shot from a highwayman's pistol is more effective than alchemical fire in transmuting lead—in the highwayman's case, that of his bullet—into gold.

SCENE III.

MACHEATH, DRAWER.

Mach. What a fool is a fond wench! *Polly* is most confoundedly bit.——I
love the sex. And a man who loves money, might as well be contented with
one guinea, as I with one woman. The town perhaps hath been as much
oblig'd to me, for recruiting it with free-hearted ladies, as to any recruiting
Officer in the army. If it were not for us and the other gentlemen of the
sword, *Drury-lane* would be uninhabited.

AIR XXI.   Would you have a young Virgin, *&c.*

If the heart of a man is deprest with cares,
The mist is dispell'd when a woman appears;
Like the notes of a fiddle, she sweetly, sweetly
Raises the spirits, and charms our ears.   10
  Roses and lillies her cheeks disclose,
  But her ripe lips are more sweet than those.
    Press her,
    Caress her,
    With blisses,
    Her kisses
  Dissolve us in pleasure, and soft repose.

I must have women. There is nothing unbends the mind like them. Money is
not so strong a cordial for the time.——Drawer.——[*Enter Drawer.*] Is the
Porter gone for all the ladies, according to my directions?   20
    Draw. I expect him back every minute. But you know, Sir, you sent him
as far as *Hockley in the Hole*, for three of the ladies, for one in *Vinegar Yard*,
and for the rest of them somewhere about *Lewkner's Lane.* Sure some of
them are below, for I hear the barr bell. As they come I will show them up.
——Coming, coming.

---

1 bit] Taken in, deceived.   6 *Drury-lane*] The 'mazy courts' in the vicinity of Drury
Lane were the favourite haunts of lower-class prostitutes.   22 *Vinegar Yard*] On the site
of the present Drury Lane Theatre: a notorious haunt of prostitutes and thieves.
23 *Lewkner's Lane*] Now Charles Street, Drury Lane: also of long-standing unsavoury
reputation.

SCENE IV.

Macheath, *Mrs*. Coaxer, Dolly Trull, *Mrs*. Vixen, Betty Doxy, Jenny Diver, *Mrs*. Slammekin, Suky Tawdry, *and* Molly Brazen.

Mach. Dear Mrs. *Coaxer*, you are welcome. You look charmingly to-day. I hope you don't want the repairs of quality, and lay on paint——*Dolly Trull!* kiss me, you slut; are you as amorous as ever, hussy? You are always so taken up with stealing hearts, that you don't allow your self time to steal any thing else.—Ah *Dolly*, thou wilt ever be a Coquette!——Mrs. *Vixen*, I'm yours, I always lov'd a woman of wit and spirit; they make charming mistresses, but plaguy wives.——*Betty Doxy!* Come hither, hussy. Do you drink as hard as ever? You had better stick to good wholesome beer; for in troth, *Betty*, strong-waters will in time ruin your constitution. You should leave those to your betters.——What! and my pretty *Jenny Diver* too! As prim and demure as ever! There is not any Prude, though ever so high bred, hath a more sanctify'd look, with a more mischievous heart. Ah! thou art a dear artful hypocrite.——Mrs. *Slammekin!* as careless and genteel as ever! all you fine ladies, who know your own beauty, affect an undress——But see, here's *Suky Tawdry* come to contradict what I was saying. Every thing she gets one way she lays out upon her back. Why, *Suky*, you must keep at least a dozen Tally-men. *Molly Brazen!* [*She kisses him.*] That's well done. I love a free-hearted wench. Thou hast a most agreeable assurance, girl, and art as willing as a Turtle.——But hark! I hear musick. The Harper is at the door. *If musick be the food of Love, play on.* E'er you seat your selves, ladies, what think you of a dance? Come in. [*Enter Harper.*] Play the *French* Tune, that Mrs. *Slammekin* was so fond of.   22

[*A Dance* a la ronde *in the* French *manner; near the end of it this Song and Chorus.*

AIR XXII.   Cotillon.

> *Youth's the season made for joys,*
>   *Love is then our duty;*
> *She alone who that employs,*
>   *Well deserves her beauty.*
>   *Let's be gay,*
>   *While we may,*
>   *Beauty's a flower despis'd in decay.*

Chorus.   *Youth's the season, &c.*   30

17 Tally-men] Men supplying goods on instalment-credit: in the clothing trade, the worst paid work.

> *Let us drink and sport to-day,*
> *Ours is not to-morrow.*
> *Love with youth flies swift away,*
> *Age is nought but sorrow.*
> > *Dance and sing,*
> > *Time's on the wing,*
> > *Life never knows the return of spring.*

Chorus.   *Let us drink,* &c.

Mach. Now, pray ladies, take your places. Here Fellow, [*Pays the Harper.*] Bid the Drawer bring us more wine. [*Ex. Harper.*] If any of the ladies chuse gin, I hope they will be so free to call for it.   41

Jenny. You look as if you meant me. Wine is strong enough for me. Indeed, Sir, I never drink strong-waters, but when I have the Cholic.

Mach. Just the excuse of the fine ladies! Why, a lady of quality is never without the Cholic. I hope, Mrs. *Coaxer*, you have had good success of late in your visits among the Mercers.

Coax. We have so many interlopers——Yet with industry, one may still have a little picking. I carried a silver-flower'd lutestring and a piece of black padesoy to Mr. *Peachum*'s Lock but last week.

Vix. There's *Molly Brazen* hath the ogle of a Rattle-snake. She rivitted a Linnen-draper's eye so fast upon her, that he was nick'd of three pieces of cambric before he could look off.   52

Braz. O dear madam!——But sure nothing can come up to your handling of laces! And then you have such a sweet deluding tongue! To cheat a man is nothing; but the woman must have fine parts indeed who cheats a woman!

Vix. Lace, madam, lyes in a small compass, and is of easy conveyance. But you are apt, madam, to think too well of your friends.

Coax. If any woman hath more art than another, to be sure, 'tis *Jenny Diver*. Though her fellow be never so agreeable, she can pick his pocket as cooly, as if money were her only pleasure. Now that is a command of the passions uncommon in a woman!   61

Jenny. I never go to the tavern with a man, but in the view of business. I have other hours, and other sort of men for my pleasure. But had I your address, madam——

Mach. Have done with your compliments, ladies; and drink about: You are not so fond of me, *Jenny*, as you use to be.

41 gin] In general, successful thieves and prostitutes, needing to keep their wits about them, would have avoided this spirit: thus, Macheath's invitation is in part ironical. The cheapness and easy availability of gin—by 1750 one in four houses in the Parish of St. Giles were gin-shops—made it the drink of the destitute. Only Mrs. Trapes (Act III, Scene vi) confesses an addiction to it in this play.   48 lutestring] A glossy silk fabric.   49 padesoy] Paduasoy: a heavy, corded silk material.

Jenny. 'Tis not convenient, Sir, to show my fondness among so many rivals. 'Tis your own choice, and not the warmth of my inclination, that will determine you.

AIR XXIII.   All in a misty morning.

Before the barn-door crowing,   70
 The Cock by Hens attended,
His eyes around him throwing,
 Stands for a while suspended.
Then one he singles from the crew,
 And cheers the happy Hen;
With how do you do, and how do you do,
 And how do you do again.

Mach. Ah *Jenny!* thou art a dear slut.

Trull. Pray, madam, were you ever in keeping?

Tawd. I hope, madam, I ha'nt been so long upon the town, but I have met with some good fortune as well as my neighbours.   81

Trull. Pardon me, madam, I meant no harm by the question; 'twas only in the way of conversation.

Tawd. Indeed, madam, if I had not been a fool, I might have liv'd very handsomely with my last friend. But upon his missing five guineas, he turn'd me off. Now I never suspected he had counted them.

Slam. Who do you look upon, madam, as your best sort of keepers?

Trull. That, madam, is thereafter as they be.

Slam. I, madam, was once kept by a *Jew*; and bating their religion, to women they are a good sort of people.   90

Tawd. Now for my part, I own I like an old fellow: for we always make them pay for what they can't do.

Vix. A spruce Prentice, let me tell you, ladies, is no ill thing, they bleed freely. I have sent at least two or three dozen of them in my time to the Plantations.

Jenny. But to be sure, Sir, with so much good fortune as you have had upon the road, you must be grown immensely rich.

Mach. The road, indeed, hath done me justice, but the gaming-table hath been my ruin.

AIR XXIV.   When once I lay with another man's wife.

Jen. *The Gamesters and Lawyers are jugglers alike,*   100
  If they meddle your all is in danger:
  Like Gypsies, if once they can finger a souse,

89 bating their religion] But for their religion.   102 finger a souse] Get their hands on a small coin—literally, a sou.

> *Your pockets they pick, and they pilfer your house,*
> *And give your estate to a stranger.*

A man of courage should never put any thing to the risque, but his life. These are the tools of a man of honour. Cards and Dice are only fit for cowardly cheats, who prey upon their friends.

[*She takes up his Pistol.* Tawdry *takes up the other.*

Tawd. This, Sir, is fitter for your hand. Besides your loss of money, 'tis a loss to the ladies. Gaming takes you off from women. How fond could I be of you! but before company, 'tis ill bred.   110

Mach. Wanton hussies!

Jen. I must and will have a kiss to give my wine a zest.

[*They take him about the neck, and make signs to* Peachum *and Constables; who rush in upon him.*

SCENE V.

To them PEACHUM and Constables.

Peach. I seize you, Sir, as my prisoner.

Mach. Was this well done, *Jenny?*——Women are decoy Ducks; who can trust them! Beasts, Jades, Jilts, Harpies, Furies, Whores!

Peach. Your case, Mr. *Macheath*, is not particular. The greatest Heroes have been ruin'd by women. But, to do them justice, I must own they are a pretty sort of creatures, if we could trust them. You must now, Sir, take your leave of the ladies, and if they have a mind to make you a visit, they will be sure to find you at home. The gentleman, ladies, lodges in *Newgate.* Constables, wait upon the Captain to his lodgings.

AIR XXV.   When first I laid siege to my *Chloris:*

Mach.   *At the Tree I shall suffer with pleasure,*   10
                 At the Tree I shall suffer with pleasure,
                    Let me go where I will,
                    In all kinds of ill,
                 I shall find no such Furies as these are.

Peach. Ladies, I'll take care the reckoning shall be discharg'd.

[*Ex.* Macheath, *guarded with* Peachum *and Constables.*

SCENE VI.

The Women remain.

Vix. Look ye, Mrs. *Jenny*, though Mr. *Peachum* may have made a private bargain with you and *Suky Tawdry* for betraying the Captain, as we were all assisting, we ought all to share alike.

Coax. I think Mr. *Peachum*, after so long an acquaintance, might have trusted me as well as *Jenny Diver*.

Slam. I am sure at least three men of his hanging, and in a year's time too, (if he did me justice) should be set down to my account.

Trull. Mrs. *Slammekin*, that is not fair. For you know one of them was taken in bed with me.

Jenny. As far as a bowl of punch or a treat, I believe Mrs. *Suky* will join with me.——As for any thing else, ladies, you cannot in conscience expect it.

Slam. Dear madam——   12
Trull. I would not for the world——
Slam. 'Tis impossible for me——
Trull. As I hope to be sav'd, madam——
Slam. Nay, then I must stay here all night——
Trull. Since you command me.

                                   [*Exeunt with great Ceremony.*

SCENE VII.   *Newgate.*

LOCKIT, Turnkeys, MACHEATH, Constables.

Lock. Noble Captain, you are welcome. You have not been a lodger of mine this year and half. You know the custom, Sir. Garnish, Captain, garnish. Hand me down those fetters there.

Mach. Those, Mr. *Lockit*, seem to be the heaviest of the whole set. With your leave, I should like the further pair better.

Lock. Look ye, Captain, we know what is fittest for our prisoners. When a gentleman uses me with civility, I always do the best I can to please him— Hand them down I say—We have them of all prices, from one guinea to ten, and 'tis fitting every gentleman should please himself.   9

Mach. I understand you, Sir. [*Gives money.*] The fees here are so many,

II. vii, 2 Garnish] The bribe demanded by jailers from newly-arrived inmates.

and so exorbitant, that few fortunes can bear the expence of getting off
handsomly, or of dying like a gentleman.   12

Lock. Those, I see, will fit the Captain better.——Take down the further
pair. Do but examine them, Sir—Never was better work.——How genteely
they are made!——They will fit as easy as a glove, and the nicest man in
England might not be asham'd to wear them. [*He puts on the chains.*] If I
had the best gentleman in the land in my custody I could not equip him more
handsomly. And so, Sir—I now leave you to your private meditations.

SCENE VIII.

MACHEATH.

AIR XXVI.   Courtiers, Courtiers think it no harm.

Man may escape from rope and gun;
  Nay, some have out-liv'd the Doctor's pill:
Who takes a woman must be undone,
  That Basilisk is sure to kill.
The Fly that sips treacle is lost in the sweets,
So he that tastes woman, woman, woman,
  He that tastes woman, ruin meets.   7

To what a woful plight have I brought my self! Here must I (all day long,
'till I am hang'd) be confin'd to hear the reproaches of a wench who lays her
ruin at my door.——I am in the custody of her father, and to be sure if he
knows of the matter, I shall have a fine time on't betwixt this and my execution.——But I promis'd the wench marriage.——What signifies a promise
to a woman? does not man in marriage itself promise a hundred things that
he never means to perform? Do all we can, women will believe us; for they
look upon a promise as an excuse for following their own inclinations.——
But here comes *Lucy*, and I cannot get from her——wou'd I were deaf!

SCENE IX.

MACHEATH, LUCY.

Lucy. You base man you,——how can you look me in the face after what
hath past between us?——See here, perfidious wretch, how I am forc'd
to bear about the load of Infamy you have laid upon me——O *Macheath*!

G

thou hast robb'd me of my quiet——to see thee tortur'd would give me pleasure.

AIR XXVII.   A lovely Lass to a Friar came.

> *Thus when a good huswife sees a Rat*
> *In her trap in the morning taken,*
> *With pleasure her heart goes pit a pat,*
> *In revenge for her loss of bacon.*
> *Then she throws him*   10
> *To the Dog or Cat,*
> *To be worried, crush'd and shaken.*

Mach. Have you no bowels, no tenderness, my dear *Lucy*, to see a husband in these circumstances?

Lucy. A husband!

Mach. In ev'ry respect but the form, and that, my dear, may be said over us at any time.——Friends should not insist upon ceremonies. From a man of honour, his word is as good as his bond.

Lucy. 'Tis the pleasure of all you fine men to insult the women you have ruin'd.   20

AIR XXVIII.   'Twas when the Sea was roaring.

> *How cruel are the traytors,*
> *Who lye and swear in jest,*
> *To cheat unguarded creatures*
> *Of virtue, fame, and rest!*
> *Whoever steals a shilling,*
> *Thro' shame the guilt conceals:*
> *In love the perjur'd villain*
> *With boasts the theft reveals.*

Mach. The very first opportunity, my dear, (have but patience) you shall be my wife in whatever manner you please.   30

Lucy. Insinuating monster! And so you think I know nothing of the affair of Miss *Polly Peachum*.——I could tear thy eyes out!

Mach. Sure *Lucy*, you can't be such a fool as to be jealous of *Polly*!

Lucy. Are you not married to her, you brute, you?

Mach. Married! Very good. The wench gives it out only to vex thee, and to ruin me in thy good opinion. 'Tis true, I go to the house; I chat with the girl, I kiss her, I say a thousand things to her (as all gentlemen do) that mean nothing, to divert my self; and now the silly jade hath set it about that I am married to her, to let me know what she would be at. Indeed, my dear *Lucy*, these violent passions may be of ill consequence to a woman in your condition.   41

Lucy. Come, come, Captain, for all your assurance, you know that Miss *Polly* hath put it out of your power to do me the justice you promis'd me.

Mach. A jealous woman believes ev'ry thing her passion suggests. To convince you of my sincerity, if we can find the Ordinary, I shall have no scruples of making you my wife; and I know the consequence of having two at a time.

Lucy. That you are only to be hang'd, and so get rid of them both.

Mach. I am ready, my dear *Lucy*, to give you satisfaction——if you think there is any in marriage.——What can a man of honour say more?   50

Lucy. So then it seems, you are not married to Miss *Polly*.

Mach. You know, *Lucy*, the girl is prodigiously conceited. No man can say a civil thing to her, but (like other fine ladies) her vanity makes her think he's her own for ever and ever.

AIR XXIX.   The Sun had loos'd his weary teams.

The first time at the looking-glass
The mother sets her daughter,
The Image strikes the smiling lass
With self-love ever after.
Each time she looks, she, fonder grown,
Thinks ev'ry charm grows stronger: 60
But alas, vain maid, all eyes but your own
Can see you are not younger.

When women consider their own beauties, they are all alike unreasonable in their demands; for they expect their lovers should like them as long as they like themselves.

Lucy. Yonder is my father——perhaps this way we may light upon the Ordinary, who shall try if you will be as good as your word.——For I long to be made an honest woman.

SCENE X.

PEACHUM, LOCKIT with an Account-Book.

Lock. In this last affair, brother *Peachum*, we are agreed. You have consented to go halves in *Macheath*.

Peach. We shall never fall out about an execution.—But as to that article, pray how stands our last year's account?

Lock. If you will run your eye over it, you'll find 'tis fair and clearly stated.

Peach. This long arrear of the government is very hard upon us! Can it be expected that we should hang our acquaintance for nothing, when our betters will hardly save theirs without being paid for it. Unless the people in employment pay better, I promise them for the future, I shall let other rogues live besides their own.   10

Lock. Perhaps, brother, they are afraid these matters may be carried too far. We are treated too by them with contempt, as if our profession were not reputable.

Peach. In one respect indeed, our employment may be reckon'd dishonest, because, like great Statesmen, we encourage those who betray their friends.

Lock. Such language, brother, any where else, might turn to your prejudice. Learn to be more guarded, I beg you.

AIR XXX.   How happy are we, *&c.*

> *When you censure the age,*
> *Be cautious and sage,*
> *Lest the Courtiers offended should be :*   20
> *If you mention vice or bribe,*
> *'Tis so pat to all the tribe ;*
> *Each cries—That was levell'd at me.*

Peach. Here's poor *Ned Clincher*'s name, I see. Sure, brother *Lockit*, there was a little unfair proceeding in *Ned*'s case: for he told me in the condemn'd hold, that for value receiv'd, you had promis'd him a Session or two longer without molestation.

Lock. Mr. *Peachum*,—this is the first time my honour was ever call'd in question.

Peach. Business is at an end—if once we act dishonourably.   30

Lock. Who accuses me?

Peach. You are warm, brother.

Lock. He that attacks my honour, attacks my livelyhood.—And this usage —Sir—is not to be born.

Peach. Since you provoke me to speak—I must tell you too, that Mrs. *Coaxer* charges you with defrauding her of her information-money, for the apprehending of curl-pated *Hugh.* Indeed, indeed, brother, we must punctually pay our Spies, or we shall have no Information.

Lock. Is this language to me, Sirrah——who have sav'd you from the gallows, Sirrah!   [*Collaring each other.*

Peach. If I am hang'd, it shall be for ridding the world of an arrant rascal.

Lock. This hand shall do the office of the halter you deserve, and throttle you—you dog!—   43

26 promis'd him a Session or two longer] That is, agreed to hold off his execution until one or two more quarter-sessions had passed.

Peach. Brother, brother,—we are both in the wrong—we shall be both losers in the dispute—for you know we have it in our power to hang each other. You should not be so passionate.

Lock. Nor you so provoking.

Peach. 'Tis our mutual interest; 'tis for the interest of the world we should agree. If I said any thing, brother, to the prejudice of your character, I ask pardon. 50

Lock. Brother *Peachum*—I can forgive as well as resent.—Give me your hand. Suspicion does not become a friend.

Peach. I only meant to give you occasion to justifie yourself: But I must now step home, for I expect the gentleman about this Snuff-box, that *Filch* nimm'd two nights ago in the Park. I appointed him at this hour.

SCENE XI.

LOCKIT, LUCY.

Lock. Whence come you, hussy?

Lucy. My tears might answer that question.

Lock. You have then been whimpering and fondling, like a Spaniel, over the fellow that hath abus'd you.

Lucy. One can't help love; one can't cure it. 'Tis not in my power to obey you, and hate him.

Lock. Learn to bear your husband's death like a reasonable woman. 'Tis not the fashion, now-a-days, so much as to affect sorrow upon these occasions. No woman would ever marry, if she had not the chance of mortality for a release. Act like a woman of spirit, hussy, and thank your father for what he is doing. 11

AIR XXXI.   Of a noble Race was *Shenkin*.

Polly.   *Is then his fate decreed, Sir?*
                   Such a man can I think of quitting?
                When first we met, so moves me yet,
                   O see how my heart is splitting!

Lock. Look ye, *Lucy*—there is no saving him.——So, I think, you must ev'n do like other widows—buy your self weeds, and be cheerful.

55 nimm'd] Stole.   II. xi, 12 Polly] This song should, correctly, be assigned to Lucy.

AIR XXXII.

You'll think, e'er many days ensue,
This sentence not severe;
I hang your husband, child, 'tis true,   20
But with him hang your care.
Twang dang dillo dee.

Like a good wife, go moan over your dying husband. That, child, is your
duty—consider, girl, you can't have the man and the money too—so make
yourself as easy as you can by getting all you can from him.

SCENE XII.

LUCY, MACHEATH.

Lucy. Though the Ordinary was out of the way to-day, I hope, my dear,
you will, upon the first opportunity, quiet my scruples—Oh Sir!—my father's
hard heart is not to be soften'd, and I am in the utmost despair.

Mach. But if I could raise a small sum—would not twenty Guineas, think
you, move him?—Of all the arguments in the way of business, the perquisite
is the most prevailing.——Your father's perquisites for the escape of
prisoners must amount to a considerable sum in the year. Money well tim'd,
and properly apply'd, will do any thing.

AIR XXXIII.   *London* Ladies.

If you at an Office solicit your due,
And would not have matters neglected;   10
You must quicken the Clerk with the perquisite too,
To do what his duty directed.
Or would you the frowns of a lady prevent,
She too has this palpable failing,
The perquisite softens her into consent;
That reason with all is prevailing.

Lucy. What love or money can do shall be done: for all my comfort
depends upon your safety.

SCENE XIII.

LUCY, MACHEATH, POLLY.

Polly. Where is my dear husband?—Was a rope ever intended for this neck!—O let me throw my arms about it, and throttle thee with love!—Why dost thou turn away from me?—'Tis thy *Polly*—'tis thy wife.

Mach. Was ever such an unfortunate rascal as I am!

Lucy. Was there ever such another villain!

Polly. O *Macheath*! was it for this we parted? Taken! Imprison'd! Try'd! Hang'd!—cruel reflection! I'll stay with thee 'till death—no force shall tear thy dear wife from thee now.—What means my love?—Not one kind word! not one kind look! think what thy *Polly* suffers to see thee in this condition.

AIR XXXIV.   All in the Downs, &c.

> *Thus when the Swallow, seeking prey,*   10
> *Within the sash is closely pent,*
> *His consort with bemoaning lay,*
> *Without sits pining for th' event.*
> *Her chatt'ring lovers all around her skim;*
> *She heeds them not (poor bird) her soul's with him.*

Mach. I must disown her. [*Aside.*] The wench is distracted.

Lucy. Am I then bilk'd of my virtue? Can I have no reparation? Sure men were born to lye, and women to believe them! O Villain! Villain!

Polly. Am I not thy wife?—Thy neglect of me, thy aversion to me too severely proves it.—Look on me.—Tell me, am I not thy wife?   20

Lucy. Perfidious wretch!

Polly. Barbarous husband!

Lucy. Hadst thou been hang'd five months ago, I had been happy.

Polly. And I too—If you had been kind to me 'till death, it would not have vex'd me—And that's no very unreasonable request, (though from a wife) to a man who hath not above seven or eight days to live.

Lucy. Art thou then married to another? Hast thou two wives, monster?

Mach. If women's tongues can cease for an answer—hear me.

Lucy. I won't.—Flesh and blood can't bear my usage.

Polly. Shall I not claim my own? Justice bids me speak.   30

SCENE XIII] The most direct satire on Italian opera in the play, the quarrel between Lucy and Polly burlesques that between two of Handel's mezzo-sopranos, Cuzzoni and Faustina, over their relative merits.

AIR XXXV. Have you heard of a frolicksome ditty.

Mach.   *How happy could I be with either,*
                         Were t'other dear charmer away!
                         But while you thus teaze me together,
                         To neither a word will I say;
                         But tol de rol, &c.

Polly. Sure, my dear, there ought to be some preference shown to a wife!
At least she may claim the appearance of it. He must be distracted with his
misfortunes, or he cou'd not use me thus!

Lucy. O Villain, Villain! thou hast deceiv'd me—I could even inform
against thee with pleasure. Not a Prude wishes more heartily to have facts
against her intimate acquaintance, than I now wish to have facts against thee.
I would have her satisfaction, and they should all out.   42

AIR XXXVI.   Irish Trot.

Polly. *I'm bubbled.*
Lucy. ————*I'm bubbled.*
Polly. *Oh how I am troubled!*
Lucy. *Bambouzled, and bit!*
Polly. ————————————*My distresses are doubled.*
Lucy. *When you come to the Tree, should the Hangman refuse,*
       These fingers, with pleasure, could fasten the noose.
Polly. *I'm bubbled, &c.*   50

Mach. Be pacified, my dear *Lucy*—This is all a fetch of *Polly's* to make me
desperate with you in case I get off. If I am hang'd, she would fain have the
credit of being thought my widow—Really, *Polly*, this is no time for a dispute
of this sort; for whenever you are talking of marriage, I am thinking of
hanging.

Polly. And hast thou the heart to persist in disowning me?

Mach. And hast thou the heart to persist in persuading me that I am
married? Why, *Polly*, dost thou seek to aggravate my misfortunes?

Lucy. Really, Miss *Peachum*, you but expose yourself. Besides, 'tis barbarous in you to worry a gentleman in his circumstances.   60

AIR XXXVII.

Polly.   *Cease your funning;*
                         Force or cunning
                         Never shall my heart trapan.

43 *bubbled*] Duped, swindled.   51 a fetch] A trick, stratagem.   63 *trapan*] Ensnare,
trap.

>   *All these sallies*
>   *Are but malice*
>   *To seduce my constant man.*
>   *'Tis most certain,*
>   *By their flirting*
>   *Women oft have envy shown:*
>   *Pleas'd, to ruin*   70
>   *Others wooing;*
>   *Never happy in their own!*

Polly. Decency, madam, methinks might teach you to behave yourself
with some reserve with the husband, while his wife is present.

Mach. But seriously, *Polly*, this is carrying the joke a little too far.

Lucy. If you are determin'd, madam, to raise a disturbance in the prison, I
shall be oblig'd to send for the Turnkey to shew you the door. I am sorry,
madam, you force me to be so ill-bred.

Polly. Give me leave to tell you, madam; these forward Airs don't become
you in the least, madam. And my duty, madam, obliges me to stay with my
husband, madam.   81

AIR XXXVIII.   Good-morrow, Gossip *Joan.*

Lucy.	*Why how now, madam* Flirt?
	If you thus must chatter,
	And are for flinging dirt,
	Let's try who best can spatter;
	Madam Flirt!
Polly.	*Why how now, saucy Jade;*
	Sure the wench is tipsy!
	How can you see me made [*To him.*
	The scoff of such a Gipsy?
	Saucy Jade! [*To her.*

SCENE XIV.

LUCY, MACHEATH, POLLY, PEACHUM.

Peach. Where's my wench? Ah hussy! hussy!—Come you home, you slut;
and when your fellow is hang'd, hang yourself, to make your family some
amends.

Polly. Dear, dear father, do not tear me from him—I must speak; I have more to say to him—Oh! twist thy fetters about me, that he may not haul me from thee!

Peach. Sure all women are alike! If ever they commit the folly, they are sure to commit another by exposing themselves—Away—Not a word more—You are my prisoner now, hussy.

AIR XXXIX.   Irish Howl.

Polly.
> *No power on earth can e'er divide*   10
> *The knot that sacred Love hath ty'd.*
> *When parents draw against our mind,*
> *The true-love's knot they faster bind.*
> > *Oh, oh ray, oh Amborah—oh, oh, &c.*

[Holding Macheath, Peachum pulling her.

SCENE XV.

LUCY, MACHEATH.

Mach. I am naturally compassionate, wife; so that I could not use the wench as she deserv'd; which made you at first suspect there was something in what she said.

Lucy. Indeed, my dear, I was strangely puzzled.

Mach. If that had been the case, her father would never have brought me into this circumstance—No, *Lucy,*—I had rather dye than be false to thee.

Lucy. How happy am I, if you say this from your heart! For I love thee so, that I could sooner bear to see thee hang'd than in the arms of another.

Mach. But couldst thou bear to see me hang'd?   10

Lucy. O *Macheath,* I can never live to see that day.

Mach. You see, *Lucy,* in the account of Love you are in my debt; and you must now be convinc'd, that I rather chuse to die than be another's.—Make me, if possible, love thee more, and let me owe my life to thee—If you refuse to assist me, *Peachum* and your father will immediately put me beyond all means of escape.

Lucy. My father, I know, hath been drinking hard with the Prisoners: and I fancy he is now taking his nap in his own room—If I can procure the keys, shall I go off with thee, my dear?

Mach. If we are together, 'twill be impossible to lye conceal'd. As soon as the search begins to be a little cool, I will send to thee—'Till then my heart is thy prisoner.   22

Lucy. Come then, my dear husband—owe thy life to me—and though you love me not—be grateful—But that *Polly* runs in my head strangely.

Mach. A moment of time may make us unhappy for-ever.

AIR XL.   The Lass of *Patie*'s Mill.

Lucy.
>   I like the Fox shall grieve,
>   Whose mate hath left her side,
>   Whom Hounds, from morn to eve,
>   Chase o'er the country wide.
>   Where can my lover hide?
>   Where cheat the wary pack?
>   If Love be not his guide,
>   He never will come back!

30

ACT III.   SCENE I.

SCENE *Newgate.*

LOCKIT, LUCY.

LOCKIT.

TO be sure, wench, you must have been aiding and abetting to help him to this escape.

Lucy. Sir, here hath been *Peachum* and his daughter *Polly*, and to be sure they know the ways of *Newgate* as well as if they had been born and bred in the place all their lives. Why must all your suspicion light upon me?

Lock. *Lucy*, *Lucy*, I will have none of these shuffling answers.

Lucy. Well then——If I know any thing of him I wish I may be burnt!

Lock. Keep your temper, *Lucy*, or I shall pronounce you guilty.

Lucy. Keep yours, Sir,——I do wish I may be burnt. I do——And what can I say more to convince you?   10

Lock. Did he tip handsomely?——How much did he come down with? Come hussy, don't cheat your father; and I shall not be angry with you—— Perhaps, you have made a better bargain with him than I could have done ——How much, my good girl?

Lucy. You know, Sir, I am fond of him, and would have given money to have kept him with me.

Lock. Ah *Lucy*! thy education might have put thee more upon thy guard; for a girl in the bar of an Ale-house is always besieg'd.

Lucy. Dear Sir, mention not my education——for 'twas to that I owe my ruin.   20

AIR XLI.   If Love's a sweet passion, &c.

When young at the bar you first taught me to score,
And bid me be free of my lips, and no more;
I was kiss'd by the Parson, the Squire, and the Sot:
When the guest was departed, the kiss was forgot.
But his kiss was so sweet, and so closely he prest,
That I languish'd and pin'd 'till I granted the rest.

If you can forgive me, Sir, I will make a fair confession, for to be sure he hath been a most barbarous villain to me.

Lock. And so you have let him escape, hussy——have you?

Lucy. When a woman loves; a kind look, a tender word can persuade her to any thing——and I could ask no other bribe.   31

Lock. Thou wilt always be a vulgar slut, *Lucy*——If you would not be look'd upon as a fool, you should never do any thing but upon the foot of interest. Those that act otherwise are their own bubbles.

Lucy. But Love, Sir, is a misfortune that may happen to the most discreet woman, and in love we are all fools alike.——Notwithstanding all he swore, I am now fully convinc'd that *Polly Peachum* is actually his wife.——Did I let him escape, (fool that I was!) to go to her?——*Polly* will wheedle her self into his money, and then *Peachum* will hang him, and cheat us both.

Lock. So I am to be ruin'd, because, forsooth, you must be in love!——a very pretty excuse!   41

Lucy. I could murder that impudent happy strumpet:——I gave him his life, and that creature enjoys the sweets of it.——Ungrateful *Macheath*!

AIR XLII.   *South-Sea* Ballad.

My love is all madness and folly,
Alone I lye,
Toss, tumble, and cry,
What a happy creature is Polly!
Was e'er such a wretch as I!
With rage I redden like scarlet,
That my dear inconstant Varlet,   50
Stark blind to my charms,
Is lost in the arms
Of that Jilt, that inveigling Harlot!
Stark blind to my charms,
Is lost in the arms
Of that Jilt, that inveigling Harlot!
This, this my resentment alarms.

Lock. And so, after all this mischief, I must stay here to be entertain'd with your catterwauling, mistress Puss!——Out of my sight, wanton Strumpet! you shall fast and mortify yourself into reason, with now and then a little handsome discipline to bring you to your senses.——Go.   61

SCENE II.

LOCKIT.

Peachum then intends to outwit me in this affair; but I'll be even with him.——The dog is leaky in his liquor, so I'll ply him that way, get the secret from him, and turn this affair to my own advantage.——Lions, Wolves, and Vulturs don't live together in herds, droves or flocks.——Of all animals of prey, man is the only sociable one. Every one of us preys upon his neighbour, and yet we herd together.——*Peachum* is my companion, my friend ——According to the custom of the world, indeed, he may quote thousands of Precedents for cheating me——And shall not I make use of the privilege of friendship to make him a return?

AIR XLIII.   *Packington*'s Pound.

> *Thus Gamesters united in friendship are found,*   10
> *Though they know that their industry all is a cheat;*
> *They flock to their prey at the Dice-box's sound,*
> *And join to promote one another's deceit.*
>   *But if by mishap*
>   *They fail of a chap,*
> *To keep in their hands, they each other entrap.*
> *Like Pikes, lank with hunger, who miss of their ends,*
> *They bite their companions, and prey on their friends.*

Now, *Peachum*, you and I, like honest Tradesmen, are to have a fair tryal which of us two can over-reach the other.——*Lucy.*——[*Enter* Lucy.] Are there any of *Peachum*'s people now in the house?   21

Lucy. *Filch*, Sir, is drinking a quartern of Strong-waters in the next room with black *Moll.*

Lock. Bid him come to me.

III. ii, 17 *Pikes*] Tramps, runaways.   18 *bite*] Cheat.

SCENE III.

LOCKIT, FILCH.

Lock. Why, boy, thou lookest as if thou wert half starv'd; like a shotten Herring.

Filch. One had need have the constitution of a horse to go thorough the business.——Since the favourite Child-getter was disabled by a mis-hap, I have pick'd up a little money by helping the ladies to a pregnancy against their being call'd down to sentence.——But if a man cannot get an honest livelihood any easier way, I am sure, 'tis what I can't undertake for another Session.

Lock. Truly, if that great man should tip off, 'twould be an irreparable loss. The vigor and prowess of a Knight-errant never sav'd half the ladies in distress that he hath done.——But, boy, can'st thou tell me where thy master is to be found?   12

Filch. At his *Lock, Sir, at the *Crooked Billet.*

Lock. Very well.——I have nothing more with you. [*Ex.* Filch.] I'll go to him there, for I have many important affairs to settle with him; and in the way of those transactions, I'll artfully get into his secret.——So that *Macheath* shall not remain a day longer out of my clutches.

* A Cant word, signifying, a Warehouse where stolen goods are deposited.

SCENE IV.   *A Gaming-House.*

MACHEATH in a fine tarnish'd Coat, BEN BUDGE,
MATT of the Mint.

Mach. I am sorry, gentlemen, the road was so barren of money. When my friends are in difficulties, I am always glad that my fortune can be serviceable to them. [*Gives them money.*] You see, gentlemen, I am not a meer Court friend, who professes every thing and will do nothing.

1 like a shotten Herring] Like a herring that has spawned—hence, figuratively, a person exhausted of his powers. The simile is only too appropriate to Filch's physical condition. 4 Child-getter] A person employed to make convicted women pregnant, and thus to save them from the gallows. 9 that great man] Another ironic allusion to Walpole. 9 tip off] Die.

AIR XLIV.   Lillibulero.

The modes of the Court so common are grown,
  That a true friend can hardly be met;
Friendship for interest is but a loan,
  Which they let out for what they can get.
    'Tis true, you find
    Some friends so kind,   10
Who will give you good counsel themselves to defend.
    In sorrowful ditty,
    They promise, they pity,
But shift you for money, from friend to friend.

But we, gentlemen, have still honour enough to break through the corruptions of the world.—And while I can serve you, you may command me.

Ben. It grieves my heart that so generous a man should be involv'd in such difficulties, as oblige him to live with such ill company, and herd with gamesters.

Matt. See the partiality of mankind!—One man may steal a horse, better than another look over a hedge.—Of all mechanics, of all servile handycraftsmen, a gamester is the vilest. But yet, as many of the Quality are of the profession, he is admitted amongst the politest company. I wonder we are not more respected.   24

Mach. There will be deep play to-night at *Marybone*, and consequently money may be pick'd up upon the road. Meet me there, and I'll give you the hint who is worth setting.

Matt. The fellow with a brown coat with a narrow gold binding, I am told, is never without money.

Mach. What do you mean, *Matt*?—Sure you will not think of meddling with him!—He's a good honest kind of a fellow, and one of us.   31

Ben. To be sure, Sir, we will put our selves under your direction.

Mach. Have an eye upon the money-lenders.—A *Rouleau*, or two, would prove a pretty sort of an expedition. I hate extortion.

Matt. Those *Rouleaus* are very pretty things.—I hate your Bank bills—there is such a hazard in putting them off.

Mach. There is a certain man of distinction, who in his time hath nick'd me out of a great deal of the ready. He is in my cash, *Ben*;—I'll point him out to you this evening, and you shall draw upon him for the debt.—The company are met; I hear the Dice-box in the other room. So, gentlemen, your servant. You'll meet me at *Marybone*.   41

---

33 A *Rouleau*] A cylindrical package of gold coins.   38 the ready] Ready money, cash in hand.   38 in my cash] Living off my money.

SCENE V. Peachum's *Lock*.

A Table with Wine, Brandy, Pipes and Tobacco.

PEACHUM, LOCKIT.

Lock. The Coronation account, brother *Peachum*, is of so intricate a nature, that I believe it will never be settled.

Peach. It consists indeed of a great variety of articles.—It was worth to our people, in fees of different kinds, above ten instalments.—This is part of the account, brother, that lies open before us.

Lock. A lady's tail of rich Brocade—that, I see, is dispos'd of.

Peach. To Mrs. *Diana Trapes*, the Tally-woman, and she will make a good hand on't in shoes and slippers, to trick out young ladies, upon their going into keeping.—

Lock. But I don't see any article of the Jewels.   10

Peach. Those are so well known, that they must be sent abroad—you'll find them enter'd under the article of Exportation.—As for the Snuff-boxes, Watches, Swords, *&c.*—I thought it best to enter them under their several heads.

Lock. Seven and twenty women's pockets compleat; with the several things therein contain'd; all seal'd, number'd, and enter'd.

Peach. But, brother, it is impossible for us now to enter upon this affair.— We should have the whole day before us.—Besides, the account of the last half year's Plate is in a book by it self, which lies at the other Office.

Lock. Bring us then more liquor.—To-day shall be for pleasure—to-morrow for business.—Ah brother, those daughters of ours are two slippery hussies—keep a watchful eye upon *Polly*, and *Macheath* in a day or two shall be our own again.   23

AIR XLV. Down in the North Country.

Lock.   *What Gudgeons are we men!*
                Ev'ry woman's easy prey.

---

1 The Coronation account] That is, the inventory of goods stolen during the Coronation celebrations. George II had succeeded to the throne on 22 June 1727, and the first night of *The Beggar's Opera* was 29 January 1728.   4 instalments] That is, occasions on which honours and titles were formally bestowed, such as the Lord Mayor's induction at St. Paul's.   7 Tally-woman] Cf. note on Act II, Scene iv, line 17. Mrs. Trapes combines the profession of bawd with that of outfitter to gentlemen's mistresses.   24 *Gudgeons*] Dupes, easy bait.

> *Though we have felt the hook, agen*
> *We bite, and they betray.*
>
> *The bird that hath been trapt,*
> *When he hears his calling mate,*
> *To her he flies, again he's clapt*   30
> *Within the wiry grate.*

Peach. But what signifies catching the Bird, if your daughter *Lucy* will set open the door of the Cage?

Lock. If men were answerable for the follies and frailties of their wives and daughters, no friends could keep a good correspondence together for two days.—This is unkind of you, brother; for among good friends, what they say or do goes for nothing.

Enter a Servant.

Serv. Sir, here's Mrs. *Diana Trapes* wants to speak with you.

Peach. Shall we admit her, brother *Lockit*?

Lock. By all means—she's a good customer, and a fine-spoken woman—and a woman who drinks and talks so freely will enliven the conversation.

Peach. Desire her to walk in.   [*Exit Servant.*

SCENE VI.

PEACHUM, *LOCKIT*, Mrs. *TRAPES*.

Peach. Dear Mrs. *Dye*, your servant—one may know by your kiss, that your Ginn is excellent.

Trap. I was always very curious in my liquors.

Lock. There is no perfum'd breath like it—I have been long acquainted with the flavour of those lips—han't I, Mrs. *Dye*?

Trap. Fill it up.—I take as large draughts of liquor, as I did of love.—I hate a Flincher in either.

AIR XLVI.   A Shepherd kept sheep, &c.

> *In the days of my youth I could bill like a Dove,* fa, la, la, &c.
> *Like a Sparrow at all times was ready for love,* fa, la, la, &c.
> *The life of all mortals in kissing should pass,*   10
> *Lip to lip while we're young—then the lip to the glass,* fa, la, &c.

But now, Mr. *Peachum*, to our business.—If you have blacks of any kind, brought in of late; Mantoes—Velvet Scarfs—Petticoats—let it be what it will—I am your chap—for all my ladies are very fond of mourning.

Peach. Why, look ye, Mrs. *Dye*—you deal so hard with us, that we can afford to give the gentlemen, who venture their lives for the goods, little or nothing.

Trap. The hard times oblige me to go very near in my dealing.—To be sure, of late years I have been a great sufferer by the Parliament.—Three thousand pounds would hardly make me amends.—The Act for destroying the Mint was a severe cut upon our business—'till then, if a customer stept out of the way—we knew where to have her—no doubt you know Mrs. *Coaxer*—there's a wench now ('till to-day) with a good suit of cloaths of mine upon her back, and I could never set eyes upon her for three months together.—Since the Act too against imprisonment for small sums, my loss there too hath been very considerable, and it must be so, when a lady can borrow a handsome petticoat, or a clean gown, and I not have the least hank upon her! And, o' my conscience, now-a-days most ladies take a delight in cheating, when they can do it with safety.   29

Peach. Madam, you had a handsome gold watch of us t'other day for seven Guineas.—Considering we must have our profit—to a gentleman upon the road, a gold watch will be scarce worth the taking.

Trap. Consider, Mr. *Peachum*, that watch was remarkable, and not of very safe sale.—If you have any black Velvet Scarfs—they are a handsome winter wear; and take with most gentlemen who deal with my customers.—'Tis I that put the ladies upon a good foot. 'Tis not youth or beauty that fixes their price. The gentlemen always pay according to their dress, from half a crown to two guineas; and yet those hussies make nothing of bilking of me.—Then too, allowing for accidents.—I have eleven fine customers now down under the Surgeon's hands,—what with fees and other expences, there are great goings-out, and no comings-in, and not a farthing to pay for at least a month's cloathing.—We run great risques—great risques indeed.   42

Peach. As I remember, you said something just now of Mrs. *Coaxer*.

Trap. Yes, Sir.—To be sure I stript her of a suit of my own cloaths about two hours ago; and have left her as she should be, in her shift, with a lover of hers at my house. She call'd him up stairs, as he was going to *Marybone* in a hackney-coach.—And I hope, for her own sake and mine, she will per-

12 blacks] Mourning garb.   14 your chap] That is, your chapman, your customer. 20 The Act for destroying the Mint] Passed in 1722, this abolished the traditional right of sanctuary in a place commonly known as the Mint, in the Parish of St. George's, Surrey. 25 the Act . . . against imprisonment for small sums] This prevented money-lenders and bailiffs acting in complicity—by apprehending a creditor for a relatively small debt, and then proceeding to exact many times its value in fees for the victim's compulsory board and lodgings.   40 under the Surgeon's hands] That is, lying-in.

swade the Captain to redeem her, for the Captain is very generous to the ladies.

Lock. What Captain?   50

Trap. He thought I did not know him.—An intimate acquaintance of yours, Mr. *Peachum*—only Captain *Macheath*—as fine as a Lord.

Peach. To-morrow, dear Mrs. *Dye*, you shall set your own price upon any of the goods you like—we have at least half a dozen Velvet Scarfs, and all at your service. Will you give me leave to make you a present of this suit of night-cloaths for your own wearing?—But are you sure it is Captain *Macheath*?

Trap. Though he thinks I have forgot him; no body knows him better. I have taken a great deal of the Captain's money in my time at second-hand, for he always lov'd to have his ladies well drest.   60

Peach. Mr. *Lockit* and I have a little business with the Captain;—you understand me—and we will satisfie you for Mrs. *Coaxer*'s debt.

Lock. Depend upon it—we will deal like men of honour.

Trap. I don't enquire after your affairs—so whatever happens, I wash my hands on't.—It hath always been my Maxim, that one friend should assist another.—But if you please—I'll take one of the Scarfs home with me, 'tis always good to have something in hand.

SCENE VII.   *Newgate.*

LUCY.

Jealousy, rage, love and fear are at once tearing me to pieces. How I am weather-beaten and shatter'd with distresses!

> AIR XLVII.   One evening having lost my way.
>
> *I'm like a skiff on the Ocean tost,*
> *   Now high, now low, with each billow born,*
> *With her rudder broke, and her anchor lost,*
> *   Deserted and all forlorn.*
> *While thus I lie rolling and tossing all night,*
> *That* Polly *lyes sporting on seas of delight!*
> *   Revenge, revenge, revenge,*
> *Shall appease my restless sprite.*   10

I have the Rats-bane ready.—I run no risque; for I can lay her death upon the Ginn, and so many dye of that naturally that I shall never be call'd in question.—But say I were to be hang'd—I never could be hang'd for any thing that would give me greater comfort, than the poysoning that slut.

Enter Filch.

Filch. Madam, here's our Miss *Polly* come to wait upon you.
Lucy. Show her in.

SCENE VIII.

LUCY, POLLY.

Lucy. Dear madam, your servant.—I hope you will pardon my passion, when I was so happy to see you last.—I was so over-run with the spleen, that I was perfectly out of my self. And really when one hath the spleen, every thing is to be excus'd by a friend.

AIR XLVIII.   Now *Roger*, I'll tell thee, because thou'rt my son.

> *When a wife's in her pout,*
> *(As she's sometimes, no doubt)*
> *The good husband as meek as a lamb,*
> *Her vapours to still,*
> *First grants her her will,*
> *And the quieting draught is a dram.*   10
> *Poor man! And the quieting draught is a dram.*

—I wish all our quarrels might have so comfortable a reconciliation.
Polly. I have no excuse for my own behaviour, madam, but my misfortunes.—And really, madam, I suffer too upon your account.
Lucy. But, Miss *Polly*—in the way of friendship, will you give me leave to propose a glass of Cordial to you?
Polly. Strong-waters are apt to give me the head-ache—I hope, Madam, you will excuse me.
Lucy. Not the greatest lady in the land could have better in her closet, for her own private drinking.—You seem mighty low in Spirits, my dear.   20
Polly. I am sorry, madam, my health will not allow me to accept of your offer.—I should not have left you in the rude manner I did when we met last, madam, had not my Papa haul'd me away so unexpectedly.—I was indeed somewhat provok'd, and perhaps might use some expressions that were disrespectful.—But really, madam, the Captain treated me with so much contempt and cruelty, that I deserv'd your pity, rather than your resentment.
Lucy. But since his escape, no doubt all matters are made up again.—Ah

Polly! Polly! 'tis I am the unhappy wife; and he loves you as if you were only his mistress.

Polly. Sure, madam, you cannot think me so happy as to be the object of your jealousy.—A man is always afraid of a woman who loves him too well—so that I must expect to be neglected and avoided.   32

Lucy. Then our cases, my dear *Polly*, are exactly alike. Both of us indeed have been too fond.

AIR XLIX. O Bessy Bell, &c.

Polly.	*A curse attends that woman's love*
	Who always would be pleasing.
Lucy.	*The pertness of the billing Dove,*
	Like tickling, is but teazing.
Polly.	*What then in love can woman do?*
Lucy.	*If we grow fond they shun us.* 40
Polly.	*And when we fly them, they pursue:*
Lucy.	*But leave us when they've won us.*

Lucy. Love is so very whimsical in both sexes, that it is impossible to be lasting.—But my heart is particular, and contradicts my own observation.

Polly. But really, mistress *Lucy*, by his last behaviour, I think I ought to envy you.—When I was forc'd from him, he did not shew the least tenderness.—But perhaps, he hath a heart not capable of it.

AIR L. Wou'd Fate to me Belinda give.

Among the men, Coquets we find,
Who court by turns all woman-kind;
And we grant all their hearts desir'd,   50
When they are flatter'd and admir'd.

The Coquets of both sexes are self-lovers, and that is a love no other whatever can dispossess. I fear, my dear *Lucy*, our husband is one of those.

Lucy. Away with these melancholy reflections,——indeed, my dear *Polly*, we are both of us a cup too low.—Let me prevail upon you, to accept of my offer.

AIR LI. Come, sweet lass.

Come, sweet lass,
Let's banish sorrow
'Till to-morrow;
Come, sweet lass,   60
Let's take a chirping glass.

61 *a chirping glass*] A drink to cheer us.

> *Wine can clear*
> *The vapours of despair ;*
> *And make us light as air ;*
> *Then drink, and banish care.*

I can't bear, child, to see you in such low spirits.—And I must persuade you to what I know will do you good.—I shall now soon be even with the hypocritical Strumpet.   [*Aside.*

SCENE IX.

POLLY.

Polly. All this wheedling of *Lucy* cannot be for nothing.—At this time too! when I know she hates me!—The dissembling of a woman is always the forerunner of mischief.—By pouring Strong-waters down my throat, she thinks to pump some secrets out of me—I'll be upon my guard, and won't taste a drop of her liquor, I'm resolv'd.   5

SCENE X.

LUCY, with Strong-waters. POLLY.

Lucy. Come, Miss *Polly.*
Polly. Indeed, child, you have given yourself trouble to no purpose.—You must, my dear, excuse me.
Lucy. Really, Miss *Polly*, you are so squeamishly affected about taking a cup of Strong-waters, as a lady before company. I vow, *Polly*, I shall take it monstrously ill if you refuse me.—Brandy and Men (though women love them never so well) are always taken by us with some reluctance—unless 'tis in private.
Polly. I protest, madam, it goes against me.—What do I see! *Macheath* again in custody!—Now every glimmering of happiness is lost.   10
                              [*Drops the glass of liquor on the ground.*
Lucy. Since things are thus, I'm glad the wench hath escap'd: for by this event, 'tis plain, she was not happy enough to deserve to be poison'd.

SCENE XI.

LOCKIT, MACHEATH, PEACHUM,
LUCY, POLLY.

Lock. Set your heart to rest, Captain.—You have neither the chance of Love or Money for another escape—for you are order'd to be call'd down upon your Tryal immediately.

Peach. Away, hussies!—This is not a time for a man to be hamper'd with his wives.—You see, the gentleman is in chains already.

Lucy. O husband, husband, my heart long'd to see thee; but to see thee thus distracts me!

Polly. Will not my dear husband look upon his *Polly*? Why hadst thou not flown to me for protection? with me thou hadst been safe.

AIR LII.   The last time I went o'er the Moor.

Polly.	*Hither, dear husband, turn your eyes.* 10
Lucy.	*Bestow one glance to cheer me.*
Polly.	*Think with that look, thy* Polly *dyes.*
Lucy.	*O shun me not,—but hear me.*
Polly.	*'Tis* Polly *sues.*
Lucy.	—————————*'Tis* Lucy *speaks.*
Polly.	*Is thus true love requited?*
Lucy.	*My heart is bursting.*
Polly.	—————————*Mine too breaks.*
Lucy.	*Must I,*
Polly.	—————————*Must I be slighted?*

Mach. What would you have me say, ladies?——You see, this affair will soon be at an end, without my disobliging either of you.

Peach. But the settling this point, Captain, might prevent a Law-suit between your two widows.   21

AIR LIII.   *Tom Tinker*'s my true love, *&c.*

Mach.	*Which way shall I turn me—how can I decide?*
	Wives, the day of our death, are as fond as a bride.
	One wife is too much for most husbands to hear,
	But two at a time there's no mortal can bear.
	This way, and that way, and which way I will,
	What would comfort the one, t'other wife would take ill.

Polly. But if his own misfortunes have made him insensible to mine—
a Father sure will be more compassionate.—Dear, dear Sir, sink the material
evidence, and bring him off at his Tryal—*Polly* upon her knees begs it of you.

AIR LIV.   I am a poor Shepherd undone.

> *When my Hero in court appears,*   31
>   *And stands arraign'd for his life,*
> *Then think of poor* Polly's *tears;*
>   *For ah! poor* Polly's *his wife.*
> *Like the Sailor he holds up his hand,*
>   *Distrest on the dashing wave.*
> *To die a dry death at land,*
>   *Is as bad as a watry grave.*
> *And alas, poor* Polly!
> *Alack, and well-a-day!*   40
> *Before I was in love,*
>   *Oh! every month was* May.

Lucy. If *Peachum*'s heart is harden'd; sure you, Sir, will have more
compassion on a daughter.——I know the evidence is in your power.——
How then can you be a tyrant to me?   [*Kneeling*.

AIR LV.   *Ianthe* the lovely, *&c.*

> *When he holds up his hand arraign'd for his life,*
> *O think of your daughter, and think I'm his wife!*
> *What are cannons, or bombs, or clashing of swords?*
> *For death is more certain by witnesses words.*
> *Then nail up their lips; that dread thunder allay;*   50
> *And each month of my life will hereafter be* May.

Lock. Macheath's time is come, *Lucy*.—We know our own affairs, therefore
let us have no more whimpering or whining.

AIR LVI.   A Cobler there was, *&c.*

> *Our selves, like the Great, to secure a retreat,*
> *When matters require it, must give up our gang:*
>   *And good reason why,*
>   *Or, instead of the fry,*
>   *Ev'n* Peachum *and I,*
> *Like poor petty rascals, might hang, hang;*
> *Like poor petty rascals, might hang.*   60

29 sink the material evidence] Pass over, avoid mention of the evidence likely to prejudice
Macheath's fate.

Peach. Set your heart at rest, *Polly.*——Your husband is to dye to day.——
Therefore, if you are not already provided, 'tis high time to look about for
another. There's comfort for you, you slut.

Lock. We are ready, Sir, to conduct you to the *Old Baily.*

AIR LVII.   Bonny *Dundee.*

Mach.
> *The charge is prepar'd; the Lawyers are met;*
> *The Judges all rang'd (a terrible show!)*
> *I go, undismay'd.—For death is a debt,*
> *A debt on demand.—So, take what I owe.*
> *Then farewell, my love—dear charmers, adieu.*
> *Contented I die—'tis the better for you.*   70
> *Here ends all dispute the rest of our lives,*
> *For this way at once I please all my wives.*

Now, Gentlemen, I am ready to attend you.

SCENE XII.

LUCY, POLLY, FILCH.

Polly. Follow them, *Filch,* to the Court. And when the Tryal is over,
bring me a particular account of his behaviour, and of every thing that
happen'd.—You'll find me here with Miss *Lucy.* [*Ex.* Filch.] But why is all
this Musick?

Lucy. The Prisoners, whose tryals are put off till next Session, are diverting
themselves.

Polly. Sure there is nothing so charming as Musick! I'm fond of it to
distraction—But alas!—now, all mirth seems an insult upon my affliction.
——Let us retire, my dear *Lucy,* and indulge our sorrows.—The noisy crew,
you see, are coming upon us.   [*Exeunt.*

A Dance of Prisoners in chains, &c.

SCENE XIII.   *The Condemn'd Hold.*

MACHEATH, in a melancholy posture.

AIR LVIII.   Happy Groves.

> *O cruel, cruel, cruel case!*
> *Must I suffer this disgrace?*

AIR LIX.   Of all the girls that are so smart.

> *Of all the friends in time of grief,*
>   *When threat'ning Death looks grimmer,*
> *Not one so sure can bring relief,*
>   *As this best friend a brimmer.*   [Drinks.

AIR LX.   *Britons* strike home.

Since I must swing,—I scorn, I scorn to wince or whine.   [Rises.

AIR LXI.   Chevy Chase.

> *But now again my spirits sink;*
> *I'll raise them high with wine.*
>   [Drinks a glass of wine.

AIR LXII.   To old Sir *Simon* the King.

> *But valour the stronger grows,*   10
>   *The stronger liquor we're drinking.*
> *And how can we feel our woes,*
>   *When we've lost the trouble of thinking?*   [Drinks.

AIR LXIII.   Joy to great *Caesar*.

> *If thus—A man can die*
> *Much bolder with brandy.*
>   [Pours out a bumper of brandy.

AIR LXIV.   There was an old woman, *&c.*

So I drink off this bumper—And now I can stand the test,
And my Comrades shall see, that I die as brave as the best.
                                                          [Drinks.

AIR LXV.   Did you ever hear of a gallant sailor.

> *But can I leave my pretty hussies,*
> *Without one tear, or tender sigh?*

AIR LXVI.   Why are mine eyes still flowing.

> *Their eyes, their lips, their busses*   20
> *Recall my love—Ah must I die!*

AIR LXVII.   Green sleeves.

Since laws were made for ev'ry degree,
To curb vice in others, as well as me,

6 *a brimmer*] A goblet filled to the brim with wine.

> *I wonder we han't better company*
>   *Upon* Tyburn *tree!*
> *But gold from law can take out the sting;*
> *And if rich men like us were to swing,*
> *'Twould thin the land, such numbers to string*
>   *Upon* Tyburn *tree!*

Jailor. Some friends of yours, Captain, desire to be admitted—I leave you together.   31

SCENE XIV.

MACHEATH, BEN BUDGE, MAT of the Mint.

Mach. For my having broke Prison, you see, gentlemen, I am order'd immediate execution.——The Sheriffs officers, I believe, are now at the door. ——That *Jemmy Twitcher* should peach me, I own surpriz'd me!—'Tis a plain proof that the world is all alike, and that even our Gang can no more trust one another than other people. Therefore, I beg you, gentlemen, look well to your selves, for in all probability you may live some months longer.

Mat. We are heartily sorry, Captain, for your misfortune.—But 'tis what we must all come to.

Mach. Peachum and *Lockit*, you know, are infamous Scoundrels. Their lives are as much in your power, as yours are in theirs——Remember your dying friend!——'Tis my last request.——Bring those villains to the Gallows before you, and I am satisfied.   12

Mat. We'll do't.

Jailor. Miss *Polly* and Miss *Lucy* intreat a word with you.

Mach. Gentlemen, adieu.

SCENE XV.

LUCY, MACHEATH, POLLY.

Mach. My dear *Lucy*——my dear *Polly*——Whatsoever hath past between us is now at an end.—If you are fond of marrying again, the best advice I can give you, is to ship yourselves off for the *West-Indies*, where you'll have a fair chance of getting a husband a-piece; or by good luck, two or three, as you like best.

Polly. How can I support this sight!
Lucy. There is nothing moves one so much as a great man in distress.

AIR LXVIII.   *All you that must take a leap, &c.*

Lucy.	*Would I might be hang'd!*
Polly.	————————————————*And I would so too!*
Lucy.	*To be hang'd with you,*
Polly.	——————————————*My dear, with you.*
Mach.	*O leave me to thought! I fear! I doubt!* 10
	I tremble! I droop!——See, my courage is out.
	[*Turns up the empty bottle.*
Polly.	*No token of love?*
Mach.	——————————*See, my courage is out.*
	[*Turns up the empty pot.*
Lucy.	*No token of love?*
Polly.	——————————*Adieu.*
Lucy.	——————————————*Farewell.*
Mach.	*But hark! I hear the toll of the bell.*
Chorus.	*Tol de rol lol,* &c.

Jailor. Four women more, Captain, with a child a-piece! See, here they come.   [*Enter women and children.*
Mach. What—four wives more!—This is too much.—Here—tell the Sheriffs officers I am ready.   [*Exit* Macheath *guarded.*

═══

SCENE XVI.

To them, Enter PLAYER and BEGGAR.

Play. But, honest friend, I hope you don't intend that *Macheath* shall be really executed.
Beg. Most certainly, Sir.—To make the piece perfect, I was for doing strict poetical Justice.—*Macheath* is to be hang'd; and for the other personages of the Drama, the Audience must have suppos'd they were all either hang'd or transported.
Play. Why then, friend, this is a down-right deep Tragedy. The catastrophe is manifestly wrong, for an Opera must end happily.   8
Beg. Your objection, Sir, is very just; and is easily remov'd. For you must

III. xvi, 3 strict poetical Justice] The recently formulated critical doctrine that a play's climax must be morally fitting, even at the expense of its dramatic probability.

allow, that in this kind of Drama, 'tis no matter how absurdly things are brought about—So—you rabble there—run and cry a Reprieve—let the prisoner be brought back to his wives in triumph.

Play. All this we must do, to comply with the taste of the town.

Beg. Through the whole piece you may observe such a similitude of manners in high and low life, that it is difficult to determine whether (in the fashionable vices) the fine gentlemen imitate the gentlemen of the road, or the gentlemen of the road the fine gentlemen.——Had the Play remain'd, as I at first intended, it would have carried a most excellent moral. 'Twould have shown that the lower sort of people have their vices in a degree as well as the rich: And that they are punish'd for them.   20

SCENE XVII.

To them MACHEATH with Rabble, &c.

Mach. So, it seems, I am not left to my choice, but must have a wife at last.——Look ye, my dears, we will have no controversie now. Let us give this day to mirth, and I am sure she who thinks her self my wife will testifie her joy by a dance.

All. Come, a Dance——a Dance.

Mach. Ladies, I hope you will give me leave to present a Partner to each of you. And (if I may without offence) for this time, I take *Polly* for mine.— And for life, you slut,—for we were really marry'd.——As for the rest.—— But at present keep your own secret.   [*To Polly.*

A DANCE.
AIR LXIX.   Lumps of Pudding, &c.

Thus I stand like the Turk, *with his doxies around;*   10
From all sides their glances his passion confound;
For black, brown, and fair, his inconstancy burns,
And the different beauties subdue him by turns:
Each calls forth her charms, to provoke his desires:
Though willing to all; with but one he retires.
But think of this maxim, and put off your sorrow,
The wretch of to-day, may be happy to morrow.

Chorus.   *But think of this maxim,* &c.

FINIS.

THE
TRAGEDY OF TRAGEDIES

Henry Fielding

1707–1754

It was partly the fault of a bad first biographer, and partly the fact of Fielding's later pre-eminence as a novelist, that his plays have commonly been dismissed as the works of a hasty hack. The sheer hard work evidently involved in preparing the mock-annotations to his *Tragedy of Tragedies* may help to refute this legend of laziness. It is, however, paradoxically true that some of the two dozen dramas over which he took least time or trouble—the fast-moving one- or two-act farces—are among his better works, and the regular five-act comedies which he tried so assiduously to perfect among the less interesting. But Fielding also explored two lesser-known forms, dramatic satire and burlesque. Indeed, it was some of his satires—*The Historical Register*, a political cabaret of its age, probably best known among them—which provided Walpole with an excuse to impose the Lord Chamberlain's stage censorship in 1737, and thus to end Fielding's prolific seven-year spell as a playwright. But these satires, however powerful, were by nature ephemeral, and it is in the plays which deflate theatrical rather than political pretensions that his powers at once to amuse and to stimulate are best preserved.

Sadly, Fielding wrote only a couple of plays in this style, though elements of formal parody are preserved in many of the politically oriented pieces. In his second and last burlesque, *The Covent-Garden Tragedy*, he ridiculed the debased blank verse of pseudo-classical tragedy, and reduced Lillo's daring introduction of merchant-class characters into tragedy *ad absurdum*, by peopling his own play with declamatory pimps, prostitutes, and rakes. *Tom Thumb*, the earlier version of the present play and Fielding's first attempt at burlesque, was mainly a pastiche of heroic tragedy—most of its exponents long dead, but their plays as popular as ever. Intended to evoke admiration rather than pity and terror, their exotic heroes were literally cut down to size by the warrior-midget, Tom Thumb—who aptly personified the technique of bathos recently re-defined by Pope in his *Art of Sinking in Poetry*.

The original *Tom Thumb*, first staged at the Haymarket on 25 April 1730, proved so popular that Fielding revised and expanded its text into *The Tragedy of Tragedies* here reprinted, which was first performed on 24 March 1731. True to his Scriblerian pseudonym, Fielding embellished the play's printed text with copious mock-annotations, in which he identified the authors who had 'plagiarized' his supposedly Elizabethan author. He also provided a Preface, solemnly setting out to prove the play's regularity—and sprinkling it liberally with the classical tags beloved by the pedants he was ridiculing. For the lay reader this Preface is probably the least rewarding part of the burlesque—since even the annotations to the play proper, unfamiliar though their sources may be, are at least evidence of the accuracy of Fielding's own heightening of bombastic rhetoric.

Not that the play entirely accords with its heroic models. It is in burlesqued blank verse rather than mock-heroic couplets—although the latter idiom, offering the ready-made bathos of ludicrous rhyme, is the easier to sustain. And the mass slaughter with which the play concludes is not, strictly speaking, an heroic habit. Rather, it is a dramatic convenience—and, subject to its timing, a theatrically effective climax—which accords more closely with the conventions of the Elizabethan tragedies among which the work pretends to be numbered, and of their eighteenth-century imitations. The lay reader is best advised to ignore all the mock-critical appendages on a first reading, relying on his own acquaintance with tragic pentameters to add stylistic relish to mounting absurdities that achieve their own kind of self-containment. The glosses, ironical and actual, can come later: for *The Tragedy of Tragedies* deserves first and foremost the tribute of belly-laughter, before closer acquaintance begins to tempt tongues into cheeks, in wry appreciation of its more academic jokes.

The present text of *The Tragedy of Tragedies* follows that of the first edition of 1731. The fullest, though over-ambitiously titled *Complete Works of Henry Fielding*, was edited in sixteen volumes by W. E. Henley for the Yale University Press in 1903, and the definitive Wesleyan Edition of the complete works is in active preparation. J. T. Hillhouse's edition of *The Tragedy of Tragedies*, published by Yale University Press in 1918 and now out of print, contains both the original and revised versions of the play—and provides copious annotations on Fielding's annotations. The text of the unrevised *Tom Thumb*, together with *The Covent-Garden Tragedy*, is included in my own edition of *Burlesque Plays of the Eighteenth Century* (Oxford Paperbacks, 1969).

THE
TRAGEDY

OF

TRAGEDIES;

OR THE

LIFE *and* DEATH

OF

TOM THUMB *the Great.*

As it is Acted at the

THEATRE in the *Hay-Market.*

With the ANNOTATIONS of
H. SCRIBLERUS SECUNDUS.

LONDON,
Printed; And Sold by *J. Roberts* in *Warwick-Lane.*
M DCC XXXI.
Price One Shilling.

H

H. Scriblerus Secundus;

HIS

PREFACE.

THE Town hath seldom been more divided in its Opinion, than concerning the Merit of the following Scenes. Whilst some publickly affirmed, That no Author could produce so fine a Piece but Mr. *P—*, others have with as much Vehemence insisted, That no one could write any thing so bad, but Mr. *F—*.

Nor can we wonder at this Dissention about its Merit, when the learned World have not unanimously decided even the very Nature of this Tragedy. For tho' most of the Universities in *Europe* have honoured it with the Name of *Egregium & maximi pretii opus, Tragoediis tam antiquis quam novis longe anteponendum*; nay, Dr. *B——* hath pronounced, *Citiùs Maevii Æneadem quam Scribleri istius Tragoediam hanc crediderim, cujus Autorem Senecam ipsum tradidisse haud dubitârim*; and the great Professor *Burman*, hath stiled *Tom Thumb, Heroum omnium Tragicorum facilè Principem*. Nay, tho' it hath, among other Languages, been translated into *Dutch*, and celebrated with great Applause at *Amsterdam* (where Burlesque never came) by the Title of *Mynheer Vander Thumb*, the Burgomasters receiving it with that reverent and silent Attention, which becometh an Audience at a deep Tragedy: Notwithstanding all this, there have not been wanting some who have represented these Scenes in a ludicrous Light; and Mr. *D——* hath been heard to say, with some Concern, That he wondered a Tragical and Christian Nation would permit a Representation on its Theatre, so visibly designed to ridicule and extirpate every thing that is Great and Solemn among us. 22

This learned Critick, and his Followers, were led into so great an Error, by that surreptitious and piratical Copy which stole last Year into the World; with what Injustice and Prejudice to our Author, I hope will be acknowledged by every one who shall happily peruse this genuine and original Copy. Nor can I help remarking, to the great Praise of our Author, that, however im-

---

3 Mr. *P—*] Pope.   5 Mr. *F—*] Fielding himself, of course.   10 Dr. *B——*] Richard Bentley, the classical scholar.   12 Professor *Burman*] A Dutch scholar, under whom Fielding had studied during his brief residence at Leyden.   19 Mr. *D——*] John Dennis, the dramatic critic—whose notices of particular plays were more perceptive than his general aesthetic pronouncements, which Fielding is here parodying.   24 that surreptitious and piratical Copy] Fielding's own, earlier version of *The Tragedy of Tragedies*, substantively shorter, lacking the *Tragedy*'s mock-critical apparatus, and called simply *Tom Thumb*.

perfect the former was, still did even that faint Resemblance of the true *Tom Thumb*, contain sufficient Beauties to give it a Run of upwards of Forty Nights, to the politest Audiences. But, notwithstanding that Applause which it receiv'd from all the best Judges, it was as severely censured by some few bad ones, and I believe, rather maliciously than ignorantly, reported to have been intended a Burlesque on the loftiest Parts of Tragedy, and designed to banish what we generally call Fine Things, from the Stage.   34

Now, if I can set my Country right in an Affair of this Importance, I shall lightly esteem any Labour which it may cost. And this I the rather undertake, First, as it is indeed in some measure incumbent on me to vindicate myself from that surreptitious Copy beforementioned, published by some ill-meaning People, under my Name: Secondly, as knowing my self more capable of doing Justice to our Author, than any other Man, as I have given my self more Pains to arrive at a thorough Understanding of this little Piece, having for ten Years together read nothing else; in which time, I think I may modestly presume, with the help of my *English* Dictionary, to comprehend all the Meanings of every Word in it.   44

But should any Error of my Pen awaken *Clariss. Bentleium* to enlighten the World with his Annotations on our Author, I shall not think that the least Reward or Happiness arising to me from these my Endeavours.

I shall wave at present, what hath caused such Feuds in the learned World, Whether this Piece was originally written by *Shakespear*, tho' certainly That, were it true, must add a considerable Share to its Merit; especially, with such who are so generous as to buy and to commend what they never read, from an implicit Faith in the Author only: A Faith! which our Age abounds in as much, as it can be called deficient in any other.   53

Let it suffice, that the *Tragedy of Tragedies*, or, *The Life and Death of Tom Thumb*, was written in the Reign of Queen *Elizabeth*. Nor can the Objection made by Mr. *D*———, That the Tragedy must then have been antecedent to the History, have any Weight, when we consider, That tho' the *History of Tom Thumb*, printed by and for *Edward M*———*r*, at the Looking-Glass on *London-Bridge*, be of a later date; still must we suppose this History to have been transcribed from some other, unless we suppose the Writer thereof to be inspired: A Gift very faintly contended for by the Writers of our Age. As to this History's not bearing the Stamp of Second, Third, or Fourth Edition, I see but little in that Objection; Editions being

---

46 his Annotations] Bentley's real classical scholarship was marred by his pedantry. Undoubtedly correct in doubting the authenticity of the so-called *Epistles* of Phalaris, he was held in scant respect by the better-known literary figures of the age, and was one of Swift's main targets in *The Battle of the Books*.   48 wave] Waive, ignore.   57 the History] That is, the *History of Tom Thumb* in chapbook form.   58 *Edward M*———*r*] Edward Midwinter, later assumed by the mock-annotator to be the author of the *Ballad of Tom Thumb*.   62 the Stamp] That is, the date or number of its edition.

very uncertain Lights to judge of Books by: And perhaps Mr. *M*———*r* may have joined twenty Editions in one, as Mr. *C*———*l* hath ere now divided one into twenty.   66

Nor doth the other Argument, drawn from the little Care our Author hath taken to keep up to the Letter of the History, carry any greater Force. Are there not Instances of Plays, wherein the History is so perverted, that we can know the Heroes whom they celebrate by no other Marks than their Names? Nay, do we not find the same Character placed by different Poets in such different Lights, that we can discover not the least Sameness, or even Likeness in the Features. The *Sophonisba* of *Mairet*, and of *Lee*, is a tender, passionate, amorous Mistress of *Massinissa*; *Corneille*, and Mr. *Thomson* give her no other Passion but the Love of her Country, and make her as cool in her Affection to *Massinissa*, as to *Syphax*. In the two latter, she resembles the Character of Queen *Elizabeth*; in the two former, she is the Picture of *Mary* Queen of *Scotland*. In short, the one *Sophonisba* is as different from the other, as the *Brutus* of *Voltaire*, is from the *Marius* Jun. of *Otway*; or as the *Minerva* is from the *Venus* of the Ancients.   80

Let us now proceed to a regular Examination of the Tragedy before us. In which I shall treat separately of the Fable, the Moral, the Characters, the Sentiments, and the Diction. And first of the

Fable; which I take to be the most simple imaginable; and, to use the Words of an eminent Author, 'One, regular, and uniform, not charged with 'a Multiplicity of Incidents, and yet affording several Revolutions of Fortune; 'by which the Passions may be excited, varied, and driven to their full 'Tumult of Emotion.'———Nor is the *Action* of this Tragedy less great than uniform. The Spring of all, is the love of *Tom Thumb* for *Huncamunca*; which causeth the Quarrel between their Majesties in the first Act; the Passion of Lord *Grizzle* in the Second; the Rebellion, Fall of Lord *Grizzle*, and *Glumdalca*, Devouring of *Tom Thumb* by the Cow, and that bloody Catastrophe, in the Third.   93

Nor is the *Moral* of this excellent Tragedy less noble than the *Fable*; it teaches these two instructive Lessons, *viz*. That Human Happiness is exceeding transient, and, That Death is the certain End of all Men; the former

---

65 Mr. *C*———*l*] Edmund Curll, the hack publisher attacked by Pope in the *Dunciad*. 65 divided one into twenty] That is, split up a single impression of a book into so-called second and subsequent editions, to make the work appear to be in public demand. 73 *Sophonisba*] Mairet was the first dramatist to attempt a play on this theme, in 1634. Subsequent versions were those of Corneille in 1663, of Lee in 1676, and of Thomson in 1730.   81 a regular Examination] That is, an examination of the play's formal regularity. The mock-critic proceeds to illustrate his 'author's' conformity to the characteristics of tragedy described—or, as the neo-classicists supposed, ordained—by Aristotle.   85 an eminent Author] Namely, James Thomson, in the Preface to his own version of *Sophonisba*.

whereof is inculcated by the fatal End of *Tom Thumb*; the latter, by that of all the other Personages.

The *Characters* are, I think, sufficiently described in the *Dramatis Personæ*; and I believe we shall find few Plays, where greater Care is taken to maintain them throughout, and to preserve in every Speech that Characteristical Mark which distinguishes them from each other. 'But (says Mr. *D*—) how well 'doth the Character of *Tom Thumb*, whom we must call the Hero of this 'Tragedy, if it hath any Hero, agree with the Precepts of *Aristotle*, who 'defineth *Tragedy to be the Imitation of a short, but perfect Action, containing a 'just Greatness in it self,* &c. What Greatness can be in a Fellow, whom History relateth to have been no higher than a Span?' This Gentleman seemeth to think, with Serjeant *Kite*, that the Greatness of a Man's Soul is in proportion to that of his Body, the contrary of which is affirmed by our *English* Physognominical Writers. Besides, if I understand *Aristotle* right, he speaketh only of the Greatness of the Action, and not of the Person.   111

As for the *Sentiments* and the *Diction*, which now only remain to be spoken to; I thought I could afford them no stronger Justification, than by producing parallel Passages out of the best of our *English* Writers. Whether this Sameness of Thought and Expression which I have quoted from them, proceeded from an Agreement in their Way of Thinking; or whether they have borrowed from our Author, I leave the Reader to determine. I shall adventure to affirm this of the Sentiments of our Author; That they are generally the most familiar which I have ever met with, and at the same time delivered with the highest Dignity of Phrase; which brings me to speak of his *Diction.*—Here I shall only beg one Postulatum, *viz.* That the greatest Perfection of the Language of a Tragedy is, that it is not to be understood; which granted (as I think it must be) it will necessarily follow, that the only ways to avoid this, is by being too high or too low for the Understanding, which will comprehend every thing within its Reach. Those two Extremities of Stile Mr. *Dryden* illustrates by the familiar Image of two Inns, which I shall term the Aerial and the Subterrestrial.   127

Horace goeth farther, and sheweth when it is proper to call at one of these Inns, and when at the other;

> *Telephus & Peleus, cùm pauper & exul uterque,*   130
> *Projicit Ampullas & Sesquipedalia Verba.*

That he approveth of the *Sesquipedalia Verba,* is plain; for had not *Telephus & Peleus* used this sort of Diction in Prosperity, they could not have dropt it in Adversity. The Aerial Inn, therefore (says *Horace*) is proper only to be

---

108 Serjeant *Kite*] A character in Farquhar's *Recruiting Officer,* who declares that 'he that has the good fortune to be born six feet high was born to be a great man'.   125 Mr. *Dryden* illustrates] In the essay on heroic drama which prefaces his *Conquest of Granada.*

frequented by Princes and other great Men, in the highest Affluence of Fortune; the Subterrestrial is appointed for the Entertainment of the poorer sort of People only, whom *Horace* advises,

> —— *dolere Sermone pedestri.*

The true Meaning of both which Citations is, That Bombast is the proper Language for Joy, and Doggrel for Grief, the latter of which is literally imply'd in the *Sermo pedestris*, as the former is in the *Sesquipedalia Verba*.

Cicero recommendeth the former of these. *Quid est tam furiosum vel tragicum quàm verborum sonitus inanis, nullâ subjectâ Sententiâ neque Scientiâ.* What can be so proper for Tragedy as a Set of big sounding Words, so contrived together, as to convey no Meaning; which I shall one Day or other prove to be the Sublime of *Longinus*. Ovid declareth absolutely for the latter Inn: 147

> *Omne genus scripti Gravitate Tragoedia vincit.*

Tragedy hath of all Writings the greatest Share in the *Bathos*, which is the Profound of *Scriblerus*.   150

I shall not presume to determine which of these two Stiles be properer for Tragedy.——— It sufficeth, that our Author excelleth in both. He is very rarely within sight through the whole Play, either rising higher than the Eye of your Understanding can soar, or sinking lower than it careth to stoop. But here it may perhaps be observed, that I have given more frequent Instances of Authors who have imitated him in the Sublime, than in the contrary. To which I answer, First, Bombast being properly a Redundancy of Genius, Instances of this Nature occur in Poets whose Names do more Honour to our Author, than the Writers in the Doggrel, which proceeds from a cool, calm, weighty Way of Thinking. Instances whereof are most frequently to be found in Authors of a lower Class. Secondly, That the Works of such Authors are difficultly found at all. Thirdly, That it is a very hard Task to read them, in order to extract these Flowers from them. And Lastly, It is very often difficult to transplant them at all; they being like some Flowers of a very nice Nature, which will flourish in no Soil but their own: For it is easy to transcribe a Thought, but not the Want of one. The *Earl of Essex*, for Instance, is a little Garden of choice Rarities, whence you can scarce transplant one Line so as to preserve its original Beauty. This must account to the Reader for his missing the Names of several of his Acquaintance, which he had certainly found here, had I ever read their Works; for which, if I

---

150 the Profound of *Scriblerus*] That is, bathos as re-defined by Pope in *The Art of Sinking in Poetry*. Taking advantage of the critical controversy over the interpretation of the word, as used by Longinus, Pope effectively bestowed upon it its modern, inverted meaning: of a ludicrous descent from the high-flown into the ridiculous.   166 The *Earl of Essex*] By John Banks.

have not a just Esteem, I can at least say with *Cicero, Quae non contemno,*
quippè quae nunquam legerim. However, that the Reader may meet with due
Satisfaction in this Point, I have a young Commentator from the University,
who is reading over all the modern Tragedies, at Five Shillings a Dozen, and
collecting all that they have stole from our Author, which shall shortly be
added as an Appendix to this Work.   176

Dramatis Personæ.

King *Arthur*, A passionate sort of King, Husband to Queen *Dollallolla*, of whom he stands a little in Fear; Father to *Huncamunca*, whom he is very fond of; and in Love with *Glumdalca*.   } Mr. *Mullart*.

Tom Thumb the Great, A little Hero with a great Soul, something violent in his Temper, which is a little abated by his Love for *Huncamunca*.   } Young *Verhuyck*.

Ghost of Gaffar Thumb, A whimsical sort of Ghost.   Mr. *Lacy*.

Lord *Grizzle*, Extremely zealous for the Liberty of the Subject, very cholerick in his Temper, and in Love with *Huncamunca*.   } Mr. *Jones*.

Merlin, A Conjurer, and in some sort Father to *Tom Thumb*.   } Mr. *Hallam*.

Noodle, } Courtiers in Place, and consequently of *Doodle,* } that Party that is uppermost.   } Mr. *Reynolds*. Mr. *Wathan*.

Foodle, A Courtier that is out of Place, and consequently of that Party that is undermost.   } Mr. *Ayres*.

Bailiff, and } Of the Party of the Plaintiff.   } Mr. *Peterson*. *Follower,* }   } Mr. *Hicks*.

Parson, Of the Side of the Church.   Mr. *Watson*.

WOMEN.

Queen *Dollallolla*, Wife to King *Arthur*, and Mother to *Huncamunca*, a Woman entirely faultless, saving that she is a little given to Drink; a little too much a *Virago* towards her Husband, and in Love with *Tom Thumb*.   } Mrs. *Mullart*.

The Princess *Huncamunca*, Daughter to their ⎫
Majesties King *Arthur* and Queen *Dollallolla*, of │
a very sweet, gentle, and amorous Disposition, ⎬ Mrs. *Jones*.
equally in Love with Lord *Grizzle* and *Tom* │
Thumb, and desirous to be married to them both. ⎭

Glumdalca, of the Giants, a Captive Queen, be- ⎱
lov'd by the King, but in Love with *Tom Thumb*. ⎰ Mrs. *Dove*.

Cleora,   ⎱ Maids of Honour, in ⎱ Noodle. ⎱
Mustacha, ⎰   Love with   ⎰ Doodle. ⎰

Courtiers, Guards, Rebels, Drums, Trumpets, Thunder and Lightning.

SCENE *the Court of King* Arthur, *and a Plain thereabouts.*

TOM THUMB *the Great.*

ACT I.   SCENE I.

SCENE, *The Palace.*

Doodle, Noodle.

DOODLE.

SURE, such a (*a*) Day as this was never seen!
   The Sun himself, on this auspicious Day,
Shines, like a Beau in a new Birth-Day Suit:
This down the Seams embroider'd, that the Beams.

                  4

   (*a*) *Corneille* recommends some very remarkable Day, wherein to fix the Action of a Tragedy. This the best of our Tragical Writers have understood to mean a Day remarkable for the Serenity of the Sky, or what we generally call a fine Summer's Day: So that according to this their Exposition, the same Months are proper for Tragedy, which are proper for Pastoral. Most of our celebrated *English* Tragedies, as *Cato, Mariamne, Tamerlane,* &c. begin with their Observations on the Morning. *Lee* seems to have come the nearest to this beautiful Description of our Authors;

> *The Morning dawns with an unwonted Crimson,*
> *The Flowers all odorous seem, the Garden Birds*
> *Sing louder, and the laughing Sun ascends,*
> *The gaudy Earth with an unusual brightness,*
> *All Nature smiles.*   Caes. Borg.

Massinissa in the new *Sophonisba* is also a Favourite of the Sun;

> *—The Sun too seems*
> *As conscious of my Joy with broader Eye*
> *To look abroad the World, and all things smile*
> *Like Sophonisba.*

Memnon in the *Persian Princess,* makes the Sun decline rising, that he may not peep on Objects, which would prophane his Brightness.

> *——————————— The Morning rises slow,*
> *And all those ruddy Streaks that us'd to paint*
> *The Days Approach, are lost in Clouds as if*
> *The Horrors of the Night had sent 'em back,*
> *To warn the Sun, he should not leave the Sea,*
> *To Peep,* &c.

---

3 a new Birth-Day Suit] A new suit worn in celebration of the king's birthday.

All Nature wears one universal Grin.

   Nood. This Day, O Mr. *Doodle*, is a Day
Indeed, (*b*) a Day we never saw before.
The mighty (*c*) *Thomas Thumb* victorious comes;
Millions of Giants crowd his Chariot Wheels,
(*d*) Giants! to whom the Giants in *Guild-hall*   10
Are Infant Dwarfs. They frown, and foam, and roar,

   (*b*) This Line is highly conformable to the beautiful Simplicity of the Antients.
It hath been copied by almost every Modern,

Not to be is not to be in Woe.	State of Innocence.
Love is not Sin but where 'tis sinful Love.	Don Sebastian.
Nature is Nature, Laelius.	Sophonisba.
Men are but Men, we did not make our selves.	Revenge.

   (*c*) Dr. *B—y* reads the mighty Tall-mast Thumb. Mr. *D—s* the mighty Thump-
ing Thumb. Mr. *T——d* reads Thundering. I think *Thomas* more agreeable to the
great Simplicity so apparent in our Author.

   (*d*) That learned Historian Mr. *S——n* in the third Number of his Criticism
on our Author, takes great Pains to explode this Passage. It is, says he, difficult to
guess what Giants are here meant, unless the Giant *Despair* in the *Pilgrim's
Progress*, or the Giant *Greatness* in the *Royal Villain*; for I have heard of no other
sort of Giants in the Reign of King *Arthur*. *Petrus Burmanus* makes three *Tom
Thumbs*, one whereof he supposes to have been the same Person whom the *Greeks*
called *Hercules*, and that by these Giants are to be understood the *Centaurs* slain
by that Heroe. Another *Tom Thumb* he contends to have been no other than the
Hermes Trismegistus of the Antients. The third *Tom Thumb* he places under the
Reign of King *Arthur*, to which third *Tom Thumb*, says he, the Actions of the other
two were attributed. Now tho' I know that this Opinion is supported by an Assertion
of *Justus Lipsius, Thomam illum Thumbum non alium quam Herculem fuisse satis
constat*; yet shall I venture to oppose one Line of Mr. *Midwinter*, against them all,
                  In Arthur's *Court* Tom Thumb *did live.*
But then, says, Dr. *B—y*, if we place *Tom Thumb* in the Court of King *Arthur*, it
will be proper to place that Court out of *Britain*, where no Giants were ever heard of.
Spencer, in his *Fairy Queen*, is of another Opinion, where describing *Albion* he says,
           ——— *Far within a salvage Nation dwelt*
           Of hideous Giants.
And in the same Canto,
           Then Elfar, *who two Brethren Giants had,*
           The one of which had two Heads ———
                The other three.
Risum teneatis, Amici.

---

   10 the Giants in *Guild-hall*] The two wooden figures, popularly known as Gog and
Magog, erected in the Guildhall in 1708. (*c*) Mr. *T——d*] Lewis Theobald, who preceded
Cibber as mock-hero of *The Dunciad*. (*d*) Mr. *S——n*] Nathanael Salmon, the antiquarian.

While *Thumb* regardless of their Noise rides on.
So some Cock-Sparrow in a Farmer's Yard,
Hops at the Head of an huge Flock of Turkeys.
   Dood. When Goody *Thumb* first brought this *Thomas* forth,
The *Genius* of our Land triumphant reign'd;
Then, then, Oh *Arthur*! did thy *Genius* reign.
   Nood. They tell me it is (*e*) whisper'd in the Books
Of all our Sages, that this mighty Hero
By *Merlin*'s Art begot, hath not a Bone   20
Within his Skin, but is a Lump of Gristle.
   Dood. Then 'tis a Gristle of no mortal kind,
Some God, my *Noodle*, stept into the Place
Of Gaffer *Thumb*, and more than (*f*) half begot,
This mighty *Tom*.
   Nood. —————— (*g*) Sure he was sent Express
From Heav'n, to be the Pillar of our State.
Tho' small his Body be, so very small,
A Chairman's Leg is more than twice as large;
Yet is his Soul like any Mountain big,
And as a Mountain once brought forth a Mouse,   30
(*h*) So doth this Mouse contain a mighty Mountain.

   (*e*) To Whisper in Books says Mr. *D—s* is errant Nonsense. I am afraid this
learned Man does not sufficiently understand the extensive meaning of the Word
Whisper. If he had rightly understood what is meant by the *Senses Whisp'ring the
Soul* in the *Persian Princess*, or what *Whisp'ring like Winds* is in *Aurengzebe*, or like
Thunder in another Author, he would have understood this. *Emmeline* in *Dryden*
sees a Voice, but she was born blind, which is an Excuse *Panthea* cannot plead in
Cyrus, who hears a sight.
             —————— *Your Description will surpass,
       All Fiction, Painting, or dumb Shew of Horror,
        That ever Ears yet heard, or Eyes beheld.*
When Mr. *D — s* understands these he will understand Whisp'ring in Books.
   (*f*)   *—Some Ruffian stept into his Father's Place,
        And more than half begot him.*   *Mary Q. of Scots.*
   (*g*) *—For* Ulamar *seems* sent Express from Heaven,
      To civilize this rugged Indian *Clime.*   Liberty Asserted.
   (*h*) *Omne majus continet in se minus, sed minus non in se majus continere potest,*
says *Scaliger* in *Thumbo.*—I suppose he would have cavilled at these beautiful Lines
in the Earl of *Essex*;
            ——*Thy most inveterate Soul,
       That looks through the foul Prison of thy Body.*

---

   28 A Chairman] One of the carriers of a sedan-chair—whose leg muscles would be
occupationally well-developed.

Dood. Mountain indeed! So terrible his Name,
(*i*) The Giant Nurses frighten Children with it;
And cry *Tom Thumb* is come, and if you are
Naughty, will surely take the Child away.
    Nood. But hark! (*k*) these Trumpets speak the King's Approach.
    Dood. He comes most luckily for my Petition.

Flourish.

SCENE II.

King, Queen, Grizzle, Noodle, Doodle, Foodle.

    King. (*l*) Let nothing but a Face of Joy appear;
The Man who frowns this Day shall lose his Head,
That he may have no Face to frown withal.
Smile, *Dollalolla*—Ha! what wrinkled Sorrow,
(*m*) Hangs, sits, lies, frowns upon thy knitted Brow?
Whence flow those Tears fast down thy blubber'd Cheeks,
Like a swoln Gutter, gushing through the Streets?

And at those of *Dryden,*

> *The Palace is without too well design'd,*
> *Conduct me in, for I will view thy Mind.*   Aurengzebe.

(*i*) Mr. *Banks* hath copied this almost Verbatim,
> *It was enough to say, here's* Essex *come,*
> *And Nurses still'd their Children with the fright.*   E. of *Essex.*

(*k*) The Trumpet in a Tragedy is generally as much as to say enter King: Which makes Mr. *Banks* in one of his Plays call it the Trumpet's formal Sound.

(*l*) *Phraortes* in the *Captives* seems to have been acquainted with King *Arthur.*
> *Proclaim a Festival for seven Days space,*
> *Let the Court shine in all its Pomp and Lustre,*
> *Let all our Streets resound with Shouts of Joy;*
> *Let Musick's Care-dispelling Voice be heard,*
> *The sumptuous Banquet, and the flowing Goblet*
> *Shall warm the Cheek, and fill the Heart with Gladness.*
> *Astarbe shall sit Mistress of the Feast.*

(*m*) *Repentance* frowns *on thy contracted Brow.*   Sophonisba.
Hung on his clouded Brow, I mark'd Despair.   Ibid.
>   —*A sullen Gloom,*
Scowls on his Brow.   Busiris.

 Queen. (*n*) Excess of Joy, my Lord, I've heard Folks say,
Gives Tears as certain as Excess of Grief.
 King. If it be so, let all Men cry for Joy,   10
(*o*) 'Till my whole Court be drowned with their Tears;
Nay, till they overflow my utmost Land,
And leave me Nothing but the Sea to rule.
 Dood. My Liege, I a Petition have here got.
 King. Petition me no Petitions, Sir, to-day;
Let other Hours be set apart for Business.
To-day it is our Pleasure to be (*p*) drunk,
And this our Queen shall be as drunk as We.

 (*n*) *Plato* is of this Opinion, and so is Mr. *Banks;*
Behold these Tears sprung from fresh Pain and Joy.   E. of *Essex.*
 (*o*) These Floods are very frequent in the Tragick Authors.
Near to some murmuring Brook I'll lay me down,
Whose Waters if they should too shallow flow,
My Tears shall swell them up till I will drown.   Lee's Sophonisba.
Pouring forth Tears at such a lavish Rate,
That were the World on Fire, they might have drown'd
The Wrath of Heav'n, and quench'd the mighty Ruin.   Mithridates.
One Author changes the Waters of Grief to those of Joy,
   ——*These Tears that sprung from Tides of Grief,*
Are now augmented to a Flood of Joy.   Cyrus the Great.
Another,
Turns all the Streams *of Hate, and makes them flow*
In Pity's *Channel.*   Royal Villain.
One drowns himself,
   ——*Pity like a Torrent* pours *me down,*
Now I am drowning all within a Deluge.   Anna Bullen.
Cyrus drowns the whole World,
  Our swelling Grief
  Shall melt into a Deluge, and the World
  Shall drown in Tears.   Cyrus the Great.
 (*p*) An Expression vastly beneath the Dignity of Tragedy, says Mr. *D*——*s*, yet
we find the Word he cavils at in the Mouth of *Mithridates* less properly used and
applied to a more terrible Idea;
   I would be drunk with Death.   Mithrid.
The Author of the New *Sophonisba* taketh hold of this Monosyllable, and uses it
pretty much to the same purpose,
   The Carthaginian *Sword with* Roman *Blood*
   Was drunk.
I would ask Mr. *D*——*s* which gives him the best Idea, a drunken King, or a
drunken Sword?

Queen. (Tho' I already (*q*) half Seas over am)
If the capacious Goblet overflow   20
With *Arrack-Punch*— 'fore *George!* I'll see it out;
Of *Rum*, and *Brandy*, I'll not taste a Drop.
   King. Tho' *Rack*, in *Punch*, Eight Shillings be a Quart,
And *Rum* and *Brandy* be no more than Six,
Rather than quarrel, you shall have your Will.

                                                                  [*Trumpets.*

But, ha! the Warrior comes; the Great *Tom Thumb*;
The little Hero, Giant-killing Boy,
Preserver of my Kingdom, is arrived.

SCENE III.

Tom Thumb, *to them with Officers, Prisoners, and Attendants.*

   King. (*r*) Oh! welcome most, most welcome to my Arms,
What Gratitude can thank away the Debt,
Your Valour lays upon me.
   Queen. ——————————— (*s*) Oh! ye Gods!   [*Aside.*
Thumb. When I'm not thank'd at all, I'm thank'd enough,
(*t*) I've done my Duty, and I've done no more.
   Queen. Was ever such a Godlike Creature seen!   [*Aside.*
   King. Thy Modesty's a (*) Candle to thy Merit,
It shines itself, and shews thy Merit too.

Mr. *Tate* dresses up King *Arthur*'s Resolution in Heroicks,
         Merry, my Lord, o' th' Captain's Humour right,
         I am resolv'd to be dead drunk to Night.
Lee also uses this charming Word;
         Love's the Drunkenness of the Mind.   Gloriana.
   (*q*) *Dryden* hath borrowed this, and applied it improperly,
         I'm half Seas o'er in Death.   Cleom.
   (*r*) This Figure is in great use among the Tragedians;
         'Tis therefore, therefore 'tis.   Victim.
         I long repent, repent and long again.   Busiris.
   (*s*) A Tragical Exclamation.
   (*t*) This Line is copied verbatim in the *Captives.*
   (*) We find a Candlestick for this Candle in two celebrated Authors;
         —— *Each Star withdraws*
         His golden Head and burns within the Socket.   Nero.
         A Soul grown old and sunk into the Socket.   Sebastian.

---

   21 *Arrack-Punch*] Originally an East Indian fermentation, based on dates. Rum and
brandy were later substitutes.

But say, my Boy, where did'st thou leave the Giants?

   Thumb. My Liege, without the Castle Gates they stand,   10
The Castle Gates too low for their Admittance.

   King. What look they like?

   Thumb. Like Nothing but Themselves.

   Queen. (*u*) And sure thou art like nothing but thy Self.   [*Aside.*

   King. Enough! the vast Idea fills my Soul.
I see them, yes, I see them now before me.
The monst'rous, ugly, barb'rous Sons of Whores.
But, Ha! what Form Majestick strikes our Eyes?
(*x*) So perfect, that it seems to have been drawn
By all the Gods in Council: So fair she is,   20
That surely at her Birth the Council paus'd,
And then at length cry'd out, This is a Woman!

   Thumb. Then were the Gods mistaken.—She is not
A Woman, but a Giantess—whom we
(*y*) With much ado, have made a shift to hawl
Within the Town: (*z*) for she is by a Foot,

   (*u*) This Simile occurs very frequently among the Dramatick Writers of both Kinds.

   (*x*) Mr. *Lee* hath stolen this Thought from our Author;

   ————*This perfect Face, drawn by the Gods in Council,*
Which they were long a making.   Lu. Jun. Brut.

   ————*At his Birth, the heavenly Council paus'd,*
And then at last cry'd out, This is a Man!
Dryden hath improved this Hint to the utmost Perfection:

   So perfect, that the very Gods who form'd you, wonder'd
   At their own Skill, and cry'd, a lucky Hit
   Has mended our Design! Their Envy hindred,
   Or you had been immortal, and a Pattern,
   When Heaven would work for Ostentation sake,
   To copy out again.   All for Love.
Banks prefers the Works of *Michael Angelo* to that of the Gods;

   A Pattern for the Gods to make a Man by,
   Or Michael Angelo *to form a Statue.*

   (*y*) It is impossible says Mr. *W*—— sufficiently to admire this natural easy Line.

   (*z*) This Tragedy which in most Points resembles the Antients differs from them in this, that it assigns the same Honour to Lowness of Stature, which they did to Height. The Gods and Heroes in *Homer* and *Virgil* are continually described higher by the Head than their Followers, the contrary of which is observ'd by our Author: In short, to exceed on either side is equally admirable, and a Man of three Foot is as wonderful a sight as a Man of nine.

   (*y*) Mr. *W*——] Leonard Welsted, a minor poet, best known as one of Pope's satirical butts.

Shorter than all her Subject Giants were.

    Glum. We yesterday were both a Queen and Wife,
One hundred thousand Giants own'd our Sway,
Twenty whereof were married to our self.   30

    Queen. Oh! happy State of Giantism—where Husbands
Like Mushrooms grow, whilst hapless we are forc'd
To be content, nay, happy thought with one.

    Glum. But then to lose them all in one black Day,
That the same Sun, which rising, saw me wife
To Twenty Giants, setting, should behold
Me widow'd of them all.—— (*a*) My worn out Heart,
That Ship, leaks fast, and the great heavy Lading,
My Soul, will quickly sink.

    Queen. —— Madam, believe,
I view your Sorrows with a Woman's Eye;   40
But learn to bear them with what Strength you may,
To-morrow we will have our Grenadiers
Drawn out before you, and you then shall chose
What Husbands you think fit.

    Glum. —— (*b*) Madam, I am
Your most obedient, and most humble Servant.

    King. Think, mighty Princess, think this Court your own,
Nor think the Landlord me, this House my Inn;
Call for whate'er you will, you'll Nothing pay.
(*c*) I feel a sudden Pain within my Breast,
Nor know I whether it arise from Love,   50
Or only the Wind-Cholick. Time must shew.
Oh *Thumb!* What do we to thy Valour owe?
Ask some Reward, great as we can bestow.

    Thumb. (*d*) I ask not Kingdoms, I can conquer those,

(*a*) *My Blood leaks fast, and the great heavy lading*
      My Soul will quickly sink.   Mithrid.
      My Soul is like a Ship.   Injur'd Love.

(*b*) This well-bred Line seems to be copied in the *Persian Princess;*
        To be your humblest, and most faithful Slave.

(*c*) This Doubt of the King puts me in mind of a Passage in the *Captives,* where
the Noise of Feet is mistaken for the Rustling of Leaves,
        —— *Methinks I hear*
      The sound of Feet
      No, 'twas the Wind that shook yon Cypress Boughs.

(*d*) Mr. *Dryden* seems to have had this Passage in his Eye in the first Page of
Love Triumphant.

---

38 Lading] Loading: the cargo of the 'ship' of Glumdalca's heart.

I ask not Money, Money I've enough;
For what I've done, and what I mean to do,
For Giants slain, and Giants yet unborn,
Which I will slay —— if this be call'd a Debt,
Take my Receipt in full —— I ask but this,
(e) To Sun my self in *Huncamunca*'s Eyes.   60
  King. Prodigious bold Request. ⎱
  Queen. —(f) Be still my Soul. ⎰   [*Aside.*
  Thumb. (g) My Heart is at the Threshold of your Mouth,
And waits its answer there—Oh! do not frown,
I've try'd, to Reason's Tune, to tune my Soul,
But Love did overwind and crack the String.
Tho' *Jove* in Thunder had cry'd out, YOU SHAN'T,
I should have lov'd her still—for oh strange fate,
Then when I lov'd her least, I lov'd her most.
  King. It is resolv'd—the Princess is your own.
  Thumb. (h) Oh! happy, happy, happy, happy, *Thumb!*   70
  Queen. Consider, Sir, reward your Soldiers Merit,
But give not *Huncamunca* to *Tom Thumb.*
  King. Tom Thumb! Odzooks, my wide extended Realm
Knows not a Name so glorious as *Tom Thumb.*
Let *Macedonia, Alexander* boast,
Let *Rome* her *Caesar's* and her *Scipio's* show,
Her Messieurs *France*, let *Holland* boast *Mynheers,*
Ireland her *O's*, her *Mac's* let *Scotland* boast,
Let England boast no other than *Tom Thumb.*
  Queen. Tho' greater yet his boasted Merit was,   80

(e) *Don Carlos* in the Revenge suns himself in the Charms of his Mistress,
      While in the Lustre of her Charms I lay.
(f) A Tragical Phrase much in use.
(g) This Speech hath been taken to pieces by several Tragical Authors who seem
to have rifled it and shared its Beauties among them.
My Soul waits at the Portal of thy Breast,
To ravish from thy Lips the welcome News.   Anna Bullen.
My Soul stands listning at my Ears.   Cyrus the Great.
Love to his Tune my jarring Heart would bring,
But Reason overwinds and cracks the String.   D. of Guise.
  —————— *I should have lov'd*
Tho' Jove in muttering Thunder had forbid it.   New Sophonisba.
And when it (my Heart) *wild resolves to love no more,*
Then is the Triumph of excessive Love.   Ibidem.
(h) *Massinissa* is one fourth less happy than *Tom Thumb.*
  Oh! happy, happy, happy.   New Sophonisba.

He shall not have my Daughter, that is Pos'.

    King. Ha! sayst thou *Dollalolla?*

    Queen. —— I say he shan't.

    King. (*i*) Then by our Royal Self we swear you lye.

    Queen. (*k*) Who but a Dog, who but a Dog,
Would use me as thou dost. Me, who have lain
(*l*) These twenty Years so loving by thy Side.
But I will be reveng'd. I'll hang my self,
Then tremble all who did this Match persuade,
(*m*) For riding on a Cat, from high I'll fall,   90
And squirt down Royal Vengeance on you all.

    Food. (*n*) Her Majesty the Queen is in a Passion.

    King. (*o*) Be she, or be she not—I'll to the Girl
And pave the Way, oh *Thumb*—Now, by our self,
We were indeed a pretty King of Clouts,
To truckle to her Will—For when by Force
Or Art the Wife her Husband over-reaches,
Give him the Peticoat, and her the Breeches.

    Thumb. (*p*) Whisper, ye Winds, that *Huncamunca*'s mine;
Echoes repeat, that *Huncamunca*'s mine!   100
The dreadful Bus'ness of the War is o'er,
And Beauty, heav'nly Beauty! crowns my Toils,
I've thrown the bloody Garment now aside,
And *Hymeneal* Sweets invite my Bride.

So when some Chimney-Sweeper, all the Day,
Hath through dark Paths pursu'd the sooty Way,
At Night, to wash his Hands and Face he flies,
And in his t'other Shirt with his *Brickdusta* lies.

    (*i*) *No by my self.*   Anna Bullen.

    (*k*) —————— *Who caus'd,*
       This dreadful Revolution in my Fate,
       Ulamar. *Who but a Dog, who but a Dog.*   Liberty Asserted.

    (*l*) —————— *A Bride,*
       Who twenty Years lay loving by your Side.   Banks.

    (*m*) *For born upon a Cloud, from high I'll fall,*
       And rain down Royal Vengeance on you all.   Albion Queen.

    (*n*) An Information very like this we have in the *Tragedy of Love,* where *Cyrus*
having stormed in the most violent manner, *Cyaxares* observes very calmly,
                       Why, Nephew Cyrus—*you are mov'd.*

    (*o*) *'Tis in your Choice,*
       Love me, or love me not.   Conquest of Granada.

    (*p*) There is not one Beauty in this Charming Speech, but hath been borrowed
by almost every Tragick Writer.

SCENE IV.

Grizzle *solus*.

(*q*) Where art thou *Grizzle*? where are now thy Glories?
Where are the Drums that waken'd thee to Honour?
Greatness is a lac'd Coat from *Monmouth-Street*,
Which Fortune lends us for a Day to wear,
To-morrow puts it on another's Back.
The spiteful Sun but yesterday survey'd
His Rival, high as Saint *Paul*'s Cupola;
Now may he see me as *Fleet-Ditch* laid low.   8

SCENE V.

Queen, Grizzle.

Queen. (*r*) Teach me to scold, prodigious-minded *Grizzle*.
Mountain of Treason, ugly as the Devil,
Teach this confounded hateful Mouth of mine,
To spout forth Words malicious as thy self,
Words, which might shame all *Billingsgate* to speak.
  Griz. Far be it from my Pride, to think my Tongue
Your Royal Lips can in that Art instruct,
Wherein you so excel. But may I ask,
Without Offence, wherefore my Queen would scold?
  Queen. Wherefore, Oh! Blood and Thunder! han't you heard   10
(What ev'ry Corner of the Court resounds)
That little *Thumb* will be a great Man made.
  Griz. I heard it, I confess—for who, alas!

(*q*) Mr. *Banks* has (I wish I could not say too servilely) imitated this of *Grizzle*
in his *Earl of Essex*.
Where art thou Essex, &c.
(*r*) The Countess of *Nottingham* in the *Earl of Essex* is apparently acquainted
with *Dollalolla*.

---

3 *Monmouth-Street*] The centre of the trade in second-hand clothing. 8 as *Fleet-Ditch*] The Fleet river had by this time become little more than an open sewer. I. v, 5 *Billingsgate*] Already a fish market, notorious for the foul language of its fishwives and porters. 12 a great Man] Probably an incidental hit at Sir Robert Walpole, styled thus ironically in *The Beggar's Opera*, *Jonathan Wild*, and many lesser works of the period.

(*s*) Can always stop his Ears—but wou'd my Teeth,
By grinding Knives, had first been set on Edge.
    Queen. Would I had heard at the still Noon of Night,
The Hallaloo of Fire in every Street!
Odsbobs! I have a mind to hang my self,
To think I shou'd a Grandmother be made
Bu such a Raskal. —— Sure the King forgets,   20
When in a Pudding, by his Mother put,
The Bastard, by a Tinker, on a Stile
Was drop'd. —— O, good Lord *Grizzle!* can I bear
To see him from a Pudding, mount the Throne?
Or can, Oh can! my *Huncamunca* bear,
To take a Pudding's Offspring to her Arms?
    Griz. Oh Horror! Horror! Horror! cease my Queen,
(*t*) Thy Voice like twenty Screech-Owls, wracks my Brain.
    Queen. Then rouse thy Spirit—we may yet prevent
This hated Match.————
    Griz. —— We will (*u*) not Fate it self,   30
Should it conspire with *Thomas Thumb*, should cause it.
I'll swim through Seas; I'll ride upon the Clouds;
I'll dig the Earth; I'll blow out ev'ry Fire;
I'll rave; I'll rant; I'll rise; I'll rush; I'll roar;
Fierce as the Man whom (*x*) smiling Dolphins bore,
From the Prosaick to Poetick Shore.
I'll tear the Scoundrel into twenty Pieces.
    Queen. Oh, no! prevent the Match, but hurt him not;
For, tho' I would not have him have my Daughter,
Yet can we kill the Man that kill'd the Giants?   40

(*s*) *Grizzle* was not probably possessed of that Glew, of which Mr. *Banks* speaks
in his *Cyrus.*
I'll glew my Ears to ev'ry Word.

  (*t*) *Screech-Owls, dark Ravens and amphibious Monsters,*
    Are screaming in that Voice.   Mary Q. of Scots.
  (*u*) The Reader may see all the Beauties of this Speech in a late Ode called the
Naval Lyrick.
  (*x*) This Epithet to a Dolphin doth not give one so clear an Idea as were to be
wished, a smiling Fish seeming a little more difficult to be imagined than a flying
Fish. Mr. *Dryden* is of Opinion, that smiling is the Property of Reason, and that no
irrational Creature can smile.
    Smiles not allowed to Beasts from Reason move.   State of Innocence.

————

  (*u*) the *Naval Lyrick*] A Pindaric ode by Edward Young.

Griz. I tell you, Madam, it was all a Trick,
He made the Giants first, and then he kill'd them;
As Fox-hunters bring Foxes to the Wood,
And then with Hounds they drive them out again.
  Queen. How! have you seen no Giants? Are there not
Now, in the Yard, ten thousand proper Giants?
  Griz. (*y*) Indeed, I cannot positively tell,
But firmly do believe there is not One.
  Queen. Hence! from my Sight! thou Traitor, hie away;
By all my Stars! thou enviest *Tom Thumb*.   50
Go, Sirrah! go, (*z*) hie away! hie! —— thou art,
A setting Dog be gone.
  Griz. Madam, I go.
Tom Thumb shall feel the Vengeance you have rais'd:
So, when two Dogs are fighting in the Streets,
With a third Dog, one of the two Dogs meets,
With angry Teeth, he bites him to the Bone,
And this Dog smarts for what that Dog had done.

SCENE VI.

Queen *sola.*

And whither shall I go? —— Alack-a-day!
I love *Tom Thumb*—but must not tell him so;

  (*y*) These Lines are written in the same Key with those in the *Earl of Essex*;
        Why sayst thou so, I love thee well, indeed
        I do, and thou shalt find by this, 'tis true.
Or with this in *Cyrus*;
        The most heroick Mind that ever was.
And with above half of the modern Tragedies.
  (*z*) *Aristotle* in that excellent Work of his which is very justly stiled his Master-
piece, earnestly recommends using the Terms of Art, however coarse or even
indecent they may be. Mr. *Tate* is of the same Opinion.
  Bru. *Do not, like young Hawks, fetch a Course about,*
        Your Game flies fair.
  Fra. *Do not fear it.*
        He answers you in your own *Hawking Phrase.*   Injur'd Love.

I think these two great Authorities are sufficient to justify *Dollalolla* in the use of the
Phrase ——*Hie away hie*; when in the same Line she says she is speaking to a
setting Dog.

For what's a Woman, when her Virtue's gone?
A Coat without its Lace; Wig out of Buckle;
A Stocking with a Hole in't —— I can't live
Without my Virtue, or without *Tom Thumb*.
(*zz*) Then let me weigh them in two equal Scales,
In this Scale put my Virtue, that, *Tom Thumb*.
Alas! *Tom Thumb* is heavier than my Virtue.
But hold! —— perhaps I may be left a Widow: 10
This Match prevented, then *Tom Thumb* is mine:
In that dear Hope, I will forget my Pain.

   So, when some Wench to *Tothill-Bridewell*'s sent,
With beating Hemp, and Flogging she's content:
She hopes in time to ease her present Pain,
At length is free, and walks the Streets again.

The End of the First ACT.

ACT II.   SCENE I.

SCENE *The Street.*

Bailiff, Follower.

Bail. COME on, my trusty Follower, come on,
     This Day discharge thy Duty, and at Night
A Double Mug of Beer, and Beer shall glad thee.
Stand here by me, this Way must *Noodle* pass.
   Follow. No more, no more, Oh Bailiff! every Word
Inspires my Soul with Virtue.—— Oh! I long
To meet the Enemy in the Street—and nab him;
To lay arresting Hands upon his Back,

  (*zz*) We meet with such another Pair of Scales in *Dryden*'s King *Arthur*.
        Arthur and Oswald *and their different Fates,*
         Are weighing now within the Scales of Heav'n.
Also in *Sebastian*.
        This Hour my Lot is weighing in the Scales.

---

13 *Tothill-Bridewell*] A Bridewell was by this time a term for a kind of prison, derived
from the situation of the first such place of correction near St. Bride's Church. Whores and
other minor offenders were often committed there. The Tothill Bridewell was in Westminster.   14 beating Hemp] One of the intentionally monotonous occupations to which
the prisoners of a Bridewell were put.

And drag him trembling to the Spunging-House.

Bail. There, when I have him, I will spunge upon him.   10
(*a*) Oh! glorious Thought! by the Sun, Moon, and Stars,
I will enjoy it, tho it be in Thought!
Yes, yes, my Follower, I will enjoy it.

Follow. Enjoy it then some other time, for now
Our Prey approaches.

Bail. Let us retire.

SCENE II.

Tom Thumb, Noodle, Bailiff, Follower.

Thumb. Trust me my *Noodle*, I am wondrous sick;
For tho' I love the gentle *Huncamunca*,
Yet at the Thought of Marriage, I grow pale;
For Oh! —— (*b*) but swear thoul't keep it ever secret,
I will unfold a Tale will make thee stare.

Nood. I swear by lovely *Huncamunca*'s Charms.

Thumb. Then know —— (*c*) my Grand-mamma hath often said,
Tom Thumb, beware of Marriage.

Nood. Sir, I blush
To think a Warrior great in Arms as you,
Should be affrighted by his Grand-mamma;   10
Can an old Woman's empty Dreams deter
The blooming Hero from the Virgin's Arms?
Think of the Joy that will your Soul alarm,

(*a*) Mr. *Rowe* is generally imagin'd to have taken some Hints from this Scene in his Character of *Bajazet*; but as he, of all the Tragick Writers, bears the least Resemblance to our Author in his Diction, I am unwilling to imagine he would condescend to copy him in this Particular.

(*b*) This Method of surprizing an Audience by raising their Expectation to the highest Pitch, and then baulking it, hath been practis'd with great Success by most of our Tragical Authors.

(*c*) *Almeyda* in *Sebastian* is in the same Distress;
> *Sometimes methinks I hear the Groan of Ghosts,*
> *Thin hollow Sounds and lamentable Screams;*
> *Then, like a dying Echo from afar,*
> *My Mother's Voice that cries, wed not* Almeyda
> *Forewarn'd,* Almeyda, *Marriage is thy Crime.*

---

9 the Spunging-House] The bailiff's residence, where debtors were forcibly detained, at their own expense, until committal or discharge.

When in her fond Embraces clasp'd you lie,
While on her panting Breast dissolv'd in Bliss,
Your pour out all *Tom Thumb* in every Kiss.
   Thumb. Oh! *Noodle*, thou hast fir'd my eager Soul;
Spight of my Grandmother, she shall be mine;
I'll hug, caress, I'll eat her up with Love.
Whole Days, and Nights, and Years shall be too short   20
For our Enjoyment, every Sun shall rise
(*d*) Blushing, to see us in our Bed together.
   Nood. Oh Sir! this Purpose of your Soul pursue.
   Bail. Oh, Sir! I have an Action against you.
   Nood. At whose Suit is it?
   Bail. At your Taylor's, Sir.
Your Taylor put this Warrant in my Hands,
And I arrest you, Sir, at his Commands.
   Thumb. Ha! Dogs! Arrest my Friend before my Face!
Think you *Tom Thumb* will suffer this Disgrace!
But let vain Cowards threaten by their Word,   30
Tom Thumb shall shew his Anger by his Sword.
                     [*Kills the Bailiff and his Follower.*
   Bail. Oh, I am slain!
   Follow. I am murthered also,
And to the Shades, the dismal Shades below,
My Bailiff's faithful Follower I go.
   Nood. (*e*) Go then to Hell, like Rascals as you are,

(*d*) As very well he may if he hath any Modesty in him, says Mr. *D——s*. The Author of *Busiris*, is extremely zealous to prevent the Sun's blushing at any indecent object; and therefore on all such Occasions he addresses himself to the Sun, and desires him to keep out of the way.
     Rise never more, O Sun! let Night prevail,
     Eternal Darkness close the World's wide Scene.   Busiris.
     Sun hide thy Face and put the World in Mourning.   Ibid.
Mr. *Banks* makes the Sun perform the Office of *Hymen*; and therefore not likely to be disgusted at such a Sight;
     The Sun sets forth like a gay Brideman with you.
                          Mary Q. of Scots.

(*e*) *Nourmahal* sends the same Message to Heaven;
     For I would have you, when you upwards move,
     Speak kindly of us, to our Friends above.   Aurengzebe.
We find another to Hell, in the *Persian* Princess;
     Villian, get thee down
     To Hell, and tell them that the Frays begun.

———————————
18 Spight of] Despite, in spite of.

And give our Service to the Bailiffs there.
  Thumb. Thus perish all the Bailiffs in the Land,
Till Debtors at Noon-Day shall walk the Streets,
And no one fear a Bailiff or his Writ.

SCENE III.

The Princess Huncamunca's *Apartment.*

Huncamunca, Cleora, Mustacha.

Hunc. (*f*) Give me some Musick—see that it be sad.

Cleora *sings.*

Cupid, *ease a Love-sick Maid,*
Bring thy Quiver to her Aid ;
With equal Ardor wound the Swain :
Beauty should never sigh in vain.

II.

Let him feel the pleasing Smart,
Drive thy Arrow thro' his Heart ;
When One you wound, you then destroy ;
When Both you kill, you kill with Joy.

Hunc. (*g*) O, *Tom Thumb ! Tom Thumb !* wherefore art thou *Tom Thumb ?*
Why had'st thou not been born of Royal Race?   11
Why had not mighty *Bantam* been thy Father?
Or else the King of *Brentford, Old* or *New*?
  Must. I am surpriz'd that your highness can give your self a Moment's
Uneasiness about that little insignificant Fellow, (*h*) *Tom Thumb the Great*—
One properer for a Play-thing, than a Husband.—— Were he my Husband,

  (*f*) *Anthony* gives the same Command in the same Words.
  (*g*) Oh! *Marius, Marius* ; wherefore art thou *Marius* ?
                                                            Otway's Marius.
  (*h*) Nothing is more common than these seeming Contradictions ; such as,
                   Haughty Weakness.   Victim.
                   Great small World.   Noah's Flood.
  _____

  12 mighty *Bantam*] The hero of the play-within-the-play in Fielding's earlier *Author's
Farce.* 13 the King of *Brentford, Old* or *New*] Two more characters from Fielding's
Author's Farce. The idea of their divided suburban kingdom was borrowed from
Buckingham's *Rehearsal.*

his Horns should be as long as his Body.—— If you had fallen in Love with a
Grenadier, I should not have wonder'd at it —— If you had fallen in Love
with Something; but to fall in Love with Nothing!

    Hunc. Cease, my *Mustacha*, on thy Duty cease.   20
The *Zephyr*, when in flowry Vales it plays,
Is not so soft, so sweet as *Thummy's* Breath.
The Dove is not so gentle to its Mate.

    Must. The Dove is every bit as proper for a Husband——Alas! Madam,
there's not a Beau about the Court looks so little like a Man —— He is a
perfect Butterfly, a Thing without Substance, and almost without Shadow
too.

    Hunc. This Rudeness is unseasonable, desist;
Or, I shall think this Railing comes from Love.
Tom Thumb's a Creature of that charming Form,   30
That no one can abuse, unless they love him.

    Must. Madam, the King.

SCENE IV.

King, Huncamunca.

    King. Let all but *Huncamunca* leave the Room.

                                      [*Ex.* Cleora, *and* Mustacha.
Daughter, I have observ'd of late some Grief,
Unusual in your Countenance—your Eyes,
(*i*) That, like two open Windows, us'd to shew
The lovely Beauty of the Rooms within,
Have now two Blinds before them—What is the Cause?
Say, have you not enough of Meat and Drink?
We've giv'n strict Orders not to have you stinted.

    Hunc. Alas! my Lord, I value not my self,
That once I eat two Fowls and half a Pig;   10
(*k*) Small is that Praise; but oh! a Maid may want,

    (*i*) *Lee* hath improv'd this Metaphor.
        Dost thou not view Joy peeping from my Eyes,
        The Casements open'd wide to gaze on thee;
        So Rome's *glad Citizens to Windows rise,*
        When they some young Triumpher fain would see.   Gloriana.
    (*k*) *Almahide* hath the same Contempt for these Appetites;
        To eat and drink can no Perfection be.

                                        Conquest of Granada.

What she can neither eat nor drink.
   King. What's that?
   Hunc. (*l*) O spare my Blushes; but I mean a Husband.
   King. If that be all, I have provided one,
A Husband great in Arms, whose warlike Sword
Streams with the yellow Blood of slaughter'd Giants.
Whose Name in *Terrâ Incognitâ* is known,
Whose Valour, Wisdom, Virtue make a Noise,
Great as the Kettle-Drums of twenty Armies.   20
   Hunc. Whom does my Royal Father mean?
   King. Tom Thumb.
   Hunc. Is it possible?
   King. Ha! the Window-Blinds are gone,
(*m*) A Country Dance of Joy is in your Face,
Your Eyes spit Fire, your Cheeks grow red as Beef.
   Hunc. O, there's a Magick-musick in that Sound,
Enough to turn me into Beef indeed.
Yes, I will own, since licens'd by your Word,
I'll own *Tom Thumb* the Cause of all my Grief.   30
For him I've sigh'd, I've wept, I've gnaw'd my Sheets.

The Earl of *Essex* is of a different Opinion, and seems to place the chief Happiness
of a General therein.
     Were but Commanders half so well rewarded,
     Then they might eat.   Banks's Earl of Essex.
But if we may believe one, who knows more than either, the Devil himself; we
shall find Eating to be an Affair of more moment than is generally imagined.
     Gods are immortal only by their Food.
                        Lucifer in the State of Innocence.
   (*l*) This Expression is enough of it self (says Mr. *D—s*) utterly to destroy the
Character of *Huncamunca*; yet we find a Woman of no abandon'd Character in
Dryden, adventuring farther and thus excusing her self;
         To speak our Wishes first, forbid it Pride,
         Forbid it Modesty: True, they forbid it,
         But Nature does not, when we are athirst,
         Or hungry, will imperious Nature stay,
         Nor eat, nor drink, before 'tis bid fall on.   Cleomenes.
Cassandra speaks before she is asked. *Huncamunca* afterwards.
   Cassandra speaks her Wishes to her Lover.
Huncamunca *only to her Father.*
   (*m*) *Her Eyes resistless Magick bear,*
     Angels I see, and Gods are dancing there.   Lee's Sophonisba.

---

31 I've gnaw'd my Sheets] Apparently a proverbial manner of expressing frustration.

King. Oh! thou shalt gnaw thy tender Sheets no more,
A Husband thou shalt have to mumble now.
   Hunc. Oh! happy Sound! henceforth, let no one tell,
That *Huncamunca* shall lead Apes in Hell.
Oh! I am over-joy'd!
   King. I see thou art.
(*n*) Joy lightens in thy Eyes, and thunders from thy Brows;
Transports, like Lightning, dart along thy Soul,
As Small-shot thro' a Hedge.
   Hunc. Oh! say not small.
   King. This happy News shall on our Tongue ride Post,   40
Our self will bear the happy News to *Thumb.*
Yet think not, Daughter, that your powerful Charms
Must still detain the Hero from his Arms;
Various his Duty, various his Delight;
Now is his Turn to kiss, and now to fight;
And now to kiss again. So, mighty (*o*) *Jove,*
When with excessive thund'ring tir'd above,
Comes down to Earth, and takes a Bit—and then,
Flies to his Trade of Thund'ring, back again.

   (*n*) Mr. *Dennis* in that excellent Tragedy, call'd *Liberty Asserted*, which is thought
to have given so great a Stroke to the late *French* King, hath frequent Imitations of
this beautiful Speech of King *Arthur*;
          Conquest light'ning in his Eyes, and thund'ring in his Arm.
          Joy lighten'd in her Eyes.
          Joys like Light'ning dart along my Soul.
   (*o*) Jove *with excessive Thund'ring tir'd above,*
          Comes down for Ease, enjoys a Nymph, and then
          Mounts dreadful, and to Thund'ring goes again.

Gloriana.

---

   35 *Huncamanca* shall lead Apes in Hell] The traditional fate of the spinster in after-life.
(*n*) the late *French* King] Louis XIV. Dennis suffered from a paranoiac fear of the French,
and was said to live in constant fear of retribution for the slurs cast upon their nation in his
Liberty Asserted.

SCENE V.

Grizzle, Huncamunca.

(*p*) *Griz.* Oh! *Huncamunca, Huncamunca*, oh,
Thy pouting Breasts, like Kettle-Drums of Brass,
Beat everlasting loud Alarms of Joy;
As bright as Brass they are, and oh, as hard;
Oh *Huncamunca, Huncamunca!* oh!
  Hunc. Ha! do'st thou know me, Princess as I am,
*That thus of me you dare to make your Game.
  Griz. Oh *Huncamunca*, well I know that you
A Princess are, and a King's Daughter too.
But Love no Meanness scorns, no Grandeur fears, ⎫   10
Love often Lords into the Cellar bears,   ⎬
And bids the sturdy Porter come up Stairs.   ⎭
For what's too high for Love, or what's too low?
Oh *Huncamunca, Huncamunca*, oh!
  Hunc. But granting all you say of Love were true,
My Love, alas! is to another due!
In vain to me, a Suitoring you come;
For I'm already promis'd to *Tom Thumb*.
  Griz. And can my Princess such a Durgen wed,
One fitter for your Pocket than your Bed!   20
Advis'd by me, the worthless Baby shun,
Or you will ne'er be brought to bed of one.
Oh take me to thy Arms and never flinch,
Who am a Man by *Jupiter* ev'ry Inch.

  (*p*) This beautiful Line, which ought, says Mr. *W——* to be written in Gold, is
imitated in the New *Sophonisba*;
                Oh! *Sophonisba, Sophonisba*, oh!
                Oh! *Narva, Narva*, oh!
The Author of a Song call'd Duke upon Duke, hath improv'd it.
                Alas! O Nick, *O* Nick, *alas!*
Where, by the help of a little false Spelling, you have two Meanings in the repeated
Words.
  *Edith, in the *Bloody Brother*, speaks to her Lover in the same familiar Language.
           Your Grace is full of Game.

---

19 Durgen] Dwarf, midget.

(*q*) Then while in Joys together lost we lie
I'll press thy Soul while Gods stand wishing by.
   Hunc. If, Sir, what you insinuate you prove
All Obstacles of Promise you remove;
For all Engagements to a Man must fall,
Whene'er that Man is prov'd no Man at all.   30
   Griz. Oh let him seek some Dwarf, some fairy Miss,
Where no Joint-stool must lift him to the Kiss.
But by the Stars and Glory, you appear
Much fitter for a *Prussian* Grenadier;
One Globe alone, on *Atlas* Shoulders rests,
Two Globes are less than *Huncamunca*'s Breasts:
The Milky-way is not so white, that's flat,
And sure thy Breasts are full as large as that.
   Hunc. Oh, Sir, so strong your Eloquence I find,
It is impossible to be unkind.   40
   Griz. Ah! speak that o'er again, and let the (*r*) Sound
From one Pole to another Pole rebound;
The Earth and Sky, each be a Battledoor
And keep the Sound, that Shuttlecock, up an Hour;
To *Doctors Commons*, for a License I,
Swift as an Arrow from a Bow will fly.
   Hunc. Oh no! lest some Disaster we should meet,
'Twere better to be marry'd at the Fleet.
   Griz. Forbid it, all ye Powers, a Princess should
By that vile Place, contaminate her Blood;   50
My quick Return shall to my Charmer prove,
I travel on the (*s*) Post-Horses of Love.

   (*q*) *Traverse the glitt'ring Chambers of the Sky,*
     Born on a Cloud in view of Fate I'll lie,   ⎫
     And press her Soul while Gods stand wishing by. ⎬   Hannibal.
   (*r*) *Let the four Winds from distant Corners meet,* ⎭
     And on their Wings first bear it into France;
     The back again to Edina's *proud Walls,*
     Till Victim to the Sound th' aspiring City falls.

                                        Albion Queen.
   (*s*) I do not remember any Metaphors so frequent in the Tragick Poets as those
borrow'd from Riding Post;

---

   45 *Doctors Commons*] The College of Doctors of Civil Law in London, which dealt,
amongst other things, with the licensing of marriages.   48 marry'd at the Fleet] That is,
disreputably or covertly married. The clergymen at the Fleet Prison were notoriously
corruptible.

Hunc. Those Post-Horses to me will seem too slow,
Tho' they should fly swift as the Gods, when they
Ride on behind that Post-Boy, Opportunity.

SCENE VI.

Tom Thumb, Huncamunca.

Thumb. Where is my Princess, where's my *Huncamunca*?
Where are those Eyes, those Cardmatches of Love,
That (*t*) Light up all with Love my waxen Soul?
Where is that Face which artful Nature made.
(*u*) In the same Moulds where *Venus* self was cast?

The Gods and Opportunity ride Post.	Hannibal.
———— *Let's rush together,*	
For Death rides Post.	Duke of Guise.
Destruction gallops to thy murther Post.	Gloriana.

(*t*) This Image too very often occurs;
—— *Bright as when thy Eye*
'First lighted up our Loves. — Aurengzebe.
This not a Crown alone lights up my Name. — Busiris.

(*u*) There is great Dissension among the Poets concerning the Method of making Man. One tells his Mistress that the Mold she was made in being lost, Heaven cannot form such another. *Lucifer*, in *Dryden*, gives a merry Description of his own Formation;

Whom Heaven neglecting, made and scarce design'd,
But threw me in for Number to the rest.

State of Innocency.

In one Place, the same Poet supposes Man to be made of Metal;
I was form'd
Of that coarse Metal, which when she was made,
The Gods threw by for Rubbish. — All for Love.
In another, of Dough;
When the Gods moulded up the Paste of Man,
Some of their Clay was left upon their Hands,
And so they made Egyptians. — Cleomenes.
In another of Clay;
————————*Rubbish of remaining Clay.* — Sebastian.
One makes the Soul of Wax;
Her waxen Soul begins to melt apace. — Anna Bullen.
Another of Flint.

II. vi, 2 Cardmatches] Sulphur-tipped matches.

I

Hunc. (*x*) Oh! What is Musick to the Ear that's deaf,
Or a Goose-Pye to him that has no taste?
What are these Praises now to me, since I
Am promis'd to another?
    Thumb. Ha! promis'd.
    Hunc. Too sure; it's written in the Book of Fate.   10
    Thumb. (*y*) Then I will tear away the Leaf
Wherein it's writ, or if Fate won't allow
So large a Gap within its Journal-Book,
I'll blot it out at least.

SCENE VII.

Glumdalca, Tom Thumb, Huncamunca.

    Glum. (*z*) I need not ask if you are *Huncamunca*,
Your Brandy Nose proclaims ———
    Hunc. I am a Princess;

> *Sure our two Souls have somewhere been acquainted*
> *In former Beings, or struck out together,*
> *One Spark to* Afric *flew, and one to* Portugal.   Sebastian.

To omit the great Quantities of Iron, Brazen and Leaden Souls which are so plenty in modern Authors —— I cannot omit the Dress of a Soul as we find it in *Dryden*;

> *Souls shirted but with Air.*   King Arthur.

Nor can I pass by a particular sort of Soul in a particular sort of Description, in the New *Sophonisba*.

> *Ye mysterious Powers,*
> *—Whether thro' your gloomy Depths I wander,*
> *Or on the Mountains walk; give me the calm,*
> *The steady smiling Soul, where Wisdom sheds*
> *Eternal Sun-shine, and eternal Joy.*

(*x*) This Line Mr. *Banks* has plunder'd entire in his *Anna Bullen.*
(*y*) *Good Heaven, the Book of Fate before me lay,*
> *But to tear out the Journal of that Day.*
> *Or if the Order of the World below,*
> *Will not the Gap of one whole Day allow,*
> *Give me that Minute when she made her Vow.*

                                   Conquest of Granada.

(*z*) I know some of the Commentators have imagined, that Mr. *Dryden*, in the *Altercative* Scene between *Cleopatra* and *Octavia*, a Scene which Mr. *Addison* inveighs against with great Bitterness, is much beholden to our Author. How just this their Observation is, I will not presume to determine.

Nor need I ask who you are.

Glum. A Giantess;
The Queen of those who made and unmade Queens.

Hunc. The Man, whose chief Ambition is to be
My Sweetheart, hath destroy'd these mighty Giants.

Glum. Your Sweetheart? do'st thou think the Man, who once
Hath worn my easy Chains, will e'er wear thine?   10

Hunc. Well may your Chains be easy, since if Fame
Says true, they have been try'd on twenty Husbands.
(*z*) The Glove or Boot, so many times pull'd on,
May well sit easy on the Hand or Foot.

Glum. I glory in the Number, and when I
Sit poorly down, like thee, content with one,
Heaven change this Face for one as bad as thine.

Hunc. Let me see nearer what this Beauty is,
That captivates the Heart of Men by Scores.

                                    [*Holds a Candle to her Face.*

Oh! Heaven, thou art as ugly as the Devil.   20

Glum. You'd give the best of Shoes within your Shop,
To be but half so handsome.

Hunc. —Since you come
(*a*) To that, I'll put my Beauty to the Test;
Tom Thumb, I'm yours, if you with me will go.

Glum. Oh! stay, *Tom Thumb*, and you alone shall fill
That Bed where twenty Giants us'd to lie.

Thumb. In the Balcony that o'er-hangs the Stage,
I've seen a Whore two 'Prentices engage;
One half a Crown does in his Fingers hold,   30

(*z*) A cobling Poet indeed, says Mr. *D.* and yet I believe we may find as monstrous
Images in the Tragick-Authors: I'll put down one;

        Untie your folded Thoughts, and let them dangle loose as a
           Bride's Hair.   Injur'd Love.

Which Lines seem to have as much Title to a Milliner's Shop, as our Author's to a
Shoemaker's.

(*a*) Mr. *L—* takes occasion in this Place to commend the great Care of our
Author to preserve the Metre of Blank Verse, in which *Shakespear*, *Johnson* and
Fletcher were so notoriously negligent; and the Moderns, in Imitation of our Author,
so laudably observant;

                ——————— *Then does*
        Your Majesty believe that he can be
        A Traitor!   Earl of Essex.

Every Page of *Sophonisba* gives us Instances of this Excellence.

(*a*) Mr. *L—*] Conjecturally, Lyttelton.

The other shews a little Piece of Gold;
She the Half Guinea wisely does purloin,
And leaves the larger and the baser Coin.
    Glum. Left, scorn'd, and loath'd for such a Chit as this;
(*b*) I feel the Storm that's rising in my Mind,
Tempests, and Whirlwinds rise, and rowl and roar.
I'm all within a Hurricane, as if
(*c*) The World's four Winds were pent within my Carcass.
(*d*) Confusion, Horror, Murder, Guts and Death.

SCENE VIII.

King, Glumdalca.

    King. *Sure never was so sad a King as I,
(*e*) My Life is worn as ragged as a Coat
A Beggar wears; a Prince should put it off,
(*f*) To love a Captive and a Giantess.
Oh Love! Oh Love! how great a King art thou!
My Tongue's thy Trumpet, and thou Trumpetest,
Unknown to me, within me. (*g*) oh *Glumdalca!*
Heaven thee design'd a Giantess to make,
But an Angelick Soul was shuffled in.
(*h*) I am a Multitude of Walking Griefs,   10

> (*b*) *Love mounts and rowls about my stormy Mind.*   Aurengzebe.
>   *Tempests and Whirlwinds thro' my Bosom move.*   Cleom.
> (*c*) *With such a furious Tempest on his Brow,*
>   *As if the World's four Winds were pent within*
>   *His blustring Carcase.*   Anna Bullen.
> (*d*) *Verba Tragica.*
> * This Speech hath been terribly maul'd by the Poets.
> (*e*) —— *My Life is worn to Rags.*
>   *Not worth a Prince's wearing.*   Love Triumph.
> (*f*) *Must I beg the Pity of my Slave?*
>   *Must a King beg! But Love's a greater King,*
>   *A Tyrant, nay a Devil that possesses me.*
>   *He tunes the Organ of my Voice and speaks,*
>   *Unknown to me, within me.*   Sebastian.
> (*g*) *When thou wer't form'd, Heaven did a Man begin;*
>   *But a Brute Soul by chance was shuffled in.*   Aurengzebe.
> (*h*) —————————— *I am a Multitude.*
>   *Of walking Griefs.*   New Sophonisba.

And only on her Lips the Balm is found,
(*i*) To spread a Plaister that might cure them all.
  Glum. What do I hear?
  King. What do I see?
  Glum. Oh!
  King Ah!
  (*k*) *Glum.* Ah Wretched Queen!
  King. Oh! Wretched King!
  Glum. Ah!
  King. Oh! (*l*)

SCENE IX.

Tom Thumb, Huncamunca, Parson.

  Parson. Happy's the Wooing, that's not long adoing;
For if I guess aright, *Tom Thumb* this Night
Shall give a Being to a New *Tom Thumb*.
  Thumb. It shall be my Endeavour so to do.
  Hunc. Oh! fie upon you, Sir, you make me blush.
  Thumb. It is the Virgin's Sign, and suits you well:

(*i*) *I will take thy Scorpion Blood,*
    And lay it to my Grief till I have Ease.   Anna Bullen.
(*k*) Our Author, who every where shews his great Penetration into human
Nature, here outdoes himself: Where a less judicious Poet would have raised a long
Scene of whining Love. He who understood the Passions better, and that so
violent an Affection as this must be too big for Utterance, chooses rather to send
his Characters off in this sullen and doleful manner: In which admirable
Conduct he is imitated by the Author of the justly celebrated *Eurydice*. Dr. *Young*
seems to point at this Violence of Passion;
    ————————————— *Passion choaks*
    Their Words, and they're the Statues of Despair,
  And *Seneca* tells us, *Curae leves loquuntur, ingentes stupent.* The Story of the
Egyptian King in *Herodotus* is too well known to need to be inserted; I refer the
more curious Reader to the excellent *Montagne*, who hath written an Essay on this
Subject.
(*l*) *To part is Death* ————
  ————————————————— *'Tis Death to part.*
  ————————————————— *Ah.*
  ————————————————— *Oh.*   Don Carlos.

  (*l*) Don Carlos] A misattribution. These terse exchanges actually occur in Gay's *What
D'ye Call It*—itself a burlesque.

(*m*) I know not where, nor how, nor what I am,
(*n*) I'm so transported, I have lost my self.
   Hunc. Forbid it, all ye Stars, for you're so small,
That were you lost, you'd find your self no more.   10
So the unhappy Sempstress once, they say,
Her Needle in a Pottle, lost, of Hay;
In vain she look'd, and look'd, and made her Moan,
For ah, the Needle was for ever gone.
   Parson. Long may they live, and love, and propagate,
Till the whole Land be peopled with *Tom Thumbs*.

   (*m*) *Nor know I whether.*
     What am I, who or where,   Busiris.
     I was I know not what, and am I know not how.   Gloriana.
   (*n*) To understand sufficiently the Beauty of this Passage, it will be necessary
that we comprehend every Man to contain two Selfs. I shall not attempt to prove
this from Philosophy, which the Poets make so plainly evident.
One runs away from the other;
                    Let me demand your Majesty?
        Why fly you from your self.   Duke of Guise.
In a 2*d*. One Self is a Guardian to the other;
        Leave me the Care of me.   Conquest of Granada.
Again, *My self am to my self less near.*   Ibid.
In the same, the first Self is proud of the second;
        I my self am proud of me.
                        State of Innocence.

In a 3*d*. Distrustful of him;
        Fain I would tell, but whisper it in mine Ear,
        That none besides might hear, nay not my self.
                        Earl of Essex.

In a 4*th*. Honours him;
        I honour Rome,
        But honour too my self.   Sophonisba.
In a 5th. At Variance with him;
        Leave me not thus at Variance with my self.   Busiris.
Again, in a 6*th*. *I find my self divided from my self.*
                        Medea.
                        Banks.

        She seemed the sad Effigies of her self.
        Assist me, Zulema, if thou would'st be
        The Friend thou seemest, assist me against me.
                        Albion Queens.
   From all which it appears, that there are two Selfs; and therefore *Tom Thumb*'s
losing himself is no such Solecism as it hath been represented by Men, rather
ambitious of Criticizing, than qualify'd to Criticize.

---

   12 a Pottle] That is, a bottle—a bundle of hay.

(*p*) So when the *Cheshire* Cheese a Maggot breeds,
Another and another still succeeds.
By thousands, and ten thousands they increase,
Till one continued Maggot fills the rotten Cheese.   20

SCENE X.

Noodle, *and then* Grizzle.

Nood. (*q*) Sure Nature means to break her solid Chain,
Or else unfix the World, and in a Rage,
To hurl it from its Axle-tree and Hinges;
All things are so confus'd, the King's in Love,
The Queen is drunk, the Princess married is.
  Griz. Oh! *Noodle*, hast thou *Huncamunca* seen?
  Nood. I've seen a Thousand Sights this day, where none
Are by the wonderful Bitch herself outdone,
The King, the Queen, and all the Court are Sights.
  Griz. (*r*) D—n your Delay, you Trifler, are you drunk, ha?   10
I will not hear one Word but *Huncamunca*.
  Nood. By this time she is married to *Tom Thumb*.
  Griz. (*s*) My *Huncamunca*.
  Nood. Your *Huncamunca*.
Tom Thumb's *Huncamunca*, every Man's *Huncamunca*.
  Griz. If this be true all Womankind are damn'd.
  Nood. If it be not, may I be so my self.
  Griz. See where she comes! I'll not believe a Word

(*p*) Mr. *F*—— imagines this Parson to have been a *Welsh* one from his Simile.
(*q*) Our Author hath been plunder'd here according to Custom;
  Great Nature break thy Chain *that links together*,
  The Fabrick of the World and makes a Chaos,
  Like that within my Soul.   Love Triumphant.
  ———— *Startle Nature, unfix the Globe,*
  And hurl it from its Axle-tree *and Hinges.*
  The tott'ring Earth seems sliding off its Props.   Albion Queens.
(*r*) D—*n your Delay, ye Torturers proceed,*
  I will not hear one Word but Almahide.   Conq. of Granada.
(*s*) Mr. *Dryden* hath imitated this in *All for Love*.

---

8 the wonderful Bitch] Hillhouse identifies this as a reference to a famous French dog—
capable, according to the *Grub-street Journal*, of playing cards 'with surprizing dexterity'.
(*p*) Mr. *F*——] Fielding himself.

Against that Face, upon whose (t) ample Brow,
Sits Innocence with Majesty Enthron'd.

Grizzle, Huncamunca.

Griz. Where has my *Huncamunca* been? See here   20
The Licence in my Hand!
Hunc. Alas! *Tom Thumb.*
Griz. Why dost thou mention him?
Hunc. Ah! me *Tom Thumb.*
Griz. What means my lovely *Huncamunca?*
Hunc. Hum!
Griz. Oh! Speak.
Hunc. Hum!
Griz. Ha! your every Word is Hum.
(*u*) You force me still to answer you *Tom Thumb.*
Tom Thumb, I'm on the Rack, I'm in a Flame,
(*x*) *Tom Thumb, Tom Thumb, Tom Thumb,* you love the Name;
So pleasing is that Sound, that were you dumb
You still would find a Voice to cry *Tom Thumb.*
Hunc. Oh! Be not hasty to proclaim my Doom,   30
My ample Heart for more than one has Room,
A Maid like me, Heaven form'd at least for two,
(*y*) I married him, and now I'll marry you.
Griz. Ha! dost thou own thy Falshood to my Face?
Think'st thou that I will share thy Husband's place,
Since to that Office one cannot suffice,
And since you scorn to dine one single Dish on,

(*t*) This Miltonick Stile abounds in the New *Sophonisba.*
———————— *And on her ample Brow*
        Sat Majesty.
(*u*) *Your ev'ry Answer, still so ends in that,*
        Your force me still to answer you Morat.   Aurengzebe.
(*x*) *Morat, Morat, Morat, you love the Name.*   Aurengzebe.
(*y*) Here is a Sentiment for the Virtuous *Huncamunca* (says Mr. *D—s*) and yet
with the leave of this great Man, the Virtuous *Panthea* in *Cyrus,* hath an Heart
every Whit as ample;
        For two I must confess are Gods to me,
        Which is my Abradatus *first, and thee.*   Cyrus the Great.
Nor is the Lady in *Love Triumphant;* more reserv'd, tho' not so intelligible;
        ———————— *I am so divided,*
        That I grieve most for both, and love both most.

Go, get your Husband put into Commission,
Commissioners to discharge, (ye Gods) it fine is,
The duty of a Husband to your Highness;   40
Yet think not long, I will my Rival bear,
Or unreveng'd the slighted Willow wear;
The gloomy, brooding Tempest now confin'd,
Within the hollow Caverns of my Mind.
In dreadful Whirl, shall rowl along the Coasts,
Shall thin the Land of all the Men it boasts,
(z) And cram up ev'ry Chink of Hell with Ghosts.
(*) So have I seen, in some dark Winter's Day,
A sudden Storm rush down the Sky's High-Way,
Sweep thro' the Streets with terrible ding dong,   50
Gush thro' the Spouts, and wash whole Crowds along.
The crowded Shops, the thronging Vermin skreen,
Together cram the Dirty and the Clean,
And not one Shoe-Boy in the Street is seen.
  Hunc. Oh! fatal Rashness should his Fury slay,
My hapless Bridegroom on his Wedding Day;
I, who this Morn, of two chose which to wed,
May go again this Night alone to Bed;
  (†) So have I seen some wild unsettled Fool,

(z) A ridiculous Supposition to any one, who considers the great and extensive
Largeness of Hell, says a Commentator: But not so to those who consider the great
Expansion of immaterial Substance. Mr. *Banks* makes one Soul to be so expanded
that Heaven could not contain it;
             The Heavens are all too narrow for her Soul.   Virtue Betray'd.
The *Persian Princess* hath a Passage not unlike the Author of this;
             We will send such Shoals of murther'd Slaves,
             Shall glut Hell's empty Regions.
This threatens to fill Hell even tho' it were empty; Lord *Grizzle* only to fill up the
Chinks, supposing the rest already full.
  (*) Mr. *Addison* is generally thought to have had this Simile in his Eye, when he
wrote that beautiful one at the end of the third Act of his *Cato.*
  (†) This beautiful Simile is founded on a Proverb, which does Honour to the
English Language;
             Between two Stools the Breech falls to the Ground.
I am not so pleased with any written Remains of the Ancients, as with those little
Aphorisms, which verbal Tradition hath delivered down to us, under the Title of
Proverbs. It were to be wished that instead of filling their Pages with the fabulous
Theology of the Pagans, our modern Poets would think it worth their while to en-

_____

51 the Spouts] It was customary for these to drain directly into the streets—and thus
indeed to 'wash whole Crowds along'.   52 skreen] Hide from view.

Who had her Choice of this, and that Joint Stool;   60
To give the Preference to either, loath
And fondly coveting to sit on both:
While the two Stools her Sitting Part confound,
Between 'em both fall Squat upon the Ground.

The End of the Second ACT.

ACT III.   SCENE I.

SCENE *King* Arthur's *Palace.*

(*a*) Ghost *solus.*

HAIL! ye black Horrors of Midnight's Midnoon!
Ye Fairies, Goblins, Bats and Screech-Owls, Hail!
And Oh! ye mortal Watchmen, whose hoarse Throats
Th' Immortal Ghosts dread Croakings counterfeit,
All Hail!—— Ye dancing Fantoms, who by Day,

---

rich their Works with the Proverbial Sayings of their Ancestors. Mr. *Dryden* hath
chronicl'd one in Heroick;

    Two ifs scarce make one Possibility.   Conquest of Granada.

My Lord *Bacon* is of Opinion, that whatever is known of Arts and Sciences might
be proved to have lurked in the Proverbs of *Solomon.* I am of the same Opinion in
relation to those abovemention'd: At least I am confident that a more perfect
System of Ethicks, as well as Oeconomy, might be compiled out of them, than is at
present extant, either in the Works of the Antient Philosophers, or those more
valuable, as more voluminous, ones of the Modern Divines.

    (*a*) Of all the Particulars in which the modern Stage falls short of the ancient,
there is none so much to be lamented, as the great Scarcity of Ghosts in the latter.
Whence this proceeds, I will not presume to determine. Some are of opinion, that
the Moderns are unequal to that sublime Language which a Ghost ought to speak.
One says ludicrously, That Ghosts are out of Fashion; another, That they are
properer for Comedy; forgetting, I suppose, that *Aristotle* hath told us, That a
Ghost is the Soul of Tragedy; for so I render the ψυχή ὁ μῦθθ ξ τραγωδίας, which
M. *Dacier*, amongst others, hath mistaken; I suppose mis-led, by not understand-
ing the *Fabula* of the *Latins*, which signifies a *Ghost* as well as a *Fable.*

    ————— *Te premet nox, fabulaeque Manes.*   Hor.

Of all the Ghosts that have ever appeared on the Stage, a very learned and judicious
foreign Critick, gives the Preference to this of our Author. These are his Words,
speaking of this Tragedy;

    ———— *Nec quidquam in illâ admirabilius quam Phasma quoddam horrendum,
quod omnibus aliis Spectris, quibuscum scatet Anglorum Tragoedia, longè* (*pace D——
isii V. Doctiss. dixerim*) *praetulerim.*

Are some condemn'd to fast, some feast in Fire;
Now play in Church-yards, skipping o'er the Graves,
To the (*b*) loud Musick of the silent Bell,
All Hail!   8

SCENE II.

King, *and* Ghost.

King. What Noise is this?—— What Villain dares,
At this dread Hour, with Feet and Voice prophane,
Disturb our Royal Walls?
Ghost. One who defies
Thy empty Power to hurt him; (*c*) one who dares
Walk in thy Bed-Chamber.
King. Presumptuous Slave!
Thou diest:
Ghost. Threaten others with that Word,
(*d*) I am a Ghost, and am already dead.
King. Ye Stars! 'tis well; were they last Hour to come,
This Moment had been it; (*e*) yet by thy Shrowd

(*b*) We have already given Instances of this Figure.
(*c*) *Almanzor reasons in the same manner;*
——————————— *A Ghost I'll be,*
  And from a Ghost, you know, no Place is free.
                                        Conq. of *Granada.*
(*d*) *The Man who writ this wretched Pun* (says Mr. *D.*) *would have picked your
Pocket :* Which he proceeds to shew, not only bad in it self, but doubly so on so
solemn an Occasion. And yet in that excellent Play of *Liberty Asserted*, we find
something very much resembling a Pun in the Mouth of a Mistress, who is parting
with the Lover she is fond of;
            Ul. *Oh, mortal Woe! one Kiss, and then farewel.*
            Irene. *The Gods have given to others to farewel.*
            O miserably must Irene *fair.*
Agamemnon, in the *Victim,* is full as facetious on the most solemn Occasion, that of
Sacrificing his Daughter;
            Yes, Daughter, yes ; you will assist the Priest ;
            Yes, you must offer up your —— Vows for Greece.
(*e*) *I'll pull thee backwards by thy Shrowd to Light,*
    Or else, I'll squeeze thee, like a Bladder, there,
    And make thee groan thy self away to Air.
                                        Conquest of *Granada.*

  Snatch me, ye Gods, this Moment into Nothing.

                                        Cyrus the Great.

I'll pull thee backward, squeeze thee to a Bladder,   10
'Till thou dost groan thy Nothingness away.

                                        [Ghost retires.

Thou fly'st! 'Tis well.
(*f*) I thought what was the Courage of a Ghost!
Yet, dare not, on thy Life —— Why say I that,
Since Life thou hast not?—Dare not walk again,
Within these Walls, on pain of the *Red-Sea*.
For, if henceforth I ever find thee here,
As sure, sure as a Gun, I'll have thee laid——
   Ghost. Were the *Red-Sea*, a Sea of *Holland*'s Gin,
The Liquor (when alive) whose very Smell   20
I did detest, did loath—yet for the Sake
Of *Thomas Thumb*, I would be laid therein.
   King. Ha! said you?
   Ghost. Yes, my Liege, I said *Tom Thumb*,
Whose Father's Ghost I am —— once not unknown
To mighty *Arthur*. But, I see, 'tis true,
The dearest Friend, when dead, we all forget.
   King. 'Tis he, it is the honest Gaffer *Thumb*.
Oh! let me press thee in my eager Arms,
Thou best of Ghosts! Thou something more than Ghost!
   Ghost. Would I were Something more, that we again   30
Might feel each other in the warm Embrace.
But now I have th' Advantage of my King,
(*g*) For I feel thee, whilst thou dost not feel me.
   King. But say, (*h*) thou dearest Air, Oh! say, what Dread,
Important Business sends thee back to Earth?
   Ghost. Oh! then prepare to hear—which, but to hear,
Is full enough to send thy Spirit hence.

    (*f*) *So, art thou gone? Thou canst no Conquest boast,*
      I thought what was the Courage of a Ghost.

                            Conquest of *Granada*.
King *Arthur* seems to be as brave a Fellow as *Almanzor*, who says most heroically,
           —————————— *In spight of Ghosts, I'll on.*
    (*g*) The Ghost of *Lausaria* in *Cyrus* is a plain Copy of this, and is therefore worth
reading.
     Ah, Cyrus!
     Thou may'st as well grasp Water, or fleet Air,
      As think of touching my immortal Shade.   *Cyrus* the Great.
    (*h*) *Thou better Part of heavenly Air.*   Conquest of *Granada*.

———

16 on pain of the *Red-Sea*] Traditionally the haunting ground least favoured by ghosts.

Thy Subjects up in Arms, by *Grizzle* led,
Will, ere the rosy finger'd Morn shall ope
The Shutters of the Sky, before the Gate   40
Of this thy Royal Palace, swarming spread:
(*i*) So have I seen the Bees in Clusters swarm,
So have I seen the Stars in frosty Nights,
So have I seen the Sand in windy Days,
So have I seen the Ghosts on *Pluto*'s Shore,
So have I seen the Flowers in Spring arise,
So have I seen the Leaves in *Autumn* fall,
So have I seen the Fruits in Summer smile,
So have I seen the Snow in Winter frown.
    King. D—n all thou'st seen! —— Dost thou, beneath the Shape   50
Of Gaffer *Thumb*, come hither to abuse me,
With Similies to keep me on the Rack?
Hence ——— or by all the Torments of thy Hell,
(*k*) I'll run thee thro' the Body, tho' thou'st none.
    Ghost. Arthur, beware; I must this Moment hence,
Not frighted by your Voice, but by the Cocks;
Arthur beware, beware, beware, beware!
Strive to avert thy yet impending Fate;
For if thou'rt kill'd To-day,
To-morrow all thy Care will come too late.   60

SCENE III.

King *solus*.

    King. Oh! stay, and leave me not uncertain thus!
And whilst thou tellest me what's like my Fate,
Oh, teach me how I may avert it too!
Curst be the Man who first a Simile made!
Curst' ev'ry Bard who writes! ——— So have I seen
Those whose Comparisons are just and true,

(*i*) *A String of Similies* (says one) *proper to be hung up in the Cabinet of a Prince.*
(*k*) This Passage hath been understood several different Ways by the Commentators. For my Part, I find it difficult to understand it at all. Mr. *Dryden* says,
I have heard something how two Bodies meet,
But how two Souls join, I know not.
So that 'till the Body of a Spirit be better understood, it will be difficult to understand how it is possible to run him through it.

And those who liken things not like at all.
The Devil is happy, that the whole Creation
Can furnish out no Simile to his Fortune.   9

SCENE IV.

King, Queen.

Queen. What is the Cause, my *Arthur*, that you steal
Thus silently from *Dollallolla*'s Breast?
Why dost thou leave me in the (*l*) Dark alone,
When well thou know'st I am afraid of Sprites?
   King. Oh *Dollallolla!* do not blame my Love;
I hop'd the Fumes of last Night's Punch had laid
Thy lovely Eye-lids fast.—— But, Oh! I find
There is no Power in Drams, to quiet Wives;
Each Morn, as the returning Sun, they wake,
And shine upon their Husbands.
   Queen. Think, Oh think!   10
What a Surprize it must be to the Sun,
Rising, to find the vanish'd World away.
What less can be the wretched Wife's Surprize,
When, stretching out her Arms to fold thee fast,
She folds her useless Bolster in her Arms.
(*m*) Think, think on that —— Oh! think, think well on that.
I do remember also to have read
(*n*) In *Dryden*'s *Ovid*'s *Metamorphosis*,
That *Jove* in Form inanimate did lie
With beauteous *Danae*; and trust me, Love,   20
(*o*) I fear'd the Bolster might have been a *Jove*.
   King. Come to my Arms, most virtuous of thy Sex;
Oh *Dollallolla!* were all Wives like thee,
So many Husbands never had worn Horns.

(*l*) *Cydaria* is of the same fearful Temper with *Dollallolla*;
    I never durst in Darkness be alone.   Ind. Emp.
  (*m*) *Think well of this, think that, think every way.*   Sophonisba.
  (*n*) These Quotations are more usual in the Comick, than in the Tragick Writers.
  (*o*) *This Distress* (says Mr. *D*——) *I must allow to be extremely beautiful, and tends
to heighten the virtuous Character of* Dollallolla, *who is so exceeding delicate, that she
is in the highest Apprehension from the inanimate Embrace of a Bolster. An Example
worthy of Imitation from all our Writers of Tragedy.*

Should *Huncamunca* of thy Worth partake,
Tom Thumb indeed were blest.———— Oh fatal Name!
For didst thou know one Quarter what I know,
Then would'st thou know—Alas! what thou would'st know!
  Queen. What can I gather hence? Why dost thou speak
Like Men who carry *Raree-Shows* about,   30
Now you shall see, Gentlemen, what you shall see?
O tell me more, or thou hast told too much.

SCENE V.

King, Queen, Noodle.

  Noodle. Long Life attend your Majesties serene,
Great *Arthur*, King, and *Dollallolla*, Queen!
Lord *Grizzle*, with a bold, rebellious Crowd,
Advances to the Palace, threat'ning loud,
Unless the Princess be deliver'd straight,
And the victorious *Thumb*, without his Pate,
They are resolv'd to batter down the Gate.   7

SCENE VI.

King, Queen, Huncamunca, Noodle.

  King. See where the Princess comes! Where is *Tom Thumb*?
  Hunc. Oh! Sir, about an Hour and half ago
He sallied out to encounter with the Foe,
And swore, unless his Fate had him mis-led,
From *Grizzle*'s Shoulders to cut off his Head,
And serve't up with your Chocolate in Bed.
  King. 'Tis well, I find one Devil told us both.
Come *Dollallolla*, *Huncamunca*, come,
Within we'll wait for the victorious *Thumb*;
In Peace and Safety we secure may stay,   10
While to his Arm we trust the bloody Fray;
Tho' Men and Giants should conspire with Gods,

---

30 *Raree-Shows*] Portable peepshows.   III. v, 6 without his Pate] That is, executed.

(*p*) He is alone equal to all these Odds.

  Queen. He is indeed, a (*q*) Helmet to us all,
While he supports, we need not fear to fall;
His Arm dispatches all things to our Wish,
And serves up every Foe's Head in a Dish.
Void is the Mistress of the House of Care,
While the good Cook presents the Bill of Fare;
Whether the Cod, that Northern King of Fish,   20
Or Duck, or Goose, or Pig, adorn the Dish;
No Fears the Number of her Guests afford,
But at her Hour she sees the Dinner on the Board.

SCENE VII.   *a Plain.*

Lord Grizzle, Foodle, *and Rebels.*

  Grizzle. Thus far our Arms with Victory are crown'd;
For tho' we have not fought, yet we have found

(*p*) *Credat Judaeus Appelles*
     Non ego —(Says Mr. *D.*) — *For, passing over the Absurdity of being equal to Odds, can we possibly suppose a little insignificant Fellow—I say again, a little insignificant Fellow able to vie with a Strength which all the* Sampsons *and* Hercules's *of Antiquity would be unable to encounter.*
I shall refer this incredulous Critick to Mr. *Dryden*'s Defence of his *Almanzor*; and lest that should not satisfy him, I shall quote a few Lines from the Speech of a much braver Fellow than *Almanzor*, Mr. *Johnson*'s *Achilles*;
    Tho' Human Race rise in embattel'd Hosts,
    To force her from my Arms —— *Oh ! Son of* Atreus!
    By that immortal Pow'r, whose deathless Spirit
    Informs this Earth, I will oppose them all.   Victim.
(*q*) *I have heard of being supported by a Staff* (says Mr. *D.*) *but never of being supported by an Helmet.* I believe he never heard of Sailing with Wings, which he may read in no less a Poet than Mr. *Dryden*;
    Unless we borrow Wings, and sail thro' Air.   Love Triumphant.
What will he say to a kneeling Valley?
    —————— *I'll stand*
    Like a safe Valley, that low bends the Knee,
    To some aspiring Mountain.   Injur'd Love.
I am asham'd of so ignorant a Carper, who doth not know that an Epithet in Tragedy is very often no other than an Expletive. Do not we read in the New *Sophonisba* of *grinding Chains, blue Plagues, white Occasions* and *blue Serenity*? Nay, 'tis not the Adjective only, but sometimes half a Sentence is put by way of Expletive, as, *Beauty pointed high with Spirit*, in the same Play —— and, *In the Lap of Blessing, to be most curst.* In the Revenge.

(r) No Enemy to fight withal.
    Foodle. Yet I,
Methinks, would willingly avoid this Day,
(s) This First of *April*, to engage our Foes.
    Griz. This Day, of all the Days of th' Year, I'd choose,
For on this Day my Grandmother was born.
Gods! I will make *Tom Thumb* an *April* Fool;
(t) Will teach his Wit an Errand it ne'er knew,
And send it Post to the *Elysian* Shades.   10
    Food. I'm glad to find our Army is so stout,
Nor does it move my Wonder less than Joy.
    Griz. (u) What Friends we have, and how we came so strong,
I'll softly tell you as we march along.

SCENE VIII.

Thunder and Lightning.

Tom Thumb, Glumdalca *cum suis.*

    Thumb. Oh, *Noodle!* hast thou seen a Day like this?
(x) The unborn Thunder rumbles o'er our Heads,
(y) As if the Gods meant to unhinge the World;
And Heaven and Earth in wild Confusion hurl;
Yet will I boldly tread the tott'ring Ball.
    Merl. Tom Thumb!
    Thumb. What Voice is this I hear?
    Merl. Tom Thumb!

(r) A Victory like that of *Almanzor.*
    Almanzor *is victorious without Fight.*   Conq. of *Granada.*
(s) *Well have we chose an happy Day for Fight,*
    For every Man in course of Time has found,
    Some Days are lucky, some unfortunate.   K. *Arthur.*
(t) We read of such another in *Lee*;
    Teach his rude Wit a Flight she never made,
    And send her Post to the Elysian *Shade.*   Gloriana.
(u) These Lines are copied *verbatim* in the *Indian Emperor.*
(x) *Unborn Thunder rolling in a Cloud.*   Conq. of *Gran.*
(y) *Were Heaven and Earth in wild Confusion hurl'd,*
    Should the rash Gods unhinge the rolling World,
    Undaunted, would I tread the tott'ring Ball,
    Crush'd, but unconquer'd, in the dreadful Fall.

                                  Female Warrior.

Thumb. Again it calls.

Merl. Tom Thumb!

Glum. It calls again.

Thumb. Appear, whoe'er thou art, I fear thee not.

Merl. Thou hast no Cause to fear, I am thy Friend,   10
Merlin by Name, a Conjurer by Trade,
And to my Art thou dost thy Being owe.

Thumb. How!

Merl. Hear then the mystick Getting of *Tom Thumb.*

> (z) *His Father was a Ploughman plain,*
>   *His Mother milk'd the Cow;*
> *And yet the Way to get a Son,*
>   *This Couple knew not how.*
> *Until such time the good old Man*
>   *To learned* Merlin *goes,*   20
> *And there to him, in great Distress,*
>   *In secret manner shows;*
> *How in his Heart he wish'd to have*
>   *A Child, in time to come,*
> *To be his Heir, tho' it might be*
>   *No bigger than his Thumb:*
> *Of which old* Merlin *was foretold,*
>   *That he his Wish should have;*
> *And so a Son of Stature small,*
>   *The Charmer to him gave.*   30

Thou'st heard the past, look up and see the future.

Thumb. (a) Lost in Amazement's Gulph, my Senses sink
See there, *Glumdalca,* see another (b) Me!

Glum. O Sight of Horror! see, you are devour'd
By the expanded Jaws of a red Cow.

Merl. Let not these Sights deter thy noble Mind,
(c) For lo! a Sight more glorious courts thy Eyes;

(z) See the History of *Tom Thumb,* pag. 2.

(a) —— *Amazement swallows up my Sense,*
   And in th' impetuous Whirl of circling Fate,
   Drinks down my Reason.   *Pers.* Princess.

(b) ———————— *I have outfaced my self,*
   What! am I two? Is there another Me?   K. *Arthur.*

(c) The Character of *Merlin* is wonderful throughout, but most so in this
Prophetick Part. We find several of these Prophecies in the Tragick Authors, who
frequently take this Opportunity to pay a Compliment to their Country, and
sometimes to their Prince. None but our Author (who seems to have detested the

See from a far a Theatre arise;
There, Ages yet unborn, shall Tribute pay
To the Heroick Actions of this Day: 40
Then Buskin Tragedy at length shall choose
Thy Name the best Supporter of her Muse.
    Thumb. Enough, let every warlike Musick sound,
We fall contented, if we fall renown'd.

SCENE IX.

Lord Grizzle, Foodle, *Rebels, on one Side*. Tom
Thumb, Glumdalca, *on the other*.

    Food. At length the Enemy advances nigh,
(*d*) I hear them with my Ear, and see them with my Eye.
    Griz. Draw all your Swords, for Liberty we fight,
(*e*) And Liberty the Mustard is of Life.
    Thumb. Are you the Man whom Men fam'd *Grizzle* name?
    Griz. (*f*) Are you the much more fam'd *Tom Thumb*?
    Thumb. The same.
    Griz. Come on, our Worth upon our selves we'll prove,
For Liberty I fight.
    Thumb. And I for Love.   10
                  [*A bloody Engagement between the two Armies here,*
                  Drums beating, Trumpets sounding, Thunder and
                  Lightning. —— They fight off and on several times.
                  Some fall. Grizzle *and* Glumdalca *remain.*

---

least Appearance of Flattery) would have past by such an Opportunity of
being a Political Prophet.
    (*d*) *I saw the Villain*, Myron, *with these Eyes I saw him.*   Busiris.
In both which Places it is intimated, that it is sometimes possible to see with other
Eyes than your own.
    (*e*) *This Mustard* (says Mr. *D*.) *is enough to turn one's Stomach: I would be glad
to know what Idea the Author had in his Head when he wrote it.* This will be, I believe,
best explained by a Line of Mr. *Dennis*;
    And gave him Liberty, the Salt of Life.   Liberty asserted.
The Understanding that can digest the one, will not rise at the other.
    (*f*) Han. *Are you the Chief, whom Men fam'd* Scipio *call?*
      Scip. *Are you the much more famous* Hannibal?   *Hannib.*

---

41 Buskin] The thick sandal used by Greek tragic actors: hence, tragedy itself.

Glum. Turn, Coward, turn, nor from a Woman fly.

Griz. Away—thou art too ignoble for my Arm.

Glum. Have at thy Heart.

Griz. Nay then, I thrust at thine.

Glum. You push too well, you've run me thro' the Guts,
And I am dead.

Griz. Then there's an End of One.

Thumb. When thou art dead, then there's an End of Two,
(*g*) Villain.

    Griz. Tom Thumb?   20

    Thumb. Rebel!

    Griz. Tom Thumb!

    Thumb. Hell!

    Griz. Huncamunca!

    Thumb. Thou hast it there.

    Griz. Too sure I feel it.

    Thumb. To Hell then, like a Rebel as you are,
And give my Service to the Rebels there.

    Griz. Triumph not, *Thumb*, nor think thou shalt enjoy
Thy *Huncamunca* undisturb'd, I'll send   30
(*h*) My Ghost to fetch her to the other World;
(*i*) It shall but bait at Heaven, and then return.
(*k*) But, ha! I feel Death rumbling in my Brains,

(*g*) Dr. *Young* seems to have copied this Engagement in his *Busiris :*

    Myr. *Villain!*

    Mem. Myron!

    Myr. *Rebel!*

    Mem. Myron!

    Myr. *Hell!*

    Mem. Mandane

(*h*) This last Speech of my Lord *Grizzle*, hath been of great Service to our Poets;

    —— *I'll hold it fast*
    As Life, and when Life's gone, I'll hold this last;
    And if thou tak'st it from me when I'm slain,
    I'll send my Ghost, and fetch it back again.

                     Conquest of *Granada.*

(*i*) *My Soul should with such Speed obey,*
    It should not bait at Heaven to stop its way.
Lee seems to have had this last in his Eye;

    'Twas not my Purpose, Sir, to tarry there,
    I would but go to Heaven to take the Air.   Gloriana.

(*k*) *A rising* Vapour rumbling *in my Brains.*   Cleomenes.

(*l*) Some kinder Spright knocks softly at my Soul.
And gently whispers it to haste away:
I come, I come, most willingly I come.
(*m*) So; when some City Wife, for Country Air,
To *Hampstead*, or to *Highgate* does repair;
Her, to make haste, her Husband does implore,
And cries, My Dear, *the Coach is at the Door*.   40
With equal Wish, desirous to be gone,
She gets into the Coach, and then she cries—*Drive on!*
    Thumb. With those last Words (*n*) he vomited his Soul,
Which, (*o*) like whipt Cream, the Devil will swallow down.
Bear off the Body, and cut off the Head,
Which I will to the King in Triumph lug;
Rebellion's dead, and now I'll go to Breakfast.

SCENE X.

King, Queen, Huncamunca, *and Courtiers.*

King. Open the Prisons, set the Wretched free,
And bid our Treasurer disburse six Pounds
To pay their Debts.———— Let no one weep To-day.
Come, *Dollallolla*; (*p*) Curse that odious Name!
It is so long, it asks an Hour to speak it.
By Heavens! I'll change it into *Doll*, or *Loll*,
Or any other civil Monosyllable
That will not tire my Tongue. ———— Come, sit thee down,
Here seated, let us view the Dancer's Sports;
Bid 'em advance. This is the Wedding-Day   10

(*l*) *Some kind Spright knocks softly at my Soul,*
    To tell me Fate's at Hand.
(*m*) Mr. *Dryden* seems to have had this Simile in his Eye, when he says,
    My Soul is packing up, *and just on Wing.*
                                      Conquest of *Granada.*
                                      Cleomenes.
(*n*) *And in a purple Vomit pour'd his Soul.*
(*o*) *The Devil swallows vulgar Souls*
    Like whipp'd Cream.   Sebastian.
(*p*) *How I could curse my Name of* Ptolemy!
    It is so long, it asks an Hour to write it.
    By Heav'n! I'll change it into Jove, *or* Mars,
    Or any other civil Monosyllable,
    That will not tire my Hand.   Cleomenes.

Of Princess *Huncamunca* and *Tom Thumb*;
Tom Thumb! who wins two Victories (*q*) To-day,
And this way marches, bearing *Grizzle*'s Head.

A Dance here.

  Nood. Oh! monstrous, dreadful, terrible, Oh! Oh!
Deaf be my Ears, for ever blind, my Eyes!
Dumb be my Tongue! Feet lame! All Senses lost!
(*r*) Howl Wolves, grunt Bears, hiss Snakes, shriek all ye Ghosts!
  King. What does the Blockhead mean?
  Nood. I mean, my Liege
(*s*) Only to grace my Tale with decent Horror;
Whilst from my Garret, twice two Stories high,   20
I look'd abroad into the Streets below;
I saw *Tom Thumb* attended by the Mob,
Twice Twenty Shoe-Boys, twice two Dozen Links,
Chairmen and Porters, Hackney-Coachmen, Whores;
Aloft he bore the grizly Head of *Grizzle*;
When of a sudden thro' the Streets there came
A Cow, of larger than the usual Size,
And in a Moment—guess, Oh! guess the rest!
And in a Moment swallow'd up *Tom Thumb*.
  King. Shut up again the Prisons, bid my Treasurer   30
Not give three Farthings out —— hang all the *Culprits*,
Guilty or not—no matter—Ravish Virgins,
Go bid the Schoolmasters whip all their Boys;
Let Lawyers, Parsons, and Physicians loose,
To rob, impose on, and to kill the World.
  Nood. Her Majesty the Queen is in a Swoon.
  Queen. Not so much in a Swoon, but I have still
Strength to reward the Messenger of ill News.   [*Kills* Noodle.

  (*q*) Here is a visible Conjunction of two Days in one, by which our Author may
have either intended an Emblem of a Wedding; or to insinuate, that Men in the
Honey-Moon are apt to imagine Time shorter than it is. It brings into my Mind a
Passage in the Comedy call'd the *Coffee-House Politician*;
        We will celebrate this Day at my House To-morrow.
  (*r*) These beautiful Phrases are all to be found in one single Speech of *King
Arthur*, or *The British Worthy*.
  (*s*) *I was but teaching him to grace his Tale*
    With decent Horror.   Cleomenes.

  23 Links] That is, link-men, torch-carriers. (*q*) the *Coffee-House Politician*] A farcical
comedy by Fielding himself.

Nood. Oh! I am slain.

Cle. My Lover's kill'd, I will revenge him so.   [*Kills the* Queen.

Hunc. My Mamma kill'd! vile Murtheress, beware.   [*Kills* Cleora.

Dood. This for an old Grudge, to thy Heart.   [*Kills* Huncamunca.

Must. And this

I drive to thine, Oh *Doodle!* for a new one.   [*Kills* Doodle.

King. Ha! Murtheress vile, take that   [*Kills* Must.

(*t*) And take thou this.   [*Kills himself, and falls.*

So when the Child whom Nurse from Danger guards,

Sends *Jack* for Mustard with a Pack of Cards;

Kings, Queens and Knaves throw one another down,

'Till the whole Pack lies scatter'd and o'erthrown;   50

So all our Pack upon the Floor is cast,

And all I boast is—that I fall the last.   [*Dies.*

FINIS.

(*t*) We may say with *Dryden*,

> *Death did at length so many Slain forget,*
> *And left the Tale, and took them by the Great.*

I know of no Tragedy which comes nearer to this charming and bloody Catastrophe, than *Cleomenes*, where the Curtain covers five principal Characters dead on the Stage. These Lines too,

> *I ask no Questions then, of Who kill'd Who?*
> *The Bodies tell the Story as they lie.*

seem to have belonged more properly to this Scene of our Author.—Nor can I help imagining that they were originally his. The Rival Ladies too seem beholden to this Scene;

> *We're now a Chain of Lovers link'd in Death,*
> Julia *goes first,* Gonsalvo *hangs on her,*
> *And* Angelina *hangs upon* Gonsalvo,
> *As I on* Angelina.

No Scene, I believe, ever received greater Honours than this. It was applauded by several *Encores*, a Word very unusual in Tragedy —— And it was very difficult for the Actors to escape without a second Slaughter. This I take to be a lively Assurance of that fierce Spirit of Liberty which remains among us, and which Mr. *Dryden* in his *Essay* on *Dramatick Poetry* hath observed —— *Whether Custom* (says he) *hath so insinuated it self into our Countrymen, or Nature hath so formed them to Fierceness, I know not, but they will scarcely suffer Combats, and other Objects of Horror, to be taken from them.* —— And indeed I am for having them encouraged in this Martial Disposition: Nor do I believe our Victories over the *French* have been owing to any thing more than to those bloody Spectacles daily exhibited in our Tragedies, of which the *French* Stage is so entirely clear.

---

48 *Jack* for Mustard] Presumably a children's card-building game—though mustard, in its now-familiar powdered form, had only been introduced into England in 1720. The reference remains ambiguous.

SHE STOOPS TO CONQUER

Oliver Goldsmith

1730–1774

Half a century separates *The Conscious Lovers* from *She Stoops to Conquer*: and not even the theatrical experiments of such writers as Gay, Fielding, and Henry Carey were allowed to bear much fruit in the intervening years. The Licensing Act of 1737 effectively stifled the new forms of socio-political drama that had begun to develop: and irregular entertainment lost its spirit of adventure while five-act comedy sunk deeper into its sentimental slough. 'The Comic muse, long sick, is now a dying,' claimed Garrick, in his Prologue to *She Stoops*: and the difficulty Goldsmith encountered in getting his play staged, against all Colman's managerial misgivings, bears witness to the atrophied taste he helped to temper. Within a few years of the opening of *She Stoops* at Covent Garden on 15 March 1773 Sheridan had begun writing for the stage, and laughing comedy had been given its short lease of new life.

That the long-awaited dramatic renaissance of the seventeen-seventies so soon proved abortive may have been due to the lack of formal originality which flawed even the best work of Goldsmith and Sheridan. Neither attempted a truly contemporary comedy: instead, they tried to rework—and in the process to purify—veins that had long since been abandoned. But Goldsmith lacked Farquhar's sense of purpose: and one of his beaux is even disinclined to attempt amorous stratagems. All the same, both end up with their fortunes secured—only in an 'hour of levity' has Constance contemplated abandoning hers—even if their five acts full of adventures are less taken up with sexual encounters and more with mistaken identities than Farquhar might have considered proper. Even Tony Lumpkin is not quite the inimitable character he appears, but an improved model of Humphry Gubbin in Steele's *Lying Lovers*. Goldsmith certainly perfected all the 'old manners' that so delighted his Hardcastle: but he did nothing to change them. The suggestion of Sir Joshua Reynolds that the comedy should have been christened *The Belle's Stratagem* was entirely apt.

Of course, to cast off the dreary cloak of sentimentality was itself a considerable achievement: and *She Stoops to Conquer* is none the less a brilliant comedy for its lack of formal innovation. In retrospect, it is simply a pity that its influence could not have been seminal. But Goldsmith was never cut out to be a literary pioneer: rather, he was a genius who dabbled happily in all forms. He published his one novel, *The Vicar of Wakefield*, in 1766, and his most ambitious poem, *The Deserted Village*, in 1770: but he also excelled in belletristic prose, and had enjoyed a moderate success with his first play, *The Good Natur'd Man*, in 1768. Earlier he had studied for holy orders, for the law, and for medicine—qualifying, somewhat obscurely, only in the latter. Thus, it was not until he attempted the periodical essays later collected as *The Citizen of the World* that he discovered his literary ability. He was introduced, in consequence, to Doctor Johnson, whose life-long friend he remained, and to whom, of course, he dedicated *She Stoops to Conquer*. He was said to be contemplating the compilation of a universal dictionary of the arts and sciences, at the time of his early death in 1774. Whether the success of *She Stoops* the year before would have encouraged him to write more seriously for the stage one can only guess: as it is, the play remains one of the great sports of English literature, an isolated and almost incidental masterpiece.

The present text of *She Stoops to Conquer* follows that of the second impression of 1773—not so designated, but easily distinguished from the first impression by its regularization of accidentals. An edition by Arthur Friedman of the *Collected Works of Oliver Goldsmith* was published in five volumes by the Oxford University Press in 1966. Textually definitive, the edition is, however, critically under-annotated. But C. E. Doble's edition of the plays, together with *The Vicar of Wakefield*, first published in the Oxford Standard Authors series in 1928, contains a useful glossarial index.

She Stoops to Conquer:

OR,

The Mistakes of a Night.

A

COMEDY.

AS IT IS ACTED AT THE

THEATRE-ROYAL

IN

COVENT-GARDEN.

WRITTEN BY
Doctor GOLDSMITH.

LONDON:

Printed for F. NEWBERY, in St. Paul's Church-Yard.

M DCC LXXIII.

To SAMUEL JOHNSON, L.L.D.

Dear Sir,

BY inscribing this slight performance to you, I do not mean so much to compliment you as myself. It may do some honour to inform the public, that I have lived many years in intimacy with you. It may serve the interests of mankind also to inform them, that the greatest wit may be found in a character, without impairing the most unaffected piety.

I have, particularly, reason to thank you for your partiality to this performance. The undertaking a comedy, not merely sentimental, was very dangerous; and Mr. Colman, who saw this piece in its various stages, always thought it so. However I ventured to trust it to the public; and though it was necessarily delayed till late in the season, I have every reason to be grateful.   13

I am, Dear Sir,
Your most sincere friend,
And admirer,

OLIVER GOLDSMITH.

10 Mr. Colman] George Colman was manager of Covent Garden Theatre from 1767 to 1774. He came under strong criticism for his lack of faith in the prospects of *She Stoops to Conquer*, and the relatively mild reference to him here was possibly the result of a personal plea to Goldsmith to 'put me out of my pain one way or other'.   12 late in the season] The play was performed twelve times between its opening on 15 March 1773 and the close of the season on 31 May.

PROLOGUE

By David Garrick, Esq.

Enter Mr. WOODWARD,

Dressed in Black, and holding a Handkerchief to his Eyes.

EXCUSE *me, Sirs, I pray—I can't yet speak—*
I'm crying now—and have been all the week!
'Tis not alone this mourning suit, *good masters;*
I've that within—*for which there are no plaisters!*
Pray wou'd you know the reason why I'm crying?
The Comic muse, long sick, is now a dying!
And if she goes, my tears will never stop;
For as a play'r, I can't squeeze out one drop:
I am undone, that's all—shall lose my bread—
I'd rather, but that's nothing—lose my head.   10
When the sweet maid is laid upon the bier,
Shuter *and I shall be chief mourners here.*
To her *a mawkish drab of spurious breed,*
Who deals in sentimentals *will succeed!*
Poor Ned *and I are dead to all intents,*
We can as soon speak Greek *as sentiments!*
Both nervous grown, to keep our spirits up,
We now and then take down a hearty cup.
What shall we do?—If Comedy forsake us!
They'll turn us out, and no one else will take us,   20
But why can't I be moral?—Let me try—
My heart thus pressing—fix'd my face and eye—
With a sententious look, that nothing means,
(*Faces are blocks, in sentimental scenes*)

Mr. WOODWARD] Sharing Colman's doubts as to the play's prospects, Henry Woodward, a noted comic actor, in fact refused his intended role as Tony Lumpkin
12 Shuter] Edward Shuter took the part of Hardcastle. As Croaker, he had rescued
Goldsmith's earlier comedy, *The Good Natur'd Man*, from impending disaster.   13 *mawkish drab*] Sentimental slut.   18 *a hearty cup*] A favourite indulgence of Ned Shuter's, to
which Garrick was probably making friendly allusion.   24 *blocks*] That is, like a barber's
block: featureless, expressionless.

Thus I begin—All is not gold that glitters,
Pleasure seems sweet, but proves a glass of bitters.
When ign'rance enters, folly is at hand;
Learning is better far than house and land.
Let not your virtue trip, who trips may stumble,
And virtue is not virtue, if she tumble.   30
   I give it up—morals won't do for me;
To make you laugh I must play tragedy.
One hope remains—hearing the maid was ill,
A doctor *comes this night to shew his skill.*
To cheer her heart, and give your muscles motion,
He in five draughts *prepar'd, presents a potion:*
A kind of magic charm—for be assur'd,
If you will swallow it, *the maid is cur'd:*
But desp'rate the Doctor, and her case is,
If you reject the dose, and make wry faces!   40
This truth he boasts, will boast it while he lives,
No pois'nous drugs *are mix'd in what he gives;*
Should he succeed, you'll give him his degree;
If not, within he will receive no fee!
The college you, *must his pretensions back,*
Pronounce him regular, *or dub him* quack.

---

34 *A* doctor] Goldsmith himself.   45 *The college* you] The audience, in the terms of the
medical metaphor, has become the degree-awarding College of Physicians.   46 regular]
That is, at once 'regular' in adherence to the conventions of the comic form, and 'regular'
in lack of pretension and sham.

EPILOGUE

By Dr. GOLDSMITH.

WELL, *having stoop'd to conquer with success,*
  And gain'd a husband without aid from dress,
Still as a Bar-maid, I could wish it too,
As I have conquer'd him to conquer you:
And let me say, for all your resolution,
That pretty Bar-maids have done execution.
Our life is all a play, compos'd to please,
"We have our exits and our entrances."
The first act shews the simple country maid,
Harmless and young, of ev'ry thing afraid;   10
Blushes when hir'd, and with unmeaning action,
I hope as how to give you satisfaction.
Her second act displays a livelier scene,—
Th' unblushing Bar-maid of a country inn.
Who whisks about the house, at market caters,
Talks loud, coquets the guests, and scolds the waiters.
Next the scene shifts to town, and there she soars,
The chop house toast of ogling connoissieurs.
On 'Squires and Cits she there displays her arts,
And on the gridiron broils her lover's hearts—   20
And as she smiles, her triumphs to compleat,
Even Common Councilmen forget to eat.
The fourth act shews her wedded to the 'Squire,
And Madam now begins to hold it higher;
Pretends to taste, at Operas cries caro,
And quits her Nancy Dawson, for Che Faro.
Doats upon dancing, and in all her pride,

EPILOGUE] Goldsmith declared his own Epilogue—of which this was the third version—a 'very mawkish thing'. 6 *have done execution*] Have settled the formalities. A legal pun. 19 *On 'Squires and Cits*] On the upper and middle classes alike. 25 caro] A cry of approbation: literally, 'dear'. 26 *Nancy Dawson*] A hornpipe dancer. The popular song about her is probably here meant. 26 Che Faro] An aria from Gluck's opera *Orfeo*, 1764.

Swims round the room, *the* Heinel *of Cheapside :*
Ogles and leers with artificial skill,
Till having lost in age the power to kill, } 30
She sits all night at cards, and ogles at spadille.
Such, thro' our lives, the eventful history—
The fifth and last act still remains for me.
The Bar-maid now for your protection prays,
Turns Female Barrister, and pleads for Bayes.

28 Heinel *of Cheapside*] That is, the proudest guest at a city ball. Mlle Heinel was a popular dancer at the Haymarket Theatre. 31 *spadille*] The ace of spades, highest trump in ombre. 35 *Bayes*] The dramatist, after Buckingham's in *The Rehearsal*, 1671.

K

DRAMATIS PERSONÆ.

MEN.

Sir CHARLES MARLOW,	Mr. GARDNER.
Young MARLOW (his Son),	Mr. LEWES.
HARDCASTLE,	Mr. SHUTER.
HASTINGS,	Mr. DUBELLAMY.
TONY LUMPKIN,	Mr. QUICK.
DIGGORY,	Mr. SAUNDERS.

WOMEN.

Mrs. HARDCASTLE,	Mrs. GREEN.
Miss HARDCASTLE,	Mrs. BULKELY.
Miss NEVILLE,	Mrs. KNIVETON.
Maid,	MISS WILLEMS.

Landlord, Servants, &c. &c.

DRAMATIS PERSONAE] The *Morning Chronicle* for 16 March 1773 notes, in addition, that the Landlord of the Three Pigeons and the Drunken Servant were played by Mr. Thompson; the Leader of the Dancing Bear and Hardcastle's Servant by Mr. Saunders; and Companions to the Squire and various supernumeraries by Mr. Bates, Mr. Holtom, and Mr. Davis.

She Stoops to Conquer:

OR,

The Mistakes of a Night.

ACT I.

SCENE, *A* CHAMBER *in an old-fashioned* HOUSE.

Enter Mrs. HARDCASTLE *and* Mr. HARDCASTLE.

Mrs. HARDCASTLE.

I Vow, Mr. Hardcastle, you're very particular. Is there a creature in the whole country, but ourselves, that does not take a trip to town now and then, to rub off the rust a little? There's the two Miss Hoggs, and our neighbour, Mrs. Grigsby, go to take a month's polishing every winter.

HARDCASTLE.

Ay, and bring back vanity and affectation to last them the whole year. I wonder why London cannot keep its own fools at home. In my time, the follies of the town crept slowly among us, but now they travel faster than a stage-coach. Its fopperies come down, not only as inside passengers, but in the very basket. **9**

Mrs. HARDCASTLE.

Ay, *your* times were fine times, indeed; you have been telling us of *them* for many a long year. Here we live in an old rumbling mansion, that looks for all the world like an inn, but that we never see company. Our best visitors are old Mrs. Oddfish, the curate's wife, and little Cripplegate, the lame dancing-master: And all our entertainment your old stories of Prince Eugene and the Duke of Marlborough. I hate such old-fashioned trumpery.

9 basket] The overhanging outside compartment at the back of a stage coach, used both for luggage and for the poorest class of passengers.   11 rumbling] A form of 'rambling' already archaic in Goldsmith's time.   14 Prince Eugene and the Duke of Marlborough] François Eugène of Savoy and the Duke of Marlborough were joint commanders of the allied forces in the War of the Spanish Succession. Eugène shared in the victories of Oudenarde and Malplaquet.

HARDCASTLE.

And I love it. I love every thing that's old: old friends, old times, old
manners, old books, old wine; and, I believe, Dorothy, (*taking her hand*) you'll
own I have been pretty fond of an old wife.   18

Mrs. HARDCASTLE.

Lord, Mr. Hardcastle, you're for ever at your Dorothy's and your old
wife's. You may be a Darby, but I'll be no Joan, I promise you. I'm not so
old as you'd make me, by more than one good year. Add twenty to twenty,
and make money of that.   22

HARDCASTLE.

Let me see; twenty added to twenty, makes just fifty and seven.

Mrs. HARDCASTLE.

It's false, Mr. Hardcastle: I was but twenty when I was brought to bed of
Tony, that I had by Mr. Lumpkin, my first husband; and he's not come to
years of discretion yet.

HARDCASTLE.

Nor ever will, I dare answer for him. Ay, you have taught *him* finely.

Mrs. HARDCASTLE.

No matter, Tony Lumpkin has a good fortune. My son is not to live by his
learning. I don't think a boy wants much learning to spend fifteen hundred
a year.   30

HARDCASTLE.

Learning, quotha! A mere composition of tricks and mischief.

Mrs. HARDCASTLE.

Humour, my dear: nothing but humour. Come, Mr. Hardcastle, you must
allow the boy a little humour.

HARDCASTLE.

I'd sooner allow him an horse-pond. If burning the footmens shoes,
frighting the maids, and worrying the kittens, be humour, he has it. It was
but yesterday he fastened my wig to the back of my chair, and when I went
to make a bow, I popt my bald head in Mrs. Frizzle's face.

Mrs. HARDCASTLE.

And am I to blame? The poor boy was always too sickly to do any good.

32 Humour] Used here in a diluted Jonsonian sense, meaning ruling inclination or whim.

A school would be his death. When he comes to be a little stronger, who knows what a year or two's Latin may do for him?   40

HARDCASTLE.

Latin for him ! A cat and fiddle. No, no, the ale-house and the stable are the only schools he'll ever go to.

Mrs. HARDCASTLE.

Well, we must not snub the poor boy now, for I believe we shan't have him long among us. Any body that looks in his face may see he's consumptive.

HARDCASTLE.

Ay, if growing too fat be one of the symptoms.

Mrs. HARDCASTLE.

He coughs sometimes.

HARDCASTLE.

Yes, when his liquor goes the wrong way.

Mrs. HARDCASTLE.

I'm actually afraid of his lungs.

HARDCASTLE.

And truly so am I; for he sometimes whoops like a speaking trumpet— (*Tony hallooing behind the Scenes*)—O there he goes—A very consumptive figure, truly.   51

Enter TONY, *crossing the Stage.*

Mrs. HARDCASTLE.

Tony, where are you going, my charmer? Won't you give papa and I a little of your company, lovee?

TONY.

I'm in haste, mother, I cannot stay.

Mrs. HARDCASTLE.

You shan't venture out this raw evening, my dear: You look most shockingly.

TONY.

I can't stay, I tell you. The Three Pigeons expects me down every moment. There's some fun going forward.

49 like a speaking trumpet] That is, as if his voice were amplified by a megaphone.

HARDCASTLE.

Ay; the ale-house, the old place: I thought so.

Mrs. HARDCASTLE.

A low, paltry set of fellows.   60

TONY.

Not so low neither. There's Dick Muggins the exciseman, Jack Slang the horse doctor, Little Aminadab that grinds the music box, and Tom Twist that spins the pewter platter.

Mrs. HARDCASTLE.

Pray, my dear, disappoint them for one night at least.

TONY.

As for disappointing *them*, I should not so much mind; but I can't abide to disappoint *myself*.

Mrs. HARDCASTLE.

(*Detaining him*) You shan't go.

TONY.

I will, I tell you.

Mrs. HARDCASTLE.

I say you shan't.

TONY.

We'll see which is strongest, you or I.   70

[*Exit, hawling her out.*

HARDCASTLE. *Solus.*

HARDCASTLE.

Ay, there goes a pair that only spoil each other. But is not the whole age in a combination to drive sense and discretion out of doors? There's my pretty darling Kate; the fashions of the times have almost infected her too. By living a year or two in town, she is as fond of gauze, and French frippery, as the best of them.

Enter MISS HARDCASTLE.

62 Little Aminadab] Colloquial nickname for a Quaker.   62 music box] Barrel organ.
63 spins the pewter platter] Twirling a pewter dish was a popular accompaniment to tavern sing-songs.

HARDCASTLE.

Blessings on my pretty innocence! Drest out as usual my Kate. Goodness! What a quantity of superfluous silk has thou got about thee, girl! I could never teach the fools of this age, that the indigent world could be cloathed out of the trimmings of the vain.

Miss HARDCASTLE.

You know our agreement, Sir. You allow me the morning to receive and pay visits, and to dress in my own manner; and in the evening, I put on my housewife's dress to please you. 82

HARDCASTLE.

Well, remember I insist on the terms of our agreement; and, by the bye, I believe I shall have occasion to try your obedience this very evening.

Miss HARDCASTLE.

I protest, Sir, I don't comprehend your meaning.

HARDCASTLE.

Then, to be plain with you, Kate, I expect the young gentleman I have chosen to be your husband from town this very day. I have his father's letter, in which he informs me his son is set out, and that he intends to follow himself shortly after.

Miss HARDCASTLE.

Indeed! I wish I had known something of this before. Bless me, how shall I behave? It's a thousand to one I shan't like him; our meeting will be so formal, and so like a thing of business, that I shall find no room for friendship or esteem. 93

HARDCASTLE.

Depend upon it, child, I'll never controul your choice; but Mr. Marlow, whom I have pitched upon, is the son of my old friend, Sir Charles Marlow, of whom you have heard me talk so often. The young gentleman has been bred a scholar, and is designed for an employment in the service of his country. I am told he's a man of an excellent understanding.

Miss HARDCASTLE.

Is he?

HARDCASTLE.

Very generous. 100

95 pitched upon] Settled, decided upon.

Miss HARDCASTLE.

I believe I shall like him.

HARDCASTLE.

Young and brave.

Miss HARDCASTLE.

I'm sure I shall like him.

HARDCASTLE.

And very handsome.

Miss HARDCASTLE.

My dear Papa, say no more (*kissing his hand*) he's mine, I'll have him.

HARDCASTLE.

And to crown all, Kate, he's one of the most bashful and reserved young fellows in all the world.

Miss HARDCASTLE.

Eh! you have frozen me to death again. That word reserved, has undone all the rest of his accomplishments. A reserved lover, it is said, always makes a suspicious husband.   110

HARDCASTLE.

On the contrary, modesty seldom resides in a breast that is not enriched with nobler virtues. It was the very feature in his character that first struck me.

Miss HARDCASTLE.

He must have more striking features to catch me, I promise you. However, if he be so young, so handsome, and so every thing, as you mention, I believe he'll do still. I think I'll have him.

HARDCASTLE.

Ay, Kate, but there is still an obstacle. Its more than an even wager, he may not have *you*.

Miss HARDCASTLE.

My dear Papa, why will you mortify one so?—Well, if he refuses, instead of breaking my heart at his indifference, I'll only break my glass for its flattery. Set my cap to some newer fashion, and look out for some less difficult admirer.   122

HARDCASTLE.

Bravely resolved! In the mean time I'll go prepare the servants for his reception; as we seldom see company they want as much training as a company of recruits, the first day's muster.   [*Exit*

Miss HARDCASTLE, *Sola*.

Miss HARDCASTLE.

Lud, this news of Papa's, puts me all in a flutter. Young, handsome; these he put last; but I put them foremost. Sensible, good-natured; I like all that. But then reserved, and sheepish, that's much against him. Yet can't he be cured of his timidity, by being taught to be proud of his wife? Yes, and can't I—But I vow I'm disposing of the husband, before I have secured the lover.

Enter Miss NEVILLE.

Miss HARDCASTLE.

I'm glad you're come, Neville, my dear. Tell me, Constance, how do I look this evening? Is there any thing whimsical about me? Is it one of my well looking days, child? Am I in face to day?   133

Miss NEVILLE.

Perfectly, my dear. Yet now I look again—bless me!—sure no accident has happened among the canary birds or the gold fishes. Has your brother or the cat been meddling? Or has the last novel been too moving?

Miss HARDCASTLE.

No; nothing of all this. I have been threatened—I can scarce get it out—I have been threatened with a lover.

Miss NEVILLE.

And his name——

Miss HARDCASTLE.

Is Marlow.   140

Miss NEVILLE.

Indeed!

Miss HARDCASTLE.

The son of Sir Charles Marlow.

Miss NEVILLE.

As I live, the most intimate friend of Mr. Hastings, *my* admirer. They are never asunder. I believe you must have seen him when we lived in town.

133 in face] Looking at my best.

Miss HARDCASTLE.

Never.

Miss NEVILLE.

He's a very singular character, I assure you. Among women of reputation and virtue, he is the modestest man alive; but his acquaintance give him a very different character among creatures of another stamp: you understand me.

Miss HARDCASTLE.

An odd character, indeed. I shall never be able to manage him. What shall I do? Pshaw, think no more of him, but trust to occurrences for success. But how goes on your own affair my dear, has my mother been courting you for my brother Tony, as usual?   153

Miss NEVILLE.

I have just come from one of our agreeable tête-a-têtes. She has been saying a hundred tender things, and setting off her pretty monster as the very pink of perfection.

Miss HARDCASTLE.

And her partiality is such, that she actually thinks him so. A fortune like your's is no small temptation. Besides, as she has the sole management of it, I'm not surprized to see her unwilling to let it go out of the family.

Miss NEVILLE.

A fortune like mine, which chiefly consists in jewels, is no such mighty temptation. But at any rate if my dear Hastings be but constant, I make no doubt to be too hard for her at last. However, I let her suppose that I am in love with her son, and she never once dreams that my affections are fixed upon another.   164

Miss HARDCASTLE.

My good brother holds out stoutly. I could almost love him for hating you so.

Miss NEVILLE.

It is a good natured creature at bottom, and I'm sure would wish to see me married to any body but himself. But my aunt's bell rings for our afternoon's walk round the improvements. Allons. Courage is necessary as our affairs are critical.   170

169 the improvements] Possibly a description of land recently enclosed and cultivated: but also, more simply, a colloquialism for gardens.

Miss HARDCASTLE.

Would it were bed time and all were well.   [*Exeunt.*

SCENE, *An Alehouse Room. Several shabby fellows, with Punch and Tobacco.* TONY *at the head of the Table, a little higher than the rest: A mallet in his hand.*

OMNES.

Hurrea, hurrea, hurrea, bravo.

First FELLOW.

Now, gentlemen, silence for a song. The 'Squire is going to knock himself down for a song.

OMNES.

Ay, a song, a song.

TONY.

Then I'll sing you, gentlemen, a song I made upon this ale-house, the Three Pigeons.

SONG.

Let school-masters puzzle their brain,
    With grammar, and nonsense, and learning;
Good liquor, I stoutly maintain,
    Gives genus a better discerning.   10
Let them brag of their Heathenish Gods,
    Their Lethes, their Styxes, and Stygians;
Their Quis, and their Quæs, and their Quods,
    They're all but a parcel of Pigeons.
            Toroddle, toroddle, toroll.

When Methodist preachers come down,
    A preaching that drinking is sinful,
I'll wager the rascals a crown,
    They always preach best with a skinful.
But when you come down with your pence,   20
    For a slice of their scurvy religion,

I. ii, 2 knock himself down for a song] That is, call upon himself for a song, in his capacity as mallet-wielding master of ceremonies. 10 genus] Tony's usual malapropism for 'genius'.

> *I'll leave it to all men of sense,*
> *But you my good friend are the pigeon.*

> > Toroddle, toroddle, toroll.

> *Then come, put the jorum about,*
> *And let us be merry and clever,*
> *Our hearts and our liquors are stout,*
> *Here's the Three Jolly Pigeons for ever.*
> *Let some cry up woodcock or hare,*
> *Your bustards, your ducks, and your widgeons;*　30
> *But of all the birds in the air,*
> *Here's a health to the Three Jolly Pigeons.*

> > Toroddle, toroddle, toroll.

OMNES.

Bravo, bravo.

First FELLOW.

The 'Squire has got spunk in him.

Second FELLOW.

I loves to hear him sing, bekeays he never gives us nothing that's *low*.

Third FELLOW.

O damn any thing that's *low*, I cannot bear it.

Fourth FELLOW.

The genteel thing is the genteel thing at any time. If so be that a gentleman bees in a concatenation accordingly.

Third FELLOW.

I like the maxum of it, Master Muggins. What, tho' I am obligated to dance a bear, a man may be a gentleman for all that. May this be my poison if my bear ever dances but to the very genteelest of tunes. Water Parted, or the minuet in Ariadne.　43

Second FELLOW.

What a pity it is the 'Squire is not come to his own. It would be well for all the publicans within ten miles round of him.

23 *pigeon*] Here used in the colloquial sense of 'dupe' or 'gull'.　25 *jorum*] Punchbowl.
41 dance a bear] Play tunes to which a tamed bear can dance. The speaker is presumably 'Little Aminadab that grinds the music box'.　42 Water Parted] A song from Thomas Arne's adaptation of Metastasio's *Artaxerxes*, first performed in 1762.　43 Ariadne] Handel's opera, first performed in 1734.　44 come to his own] Entered into his inheritance.

TONY.

Ecod and so it would Master Slang. I'd then shew what it was to keep choice of company.

Second FELLOW.

O he takes after his own father for that. To be sure old 'Squire Lumpkin was the finest gentleman I ever set my eyes on. For winding the streight horn, or beating a thicket for a hare, or a wench he never had his fellow. It was a saying in the place, that he kept the best horses, dogs and girls in the whole county.   52

TONY.

Ecod, and when I'm of age I'll be no bastard I promise you. I have been thinking of Bett Bouncer and the miller's grey mare to begin with. But come, my boys, drink about and be merry, for you pay no reckoning. Well Stingo, what's the matter? *He's going to live life fast like father*

Enter LANDLORD.

LANDLORD.

There be two gentlemen in a post-chaise at the door. They have lost their way upo' the forest; and they are talking something about Mr. Hardcastle.

TONY.

As sure as can be one of them must be the gentleman that's coming down to court my sister. Do they seem to be Londoners?   60

LANDLORD.

I believe they may. They look woundily like Frenchmen. *French fashion*

TONY.

Then desire them to step this way, and I'll set them right in a twinkling. (*Exit Landlord.*) Gentlemen, as they mayn't be good enough company for you, step down for a moment, and I'll be with you in the squeezing of a lemon.   [*Exeunt Mob.*

TONY *solus.*

TONY. *more sensitivity behind [civility]*

Father-in-law has been calling me whelp, and hound, this half year. Now if I pleased, I could be so revenged upon the old grumbletonian. But then I'm afraid—afraid of what! I shall soon be worth fifteen hundred a year, and let him frighten me out of *that* if he can.

49 winding the streight horn] Blowing the hunting horn.   61 woundily] Excessively.
66 Father-in-law] Here used in the old sense of step-father.

Enter LANDLORD, *conducting Marlow and Hastings.*

MARLOW.

What a tedious uncomfortable day have we had of it! We were told it was but forty miles across the country, and we have come above threescore.

HASTINGS.

And all Marlow, from that unaccountable reserve of yours, that would not let us enquire more frequently on the way.   73

MARLOW.

I own, Hastings, I am unwilling to lay myself under an obligation to every one I meet; and often, stand the chance of an unmannerly answer.

HASTINGS.

At present, however, we are not likely to receive any answer.

TONY.

No offence, gentlemen. But I'm told you have been enquiring for one Mr. Hardcastle, in those parts. Do you know what part of the country you are in?

HASTINGS.

Not in the least Sir, but should thank you for information.

TONY.

Nor the way you came?   80

HASTINGS.

No, Sir; but if you can inform us——

TONY.

Why, gentlemen, if you know neither the road you are going, nor where you are, nor the road you came, the first thing I have to inform you is, that— You have lost your way.

MARLOW.

We wanted no ghost to tell us that.

TONY.

Pray, gentlemen, may I be so bold as to ask the place from whence you came?

MARLOW.

That's not necessary towards directing us where we are to go.

85 We wanted no ghost to tell us that] That is, Tony's information is superfluous. Marlow is adapting a reply of Horatio's to Hamlet.

TONY.

No offence; but question for question is all fair, you know. Pray, gentlemen, is not this same Hardcastle a cross-grain'd, old-fashion'd, whimsical fellow, with an ugly face; a daughter, and a pretty son? 91

HASTINGS.

We have not seen the gentleman, but he has the family you mention.

TONY.

The daughter, a tall trapesing, trolloping, talkative maypole—The son, a pretty, well-bred, agreeable youth, that every body is fond of.

MARLOW.

Our information differs in this. The daughter is said to be well-bred and beautiful; the son, an awkward booby, reared up, and spoiled at his mother's aprong-string.

TONY.

He-he-hem—Then, gentlemen, all I have to tell you is, that you won't reach Mr. Hardcastle's house this night, I believe.

HASTINGS.

Unfortunate! 100

TONY.

It's a damn'd long, dark, boggy, dirty, dangerous way. Stingo, tell the gentlemen the way to Mr. Hardcastle's; (*winking upon the Landlord*) Mr. Hardcastle's, of Quagmire Marsh, you understand me.

LANDLORD.

Master Hardcastle's! Lock-a-daisy, my masters, you're come a deadly deal wrong! When you came to the bottom of the hill, you should have cross'd down Squash-lane.

MARLOW.

Cross down Squash-lane!

LANDLORD.

Then you were to keep streight forward, 'till you came to four roads.

MARLOW.

Come to where four roads meet!

TONY.

Ay; but you must be sure to take only one of them. 110

MARLOW.

O Sir, you're facetious.

TONY.

Then keeping to the right, you are to go side-ways till you come upon Crack-skull common: there you must look sharp for the track of the wheel, and go forward, 'till you come to farmer Murrain's barn. Coming to the farmer's barn, you are to turn to the right, and then to the left, and then to the right about again, till you find out the old mill——

MARLOW.

Zounds, man! we could as soon find out the longitude.

HASTINGS.

What's to be done, Marlow?

MARLOW.

This house promises but a poor reception; though perhaps the Landlord can accommodate us.   120

LANDLORD.

Alack, master, we have but one spare bed in the whole house.

TONY.

And to my knowledge, that's taken up by three lodgers already. (*after a pause, in which the rest seem disconcerted*) I have hit it. Don't you think, Stingo, our landlady could accommodate the gentlemen by the fire-side, with——three chairs and a bolster?

HASTINGS.

I hate sleeping by the fire-side.

MARLOW.

And I detest your three chairs and a bolster.

TONY.

You do, do you?—then let me see—what—if you go on a mile further, to the Buck's Head; the old Buck's Head on the hill, one of the best inns in the whole county?   130

HASTINGS.

O ho! so we have escaped an adventure for this night, however.

117 as soon find out the longitude] The reward first offered in 1714 for an exact method of determining longitude was in fact claimed a few months after this play's first performance.

LANDLORD.

(*Apart to Tony*) Sure, you ben't sending them to your father's as an inn, be you?

TONY.

Mum, you fool you. Let *them* find that out. (*to them*) You have only to keep on streight forward, till you come to a large old house by the road side. You'll see a pair of large horns over the door. That's the sign. Drive up the yard, and call stoutly about you.

HASTINGS.

Sir, we are obliged to you. The servants can't miss the way?

TONY.

No, no: But I tell you though, the landlord is rich, and going to leave off business; so he wants to be thought a Gentleman, saving your presence, he! he! he! He'll be for giving you his company, and ecod if you mind him, he'll persuade you that his mother was an alderman, and his aunt a justice of peace.   143

LANDLORD.

A troublesome old blade to be sure; but a keeps as good wines and beds as any in the whole country.

MARLOW.

Well, if he supplies us with these, we shall want no further connexion. We are to turn to the right, did you say?

TONY.

No, no; streight forward. I'll just step myself, and shew you a piece of the way. (*to the landlord*) Mum.

LANDLORD.

Ah, bless your heart, for a sweet, pleasant——damn'd mischievous son of a whore.   [*Exeunt.*

END OF THE FIRST ACT.

---

144 blade] Mildly contemptuous term for an active, reckless person. A sharp fellow.

Shaw Falseness of being social, socialising, neo to extent to pretend to be 'good company' - vanity play behave more, more. go to great lengths - impressions make de way they deh days. These

ACT II.

SCENE, *An old-fashioned* HOUSE.

Enter HARDCASTLE, *followed by three or four aukward Servants.*

HARDCASTLE.

WELL, I hope you're perfect in the table exercise I have been teaching you these three days. You all know your posts and your places, and can shew that you have been used to good company, without ever stirring from home.

OMNES.

Ay, ay.

HARDCASTLE.

When company comes, you are not to pop out and stare, and then run in again, like frighted rabbits in a warren.

OMNES.

No, no.

HARDCASTLE.

You, Diggory, whom I have taken from the barn, are to make a shew at the side-table; and you, Roger, whom I have advanced from the plough, are to place yourself behind *my* chair. But you're not to stand so, with your hands in your pockets. Take your hands from your pockets, Roger; and from your head, you blockhead you. See how Diggory carries his hands. They're a little too stiff, indeed, but that's no great matter.   14

DIGGORY.

Ay, mind how I hold them. I learned to hold my hands this way, when I was upon drill for the militia. And so being upon drill——

HARDCASTLE.

You must not be so talkative, Diggory, You must be all attention to the guests. You must hear us talk, and not think of talking; you must see us drink, and not think of drinking; you must see us eat, and not think of eating.

DIGGORY.

By the laws, your worship, that's perfectly unpossible. Whenever Diggory sees yeating going forward, ecod he's always wishing for a mouthful himself.

HARDCASTLE.

Blockhead! Is not a belly-full in the kitchen as good as a belly-full in the parlour? Stay your stomach with that reflection.

DIGGORY.

Ecod I thank your worship, I'll make a shift to stay my stomach with a slice of cold beef in the pantry.

HARDCASTLE.

Diggory, you are too talkative. Then if I happen to say a good thing, or tell a good story at table, you must not all burst out a-laughing, as if you made part of the company.

DIGGORY.

Then ecod your worship must not tell the story of Ould Grouse in the gun-room: I can't help laughing at that—he! he! he!—for the soul of me. We have laughed at that these twenty years—ha! ha! ha!   31

HARDCASTLE.

Ha! ha! ha! The story is a good one. Well, honest Diggory, you may laugh at that—but still remember to be attentive. Suppose one of the company should call for a glass of wine, how will you behave? A glass of wine, Sir, if you please (*to Diggory*)—Eh, why don't you move?

DIGGORY.

Ecod, your worship, I never have courage till I see the eatables and drinkables brought upo' the table, and then I'm as bauld as a lion.

HARDCASTLE.

What, will no body move?

FIRST SERVANT.

I'm not to leave this pleace.

SECOND SERVANT.

I'm sure it's no pleace of mine.   40

THIRD SERVANT.

Nor mine, for sartain.

DIGGORY.

Wauns, and I'm sure it canna be mine.

42 Wauns] Wounds—an abbreviated euphemism for the oath 'by God's wounds'.

Like a ritual.

296   His exasperation is funny, it's over something that is as farcical & peculiar as them.   OLIVER GOLDSMITH   Act II

HARDCASTLE.

You numbskulls! and so while, like your betters, you are quarrelling for places, the guests must be starved. O you dunces! I find I must begin all over again.——But don't I hear a coach drive into the yard? To your posts, you blockheads. I'll go in the mean time and give my old friend's son a hearty reception at the gate.   [*Exit* Hardcastle.

DIGGORY.

By the elevens, my pleace is gone quite out of my head.

ROGER.

I know that my pleace is to be every where.

FIRST SERVANT.

Where the devil is mine?   50

SECOND SERVANT.

My pleace is to be no where at all; and so Ize go about my business.
         [*Exeunt Servants, running about as if frighted, different ways.*

Enter SERVANT *with Candles, shewing in* MARLOW *and* HASTINGS.

SERVANT.

Welcome, gentlemen, very welcome. This way.

HASTINGS.

After the disappointments of the day, welcome once more, Charles, to the comforts of a clean room and a good fire. Upon my word, a very well-looking house; antique, but creditable.

MARLOW.

The usual fate of a large mansion. Having first ruined the master by good housekeeping, it at last comes to levy contributions as an inn.

HASTINGS.

As you say, we passengers are to be taxed to pay all these fineries. I have often seen a good sideboard, or a marble chimney-piece, tho' not actually put in the bill, enflame a reckoning confoundedly.   60

MARLOW.

Travellers, George, must pay in all places. The only difference is, that in good inns, you pay dearly for luxuries; in bad inns, you are fleeced and starved.

48 By the elevens] Probably, by the eleven apostles—Judas being excluded from the twelve.   60 enflame] Add to, increase.

HASTINGS.

You have lived pretty much among them. In truth, I have been often surprized, that you have seen so much of the world, with your natural good sense, and your many opportunities, could never yet acquire a requisite share of assurance.

MARLOW.

The Englishman's malady. But tell me, George, where could I have learned that assurance you talk of? My life has been chiefly spent in a college, or an inn, in seclusion from that lovely part of the creation that chiefly teach men confidence. I don't know that I was ever familiarly acquainted with a single modest woman—except my mother—But among females of another class you know—   73

HASTINGS.

Ay, among them you are impudent enough of all conscience.

MARLOW.

They are of *us* you know.

HASTINGS.

But in the company of women of reputation I never saw such an ideot, such a trembler; you look for all the world as if you wanted an opportunity of stealing out of the room.

MARLOW.

Why man that's because I *do* want to steal out of the room. Faith, I have often formed a resolution to break the ice, and rattle away at any rate. But I don't know how, a single glance from a pair of fine eyes has totally overset my resolution. An impudent fellow may counterfeit modesty, but I'll be hanged if a modest man can ever counterfeit impudence.   83

HASTINGS.   *pretences again*

If you could but say half the fine things to them that I have heard you lavish upon the bar-maid of an inn, or even a college bed maker—

MARLOW.

Why, George, I can't say fine things to them, They freeze, they petrify me. They may talk of a comet, or a burning mountain, or some such bagatelle. But to me, a modest woman, drest out in all her finery, is the most tremendous object of the whole creation.

68 The Englishman's malady] A phrase often used at the time to convey the modish tendency to withdraw into melancholia.   87 a burning mountain] A volcano. Probably a reference to the eruption of Vesuvius in 1767.

HASTINGS.

Ha! ha! ha! At this rate, man, how can you ever expect to marry!   90

MARLOW.

Never, unless as among kings and princes, my bride were to be courted by proxy. If, indeed, like an Eastern bridegroom, one were to be introduced to a wife he never saw before, it might be endured. But to go through all the terrors of a formal courtship, together with the episode of aunts, grand-mothers and cousins, and at last to blurt out the broad staring question, of, *madam will you marry me?* No, no, that's a strain much above me I assure you.

HASTINGS.

I pity you. But how do you intend behaving to the lady you are come down to visit at the request of your father?

MARLOW.

As I behave to all other ladies. Bow very low. Answer yes, or no, to all her demands—But for the rest, I don't think I shall venture to look in her face, till I see my father's again.   101

HASTINGS.

I'm surprized that one who is so warm a friend can be so cool a lover.

MARLOW.

To be explicit, my dear Hastings, my chief inducement down was to be instrumental in forwarding your happiness, not my own. Miss Neville loves you, the family don't know you, as my friend you are sure of a reception, and let honour do the rest.

HASTINGS.

My dear Marlow! But I'll suppress the emotion. Were I a wretch, meanly seeking to carry off a fortune, you should be the last man in the world I would apply to for assistance. But Miss Neville's person is all I ask, and that is mine, both from her deceased father's consent, and her own inclina-tion.   111

MARLOW.

Happy man! You have talents and art to captivate any woman. I'm doom'd to adore the sex, and yet to converse with the only part of it I despise. This stammer in my address, and this aukward prepossessing visage of mine, can never permit me to soar above the reach of a milliner's 'prentice, or one of the dutchesses of Drury-lane. Pshaw! this fellow here to interrupt us.

114 prepossessing visage] That is, a face causing its beholder to be unfavourably impressed. 116 dutchesses of Drury-lane] Common prostitutes, who often appropriated the titles of their betters.

Marking her act to people, how class comes into it.

Enter HARDCASTLE.

HARDCASTLE.

Gentlemen, once more you are heartily welcome. Which is Mr. Marlow?
Sir, you're heartily welcome. It's not my way, you see, to receive my friends
with my back to the fire. I like to give them a hearty reception in the old stile
at my gate. I like to see their horses and trunks taken care of.   120

MARLOW (*aside.*)

He has got our names from the servants already. (*To Him*) We approve
your caution and hospitality, Sir. (*To Hastings*) I have been thinking,
George, of changing our travelling dresses in the morning. I am grown confoundedly ashamed of mine.

HARDCASTLE.

I beg, Mr. Marlow, you'll use no ceremony in this house.

HASTINGS.

I fancy, Charles, you're right: the first blow is half the battle. I intend
opening the campaign with the white and gold.

Mr. HARDCASTLE.

Mr. Marlow—Mr. Hastings—gentlemen—pray be under no constraint
in this house. This is Liberty-hall, gentlemen. You may do just as you please
here.   130

MARLOW.

Yet, George, if we open the campaign too fiercely at first, we may want
ammunition before it is over. I think to reserve the embroidery to secure a
retreat.

HARDCASTLE.

Your talking of a retreat, Mr. Marlow, puts me in mind of the Duke of
Marlborough, when we went to besiege Denain. He first summoned the
garrison.

MARLOW.

Don't you think the *ventre dor* waistcoat will do with the plain brown?

HARDCASTLE.

He first summoned the garrison, which might consist of about five thousand
men——

126 Charles] The first edition mistakenly prints 'George'.   127 with the white and gold]
That is, by donning a white and gold suit.   135 Denain] At this siege in 1712 the allied
troops under Prince Eugène were defeated by the French. But Marlborough had been
relieved of his command shortly before the battle.

[handwritten: What sig. of both talking about battles : strategies & tactics]

HASTINGS.

I think not: Brown and yellow mix but very poorly.   140

HARDCASTLE.

I say, gentlemen, as I was telling you, he summoned the garrison, which might consist of about five thousand men——

MARLOW.

The girls like finery.

HARDCASTLE.

Which might consist of about five thousand men, well appointed with stores, ammunition, and other implements of war. Now, says the Duke of Marlborough, to George Brooks, that stood next to him——You must have heard of George Brooks; I'll pawn my Dukedom, says he, but I take that garrison without spilling a drop of blood. So——

MARLOW.

What, my good friend, if you gave us a glass of punch in the mean time, it would help us to carry on the siege with vigour.   150

HARDCASTLE.

Punch, Sir! (*aside*) This is the most unaccountable kind of modesty I ever met with.   *[handwritten: told he was modest]*

MARLOW.

Yes, Sir, Punch. A glass of warm punch, after our journey, will be comfortable. This is Liberty-Hall, you know.

HARDCASTLE.

Here's Cup, Sir.

MARLOW.

(*Aside*) So this fellow, in his Liberty-hall, will only let us have just what he pleases.

HARDCASTLE.

(*Taking the Cup*) I hope you'll find it to your mind. I have prepared it with my own hands, and I believe you'll own the ingredients are tolerable. Will you, be so good as to pledge me, Sir? Here, Mr. Marlow, here is to our better acquaintance.   [*drinks.*

155 Here's Cup] That is, claret cup, and not the punch requested. Hence Marlow's following remark.

MARLOW.

(*Aside*) A very impudent fellow this! but he's a character, and I'll humour him a little. Sir, my service to you.   (*drinks*)

HASTINGS.

(*Aside*) I see this fellow wants to give us his company, and forgets that he's an innkeeper, before he has learned to be a gentleman.   165

MARLOW.

From the excellence of your cup, my old friend, I suppose you have a good deal of business in this part of the country. Warm work, now and then, at elections, I suppose.

HARDCASTLE.

No, Sir, I have long given that work over. Since our betters have hit upon the expedient of electing each other, there's no business *for us that sell ale.*

HASTINGS.

So, then you have no turn for politics I find.   171

HARDCASTLE.

Not in the least. There was a time, indeed, I fretted myself about the mistakes of government, like other people; but finding myself every day grow more angry, and the government growing no better, I left it to mend itself. Since that, I no more trouble my head about *Heyder Ally*, or *Ally Cawn*, than about *Ally Croaker*. Sir, my service to you.

HASTINGS.

So that with eating above stairs, and drinking below, with receiving your friends within, and amusing them without, you lead a good pleasant bustling life of it.

HARDCASTLE.

I do stir about a great deal, that's certain. Half the differences of the parish are adjusted in this very parlour.   181

167 Warm work] Marlow uses the phrase in its archaic sense of 'profitable employment'. Hardcastle takes it, of course, simply to mean 'much exertion'. 169 our betters] Hardcastle is presumably referring to those few members of the aristocracy who have his county's representation in their pockets. 170 *for us that sell ale*] The political sense in which Hardcastle is using this phrase, and thus confirming his own mistaken identity, is now lost. 175 *Heyder Ally*] Hyder Ali, the Maharaja of Mysore, who gave much trouble to the British administration. 175 *Ally Cawn*] Ali Khan, elevated by Clive to the position of Subah of Bengal in 1757, but subsequently deposed by the East India Company. 176 *Ally Croaker*] A popular Irish ballad.

MARLOW.

(*After drinking*) And you have an argument in your cup, old gentleman, better than any in Westminster-hall.

HARDCASTLE.

Ay, young gentleman, that, and a little philosophy.

MARLOW.

(*Aside*) Well, this is the first time I ever heard of an innkeeper's philosophy.

HASTINGS.

So then, like an experienced general, you attack them on every quarter. If you find their reason manageable, you attack it with your philosophy; if you find they have no reason, you attack them with this. Here's your health, my philosopher.   (*drinks*)

HARDCASTLE.

Good, very good, thank you; ha, ha. Your Generalship puts me in mind of Prince Eugene, when he fought the Turks at the battle of Belgrade. You shall hear.   192

MARLOW.

Instead of the battle of Belgrade, I believe it's almost time to talk about supper. What has your philosophy got in the house for supper?

HARDCASTLE.

For Supper, Sir! (*aside*) Was ever such a request to a man in his own house!

MARLOW.

Yes, Sir, supper Sir; I begin to feel an appetite. I shall make devilish work to-night in the larder, I promise you.

HARDCASTLE.

(*Aside*) Such a brazen dog sure never my eyes beheld. (*to him*) Why really, Sir, as for supper I can't well tell. My Dorothy, and the cook maid, settle these things between them. I leave these kind of things entirely to them.

MARLOW.

You do, do you?   201

HARDCASTLE.

Entirely. By-the-bye, I believe they are in actual consultation upon what's for supper this moment in the kitchen.

183 Westminster-hall] Still at that time the meeting place of the law courts.   191 the battle of Belgrade] A later victory of Prince Eugène's, in 1716.

MARLOW.

Then I beg they'll admit *me* as one of their privy council. It's a way I have got. When I travel, I always chuse to regulate my own supper. Let the cook be called. No offence I hope, Sir.

HARDCASTLE.

O no, Sir, none in the least; yet I don't know how: our Bridget, the cook maid, is not very communicative upon these occasions. Should we send for her, she might scold us all out of the house.

HASTINGS.

Let's see your list of the larder then. I ask it as a favour. I always match my appetite to my bill of fare.   211

MARLOW.

(*To Hardcastle, who looks at them with surprize*) Sir, he's very right, and it's my way too.

HARDCASTLE.

Sir, you have a right to command here. Here, Roger, bring us the bill of fare for to night's supper. I believe it's drawn out. Your manner, Mr. Hastings, puts me in mind of my uncle, Colonel Wallop. It was a saying of his, that no man was sure of his supper till he had eaten it.

HASTINGS.

(*Aside*) All upon the high ropes! His uncle a Colonel! We shall soon hear of his mother being a justice of peace. But let's hear the bill of fare.

MARLOW.

(*Perusing*) What's here? For the first course; for the second course; for the desert. The devil, Sir, do you think we have brought down the whole Joiners Company, or the Corporation of Bedford, to eat up such a supper? Two or three little things, clean and comfortable, will do.   223

HASTINGS.

But, let's hear it.

MARLOW.

(*Reading*) For the first course at the top, a pig, and pruin sauce.

217 had eaten it.] Following this, Goldsmith's manuscript version adds the stage direction: *Enter Roger, who gives a Bill of Fare.*   218 All upon the high ropes] Standing on his dignity. 221 the whole Joiners Company] A city guild famous for its banquets.   222 the Corporation of Bedford] Local corporations were proverbially gluttonous: but a particular reference may be intended to the recent creation by the Corporation of Bedford of a large number of additional freemen.

HASTINGS.

Damn your pig, I say.

MARLOW.

And damn your pruin sauce, say I.

HARDCASTLE.

And yet, gentlemen, to men that are hungry, pig, with pruin sauce, is very good eating.

MARLOW.

At the bottom, a calve's tongue and brains.   230

HASTINGS.

Let your brains be knock'd out, my good Sir; I don't like them.

MARLOW.

Or you may clap them on a plate by themselves. I do.

HARDCASTLE.

(*Aside*) Their impudence confounds me. (*to them*) Gentlemen, you are my guests, make what alterations you please. Is there any thing else you wish to retrench or alter, gentlemen?

MARLOW.

Item. A pork pie, a boiled rabbet and sausages, a florentine, a shaking pudding, and a dish of tiff—taff—taffety cream!

HASTINGS.

Confound your made dishes, I shall be as much at a loss in this house as at a green and yellow dinner at the French ambassador's table. I'm for plain eating.   240

HARDCASTLE.

I'm sorry, gentlemen, that I have nothing you like, but if there be any thing you have a particular fancy to——

MARLOW.

Why, really, Sir, your bill of fare is so exquisite, that any one part of it is full as good as another. Send us what you please. So much for supper. And now to see that our beds are air'd, and properly taken care of.

236 florentine] A kind of baked and spiced tart.   236 shaking pudding] Jelly.   237 taffety cream] Probably a kind of blancmange, of the delicate consistency of taffeta.   239 a green and yellow dinner] A meal full of colour but lacking in substance.

HARDCASTLE.

I entreat you'll leave all that to me. You shall not stir a step.

MARLOW.

Leave that to you! I protest, Sir, you must excuse me, I always look to these things myself.

HARDCASTLE.

I must insist, Sir, you'll make yourself easy on that head.

MARLOW.

You see I'm resolved on it. (*aside*) A very troublesome fellow this, as ever I met with. *Over- friendly , polite   a facade anyway.*   251

HARDCASTLE.

Well, Sir, I'm resolved at least to attend you. (*aside*) This may be modern modesty, but I never saw any thing look so like old-fashioned impudence.
Too rude   [*Exeunt* Marlow and Hardcastle.

HASTINGS solus.

HASTINGS.

So I find this fellow's civilities begin to grow troublesome. But who can be angry at those assiduities which are meant to please him? Ha! what do I see? Miss Neville, by all that's happy!

Enter Miss NEVILLE.

Miss NEVILLE.

My dear Hastings! To what unexpected good fortune? to what accident am I to ascribe this happy meeting?

HASTINGS.

Rather let me ask the same question, as I could never have hoped to meet my dearest Constance at an inn.   260

Miss NEVILLE.

An inn! sure you mistake! my aunt, my guardian, lives here. What could induce you to think this house an inn?

HASTINGS.

My friend Mr. Marlow, with whom I came down, and I, have been sent here as to an inn, I assure you. A young fellow whom we accidentally met at a house hard by directed us hither.

Miss NEVILLE.

Certainly it must be one of my hopeful cousin's tricks, of whom you have heard me talk so often, ha! ha! ha! ha!

HASTINGS.

He whom your aunt intends for you? He of whom I have such just apprehensions?

Miss NEVILLE.

You have nothing to fear from him, I assure you. You'd adore him if you knew how heartily he despises me. My aunt knows it too, and has undertaken to court me for him, and actually begins to think she has made a conquest.

HASTINGS.

Thou dear dissembler! You must know, my Constance, I have just seized this happy opportunity of my friend's visit here to get admittance into the family. The horses that carried us down are now fatigued with their journey, but they'll soon be refreshed; and then if my dearest girl will trust in her faithful Hastings, we shall soon be landed in France, where even among slaves the laws of marriage are respected.   278

Miss NEVILLE.

I have often told you, that though ready to obey you, I yet should leave my little fortune behind with reluctance. The greatest part of it was left me by my uncle, the India Director, and chiefly consists in jewels. I have been for some time persuading my aunt to let me wear them. I fancy I'm very near succeeding. The instant they are put into my possession you shall find me ready to make them and myself yours.   284

HASTINGS.

Perish the baubles! Your person is all I desire. In the meantime, my friend Marlow must not be let into his mistake. I know the strange reserve of his temper is such, that if abruptly informed of it, he would instantly quit the house before our plan was ripe for execution.

Miss NEVILLE.

But how shall we keep him in the deception? Miss Hardcastle is just returned from walking; what if we still continue to deceive him?——This, this way——   [They confer.]

278 slaves] A contemptuous term for the downtrodden French themselves.   278 the laws of marriage] Often assumed to be an incidental hit at the Royal Marriage Act of 1772, a highly unpopular measure by which George III attempted to strengthen his influence over the marriages of his descendants.   281 the India Director] A director of the East India Company.

Enter MARLOW.

MARLOW.

The assiduities of these good people teize me beyond bearing. My host seems to think it ill manners to leave me alone, and so he claps not only himself but his old-fashioned wife on my back. They talk of coming to sup with us too; and then, I suppose, we are to run the gauntlet thro' all the rest of the family.—What have we got here!—   296

HASTINGS.

My dear Charles! Let me congratulate you!—The most fortunate accident! —Who do you think is just alighted?

MARLOW.

Cannot guess.

HASTINGS.

Our mistresses boy, Miss Hardcastle and Miss Neville. Give me leave to introduce Miss Constance Neville to your acquaintance. Happening to dine in the neighbourhood, they called, on their return to take fresh horses, here. Miss Hardcastle has just stept into the next room, and will be back in an instant. Wasn't it lucky? eh!   304

MARLOW.

(*Aside*) I have just been mortified enough of all conscience, and here comes something to complete my embarrassment.

HASTINGS.

Well! but wasn't it the most fortunate thing in the world?

MARLOW.

Oh! yes. Very fortunate—a most joyful encounter——But our dresses, George, you know, are in disorder——What if we should postpone the happiness 'till to-morrow?——To-morrow at her own house——It will be every bit as convenient—And rather more respectful——To-morrow let it be.
[*offering to go.*

Miss NEVILLE.

By no means, Sir. Your ceremony will displease her. The disorder of your dress will shew the ardour of your impatience. Besides, she knows you are in the house, and will permit you to see her.   314

292 teize] Irritate, annoy.

MARLOW.

O! the devil! how shall I support it? Hem! hem! Hastings, you must not go. You are to assist me, you know. I shall be confoundedly ridiculous. Yet, hang it! I'll take courage. Hem!

HASTINGS.

Pshaw man! it's but the first plunge, and all's over. She's but a woman, you know.

MARLOW.

And of all women, she that I dread most to encounter!   320

Enter Miss HARDCASTLE as returned from walking, a Bonnet, &c.

HASTINGS, (introducing them.)

Miss Hardcastle, Mr. Marlow, I'm proud of bringing two persons of such merit together, that only want to know, to esteem each other.

Miss HARDCASTLE aside.

Now, for meeting my modest gentleman with a demure face, and quite in his own manner. (*After a pause, in which he appears very uneasy and disconcerted.*) I'm glad of your safe arrival, Sir——I'm told you had some accidents by the way.

MARLOW.

Only a few madam. Yes, we had some. Yes, Madam, a good many accidents, but should be sorry—Madam—or rather glad of any accidents—that are so agreeably concluded. Hem!

HASTINGS.

(*To him.*) You never spoke better in your whole life. Keep it up, and I'll insure you the victory.   331

Miss HARDCASTLE.

I'm afraid you flatter, Sir. You that have seen so much of the finest company can find little entertainment in an obscure corner of the country.

MARLOW.

(*Gathering courage.*) I have lived, indeed, in the world, Madam; but I have kept very little company. I have been but an observer upon life, Madam, while others were enjoying it.

Miss NEVILLE.

But that, I am told, is the way to enjoy it at last.

HASTINGS.

(*To him.*) Cicero never spoke better. Once more, and you are confirm'd in assurance for ever.

MARLOW.

(*To him.*) Hem! Stand by me then, and when I'm down, throw in a word or two to set me up again.   341

Miss HARDCASTLE.

An observer, like you, upon life, were, I fear, disagreeably employed, since you must have had much more to censure than to approve.

MARLOW.

Pardon me, Madam. I was always willing to be amused. The folly of most people is rather an object of mirth than uneasiness. *Being laughed at*

HASTINGS.

(*To him.*) Bravo, Bravo. Never spoke so well in your whole life. Well! Miss Hardcastle, I see that you and Mr. Marlow are going to be very good company. I believe our being here will but embarrass the interview.

MARLOW.

Not in the least, Mr. Hastings. We like your company of all things. (*To him.*) Zounds! George, sure you won't go? How can you leave us?   350

HASTINGS.

Our presence will but spoil conversation, so we'll retire to the next room. (*To him*) You don't consider, man, that we are to manage a little tête-à-tête of our own.   *Exeunt.*

Miss HARDCASTLE.

(*After a pause*) But you have not been wholly an observer, I presume, Sir: The ladies I should hope have employed some part of your addresses.

MARLOW.

(*Relapsing into timidity*) Pardon me, Madam, I—I—I—as yet have studied —only—to—deserve them.

Miss HARDCASTLE.

And that some say is the very worst way to obtain them.

s.d. *Exeunt*] That is, exeunt Hastings and Miss Neville, leaving Marlow and Miss Hard-castle alone.

L

MARLOW.

Perhaps so, madam. But I love to converse only with the more grave and sensible part of the sex.——But I'm afraid I grow tiresome.   360

Miss HARDCASTLE.

Not at all, Sir; there is nothing I like so much as grave conversation myself; I could hear it for ever. Indeed I have often been surprized how a man of *sentiment* could ever admire those light airy pleasures, where nothing reaches the heart.

MARLOW.

It's——a disease——of the mind, madam. In the variety of tastes there must be some who wanting a relish——for——um—a—um.

Miss HARDCASTLE.

I understand you, Sir. There must be some, who wanting a relish for refined pleasures, pretend to despise what they are incapable of tasting.

MARLOW.

My meaning, madam, but infinitely better expressed. And I can't help observing——a——   370

Miss HARDCASTLE.

(*Aside*) Who could ever suppose this fellow impudent upon some occasions. (*To him*) You were going to observe, Sir——

MARLOW.

I was observing, madam——I protest, madam, I forget what I was going to observe.

Miss HARDCASTLE.

(*Aside*) I vow and so do I. (*To him*) You were observing, Sir, that in this age of hypocrisy something about hypocrisy, Sir.

MARLOW.

Yes, madam. In this age of hypocrisy there are few who upon strict enquiry do not—a—a—a——

Miss HARDCASTLE.

I understand you perfectly, Sir.

MARLOW.

(*Aside*) Egad! and that's more than I do myself.   380

362 a man of *sentiment*] That is, a man of sensibility, ready to respond to an appeal to his emotions.

Miss HARDCASTLE.

You mean that in this hypocritical age there are few that do not condemn in public what they practise in private, and think they pay every debt to virtue when they praise it.

MARLOW.

True, madam; those who have most virtue in their mouths, have least of it in their bosoms. But I'm sure I tire you, madam.

Miss HARDCASTLE.

Not in the least, Sir; there's something so agreeable and spirited in your manner, such life and force—pray, Sir, go on.

MARLOW.

Yes, madam. I was saying——that there are some occasions——when a total want of courage, madam, destroys all the——and puts us——upon a——a——a——   390

Miss HARDCASTLE.

I agree with you entirely, a want of courage upon some occasions assumes the appearance of ignorance, and betrays us when we most want to excel. I beg you'll proceed.

MARLOW.

Yes, madam. Morally speaking, madam—But I see Miss Neville expecting us in the next room. I would not intrude for the world.

Miss HARDCASTLE.

I protest, Sir, I never was more agreeably entertained in all my life. Pray go on.

MARLOW.

Yes, madam. I was——But she beckons us to join her. Madam, shall I do myself the honour to attend you?

Miss HARDCASTLE.

Well then, I'll follow.   400

MARLOW aside.

This pretty smooth dialogue has done for me.   [*Exit.*

Miss HARDCASTLE sola.

Miss HARDCASTLE.

Ha! ha! ha! Was there ever such a sober sentimental interview? I'm certain he scarce look'd in my face the whole time. Yet the fellow, but for his unaccountable bashfulness, is pretty well too. He has good sense, but then so buried in his fears, that it fatigues one more than ignorance. If I could teach him a little confidence, it would be doing somebody that I know of a piece of service. But who is that somebody?—that, faith, is a question I can scarce answer.   [*Exit.*

Enter TONY and Miss NEVILLE, followed by Mrs. HARDCASTLE and HASTINGS.

TONY.

What do you follow me for, cousin Con? I wonder you're not ashamed to be so very engaging.   410

Miss NEVILLE.

I hope, cousin, one may speak to one's own relations, and not be to blame.

TONY.

Ay, but I know what sort of a relation you want to make me though; but it won't do. I tell you, cousin Con, it won't do, so I beg you'll keep your distance, I want no nearer relationship.

                               [*She follows coqueting him to the back scene.*

Mrs. HARDCASTLE.

Well! I vow, Mr. Hastings, you are very entertaining. There's nothing in the world I love to talk of so much as London, and the fashions, though I was never there myself.

HASTINGS.

Never there! You amaze me! From your air and manner, I concluded you had been bred all your life either at Ranelagh, St. James's, or Tower Wharf.

Mrs. HARDCASTLE.

O! Sir, you're only pleased to say so. We Country persons can have no manner at all. I'm in love with the town, and that serves to raise me above some of our neighbouring rustics; but who can have a manner, that has

---

410 engaging] That is, persistent in her attentions to her cousin.   419 Ranelagh] A public garden and fashionable place of entertainment in Chelsea.   419 St. James's, or Tower Wharf] It is apparently Hastings's intention to play upon Mrs. Hardcastle's ignorance of city life by mentioning a highly fashionable area and a wharf close to the Tower of London in a single breath. But Tower Wharf did, in fact, afford a pleasant and shaded prospect of the river.

never seen the Pantheon, the Grotto Gardens, the Borough, and such places where the Nobility chiefly resort? All I can do, is to enjoy London at second-hand. I take care to know every tête-à-tête from the Scandalous Magazine, and have all the fashions, as they come out, in a letter from the two Miss Rickets of Crooked-lane. Pray how do you like this head, Mr. Hastings? 427

HASTINGS.

Extremely elegant and degagée, upon my word, Madam. Your Friseur is a Frenchman, I suppose?

Mrs. HARDCASTLE.

I protest I dressed it myself from a print in the Ladies Memorandum-book for the last year. 431

HASTINGS.

Indeed. Such a head in a side-box, at the Playhouse, would draw as many gazers as my Lady May'ress at a City Ball.

Mrs. HARDCASTLE.

I vow, since inoculation began, there is no such thing to be seen as a plain woman; so one must dress a little particular or one may escape in the crowd.

HASTINGS.

But that can never be your case, Madam, in any dress. (*bowing*)

Mrs. HARDCASTLE.

Yet, what signifies *my* dressing when I have such a piece of antiquity by my side as Mr. Hardcastle: all I can say will never argue down a single button from his cloaths. I have often wanted him to throw off his great flaxen wig, and where he was bald, to plaister it over like my Lord Pately, with powder. 442

423 the Pantheon] A sumptuous tea house in Oxford Street, much frequented by the upper class since its opening in 1772.   423 the Grotto Gardens] A suburban imitation of Ranelagh, in Clerkenwell.   423 the Borough] That is, the Borough of Southwark—but Mrs. Hardcastle is probably thinking specifically of Southwark Fair.   423 such places where the Nobility chiefly resort] Of the three places mentioned by Mrs. Hardcastle, only the Pantheon would have been a regular haunt of the nobility.   425 the Scandalous Magazine] The *Town and Country Magazine*, then publishing a monthly engraving of a prominent figure alongside his mistress, together with a *History of the Tête-à-Tête Annexed*. 427 Crooked-lane] Cannon Street: not at all a centre of fashion.   427 this head] That is, this head of hair, this hair style.   428 degagée] Stylish.   430 the Ladies Memorandum-book] A diary-cum-almanack of the time, which included illustrations of modish hair styles.   434 since inoculation began] Inoculation against smallpox, first introduced into England in 1718, but not widely practised until the middle of the century, had drastically reduced the number of faces scarred in the aftermath of the illness.

HASTINGS.

You are right, Madam; for, as among the ladies, there are none ugly, so among the men there are none old.

Mrs. HARDCASTLE.

But what do you think his answer was? Why, with his usual Gothic vivacity, he said I only wanted him to throw off his wig to convert it into a tête for my own wearing.

HASTINGS.

Intolerable! At your age you may wear what you please, and it must become you.

Mrs. HARDCASTLE.

Pray, Mr. Hastings, what do you take to be the most fashionable age about town?   451

HASTINGS.

Some time ago, forty was all the mode; but I'm told the ladies intend to bring up fifty for the ensuing winter.

Mrs. HARDCASTLE.

Seriously. Then I shall be too young for the fashion.

HASTINGS.

No lady begins now to put on jewels 'till she's past forty. For instance, Miss there, in a polite circle, would be considered as a child, as a mere maker of samplers.

Mrs. HARDCASTLE.

And yet Mrs. Niece thinks herself as much a woman, and is as fond of jewels as the oldest of us all.

HASTINGS.

Your niece, is she? And that young gentleman, a brother of yours, I should presume?   461

Mrs. HARDCASTLE.

My son, Sir. They are contracted to each other. Observe their little sports. They fall in and out ten times a day, as if they were man and wife already. (*To them.*) Well Tony, child, what soft things are you saying to your cousin Constance this evening?

445 Gothic] Barbaric, ill-mannered.   457 samplers] Designs embroidered onto canvas, usually in cross-stitch. Most samplers were made by little girls.

TONY.

I have been saying no soft things; but that it's very hard to be followed about so. Ecod! I've not a place in the house now that's left to myself but the stable.

Mrs. HARDCASTLE. *lie more obvious*

Never mind him, Con. my dear. He's in another story behind your back.

Miss NEVILLE. *than Hastings*

There's something generous in my cousin's manner. He falls out before faces to be forgiven in private. — *sarcy*   471

TONY. *opposite of the hypocrite Madon & Kate were earlier talking about.*

That's a damned confounded——crack.

Mrs. HARDCASTLE.

Ah! he's a sly one. Don't you think they're like each other about the mouth, Mr. Hastings? The Blenkinsop mouth to a T. They're of a size too. Back to back, my pretties, that Mr. Hastings may see you. Come Tony.

TONY.

You had as good not make me, I tell you. (*measuring.*)

Miss NEVILLE.

O lud! he has almost cracked my head.

Mrs. HARDCASTLE.

O the monster! For shame, Tony. You a man, and behave so!

TONY.

If I'm a man, let me have my fortin. Ecod! I'll not be made a fool of no longer. *He has pride*   480

Mrs. HARDCASTLE.

Is this, ungrateful boy, all that I'm to get for the pains I have taken in your education? I that have rock'd you in your cradle, and fed that pretty mouth with a spoon! Did not I work that waistcoat to make you genteel? Did not I prescribe for you every day, and weep while the receipt was operating?

TONY.

Ecod! you had reason to weep, for you have been dosing me ever since

469 He's in another story] That is, he tells a different tale.   472 crack] Falsehood.
484 receipt] Prescription for a medicine.

I was born. I have gone through every receipt in the complete huswife ten times over; and you have thoughts of coursing me through *Quincy* next spring. But, Ecod! I tell you, I'll not be made a fool of no longer.

Mrs. HARDCASTLE.

Wasn't it all for your good, viper? Wasn't it all for your good?

TONY.

I wish you'd let me and my good alone then. Snubbing this way when I'm in spirits. If I'm to have any good, let it come of itself; not to keep dinging it, dinging it into one so. *His psyche / behaviour a reaction*   492

Mrs. HARDCASTLE. *to her?*

That's false; I never see you when you're in spirits. No, Tony, you then go to the alehouse or kennel. I'm never to be delighted with your agreeable, wild notes, unfeeling monster!

TONY.

Ecod! Mamma, your own notes are the wildest of the two.

Mrs. HARDCASTLE.

Was ever the like? But I see he wants to break my heart, I see he does.

HASTINGS.

Dear Madam, permit me to lecture the young gentleman a little. I'm certain I can persuade him to his duty.

Mrs. HARDCASTLE.

Well! I must retire. Come, Constance, my love. You see Mr. Hastings, the wretchedness of my situation: Was ever poor woman so plagued with a dear, sweet, pretty, provoking, undutiful boy.   502

[*Exeunt* Mrs. Hardcastle and Miss Neville.

paradox, irony
maybe some truth in
it

HASTINGS.   TONY.

TONY, *singing.*

There was a young man riding by, and fain would have his will. Rang do didlo dee. Don't mind her. Let her cry. It's the comfort of her heart. I have seen her and sister cry over a book for an hour together, and they said, they liked the book the better the more it made them cry.

HASTINGS.

Then you're no friend to the ladies, I find, my pretty young gentleman?

486 the complete huswife] *The Compleat Housewife* had been a popular domestic handbook for half a century.   487 *Quincy*] John Quincy's *Compleat English Dispensatory*, 1719. 492 dinging it into one] Forcing it upon one by constant repetition.

TONY.

That's as I find 'um. *- depends. Easy going*

HASTINGS.

Not to her of your mother's chusing, I dare answer? And yet she appears
to me a pretty well-tempered girl.   510

TONY.

That's because you don't know her as well as I. Ecod! I know every inch
about her; and there's not a more bitter cantanckerous toad in all Christen-
dom.

HASTINGS.

(*Aside*) Pretty encouragement this for a lover! *& mocking.*

TONY.

I have seen her since the height of that. She has as many tricks as a hare
in a thicket, or a colt the first day's breaking. *- she's not as seems either (to Tony)*

HASTINGS.

To me she appears sensible and silent!

TONY.

Ay, before company. But when she's with her play-mates she's as loud as a
hog in a gate.   *Like Mr & Mrs H.C*

HASTINGS.   *conversation. See*

But there is a meek modesty about her that charms me. *things diff.*   520

TONY.

Yes, but curb her never so little, she kicks up, and you're flung in a ditch.

HASTINGS.

Well, but you must allow her a little beauty.—Yes, you must allow her
some beauty.

TONY.

Bandbox! She's all a made up thing, mun. Ah! could you but see Bet
Bouncer of these parts, you might then talk of beauty. Ecod, she has two
eyes as black as sloes, and cheeks as broad and red as a pulpit cushion. She'd
make two of she.

519 a hog in a gate] That is, wedged into a gateway.   524 Bandbox!] That is: her beauty
is the product of her wardrobe, not of her person.

HASTINGS.

Well, what say you to a friend that would take this bitter bargain off your hands?

TONY.

Anon.

530

HASTINGS.

Would you thank him that would take Miss Neville and leave you to happiness and your dear Betsy?

TONY.

Ay; but where is there such a friend, for who would take *her?*

HASTINGS.

I am he. If you but assist me, I'll engage to whip her off to France, and you shall never hear more of her.

TONY.

Assist you! Ecod I will, to the last drop of my blood. I'll clap a pair of horses to your chaise that shall trundle you off in a twinkling, and may be get you a part of her fortin beside, in jewels, that you little dream of.

HASTINGS.

My dear squire, this looks like a lad of spirit.

TONY.

Come along then, and you shall see more of my spirit before you have done with me. (*singing*). We are the boys that fears no noise where the thundering cannons roar.   [*Exeunt.*

END OF SECOND ACT.

ACT III.

Enter HARDCASTLE solus.

HARDCASTLE.

WHAT could my old friend Sir Charles mean by recommending his son as the modestest young man in town? To me he appears the most impudent piece of brass that ever spoke with a tongue. He has taken possession of the easy chair by the fire-side already. He took off his boots in

530 Anon] At your service.

the parlour, and desired me to see them taken care of. I'm desirous to know how his impudence affects my daughter.—She will certainly be shocked at it.

Enter Miss HARDCASTLE, plainly dress'd.

HARDCASTLE.

Well, my Kate, I see you have changed your dress as I bid you; and yet, I believe, there was no great occasion.

Miss HARDCASTLE.

I find such a pleasure, Sir, in obeying your commands, that I take care to observe them without ever debating their propriety.   10

HARDCASTLE.

And yet, Kate, I sometimes give you some cause, particularly when I recommended my *modest* gentleman to you as a lover to-day.

Miss HARDCASTLE.

You taught me to expect something extraordinary, and I find the original exceeds the description.

HARDCASTLE.

I was never so surprized in my life! He has quite confounded all my faculties!

Miss HARDCASTLE.

I never saw any thing like it: And a man of the world too!

HARDCASTLE.

Ay, he learned it all abroad,—what a fool was I, to think a young man could learn modesty by travelling. He might as soon learn wit at a masquerade.

Miss HARDCASTLE.

It seems all natural to him.   20

HARDCASTLE.

A good deal assisted by bad company and a French dancing-master.

Miss HARDCASTLE.

Sure you mistake, papa! a French dancing-master could never have taught him that timid look,—that aukward address,—that bashful manner——

HARDCASTLE.

Whose look? whose manner? child!

Miss HARDCASTLE.

Mr. Marlow's: his meauvaise honte, his timidity struck me at the first sight.

HARDCASTLE.

Then your first sight deceived you; for I think him one of the most brazen first sights that ever astonished my senses.

Miss HARDCASTLE.

Sure, Sir, you rally! I never saw any one so modest.

HARDCASTLE.

And can you be serious! I never saw such a bouncing swaggering puppy since I was born. Bully Dawson was but a fool to him.   30

Miss HARDCASTLE.

Surprizing! He met me with a respectful bow, a stammering voice, and a look fixed on the ground.

HARDCASTLE.

He met me with a loud voice, a lordly air, and a familiarity that made my blood freeze again.

Miss HARDCASTLE.

He treated me with diffidence and respect; censured the manners of the age; admired the prudence of girls that never laughed; tired me with apologies for being tiresome; then left the room with a bow, and, madam, I would not for the world detain you.

HARDCASTLE.

He spoke to me as if he knew me all his life before. Asked twenty questions, and never waited for an answer. Interrupted my best remarks with some silly pun, and when I was in my best story of the Duke of Marlborough and Prince Eugene, he asked if I had not a good hand at making punch. Yes, Kate, he ask'd your father if he was a maker of punch!   43

Miss HARDCASTLE.

One of us must certainly be mistaken.

HARDCASTLE.

If he be what he has shewn himself, I'm determined he shall never have my consent.

25 meauvaise honte] Literally, false shame. Gauche, awkward manner. 30 Bully Dawson] A Restoration coffee house sharper.

Miss HARDCASTLE.

And if he be the sullen thing I take him, he shall never have mine.

HARDCASTLE.

In one thing then we are agreed—to reject him.

Miss HARDCASTLE.

Yes. But upon conditions. For if you should find him less impudent, and I more presuming; if you find him more respectful, and I more importunate ——I don't know——the fellow is well enough for a man—Certainly we don't meet many such at a horse race in the country.   52

HARDCASTLE.

If we should find him so——But that's impossible. The first appearance has done my business. I'm seldom deceived in that.

Miss HARDCASTLE.

And yet there may be many good qualities under that first appearance.

HARDCASTLE.

Ay, when a girl finds a fellow's outside to her taste, she then sets about guessing the rest of his furniture. With her, a smooth face stands for good sense, and a genteel figure for every virtue.

Miss HARDCASTLE.

I hope, Sir, a conversation begun with a compliment to my good sense won't end with a sneer at my understanding?   60

HARDCASTLE.

Pardon me, Kate. But if young Mr. Brazen can find the art of reconciling contradictions, he may please us both, perhaps.

Miss HARDCASTLE.

And as one of us must be mistaken, what if we go to make further discoveries?

HARDCASTLE.

Agreed. But depend on't I'm in the right.

Miss HARDCASTLE.

And depend on't I'm not much in the wrong.   [*Exeunt.*

Enter TONY running in with a Casket.

TONY.

Ecod! I have got them. Here they are. My Cousin Con's necklaces, bobs and all. My mother shan't cheat the poor souls out of their fortune neither. O! my genus, is that you?

Enter HASTINGS.

HASTINGS.

My dear friend, how have you managed with your mother? I hope you have amused her with pretending love for your cousin, and that you are willing to be reconciled at last? Our horses will be refreshed in a short time, and we shall soon be ready to set off.   73

TONY.

And here's something to bear your charges by the way, (*giving the casket.*) Your sweetheart's jewels. Keep them, and hang those, I say, that would rob you of one of them.   *Also talking about Kate*

HASTINGS.

But how have you procured them from your mother?

TONY.

Ask me no questions, and I'll tell you no fibs. I procured them by the rule of thumb. If I had not a key to every drawer in mother's bureau, how could I go to the alehouse so often as I do? An honest man may rob himself of his own at any time.   81

HASTINGS.

Thousands do it every day. But to be plain with you; Miss Neville is endeavouring to procure them from her aunt this very instant. If she succeeds, it will be the most delicate way at least of obtaining them.

TONY.

Well, keep them, till you know how it will be. But I know how it will be well enough, she'd as soon part with the only sound tooth in her head.

HASTINGS.

But I dread the effects of her resentment, when she finds she has lost them.

TONY.

Never you mind her resentment, leave *me* to manage that. I don't value her resentment the bounce of a cracker. Zounds! here they are. Morrice. Prance.

[*Exit* Hastings.

67 bobs] Ornamental earrings.   89 the bounce of a cracker] So much as the snap of a firecracker.   89 Morrice] Get going, clear out.

TONY, Mrs. HARDCASTLE, Miss NEVILLE.

Mrs. HARDCASTLE.

Indeed, Constance, you amaze me. Such a girl as you want jewels? It will be time enough for jewels, my dear, twenty years hence, when your beauty begins to want repairs. *— what Has mvs said*   92

Miss NEVILLE.

But what will repair beauty at forty, will certainly improve it at twenty, Madam.

Mrs. HARDCASTLE.

Yours, my dear, can admit of none. That natural blush is beyond a thousand ornaments. Besides, child, jewels are quite out at present. Don't you see half the ladies of our acquaintance, my lady Kill day light, and Mrs. Crump, and the rest of them, carry their jewels to town, and bring nothing but Paste and Marcasites back.

Miss NEVILLE.

But who knows, Madam, but somebody that shall be nameless would like me best with all my little finery about me?   101

Mrs. HARDCASTLE.

Consult your glass, my dear, and then see, if with such a pair of eyes, you want any better sparklers. What do you think, Tony, my dear, does your cousin Con. want any jewels, in your eyes, to set off her beauty.

TONY.

That's as thereafter may be.

Miss NEVILLE.

My dear aunt, if you knew how it would oblige me.

Mrs. HARDCASTLE.

A parcel of old-fashioned rose and table-cut things. They would make you look like the court of king Solomon at a puppet-shew. Besides, I believe I can't readily come at them. They may be missing for aught I know to the contrary.   110

TONY.

(*Apart to Mrs. Hardcastle.*) Then why don't you tell her so at once, as she's

99 Paste] Imitation jewels. 99 Marcasites] Iron pyrites in crystallized forms which resembled diamonds. 107 rose and table-cut things] Rose-cut jewels have smooth faces while table-cut diamonds have flat upper and under sides. 108 king Solomon at a puppet-shew] Solomon was apparently second only to Punch in puppet-show popularity.

They're struggling to be polite while probably look like going to hit each other.

so longing for them. Tell her they're lost. It's the only way to quiet her. Say they're lost, and call me to bear witness.

Mrs. HARDCASTLE.

(*Apart to Tony.*) You know, my dear, I'm only keeping them for you. So if I say they're gone, you'll bear me witness, will you? He! he! he!

double meaning again

TONY.

Never fear me. Ecod! I'll say I saw them taken out with my own eyes.

Miss NEVILLE.

I desire them but for a day, Madam. Just to be permitted to shew them as relicks, and then they may be lock'd up again. *But she'll be gone*

Mrs. HARDCASTLE.

To be plain with you, my dear Constance; if I could find them, you should have them. They're missing, I assure you. Lost, for aught I know; but we must have patience wherever they are.   121

Miss NEVILLE.

I'll not believe it; this is but a shallow pretence to deny me. I know they're too valuable to be so slightly kept, and as you are to answer for the loss.

Mrs. HARDCASTLE. *it would be her fault*

Don't be alarm'd, Constance. If they be lost, I must restore an equivalent. But my son knows they are missing, and not to be found.

TONY.

That I can bear witness to. They are missing, and not to be found, I'll take my oath on't.

Mrs. HARDCASTLE.

You must learn resignation, my dear; for tho' we lose our fortune, yet we should not lose our patience. See me, how calm I am.

Miss NEVILLE.

Ay, people are generally calm at the misfortunes of others.   130

Mrs. HARDCASTLE.

Now, I wonder a girl of your good sense should waste a thought upon such trumpery. We shall soon find them; and, in the mean time, you shall make use of my garnets till your jewels be found.

Miss NEVILLE.

I detest garnets.

patronizing, smug

Mrs. HARDCASTLE.

The most becoming things in the world to set off a clear complexion. You have often seen how well they look upon me. You *shall* have them.   [*Exit.*

Miss NEVILLE.

I dislike them of all things. You shan't stir.—Was ever any thing so provoking to mislay my own jewels, and force me to wear her trumpery.

TONY.

Don't be a fool. If she gives you the garnets, take what you can get. The jewels are your own already. I have stolen them out of her bureau, and she does not know it. Fly to your spark, he'll tell you more of the matter. Leave me to manage *her*.   142

Miss NEVILLE.

My dear cousin.

TONY.

Vanish. She's here, and has missed them already. Zounds! how she fidgets and spits about like a Catharine wheel.

Enter Mrs. HARDCASTLE.

Mrs. HARDCASTLE.

Confusion! thieves! robbers! We are cheated, plundered, broke open, undone.

TONY.

What's the matter, what's the matter, mamma? I hope nothing has happened to any of the good family!

Mrs. HARDCASTLE.

We are robbed. My bureau has been broke open, the jewels taken out, and I'm undone.   151

TONY.

Oh! is that all? Ha, ha, ha. By the laws, I never saw it better acted in my life. Ecod, I thought you was ruin'd in earnest, ha, ha, ha.

Mrs. HARDCASTLE.

Why boy, I *am* ruin'd in earnest. My bureau has been broke open, and all taken away.

TONY.

Stick to that; ha, ha, ha; stick to that. I'll bear witness, you know, call me to bear witness.

141 spark] Lover, gallant.

Mrs. HARDCASTLE.

I tell you, Tony, by all that's precious, the jewels are gone, and I shall be ruin'd for ever.

TONY.

Sure I know they're gone, and I am to say so.   160

Mrs. HARDCASTLE.

My dearest Tony, but hear me. They're gone, I say.

TONY.

By the laws, mamma, you make me for to laugh, ha, ha. I know who took them well enough, ha, ha, ha.

Mrs. HARDCASTLE.

Was there ever such a blockhead, that can't tell the difference between jest and earnest. I tell you I'm not in jest, booby.

TONY.

That's right, that's right: You must be in a bitter passion, and then nobody will suspect either of us. I'll bear witness that they are gone.

Mrs. HARDCASTLE.

Was there ever such a cross-grain'd brute, that won't hear me! Can you bear witness that you're no better than a fool? Was ever poor woman so beset with fools on one hand, and thieves on the other.   170

TONY.

I can bear witness to that.

Mrs. HARDCASTLE.

Bear witness again, you blockhead you, and I'll turn you out of the room directly. My poor niece, what will become of *her!* Do you laugh, you unfeeling brute, as if you enjoy'd my distress?

TONY.

I can bear witness to that.

Mrs. HARDCASTLE.

Do you insult me, monster? I'll teach you to vex your mother, I will.

TONY.

I can bear witness to that.   (*He runs off, she follows him.*

Enter Miss HARDCASTLE and Maid

Madam already mistakes Kate, gives her the idea

Miss HARDCASTLE.

What an unaccountable creature is that brother of mine, to send them to the house as an inn, ha, ha. I don't wonder at his impudence.

MAID.

But what is more, madam, the young gentleman as you passed by in your present dress, ask'd me if you were the bar maid? He mistook you for the bar maid, madam. 182

Miss HARDCASTLE.

Did he? Then as I live I'm resolved to keep up the delusion. Tell me, Pimple, how do you like my present dress. Don't you think I look something like Cherry in the Beaux Stratagem?

MAID.

It's the dress, madam, that every lady wears in the country, but when she visits or receives company.

Miss HARDCASTLE.

And are you sure he does not remember my face or person?

MAID.

Certain of it.

Miss HARDCASTLE.

I vow I thought so; for though we spoke for some time together, yet his fears were such, that he never once looked up during the interview. Indeed, if he had, my bonnet would have kept him from seeing me. 192

MAID.

But what do you hope from keeping him in his mistake?

Miss HARDCASTLE.

attract him, get to know him. Relax

In the first place, I shall be *seen*, and that is no small advantage to a girl who brings her face to market. Then I shall perhaps make an acquaintance and that's no small victory gained over one who never addresses any but the wildest of her sex. But my chief aim is to take my gentleman off his guard, and like an invisible champion of romance examine the giant's force before I offer to combat.

MAID.

The romance in comedy

But are you sure you can act your part, and disguise your voice, so that he may mistake that, as he has already mistaken your person? 201

185 Cherry in the Beaux Stratagem] The landlord's daughter in Farquhar's play. Cf. introduction, p. 269.

Miss HARDCASTLE.

Never fear me. I think I have got the true bar cant.—Did your honour call?——Attend the Lion there.——Pipes and tobacco for the Angel.—The Lamb has been outrageous this half hour.

MAID.

It will do, madam. But he's here.   [*Exit* Maid.

Enter MARLOW.

MARLOW.

What a bawling in every part of the house; I have scarce a moment's repose. If I go to the best room, there I find my host and his story. If I fly to the gallery, there we have my hostess with her curtesy down to the ground. I have at last got a moment to myself, and now for recollection.

[*Walks and muses.*

Miss HARDCASTLE.

Did you call, Sir? did your honour call?   210

MARLOW.

(*Musing.*) As for Miss Hardcastle, she's too grave and sentimental for me.

Miss HARDCASTLE.

Did your honour call?

(*She still places herself before him, he turning away.*

MARLOW.

No, child (*musing*). Besides from the glimpse I had of her, I think she squints.

Miss HARDCASTLE.

I'm sure, Sir, I heard the bell ring.

MARLOW.

No, No. (*musing*) I have pleased my father, however, by coming down, and I'll to-morrow please myself by returning.

(*Taking out his tablets, and perusing.*

Miss HARDCASTLE.

Perhaps the other gentleman called, Sir.

202 true bar cant] The jargon of inn-keeping.   203 the Lion] Like the Angel and the Lamb, the supposed name of a room in the 'inn'.   s.d. *his tablets*] His pocket-book.

MARLOW.

I tell you, no.

Miss HARDCASTLE.

I should be glad to know, Sir. We have such a parcel of servants.   220

MARLOW.

No, no, I tell you. (*Looks full in her face.*) Yes, child, I think I did call. I wanted——I wanted——I vow, child, you are vastly handsome.

Miss HARDCASTLE.

O la, Sir, you'll make one asham'd.

Tony's spirit

MARLOW.

Never saw a more sprightly malicious eye. Yes, yes, my dear, I did call. Have you got any of your—a— what d'ye call it in the house?

Miss HARDCASTLE.

No, Sir, we have been out of that these ten days.

MARLOW.

One may call in this house, I find, to very little purpose. Suppose I should call for a taste, just by way of trial, of the nectar of your lips; perhaps I might be disappointed in that too.

Miss HARDCASTLE.

Nectar! nectar! that's a liquor there's no call for in these parts. French, I suppose. We keep no French wines here, Sir.   231

MARLOW.

Of true English growth, I assure you.

Miss HARDCASTLE.

Then it's odd I should not know it. We brew all sorts of wines in this house, and I have lived here these eighteen years.

MARLOW.

Eighteen years! Why one would think, child, you kept the bar before you were born. How old are you?   *Younger than is   Older*

Miss HARDCASTLE.

O! Sir, I must not tell my age. They say women and music should never be dated.

Wildly flirting

MARLOW.

To guess at this distance, you can't be much above forty (*approaching*.) Yet nearer I don't think so much (*approaching*.) By coming close to some women they look younger still; but when we come very close indeed (*attempting to kiss her*.)   242

Miss HARDCASTLE.

Pray, Sir, keep your distance. One would think you wanted to know one's age as they do horses, by mark of mouth.

MARLOW.

I protest, child, you use me extremely ill. If you keep me at this distance, how is it possible you and I can be ever acquainted?

Miss HARDCASTLE.

And who wants to be acquainted with you? I want no such acquaintance, not I. I'm sure you did not treat Miss Hardcastle that was here awhile ago in this obstropalous manner. I'll warrant me, before her you look'd dash'd, and kept bowing to the ground, and talk'd, for all the world, as if you was before a justice of peace.   251

MARLOW.

(*Aside*.) Egad! she has hit it, sure enough. (*To her*.) In awe of her, child? Ha! ha! ha! A mere, aukward, squinting thing, no, no. I find you don't know me. I laugh'd, and rallied her a little; but I was unwilling to be too severe. No, I could not be too severe, *curse me!*

Miss HARDCASTLE.

O! then, Sir, you are a favourite, I find, among the ladies?

MARLOW.

Yes, my dear, a great favourite. And yet, hang me, I don't see what they find in me to follow. At the Ladies Club in town, I'm called their agreeable Rattle. Rattle, child, is not my real name, but one I'm known by. My name is Solomons. Mr. Solomons, my dear, at your service. (*Offering to salute her*.)

Miss HARDCASTLE.

Hold, Sir; you were introducing me to your club, not to yourself. And you're so great a favourite there you say?   262

258 the Ladies Club] That is, the club in Albemarle Street for ladies and gentlemen, where Goldsmith himself had made his mark.   259 Rattle] A name good-naturedly applied to any chatterer or idle talker.   s.d. *salute*] Kiss.

MARLOW.

Yes, my dear. There's Mrs. Mantrap, Lady Betty Blackleg, the Countess of Sligo, Mrs. Langhorns, old Miss Biddy Buckskin, and your humble servant, keep up the spirit of the place.

Miss HARDCASTLE.

Then it's a very merry place, I suppose.

MARLOW.

Yes, as merry as cards, suppers, wine, and old women can make us.

Miss HARDCASTLE.

And their agreeable Rattle, ha! ha! ha!

MARLOW.

(*Aside*) Egad! I don't quite like this chit. She looks knowing, methinks. You laugh, child!   270

Miss HARDCASTLE.

I can't but laugh to think what time they all have for minding their work or their family.

MARLOW.

(*Aside*) All's well, she don't laugh at me. (*To her*) Do *you* ever work, child?

Miss HARDCASTLE.

Ay, sure. There's not a screen or a quilt in the whole house but what can bear witness to that.

MARLOW.

Odso! Then you must shew me your embroidery. I embroider and draw patterns myself a little. If you want a judge of your work you must apply to me.   [*Seizing her hand.*

Miss HARDCASTLE.

Ay, but the colours don't look well by candle light. You shall see all in the morning.   [*Struggling.*

MARLOW.

And why not now, my angel? Such beauty fires beyond the power of resistance.————Pshaw! the father here! My old luck: I never nick'd seven that I did not throw ames ace three times following.   [*Exit* Marlow.

271 what time they all have] That is, how little time they have left over. 282 never nick'd seven] Never made one of the two winning throws—seven and eleven—at dice. 283 throw ames ace] That is, throw a double-ace at dice, the lowest score possible.

Never goes right for him

Enter HARDCASTLE, who stands in surprize.

HARDCASTLE.

So, madam! So I find *this* is your *modest* lover. This is your humble admirer that kept his eyes fixed on the ground, and only ador'd at humble distance. Kate, Kate, are thou not asham'd to deceive your father so?   286

Miss HARDCASTLE.

Never trust me, dear papa, but he's still the modest man I first took him for, you'll be convinced of it as well as I.

HARDCASTLE.

By the hand of my body I believe his impudence is infectious! Didn't I see him seize your hand? Didn't I see him hawl you about like a milk maid? and now you talk of his respect and his modesty, forsooth!   291

Miss HARDCASTLE.

But if I shortly convince you of his modesty, that he has only the faults that will pass off with time, and the virtues that will improve with age, I hope you'll forgive him.

HARDCASTLE.

The girl would actually make one run mad! I tell you I'll not be convinced. I am convinced. He has scarcely been three hours in the house, and he has already encroached on all my prerogatives. You may like his impudence, and call it modesty. But my son-in-law, madam, must have very different qualifications.

Miss HARDCASTLE.

Sir, I ask but this night to convince you.   300

HARDCASTLE.

You shall not have half the time, for I have thoughts of turning him out this very hour.

Miss HARDCASTLE.

Give me that hour then, and I hope to satisfy you.

HARDCASTLE.

Well, an hour let it be then. But I'll have no trifling with your father. All fair and open do you mind me.

Miss HARDCASTLE.

I hope, Sir, you have ever found that I considered your commands as my pride; for your kindness is such, that my duty as yet has been inclination.

[*Exeunt.*

END OF THIRD ACT.

ACT IV.

Enter HASTINGS and Miss NEVILLE.

HASTINGS.

YOU surprise me! Sir Charles Marlow expected here this night? Where have you had your information?

Miss NEVILLE.

You may depend upon it. I just saw his letter to Mr. Hardcastle, in which he tells him he intends setting out a few hours after his son.

HASTINGS.

Then, my Constance, all must be completed before he arrives. He knows me; and should he find me here, would discover my name, and perhaps my designs, to the rest of the family.

Miss NEVILLE.

The jewels, I hope, are safe.   8

HASTINGS.

Yes, yes. I have sent them to Marlow, who keeps the keys of our baggage. In the meantime, I'll go to prepare matters for our elopement. I have had the Squire's promise of a fresh pair of horses; and, if I should not see him again, will write him further directions.   [*Exit.*

Miss NEVILLE.

Well! success attend you. In the meantime, I'll go amuse my aunt with the old pretence of a violent passion for my cousin.   [*Exit.*

Enter MARLOW, followed by a Servant.

MARLOW.

I wonder what Hastings could mean by sending me so valuable a thing as a casket to keep for him, when he knows the only place I have is the seat of a

6 discover my name] In fact, both Mr. and Mrs. Hardcastle have addressed Hastings by his own name in the second act.

post-coach at an Inn-door. Have you deposited the casket with the landlady, as I ordered you? Have you put it into her own hands?

SERVANT.

Yes, your honour.

MARLOW.

She said she'd keep it safe, did she?　　　　　　　　　　　　　20

SERVANT.

Yes, she said she'd keep it safe enough; she ask'd me how I came by it? and she said she had a great mind to make me give an account of myself.

[*Exit* Servant.

MARLOW.

Ha! ha! ha! They're safe however. What an unaccountable set of beings have we got amongst! This little bar-maid though runs in my head most strangely, and drives out the absurdities of all the rest of the family. She's mine, she must be mine, or I'm greatly mistaken.

Enter HASTINGS.

HASTINGS.

Bless me! I quite forgot to tell her that I intended to prepare at the bottom of the garden. Marlow here, and in spirits too!

MARLOW.

Give me joy, George! Crown me, shadow me with laurels! Well, George, after all, we modest fellows don't want for success among the women.　30

HASTINGS.

Some women you mean. But what success has your honour's modesty been crowned with now, that it grows so insolent upon us?

MARLOW.

Didn't you see the tempting, brisk, lovely, little thing that runs about the house with a bunch of keys to its girdle?

HASTINGS.

Well! and what then?

MARLOW.

She's mine, you rogue you. Such fire, such motion, such eyes, such lips——but, egad! she would not let me kiss them though.

HASTINGS.

But are you so sure, so very sure of her?

MARLOW.

Why man, she talk'd of shewing me her work above-stairs, and I am to improve the pattern.   40

HASTINGS.

But how can *you*, Charles, go about to rob a woman of her honour?

MARLOW.

Pshaw! pshaw! we all know the honour of the bar-maid of an inn. I don't intend to *rob* her, take my word for it, there's nothing in this house, I shan't honestly *pay* for.

HASTINGS.

I believe the girl has virtue.

MARLOW.

And if she has, I should be the last man in the world that would attempt to corrupt it.

HASTINGS.

You have taken care, I hope, of the casket I sent you to lock up? It's in safety?

MARLOW.

Yes, yes. It's safe enough. I have taken care of it. But how could you think the seat of a post-coach at an Inn-door a place of safety? Ah! numbskull! I have taken better precautions for you than you did for yourself.——I have———   53

HASTINGS.

What!

MARLOW.

I have sent it to the landlady to keep for you.

HASTINGS.

To the landlady!

MARLOW.

The landlady.

HASTINGS.

You did.

MARLOW.

I did. She's to be answerable for its forth-coming, you know.

HASTINGS.

Yes, she'll bring it forth, with a witness.   60

MARLOW.

Wasn't I right? I believe you'll allow that I acted prudently upon this occasion?

HASTINGS.

(*Aside.*) He must not see my uneasiness.

MARLOW.

You seem a little disconcerted though, methinks. Sure nothing has happened?

HASTINGS.

No, nothing. Never was in better spirits in all my life. And so you left it with the landlady, who, no doubt, very readily undertook the charge?

MARLOW.

Rather too readily. For she not only kept the casket; but, thro' her great precaution, was going to keep the messenger too. Ha! ha! ha!

HASTINGS.

He! he! he! They're safe however.   70

MARLOW.

As a guinea in a miser's purse.

HASTINGS.

(*Aside.*) So now all hopes of fortune are at an end, and we must set off without it. (*To him.*) Well, Charles, I'll leave you to your meditations on the pretty bar-maid, and, he! he! he! may you be as successful for yourself as you have been for me.   [*Exit.*

MARLOW.

Thank ye, George! I ask no more. Ha! ha! ha!

Enter HARDCASTLE.

HARDCASTLE.

I no longer know my own house. It's turned all topsey-turvey. His servants have got drunk already. I'll bear it no longer, and yet, from my respect for his father, I'll be calm. (*To him.*) Mr. Marlow, your servant. I'm your very humble servant.   (*bowing low.*

MARLOW.

Sir, your humble servant. (*Aside.*) What's to be the wonder now? 81

HARDCASTLE.

I believe, Sir, you must be sensible, Sir, that no man alive ought to be more welcome than your father's son, Sir. I hope you think so?

MARLOW.

I do from my soul, Sir. I don't want much intreaty. I generally make my father's son welcome wherever he goes.

HARDCASTLE.

I believe you do, from my soul, Sir. But tho' I say nothing to your own conduct, that of your Servants is unsufferable. Their manner of drinking is setting a very bad example in this house, I assure you.

MARLOW.

I protest, my very good Sir, that's no fault of mine. If they don't drink as they ought *they* are to blame. I ordered them not to spare the cellar. I did, I assure you. (*To the side scene.*) Here, let one of my servants come up. (*To him.*) My positive directions were, that as I did not drink myself, they should make up for my deficiencies below. 93

HARDCASTLE.

Then they had your orders for what they do! I'm satisfied!

MARLOW.

They had, I assure. You shall hear from one of themselves.

Enter SERVANT drunk.

MARLOW.

You, Jeremy! Come forward, sirrah! What were my orders? Were you not told to drink freely, and call for what you thought fit, for the good of the house?

HARDCASTLE.

(*Aside.*) I begin to lose my patience.

JEREMY.

Please your honour, liberty and Fleet-street for ever! Tho' I'm but a servant, I'm as good as another man. I'll drink for no man before supper,

100 liberty and Fleet-street] A variation on the popular call for 'Wilkes and Liberty', Wilkes then being engaged in his long struggle to take his seat in the House of Commons. The substitution here of Fleet Street for Wilkes's name probably reflected the simultaneous agitation for greater press freedom in reporting parliamentary proceedings.

Sir, dammy! Good liquor will sit upon a good supper, but a good supper will not sit upon——hiccup——upon my conscience, Sir.   103

MARLOW.

You see, my old friend, the fellow is as drunk as he can possibly be. I don't know what you'd have more, unless you'd have the poor devil soused in a beer-barrel.

HARDCASTLE.

Zounds! He'll drive me distracted if I contain myself any longer. Mr. Marlow. Sir; I have submitted to your insolence for more than four hours, and I see no likelihood of its coming to an end. I'm now resolved to be master here, Sir, and I desire that you and your drunken pack may leave my house directly.   111

MARLOW.

Leave your house!——Sure you jest, my good friend? What, when I'm doing what I can to please you.

HARDCASTLE.

I tell you, Sir, you don't please me; so I desire you'll leave my house.

MARLOW.

Sure you cannot be serious? At this time o'night, and such a night. You only mean to banter me?

HARDCASTLE.

I tell you, Sir, I'm serious; and, now that my passions are rouzed, I say this house is mine, Sir; this house is mine, and I command you to leave it directly.

MARLOW.

Ha! ha! ha! A puddle in a storm. I shan't stir a step, I assure you. (*In a serious tone.*) This, your house, fellow! It's my house. This is my house. Mine, while I chuse to stay. What right have you to bid me leave this house, Sir? I never met with such impudence, curse me, never in my whole life before.   124

HARDCASTLE.

Nor I, confound me if ever I did. To come to my house, to call for what he likes, to turn me out of my own chair, to insult the family, to order his servants to get drunk, and then to tell me *This house is mine, Sir.* By all that's impudent it makes me laugh. Ha! ha! ha! Pray, Sir, (*bantering.*) as you take the house, what think you of taking the rest of the furniture? There's a pair of silver candlesticks, and there's a fire-screen, and here's a pair of brazen nosed bellows, perhaps you may take a fancy to them?   131

MARLOW.

Bring me your bill, Sir, bring me your bill, and let's make no more words about it.

HARDCASTLE.

There are a set of prints too. What think you of the rake's progress for your own apartment?

MARLOW.

Bring me your bill, I say; and I'll leave you and your infernal house directly.

HARDCASTLE.

Then there's a mahogony table, that you may see your own face in.

MARLOW.

My bill, I say.

HARDCASTLE.

I had forgot the great chair, for your own particular slumbers, after a hearty meal.   141

MARLOW.

Zounds! bring me my bill, I say, and let's hear no more on't.

HARDCASTLE.

Young man, young man, from your father's letter to me, I was taught to expect a well-bred modest man, as a visitor here, but now I find him no better than a coxcomb and a bully; but he will be down here presently, and shall hear more of it.   [*Exit.*

MARLOW.

How's this! Sure I have not mistaken the house! Every thing looks like an inn. The servants cry, coming. The attendance is aukward; the bar-maid too to attend us. But she's here, and will further inform me. Whither so fast, child. A word with you.   150

Enter Miss HARDCASTLE.

Miss HARDCASTLE.

Let it be short then. I'm in a hurry. (*Aside.*) (I believe he begins to find out his mistake, but its too soon quite to undeceive him.)

130 brazen nosed] Brass-tipped—so as to strengthen a pair of bellows against the heat.
134 the rake's progress] Hogarth's famous sequence depicting the downhill course of a rake.

MARLOW.

Pray, child, answer me one question. What are you, and what may your business in this house be?

Miss HARDCASTLE.

A relation of the family, Sir.

MARLOW.

What. A poor relation?

Miss HARDCASTLE.

Yes, Sir. A poor relation appointed to keep the keys, and to see that the guests want nothing in my power to give them.

MARLOW.

That is, you act as the bar-maid of this inn.

Miss HARDCASTLE.

Inn. O law—What brought that in your head. One of the best families in the county keep an inn. Ha, ha, ha, Mr. Hardcastle's house an inn.   161

MARLOW.

Mr. Hardcastle's house! Is this house Mr. Hardcastle's house, child!

Miss HARDCASTLE.

Ay, sure. Whose else should it be.

MARLOW.

So then all's out, and I have been damnably imposed on. O, confound my stupid head, I shall be laugh'd at over the whole town. I shall be stuck up in caricatura in all the print-shops. The Dullissimo Maccaroni. To mistake this house of all others for an inn, and my father's old friend for an inn-keeper. What a swaggering puppy must he take me for. What a silly puppy do I find myself. There again, may I be hang'd, my dear, but I mistook you for the bar-maid.   170

Miss HARDCASTLE.

Dear me! dear me! I'm sure there's nothing in my *behaviour* to put me upon a level with one of that stamp.

165 stuck up in caricatura] Set up in a display of caricatures.   166 The Dullissimo Maccaroni] Darly's series of satirical drawings. The name Maccaroni was applied generally to dandies and fops, particularly to those who affected foreign airs.

MARLOW.

Nothing, my dear, nothing. But I was in for a list of blunders, and could not help making you a subscriber. My stupidity saw every thing the wrong way. I mistook your assiduity for assurance, and your simplicity for allurement. But its over—This house I no more shew *my* face in.

Miss HARDCASTLE.

I hope, Sir, I have done nothing to disoblige you. I'm sure I should be sorry to affront any gentleman who has been so polite, and said so many civil things to me. I'm sure I should be sorry (*pretending to cry*) if he left the family upon my account. I'm sure I should be sorry, people said any thing amiss, since I have no fortune but my character.   181

MARLOW.

[*Aside.*] By heaven, she weeps. This is the first mark of tenderness I ever had from a modest woman, and it touches me; (*to her*) Excuse me, my lovely girl, you are the only part of the family I leave with reluctance. But to be plain with you, the difference of our birth, fortune and education, make an honourable connexion impossible; and I can never harbour a thought of seducing simplicity that trusted in my honour, or bringing ruin upon one, whose only fault was being too lovely.

Miss HARDCASTLE.

[*Aside.*] Generous man! I now begin to admire him. (*to him*) But I'm sure my family is as good as miss Hardcastle's, and though I'm poor, that's no great misfortune to a contented mind, and, until this moment, I never thought that it was bad to want fortune.   192

MARLOW.

And why now, my pretty simplicity?

Miss HARDCASTLE.

Because it puts me at a distance from one, that if I had a thousand pound I would give it all to.

MARLOW.

[*Aside.*] This simplicity bewitches me, so that if I stay I'm undone. I must make one bold effort, and leave her. (*to her*) Your partiality in my favour, my dear, touches me most sensibly, and were I to live for myself alone, I could easily fix my choice. But I owe too much to the opinion of the world, too much to the authority of a father, so that—I can scarcely speak it—it affects me. Farewell.   [*Exit.*

198 sensibly] Sensitively, on my senses.

M

Miss HARDCASTLE.

I never knew half his merit till now. He shall not go, if I have power or art to detain him. I'll still preserve the character in which I stoop'd to conquer, but will undeceive my papa, who, perhaps, may laugh him out of his resolution.   [*Exit.*

Enter TONY, Miss NEVILLE.

TONY.

Ay, you may steal for yourselves the next time. I have done my duty. She has got the jewels again, that's a sure thing; but she believes it was all a mistake of the servants.   208

Miss NEVILLE.

But, my dear cousin, sure you won't forsake us in this distress. If she in the least suspects that I am going off, I shall certainly be locked up, or sent to my aunt Pedigree's, which is ten times worse.   211

TONY.

To be sure, aunts of all kinds are damn'd bad things. But what can I do? I have got you a pair of horses that will fly like Whistlejacket, and I'm sure you can't say but I have courted you nicely before her face. Here she comes, we must court a bit or two more, for fear she should suspect us.
                                  [*They retire, and seem to fondle.*

Enter Mrs. HARDCASTLE.

Mrs. HARDCASTLE.

Well, I was greatly fluttered, to be sure. But my son tells me it was all a mistake of the servants. I shan't be easy, however, till they are fairly married, and then let her keep her own fortune. But what do I see! Fondling together, as I'm alive. I never saw Tony so sprightly before. Ah! have I caught you, my pretty doves! What, billing, exchanging stolen glances, and broken murmurs. Ah!   221

TONY.

As for murmurs, mother, we grumble a little now and then, to be sure. But there's no love lost between us.

Mrs. HARDCASTLE.

A mere sprinkling, Tony, upon the flame, only to make it burn brighter.

Miss NEVILLE.

Cousin Tony promises to give us more of his company at home. Indeed, he shan't leave us any more. It won't leave us cousin Tony, will it?

213 Whistlejacket] A famous racehorse owned by Lord Rockingham.

TONY.

O! it's a pretty creature. No, I'd sooner leave my horse in a pound, than leave you when you smile upon one so. Your laugh makes you so becoming.

Miss NEVILLE.

Agreeable cousin! Who can help admiring that natural humour, that pleasant, broad, red, thoughtless, (*patting his cheek*) ah! it's a bold face.

Mrs. HARDCASTLE.

Pretty innocence.   231

TONY.

I'm sure I always lov'd cousin Con's hazle eyes, and her pretty long fingers, that she twists this way and that, over the haspicholls, like a parcel of bobbins.

Mrs. HARDCASTLE.

Ah, he would charm the bird from the tree. I was never so happy before. My boy takes after his father, poor Mr. Lumpkin, exactly. The jewels, my dear Con, shall be your's incontinently. You shall have them. Isn't he a sweet boy, my dear? You shall be married to-morrow, and we'll put off the rest of his education, like Dr. Drowsy's sermons, to a fitter opportunity.

Enter DIGGORY.

DIGGORY.

Where's the 'Squire. I have got a letter for your worship.   240

TONY.

Give it to my mamma. She reads all my letters first.

DIGGORY.

I had orders to deliver it into your own hands.

TONY.

Who does it come from?

DIGGORY.

Your worship mun ask that o' the letter itself.

TONY.

I could wish to know, tho' [*turning the letter, and gazing on it.*]

233 haspicholls] Tony means, over the keys of a harpsichord.   234 bobbins] That is, the short wooden bobbins used in lace-making, which a skilled craftsman could manipulate at great speed.

Miss NEVILLE.

[*Aside.*] Undone, undone. A letter to him from Hastings. I know the hand.
If my aunt sees it, we are ruined for ever. I'll keep her employ'd a little if I
can. [*To Mrs. Hardcastle.*] But I have not told you, Madam, of my cousin's
smart answer just now to Mr. Marlow. We so laugh'd—You must know,
Madam—this way a little, for he must not hear us.   [*They confer.*

TONY.

[*Still gazing.*] A damn'd cramp piece of penmanship, as ever I saw in my
life. I can read your print-hand very well. But here there are such handles,
and shanks, and dashes, that one can scarce tell the head from the tail. *To
Anthony Lumpkin, Esquire.* It's very odd, I can read the outside of my
letters, where my own name is, well enough. But when I come to open it, it's
all—buzz. That's hard, very hard; for the inside of the letter is always the
cream of the correspondence.   257

Mrs. HARDCASTLE.

Ha, ha, ha. Very well, very well. And so my son was too hard for the
philosopher.

Miss NEVILLE.

Yes, Madam; but you must hear the rest, Madam. A little more this way,
or he may hear us. You'll hear how he puzzled him again.   261

Mrs. HARDCASTLE.

He seems strangely puzzled now himself, methinks.

TONY.

[*Still gazing.*] A damn'd up and down hand, as if it was disguised in liquor.
[*Reading.*] *Dear Sir.* Ay, that's that. Then there's an *M*, and a *T*, and an *S*,
but whether the next be an *izzard* or an *R*, confound me, I cannot tell.

Mrs. HARDCASTLE.

What's that, my dear. Can I give you any assistance?

Miss NEVILLE.

Pray, aunt, let me read it. No body reads a cramp hand better than I.
(*twitching the letter from her.*) Do you know who it is from?

TONY.

Can't tell, except from Dick Ginger the feeder.

265 an *izzard*] The letter Z.   269 the feeder] Probably, in this context, a trainer of
fighting cocks. But the name also signified a fattener of cattle for slaughter.

Miss NEVILLE.

Ay, so it is, (*pretending to read*) Dear 'Squire, Hoping that you're in health, as I am at this present. The gentlemen of the Shake-bag club has cut the gentlemen of goose-green quite out of feather. The odds—um—odd battle—um—long fighting—um here, here, it's all about cocks, and fighting; it's of no consequence, here, put it up, put it up.

> [*thrusting the crumpled letter upon him.*

TONY.

But I tell you, Miss, it's of all the consequence in the world. I would not lose the rest of it for a guinea. Here, mother, do you make it out. Of no consequence!   [*giving Mrs. Hardcastle the letter.*

Mrs. HARDCASTLE.

How's this! (*reads*) Dear 'Squire, I'm now waiting for Miss Neville, with a post-chaise and pair, at the bottom of the garden, but I find my horses yet unable to perform the journey. I expect you'll assist us with a pair of fresh horses, as your promised. Dispatch is necessary, as the *hag* (ay the hag) your mother will otherwise suspect us. Your's, Hastings. Grant me patience. I shall run distracted. My rage choaks me.   283

Miss NEVILLE.

I hope, Madam, you'll suspend your resentment for a few moments, and not impute to me any impertinence, or sinster design that belongs to another.

Mrs. HARDCASTLE.

(*Curtesying very low.*) Fine spoken, Madam, you are most miraculously polite and engaging, and quite the very pink of curtesy and circumspection, Madam. (*Changing her tone.*) And you, you great ill-fashioned oaf, with scarce sense enough to keep your mouth shut. Were you too join'd against me? But I'll defeat all your plots in a moment. As for you, Madam, since you have got a pair of fresh horses ready, it would be cruel to disappoint them. So, if you please, instead of running away with your spark, prepare, this very moment, to run off with *me*. Your old aunt Pedigree will keep you secure, I'll warrant me. You too, Sir, may mount your horse, and guard us upon the way. Here, Thomas, Roger, Diggory, I'll shew you, that I wish you better than you do yourselves.   [*Exit.*

Miss NEVILLE.

So now I'm completely ruined.   297

271 the Shake-bag club] A cock-fighting club. A shake-bag was a large fighting cock. 271-2 cut . . . out of feather] Literally, taken the shine from the plumage of 'the gentlemen of goose-green'. In the modern sense of: put their noses out of joint.

TONY.

Ay, that's a sure thing.

Miss NEVILLE.

What better could be expected from being connected with such a stupid fool, and after all the nods and signs I made him. *Tony, what else* 300 *expect?*

TONY.

By the laws, Miss, it was your own cleverness, and not my stupidity, that did your business. You were so nice and so busy with your Shake-bags and Goose-greens, that I thought you could never be making believe.

Enter HASTINGS.   *Didn't think making up*

HASTINGS.

So, Sir, I find by my servant, that you have shewn my letter, and betray'd us. Was this well done, young gentleman. *- Think Tony betrayed*

TONY.

Here's another. Ask Miss there who betray'd you. Ecod, it was her doing, not mine.

Enter MARLOW.

MARLOW.

So I have been finely used here among you. Rendered contemptible, driven into ill manners, despised, insulted, laugh'd at. *- Betrayed*

TONY.

Here's another. We shall have old Bedlam broke loose presently.   310

Miss NEVILLE.

And there, Sir, is the gentleman to whom we all owe every obligation.

MARLOW.

What can I say to him, a mere boy, an ideot, whose ignorance and age are a protection.

HASTINGS.

A poor contemptible booby, that would but disgrace correction.

Miss NEVILLE.

Yet with cunning and malice enough to make himself merry with all our embarrassments.

HASTINGS.

An insensible cub.

MARLOW.

Replete with tricks and mischief.

TONY.

Baw! damme, but I'll fight you both one after the other,——with baskets.

MARLOW.

As for him, he's below resentment. But your conduct, Mr. Hastings, requires an explanation. You knew of my mistakes, yet would not undeceive me.   323

HASTINGS.

Tortured as I am with my own disappointments, is this a time for explanations. It is not friendly, Mr. Marlow.

MARLOW.

But, Sir——

Miss NEVILLE.

Mr. Marlow, we never kept on your mistake, till it was too late to undeceive you. Be pacified.

Enter SERVANT.

SERVANT.

My mistress desires you'll get ready immediately, Madam. The horses are putting to. Your hat and things are in the next room. We are to go thirty miles before morning.   [*Exit servant.*

Miss NEVILLE.

Well, well; I'll come presently.   331

MARLOW.

[*To Hastings.*] Was it well done, Sir, to assist in rendering me ridiculous. To hang me out for the scorn of all my acquaintance. Depend upon it, Sir, I shall expect an explanation.

HASTINGS.

Was it well done, Sir, if you're upon that subject, to deliver what I entrusted to yourself, to the care of another, Sir.

Miss NEVILLE.

Mr. Hastings. Mr. Marlow. Why will you increase my distress by this groundless dispute. I implore, I intreat you——

319 baskets] Wicker-work guard on a sword to protect the hands.   326 never kept on your mistake] Had not ourselves realized your mistake.

Enter SERVANT.

SERVANT.

Your cloak, Madam. My mistress is impatient.

Miss NEVILLE.

I come. Pray be pacified. If I leave you thus, I shall die with apprehension.

Enter SERVANT.

SERVANT.

Your fan, muff, and gloves, Madam. The horses are waiting.   341

Miss NEVILLE.

O, Mr. Marlow! if you knew what a scene of constraint and ill-nature lies before me, I'm sure it would convert your resentment into pity.

MARLOW.

I'm so distracted with a variety of passions, that I don't know what I do. Forgive me, Madam. George, forgive me. You know my hasty temper, and should not exasperate it.

HASTINGS.

The torture of my situation is my only excuse.

Miss NEVILLE.

Well, my dear Hastings, if you have that esteem for me that I think, that I am sure you have, your constancy for three years will but encrease the happiness of our future connexion. If— separated for 3 years 350

Mrs. HARDCASTLE.

[*Within.*] Miss Neville. Constance, why Constance, I say.

Miss NEVILLE.

I'm coming. Well, constancy. Remember, constancy is the word.   [*Exit.*

patience
aim | moral

HASTINGS.

My heart! How can I support this. To be so near happiness, and such happiness.

MARLOW.

[*To Tony.*] You see now, young gentleman, the effects of your folly. What might be amusement to you, is here disappointment, and even distress.

TONY.

[*From a reverie.*] Ecod, I have hit it. Its here. Your hands. Yours and yours, my poor Sulky. My boots there, ho. Meet me two hours hence at the bottom of the garden; and if you don't find Tony Lumpkin a more good-natur'd fellow than you thought for, I'll give you leave to take my best horse, and Bet Bouncer into the bargain. Come along. My boots, ho.   [*Exeunt.*

END OF THE FOURTH ACT.

ACT V.

SCENE Continues.

Enter HASTINGS *and* SERVANT.

HASTINGS.

YOU saw the Old Lady and Miss Neville drive off, you say.

SERVANT.

Yes, your honour. They went off in a post coach, and the young 'Squire went on horseback. They're thirty miles off by this time.

HASTINGS.

Then all my hopes are over.

SERVANT.

Yes, Sir. Old Sir Charles is arrived. He and the Old Gentleman of the house have been laughing at Mr. Marlow's mistake this half hour. They are coming this way.

HASTINGS.

Then I must not be seen. So now to my fruitless appointment at the bottom of the garden. This is about the time.   [*Exit.*

Enter SIR CHARLES *and* HARDCASTLE.

HARDCASTLE.

Ha, ha, ha. The peremptory tone in which he sent forth his sublime commands.   11

358 my poor Sulky] The reference is presumably to Marlow.   V. i, s.d. *Exit.*] The manuscript direction reads *Exeunt*, indicating that the Servant also departs.

Sir CHARLES.

And the reserve with which I suppose he treated all your advances.

HARDCASTLE.

And yet he might have seen something in me above a common inn-keeper, too.

Sir CHARLES.

Yes, Dick, but he mistook you for an uncommon innkeeper, ha, ha, ha.

HARDCASTLE.

Well, I'm in too good spirits to think of any thing but joy. Yes, my dear friend, this union of our families will make our personal friendships hereditary; and tho' my daughter's fortune is but small——

Sir CHARLES.

Why, Dick, will you talk of fortune to *me*. My son is possessed of more than a competence already, and can want nothing but a good and virtuous girl to share his happiness and encrease it. If they like each other, as you say they do——　　　　　　　　　　　　　　　　　　　　　　　　22

HARDCASTLE.

If, man. I tell you they *do* like each other. My daughter as good as told me so.

Sir CHARLES.

But girls are apt to flatter themselves, you know.

HARDCASTLE.

I saw him grasp her hand in the warmest manner myself; and here he comes to put you out of your *iffs*, I warrant him.

Enter MARLOW.

MARLOW.

I come, Sir, once more, to ask pardon for my strange conduct. I can scarce reflect on my insolence without confusion.

HARDCASTLE.

Tut, boy, a trifle. You take it too gravely. An hour or two's laughing with my daughter will set all to rights again. She'll never like you the worse for it.

MARLOW.

Sir, I shall be always proud of her approbation.　　　　　　　　　　32

HARDCASTLE.

Approbation is but a cold word, Mr. Marlow; if I am not deceived, you have something more than approbation thereabouts. You take me.

MARLOW.

Really, Sir, I have not that happiness.

HARDCASTLE.

Come, boy, I'm an old fellow, and know what's what, as well as you that are younger. I know what has past between you; but mum.

MARLOW.

Sure, Sir, nothing has past between us but the most profound respect on my side, and the most distant reserve on her's. You don't think, Sir, that my impudence has been past upon all the rest of the family.   40

HARDCASTLE.

Impudence! No, I don't say that—Not quite impudence—Though girls like to be play'd with, and rumpled a little too sometimes. But she has told no tales, I assure you.

MARLOW.

I never gave her the slightest cause.

HARDCASTLE.

Well, well, I like modesty in its place well enough. But this is over-acting, young gentleman. You *may* be open. Your father and I will like you the better for it.

MARLOW.

May I die, Sir, if I ever——

HARDCASTLE.

I tell you, she don't dislike you; and as I'm sure you like her——

MARLOW.

Dear Sir—I protest, Sir——   50

HARDCASTLE.

I see no reason why you should not be joined as fast as the parson can tie you.

MARLOW.

But hear me, Sir——

HARDCASTLE.

Your father approves the match, I admire it, every moment's delay will be doing mischief, so——

MARLOW.

But why won't you hear me? By all that's just and true, I never gave miss Hardcastle the slightest mark of my attachment, or even the most distant hint to suspect me of affection. We had but one interview, and that was formal, modest and uninteresting.

HARDCASTLE.

(*Aside.*) This fellow's formal modest impudence is beyond bearing.   60

Sir CHARLES.

And you never grasp'd her hand, or made any protestations!

MARLOW.

As heaven is my witness, I came down in obedience to your commands. I saw the lady without emotion, and parted without reluctance. I hope you'll exact no further proofs of my duty, nor prevent me from leaving a house in which I suffer so many mortifications.   [*Exit.*

Sir CHARLES.

I'm astonish'd at the air of sincerity with which he parted.

HARDCASTLE.

And I'm astonish'd at the deliberate intrepidity of his assurance.

Sir CHARLES.

I dare pledge my life and honour upon his truth.

HARDCASTLE.

Here comes my daughter, and I would stake my happiness upon her veracity.   70

Enter Miss HARDCASTLE.

HARDCASTLE.

Kate, come hither, child. Answer us sincerely, and without reserve; has Mr. Marlow made you any professions of love and affection?

Miss HARDCASTLE.

The question is very abrupt, Sir! But since you require unreserved sincerity, I think he has.

HARDCASTLE.

(*To Sir Charles*) You see.

Sir CHARLES.

And pray, madam, have you and my son had more than one interview?

Miss HARDCASTLE.

Yes, Sir, several.

HARDCASTLE.

(*To Sir Charles*) You see.

Sir CHARLES.

But did he profess any attachment?

Miss HARDCASTLE.

A lasting one.   80

Sir CHARLES.

Did he talk of love?

Miss HARDCASTLE.

Much, Sir.

Sir CHARLES.

Amazing! And all this formally.

Miss HARDCASTLE.

Formally.

HARDCASTLE.

Now, my friend, I hope you are satisfied.

Sir CHARLES.

And how did he behave, madam?

Miss HARDCASTLE.

As most profest admirers do. Said some civil things of my face, talked much of his want of merit, and the greatness of mine; mentioned his heart, gave a short tragedy speech, and ended with pretended rapture.

Sir CHARLES.

Now I'm perfectly convinced, indeed. I know his conversation among women to be modest and submissive. This forward canting ranting manner by no means describes him, and I am confident, he never sate for the picture.

92 he never sate for the picture] That is, he is not the original of the person you describe.

Miss HARDCASTLE.

Then what, Sir, if I should convince you to your face of my sincerity?
If you and my papa, in about half an hour, will place yourselves behind that
screen, you shall hear him declare his passion to me in person.   95

Sir CHARLES.

Agreed. And if I find him what you describe, all my happiness in him must
have an end.   [*Exit.*

Miss HARDCASTLE.

And if you don't find him what I describe—I fear my happiness must
never have a beginning.   [*Exeunt.*

SCENE *changes to the Back of the Garden.*

Enter HASTINGS.

HASTINGS.

What an ideot am I, to wait here for a fellow, who probably takes a delight
in mortifying me. He never intended to be punctual, and I'll wait no longer.
What do I see. It is he, and perhaps with news of my Constance.

Enter TONY, *booted and spattered.*

HASTINGS.

My honest 'Squire! I now find you a man of your word. This looks like
friendship.

TONY.

Ay, I'm your friend, and the best friend you have in the world, if you
knew but all. This riding by night, by the bye, is cursedly tiresome. It has
shook me worse than the basket of a stage-coach.

HASTINGS.

But how? Where did you leave your fellow travellers? Are they in safety?
Are they housed?   10

TONY.

Five and twenty miles in two hours and a half is no such bad driving. The
poor beasts have smoaked for it: Rabbet me, but I'd rather ride forty miles
after a fox, than ten with such *varment.*

12 smoaked] Steamed with sweat.   12 Rabbet me] A common expletive, equivalent to
'confound me'.

HASTINGS.

Well, but where have you left the ladies? I die with impatience.

TONY.

Left them. Why where should I leave them, but where I found them.

HASTINGS.

This is a riddle.

TONY.

Riddle me this then. What's that goes round the house, and round the house, and never touches the house?

HASTINGS.

I'm still astray.

TONY.

Why that's it, mon. I have led them astray. By jingo, there's not a pond or slough within five miles of the place but they can tell the taste of.   21

HASTINGS.

Ha, ha, ha, I understand; you took them in a round, while they supposed themselves going forward. And so you have at last brought them home again.

TONY.

You shall hear. I first took them down Feather-bed-lane, where we stuck fast in the mud. I then rattled them crack over the stones of Up-and-down Hill—I then introduc'd them to the gibbet on Heavy-tree Heath, and from that, with a circumbendibus, I fairly lodged them in the horse-pond at the bottom of the garden.

HASTINGS.

But no accident, I hope.   30

TONY.

No, no. Only mother is confoundedly frightened. She thinks herself forty miles off. She's sick of the journey, and the cattle can scarce crawl. So if your own horses be ready, you may whip off with cousin, and I'll be bound that no soul here can budge a foot to follow you.

HASTINGS.

My dear friend, how can I be grateful?

28 with a circumbendibus] Completing the full circle.

TONY.

Ay, now its dear friend, noble 'Squire. Just now, it was all ideot, cub, and run me through the guts. Damn *your* way of fighting, I say. After we take a knock in this part of the country, we kiss and be friends. But if you had run me through the guts, then I should be dead, and you might go kiss the hangman.   40

HASTINGS.

The rebuke is just. But I must hasten to relieve miss Neville; if you keep the old lady employed, I promise to take care of the young one.

                          [*Exit Hastings.*

TONY.

Never fear me. Here she comes. Vanish. She's got from the pond, and draggled up to the waist like a mermaid.

Enter Mrs. HARDCASTLE.

Mrs. HARDCASTLE.

Oh, Tony, I'm killed. Shook. Battered to death. I shall never survive it. That last jolt that laid us against the quickset hedge has done my business.

TONY.

Alack, mama, it was all your own fault. You would be for running away by night, without knowing one inch of the way.

Mrs. HARDCASTLE.

I wish we were at home again. I never met so many accidents in so short a journey. Drench'd in the mud, overturn'd in a ditch, stuck fast in a slough, jolted to a jelly, and at last to lose our way. Whereabouts do you think we are, Tony?   52

TONY.

By my guess we should be upon Crackskull common, about forty miles from home.

Mrs. HARDCASTLE.

O lud! O lud! the most notorious spot in all the country. We only want a robbery to make a complete night on't.

TONY.

Don't be afraid, mama, don't be afraid. Two of the five that kept here are hanged, and the other three may not find us. Don't be afraid. Is that a man that's galloping behind us? No; its only a tree. Don't be afraid.

46 the quickset hedge] A hedge formed by a row of growing plants.

Mrs. HARDCASTLE.

The fright will certainly kill me.   60

TONY.

Do you see any thing like a black hat moving behind the thicket?

Mrs. HARDCASTLE.

O death!

TONY.

No, it's only a cow. Don't be afraid, mama; don't be afraid.

Mrs. HARDCASTLE.

As I'm alive, Tony, I see a man coming towards us. Ah! I'm sure on't. If he perceives us we are undone.

TONY.

[*Aside.*] Father-in-law, by all that's unlucky, come to take one of his night walks. [*To her.*] Ah, it's a highwayman, with pistils as long as my arm. A damn'd ill-looking fellow.

Mrs. HARDCASTLE.

Good heaven defend us! He approaches.

TONY.

Do you hide yourself in that thicket, and leave me to manage him. If there be any danger I'll cough and cry hem. When I cough be sure to keep close.   [*Mrs. Hardcastle hides behind a tree in the back scene.*

Enter HARDCASTLE.

HARDCASTLE.

I'm mistaken, or I heard voices of people in want of help. Oh, Tony, is that you. I did not expect you so soon back. Are your mother and her charge in safety?   75

TONY.

Very safe, Sir, at my aunt Pedigree's. Hem.

Mrs. HARDCASTLE.

[*From behind.*] Ah death! I find there's danger.

HARDCASTLE.

Forty miles in three hours; sure, that's too much, my youngster.

66 Father-in-law] Again, in the old sense of step-father.

TONY.

Stout horses and willing minds make short journies, as they say. Hem.

Mrs. HARDCASTLE.

[*From behind.*] Sure he'll do the dear boy no harm.   80

HARDCASTLE.

But I heard a voice here; I should be glad to know from whence it came?

TONY.

It was I, Sir, talking to myself, Sir. I was saying that forty miles in four hours was very good going. Hem. As to be sure it was. Hem. I have got a sort of cold by being out in the air. We'll go in, if you please. Hem.

HARDCASTLE.

But if you talk'd to yourself, you did not answer yourself. I am certain I heard two voices, and am resolved (*raising his voice*) to find the other out.

Mrs. HARDCASTLE.

(*From behind.*) Oh! he's coming to find me out. Oh!

TONY.

What need you go, Sir, if I tell you. Hem. I'll lay down my life for the truth—hem—I'll tell you all, Sir.   [*detaining him.*

HARDCASTLE.

I tell you, I will not be detained. I insist on seeing. It's in vain to expect I'll believe you.   91

Mrs. HARDCASTLE.

(*Running forward from behind.*) O lud, he'll murder my poor boy, my darling. Here, good gentleman, whet your rage upon me. Take my money, my life, but spare that young gentleman, spare my child, if you have any mercy.

HARDCASTLE.

My wife! as I'm a Christian. From whence can she come, or what does she mean!

Mrs. HARDCASTLE.

(*Kneeling.*) Take compassion on us, good Mr. Highwayman. Take our money, our watches, all we have, but spare our lives. We will never bring you to justice, indeed we won't, good Mr. Highwayman.   100

HARDCASTLE.

I believe the woman's out of her senses. What, Dorothy, don't you know *me?*

Mrs. HARDCASTLE.

Mr. Hardcastle, as I'm alive! My fears blinded me. But who, my dear, could have expected to meet you here, in this frightful place, so far from home. What has brought you to follow us?

HARDCASTLE.

Sure, Dorothy, you have not lost your wits. So far from home, when you are within forty yards of your own door. (*To him.*) This is one of your old tricks, you graceless rogue you. (*To her.*) Don't you know the gate, and the mulberry-tree; and don't you remember the horsepond, my dear?

Mrs. HARDCASTLE.

Yes, I shall remember the horsepond as long as I live; I have caught my death in it. (*To* Tony.) And is it to you, you graceless varlet, I owe all this. I'll teach you to abuse your mother, I will.   112

TONY.

Ecod, mother, all the parish says you have spoil'd me, and so you may take the fruits on't.

Mrs. HARDCASTLE.

I'll spoil you, I will.   [*Follows him off the stage. Exit.*

HARDCASTLE.

There's morality, however, in his reply.   [*Exit.*

Enter HASTINGS *and Miss* NEVILLE.

HASTINGS.

My dear Constance, why will you deliberate thus? If we delay a moment, all is lost for ever. Pluck up a little resolution, and we shall soon be out of the reach of her malignity.

Miss NEVILLE.

I find it impossible. My spirits are so sunk with the agitations I have suffered, that I am unable to face any new danger. Two or three years patience will at last crown us with happiness.   122

HASTINGS.

Such a tedious delay is worse than inconstancy. Let us fly, my charmer. Let us date our happiness from this very moment. Perish fortune. Love and content will encrease what we possess beyond a monarch's revenue. Let me prevail.

Miss NEVILLE.

No, Mr. Hastings; no. Prudence once more comes to my relief, and I will obey its dictates. In the moment of passion, fortune may be despised, but it ever produces a lasting repentance. I'm resolved to apply to Mr. Hardcastle's compassion and justice for redress.   130

HASTINGS.

here 2

triumph

so caused

by confusion,

hm.

But tho' he had the will, he has not the power to relieve you.

Miss NEVILLE.

But he has influence, and upon that I am resolved to rely.

HASTINGS.

I have no hopes. But since you persist, I must reluctantly obey you.

[*Exeunt.*

SCENE *Changes.*

Enter Sir CHARLES *and Miss* HARDCASTLE.

Sir CHARLES.

What a situation am I in. If what you say appears, I shall then find a guilty son. If what he says be true, I shall then lose one that, of all others, I most wish'd for a daughter.

Miss HARDCASTLE.

I am proud of your approbation, and to shew I merit it, if you place yourself as I directed, you shall hear his explicit declaration. But he comes.

Sir CHARLES.

I'll to your father, and keep him to the appointment.   [*Exit Sir Charles.*

Enter MARLOW.

MARLOW.

Tho' prepar'd for setting out, I come once more to take leave, nor did I, till this moment, know the pain I feel in the separation.

Miss HARDCASTLE.

(*In her own natural manner.*) I believe these sufferings cannot be very great, Sir, which you can so easily remove. A day or two longer, perhaps, might lessen your uneasiness, by shewing the little value of what you now think proper to regret.   12

MARLOW.

[*Aside.*] This girl every moment improves upon me. (*To her.*) It must not be, Madam. I have already trifled too long with my heart. My very pride begins to submit to my passion. The disparity of education and fortune, the anger of a parent, and the contempt of my equals, begin to lose their weight; and nothing can restore me to myself, but this painful effort of resolution.

Miss HARDCASTLE.

Then go, Sir. I'll urge nothing more to detain you. Tho' my family be as good as her's you came down to visit, and my education, I hope, not inferior, what are these advantages without equal affluence? I must remain contented with the slight approbation of imputed merit; I must have only the mockery of your addresses, while all your serious aims are fix'd on fortune.   22

Enter HARDCASTLE *and Sir* CHARLES *from behind.*

Sir CHARLES.

Here, behind this screen.

HARDCASTLE.

Ay, Ay, make no noise. I'll engage my Kate covers him with confusion at last.

MARLOW.

By heavens, Madam, fortune was ever my smallest consideration. Your beauty at first caught my eye; for who could see that without emotion. But every moment that I converse with you, steals in some new grace, heightens the picture, and gives it stronger expression. What at first seem'd rustic plainness, now appears refin'd simplicity. What seem'd forward assurance, now strikes me as the result of courageous innocence, and conscious virtue.

Sir CHARLES.

What can it mean! He amazes me!   32

HARDCASTLE.

I told you how it would be. Hush!

MARLOW.

I am now determined to stay, Madam, and I have too good an opinion of my father's discernment, when he sees you, to doubt his approbation.

Miss HARDCASTLE.

No, Mr. Marlow, I will not, cannot detain you. Do you think I could suffer a connexion, in which there is the smallest room for repentance? Do you think I would take the mean advantage of a transient passion, to load you with confusion? Do you think I could ever relish that happiness, which was acquired by lessening your's? — *This sounds sincere, before* 40

MARLOW. *it high-lighted how stupid motives are.*

By all that's good, I can have no happiness but what's in your power to grant me. Nor shall I ever feel repentance, but in not having seen your merits before. I will stay, even contrary to your wishes; and tho' you should persist to shun me, I will make my respectful assiduities atone for the levity of my past conduct.

Miss HARDCASTLE.

Sir, I must entreat you'll desist. As our acquaintance began, so let it end, in indifference. I might have given an hour or two to levity; but seriously, Mr. Marlow, do you think I could ever submit to a connexion, where *I* must appear mercenary, and *you* imprudent? Do you think I could ever catch at the confident addresses of a secure admirer?   50

not the real Kate & Marlow relationship

MARLOW.

(*Kneeling.*) Does this look like security. Does this look like confidence. No, Madam, every moment that shews me your merit, only serves to encrease my diffidence and confusion. Here let me continue——

Sir CHARLES.

I can hold it no longer. Charles, Charles, how hast thou deceived me! Is this your indifference, your uninteresting conversation!

HARDCASTLE.

Your cold contempt; your formal interview. What have you to say now?

MARLOW.

That I'm all amazement! What can it mean!

HARDCASTLE.

It means that you can say and unsay things at pleasure. That you can
49 catch at] Be over-eager for.

address a lady in private, and deny it in public; that you have one story for us, and another for my daughter. 60

MARLOW.

Daughter!—this lady your daughter!

HARDCASTLE.

Yes, Sir, my only daughter. My Kate, whose else should she be.

MARLOW.

Oh, the devil.

Miss HARDCASTLE.

Yes, Sir, that very identical tall squinting lady you were pleased to take me for, (*curtesying*.) She that you addressed as the mild, modest, sentimental man of gravity, and the bold forward agreeable rattle of the ladies club; ha, ha, ha.

MARLOW.

Zounds, there's no bearing this; it's worse than death.

Miss HARDCASTLE.

In which of your characters, Sir, will you give us leave to address you. As the faultering gentleman, with looks on the ground, that speaks just to be heard, and hates hypocrisy; or the loud confident creature, that keeps it up with Mrs. Mantrap, and old Miss Biddy Buckskin, till three in the morning; ha, ha, ha. 73

MARLOW.

O, curse on my noisy head. I never attempted to be impudent yet, that I was not taken down. I must be gone.

HARDCASTLE.

By the hand of my body, but you shall not. I see it was all a mistake, and I am rejoiced to find it. You shall not, Sir, I tell you. I know she'll forgive you. Won't you forgive him, Kate. We'll all forgive you. Take courage, man.
                    [*They retire, she tormenting him to the back Scene.*

Enter Mrs. HARDCASTLE.   TONY.

Mrs. HARDCASTLE.

So, so, they're gone off. Let them go, I care not.

HARDCASTLE.

Who gone? 80

Mrs. HARDCASTLE.

My dutiful niece and her gentleman, Mr. Hastings, from Town. He who came down with our modest visitor here.

Sir CHARLES.

Who, my honest George Hastings. As worthy a fellow as lives, and the girl could not have made a more prudent choice.

HARDCASTLE.

Then, by the hand of my body, I'm proud of the connexion.

Mrs. HARDCASTLE.

Well, if he has taken away the lady, he has not taken her fortune, that remains in this family to console us for her loss.

HARDCASTLE.

Sure Dorothy you would not be so mercenary?

Mrs. HARDCASTLE.

Ay, that's my affair, not your's. But you know if your son, when of age, refuses to marry his cousin, her whole fortune is then at her own disposal.

HARDCASTLE.

Ay, but he's not of age, and she has not thought proper to wait for his refusal.   92

Enter HASTINGS and Miss NEVILLE.

Mrs. HARDCASTLE.

(*Aside.*) What returned so soon, I begin not to like it.

HASTINGS.

(*To Hardcastle.*) For my late attempt to fly off with your niece, let my present confusion be my punishment. We are now come back, to appeal from your justice to your humanity. By her father's consent, I first paid her my addresses, and our passions were first founded in duty.

Miss NEVILLE.

Since his death, I have been obliged to stoop to dissimulation to avoid oppression. In an hour of levity, I was ready even to give up my fortune to

89–90 But you know . . own disposal] In the first edition, as here, this is a continuation of Mrs. Hardcastle's speech. Logically, as in the manuscript, it is Hardcastle's reply.

HARDCASTLE] Thus the first edition. The manuscript assigns this speech to Mrs. Hardcastle.

secure my choice. But I'm now recover'd from the delusion, and hope from
your tenderness what is denied me from a nearer connexion.   101

Mrs. HARDCASTLE.

Pshaw, pshaw, this is all but the whining end of a modern novel.

HARDCASTLE.

Be it what it will, I'm glad they're come back to reclaim their due. Come
hither, Tony boy. Do you refuse this lady's hand whom I now offer you?

TONY.

What signifies my refusing. You know I can't refuse her till I'm of age,
father.

HARDCASTLE.

While I thought concealing your age boy was likely to conduce to your
improvement, I concurred with your mother's desire to keep it secret. But
since I find she turns it to a wrong use, I must now declare, you have been
of age these three months.   110

TONY.

Of age! Am I of age, father?

HARDCASTLE.

Above three months.

TONY.

Then you'll see the first use I'll make of my liberty. (*taking miss Neville's
hand.*) Witness all men by these presents, that I, Anthony Lumpkin, Esquire,
of BLANK place, refuse you, Constantia Neville, spinster, of no place at all,
for my true and lawful wife. So Constance Neville may marry whom she
pleases, and Tony Lumpkin is his own man again.

Sir CHARLES.

O brave 'Squire.

HASTINGS.

My worthy friend.

Mrs. HARDCASTLE.

My undutiful offspring.   120

102 a modern novel] The title of the play in its manuscript version was *The Novel or*, *The
Mistakes of a Night*.

MARLOW.

Joy, my dear George, I give you joy sincerely. And could I prevail upon my little tyrant here to be less arbitrary, I should be the happiest man alive, if you would return me the favour.

HASTINGS.

(*To miss Hardcastle.*) Come, madam, you are now driven to the very last scene of all your contrivances. I know you like him, I'm sure he loves you, and you must and shall have him.

HARDCASTLE.

(*Joining their hands.*) And I say so too. And Mr. Marlow, if she makes as good a wife as she has a daughter, I don't believe you'll ever repent your bargain. So now to supper, to-morrow we shall gather all the poor of the parish about us, and the Mistakes of the Night shall be crowned with a merry morning; so boy take her; and as you have been mistaken in the mistress, my wish is, that you may never be mistaken in the wife.   132

FINIS.

EPILOGUE

To be Spoken in the Character of TONY LUMPKIN.

By J. CRADDOCK, Esq.

WELL—*now all's ended—and my comrades gone,*
    Pray what becomes of mother's nonly son?
A hopeful blade!—in town I'll fix my station,
And try to make a bluster in the nation.
As for my cousin Neville, I renouce her,
Off—in a crack—I'll carry big Bett Bouncer.
    Why should not I in the great world appear?
I soon shall have a thousand pounds a year;
No matter what a man may here inherit,
In London—'gad, they've some regard to spirit.   10
I see the horses prancing up the streets,
And big Bet Bouncer, bobs to all she meets;
Then hoikes to jiggs and pastimes ev'ry night—
Not to the plays—they say it a'n't polite,
To Sadler's-Wells perhaps, or Operas go,
And once by chance, to the roratorio.
Thus here and there, for ever up and down,
We'll set the fashions too, to half the town;
And then at auctions—money ne'er regard,
Buy pictures like the great, ten pounds a yard;   20
Zounds, we shall make these London gentry say,
We know what's damn'd genteel, as well as they.

This came too late to be Spoken.

---

13 *hoikes to jiggs*] That is, hikes or takes herself to dances. 15 *Sadler's-Wells*] Then a music-house and pleasure garden. 16 *the roratorio*] The oratorio—probably meaning a specifically religious opera, but perhaps to suggest 'oratory', a place of preaching.

Selected Bibliography

Allardyce Nicoll's *History of Early Eighteenth Century Drama* (Cambridge, 1925, rev. ed. 1952) and *History of Late Eighteenth Century Drama* (Cambridge, 1927, rev. ed. 1952) remain the only comprehensive studies of the drama of the period. Critically, however, Nicoll's verdicts are often contentious: and factually his material has been superseded, though in less easily accessible form, by *The London Stage 1660–1800* (Southern Illinois), a compendious and definitive study by William van Lennep and others. The work is in five parts of which the first appeared in 1965. *An Introduction to Eighteenth-Century Drama* by F. S. Boas (Oxford, 1953) is wide-ranging but synoptic. Specifically on the comedy of the period, F. S. Bateson's *English Comic Drama 1700–1750* (Oxford, 1929) is over-concise, but critically intelligent. And of the theatre and stage conventions, Richard Southern's *The Georgian Playhouse* (1948) is the fullest technical account, whilst V. C. Clinton-Baddeley's *All Right on the Night* (Putnam, 1954) is a discursive but intriguing description of the behaviour of actors and audiences.

On special aspects of the period, two books by John Loftis, *Comedy and Society from Congreve to Fielding* (Stanford, 1959) and *The Politics of Drama in Augustan England* (Oxford, 1963) are admirable within the limitations of their titles, and V. C. Clinton-Baddeley's *Burlesque Tradition in the English Theatre* (Methuen, 1952) is an appropriately cheerful introduction to its subject. J. W. Krutch's *Comedy and Conscience After the Restoration* (Columbia, 1924, rev. ed. 1949) remains the best account of the causes and consequences of the Collier controversy. And on the regular comedies of the period there are J. Palmer's *Comedy of Manners* (1913) and E. Bernbaum's *The Drama of Sensibility* (1915). E. M. Gagey's *Ballad Opera* (1937) is the fullest examination of its genre.

Of the five dramatists represented in the present collection, George Farquhar has attracted least critical attention. Willard Connely's *Young George Farquhar: the Restoration Drama at Twilight* (Cassell, 1949) is primarily a biography—readable though not always reliable. The only full-length critical study is *George Farquhar* by E. Rothstein (Twayne, 1968); but a useful pamphlet by A. J. Farmer has appeared in the *Writers and Their Work* series (Longmans, 1966). G. A. Aitken's two-volume biography of *Richard Steele*, published in 1889, is still in many respects superior to W. Connely's *Sir Richard Steele* (1934), but a more nearly definitive modern work is John Loftis's *Steele and Drury Lane* (Univ. of California, 1952).

W. H. Irving's *John Gay: Favourite of the Wits* (Duke, 1940) is the most recent biography of this author, and the same critic's *John Gay's London*

(Harvard, 1928), though referring mainly to the *Trivia*, makes excellent background reading to *The Beggar's Opera*. On the play itself, there are F. Kidson's *The Beggar's Opera: its Predecessors and Successors* (1922), W. E. Schultz's *Gay's Beggar's Opera* (1923), and, of course, the idiosyncratic but essential essay by William Empson in *Some Versions of Pastoral* (1936). Charles E. Pearce's *Polly Peachum: the Story of Polly and the Beggar's Opera*, undated, does not set out to be a scholarly work, and some of its facts need checking: but its readability and theatrical flavour are undeniable.

Wilbur L. Cross's three-volume *History of Henry Fielding* (Yale, 1918) has yet to be bettered as a critical biography. There is, unfortunately, no full-length critical study of Fielding's plays, which tend to be over-cursorily dismissed even in works not devoted exclusively to his novels. Ralph M. Wardle's *Oliver Goldsmith* (Univ. of Kansas, 1957) is the best account of a writer whose plays have been almost as neglected by critics—though thankfully not by audiences—as have Fielding's. A good recent critical study is Ricardo Quintana's *Oliver Goldsmith* (Weidenfeld 1969).

1969   S. T.